TRAINS ACROSS
THE CONTINENT

Telocaset, Oregon, October 1995. Courtesy Union Pacific Museum Collection. #1080.

TRAINS ACROSS THE CONTINENT

North American Railroad History

SECOND EDITION

by

Rudolph Daniels

WITH FOREWORDS BY

Roger Cameron
Railway Association of Canada

Thomas C. White
Association of American Railroads

Frank N. Wilner
formerly with the U.S. Surface Transportation Board

Indiana
University
Press

BLOOMINGTON AND INDIANAPOLIS

This book is a publication of
Indiana University Press
601 North Morton Street
Bloomington, IN 47404-3797 USA

http://www.indiana.edu/~iupress

Telephone orders   800-842-6796
Fax orders   812-855-7931
Orders by e-mail   iuporder@indiana.edu

Originally printed by Pacific City Graphics.
First Indiana University Press edition published in 2000.

Library of Congress Cataloging-in-Publication Data
Daniels, Rudolph L., date
Trains across the continent : North American Railroad history (second edition) / by Rudolph Daniels ;
with foreword by Roger Cameron, Thomas C. White, Frank N. Wilner.
p.   cm.
Includes bibliographical references and index.
ISBN 0-253-33762-3 (cl : alk. paper).—
ISBN 0-253-21411-4 (pbk. : alk. paper)
1. Railroads—North America—History.   2. Railroads—United States—History.   3. Railroads—Canada—History.   I. Title.
TF22 .D36   2000
385'.097—dc21   00-27801

1   2   3   4   5   05   04   03   02   01   00

I can no more conceive of a world without railroads and trains to run on them than I can imagine wishing to live in such a world.

James Norman Hall

(co-author of *Mutiny on the Bounty*)

THIS BOOK IS DEDICATED
TO ALL RAILROAD WORKERS,
MANAGERS, AND OWNERS,
PAST, PRESENT, AND FUTURE.

CONTENTS

MAPS

FOREWORDS

Canada was created on the strength of a commitment to build a national railway. Today, 40 railways, operating one of the largest networks in some of the world's worst weather conditions, are helping Canada succeed as a trading nation.

Two-thirds of their traffic moves in international trade, and north–south movements are the fastest growing. The railways know they play a more important role in Canada's economy than railroads do in the United States, but they are up to the challenge!

Roger Cameron
General Manager, Public Affairs
Railway Association of Canada

Few industries have had as much impact on American history as the railroad. John F. Kennedy placed it in perspective when he wrote: "As our frontier moved westward, it was the railroads that bore the great tide of Americans to the areas of new opportunities and hope. It was the railroads that linked together the diverse segments of this vast land so that together they might create the greatest economy the world has ever known."

Until the coming of the railroad, the nation's population centers were clustered along the East Coast and navigable waterways leading to it. Development elsewhere was stifled by geographic barriers that rendered the vast riches of the continent virtually inaccessible to all but a hardy few adventurous pioneers. The railroad changed that, unlocking vast stores of natural resources and allowing population centers to take root and flourish in areas previously home only to Native Americans. In the process, railroad agents helped unleash a new wave of immigration, filling these newly opened areas with people recruited for the purpose of providing the demand for freight and passenger transportation that the expanding rail system needed.

As this occurred, fortunes were gained . . . and lost. Legendary railroad names . . . Vanderbilt . . . Harriman . . . Hill . . . came to symbolize both the growth of the nation and the arrogance of big business. And the nation was united by a form of economic and universal transportation that was a necessary ingredient for the industrialization of North America.

Today's railroads are vastly different from those that built this continent, but just as essential. Only a few short years ago, more than 20 percent of the industry was in bankruptcy, market share was spiraling downward, and many experts declared them to be in irreversible decline. But in 1980 railroads were invigorated by the most successful transportation legislation since the legislation that created the Interstate Highway System — the Staggers Rail Act of 1980. This law partially deregulated railroads and set off a series of changes that included new emphasis on customer-driven marketing initiatives, industry-wide restructuring, unprecedented productivity gains, and embrace of new technology. As a result, the rail share of the freight transportation market is increasing for the first time since the end of World War II, accident rates have fallen to the lowest level in history, and North America's railroads are regarded as the worldwide model for successful rail freight transportation.

The journey from continent-builder to near-bankruptcy to revival is one that anyone contemplating a career in the railroad industry ought to experience. Rudy Daniels has chronicled that journey in an entertaining, yet thoughtful account of how railroads helped shape the history of North America — and how they were shaped by it — and how that process continues today.

Thomas C. White
Director, Editorial Services
Association of American Railroads

America's railroads have been compared in function and importance to the arteries in the human body.

Railroads permitted us to cobble together and defend an embryo nation, to develop a commercial base that meets our material wants, to make our manufacturers competitive worldwide, and to enjoy an ever-improving standard of living.

Indeed, whatever America mines, farms, mills, transforms, creates, assembles, and distributes moves some part of its journey via a railroad.

Railroads were America's first big business. They were the first to have their economic practices regulated by the government, to help rehabilitate employees injured on the job, to recognize labor unions, to pay pensions, and to provide unemployment insurance.

Today's railroads are even bigger businesses, with fewer than seven major systems, each at least several thousand miles long, controlling more than 90 percent of all rail traffic. This resulted from more than a century of unceasing consolidation among more than 1,000 railroads that began life but a few miles long.

Railroads primarily carry freight. But while not too long ago it looked as if automobiles and airplanes had killed the passenger train, highway and airport congestion and the advent of 150-mph trains is encouraging a revival in rail passenger service.

Professor Daniels does a superb job in tracing the history of railroads — an industry that once employed at least one member of virtually every American family — and transporting the reader to an understanding of the crucial issues facing railroads, their customers, and employees today.

Frank N. Wilner
Author, *Railroad Mergers:
History, Analysis, Insight*

PREFACE

When I accepted a position at Western Iowa Tech Community College in January 1996, the Curriculum Development Director, Charlene Balmer, told me that I would have an opportunity to teach Railroad History. She showed me the text chosen for the course, and said that, even though it left a few things to be desired, it was acceptable to the Railroad Multimedia Training Consortium (RMTC).

I casually mentioned that I wanted to write a comprehensive railroad history on into my retirement. I was finishing the paperwork on a National Endowment for the Humanities grant and my next project was to write a comparative social and political history of the United States. Besides, it would take me some time to adjust to my new position. I would also have to begin preparation to teach the railroad course.

Five months later, Charlene telephoned me to ask how much of the railroad history book I had completed! I reminded her the project was years away, and I had yet to prepare the course. She then asked me if I could complete such a text by next summer, because the current book was out of print. The RMTC needed one by August 1997! I told her I would do it. I realized what I had said only after I hung up the phone. . . .

To write a complete text from scratch in a year. So I got to work immediately.

Charlene suggested I visit with Bill Podrazik at Johnson County Community College/National Academy of Railroad Sciences. Bill was planning a curriculum revision for Railroad Technology courses. He explained his expectations for the history course and text. He made many suggestions throughout the year, and continued to encourage me in the project.

Over the summer I had to make a legal agreement with Western Iowa Tech. I agreed to continue teaching and carrying out administrative duties; in turn, I retained the copyright on the book. Western Iowa Tech would provide a no-interest loan for graphics and typing expenses. Therefore, I would write the text while continuing to work full time.

Photos posed a problem. Pictures are a natural part of any book on railroad history. I had to find institutions willing to sell me prints at low or no cost, and grant me the right to publish the same. The photo search absorbed much of my time and personal finances. Although I wanted to have a number of different railroads represented in photos, I had to settle on affordable examples. I took many photos myself to avoid costs and copyright problems. I enjoy photography anyway.

I also wanted to include an adequate amount of material on Canadian railroad history.

I must mention something about the heralds in the margins. I included them to help the reader identify the "flag" of a railroad company. I placed one for a railroad which achieved a "first," and some for decoration. These logos/heralds were printed with permission of the respective railroads and companies. They may not be reproduced in any form without the express written permission of their respective companies.

The primary intention of *Trains across the Continent* is to furnish a textbook of North American railroad history for conductor training courses at community colleges. It can also serve as a very readable account for anyone interested in railroad history.

I was glad to change my plans and write *Trains across the Continent*. I regard it as a great opportunity. I hope I did the railroad industry, students, instructors, and history a creditable service.

Rudolph Daniels
Sioux City, Iowa
June 1997

ACKNOWLEDGMENTS

Many people have provided assistance to me during the research and writing of this book. Some have gone out of their way to help. In mentioning some of them, I hope I do not inadvertently leave anyone out.

I wish to thank Bruce Eveland and Bud and Duane Miller of the Fremont & Elkhorn Valley Railroad/Fremont Dinner Train for permitting me to take photos of their train.

While several organizations furnished photos, I wish to acknowledge those who have been particularly helpful. Connie Romani of Visualarity and Anne Calhoun of the B&O Museum were most considerate. David Letourneau of BNSF Archives loaned me original prints for copying. Carol Peterson, Canadian National Reference Assistant, pointed out a number of excellent sources. At the same time, Marc Magliari, Amtrak Manager of Public Affairs, furnished me with information for the Amtrak sections of the book. Malcolm Andrews of VIA Rail Canada did the same. Bob Pennisi of Railroad Avenue Enterprises permitted me to use his photos.

I am grateful to Senator Charles Grassley of Iowa and his staff for furnishing information on railroad legislation. Darlene Richardson of the Virginia Museum of Transportation was most helpful in finding photos for the second edition as was Robert Haynes of the African American Museum and Library of Oakland.

Patty Drumeller provided me with an interview and sources on the Orphan Trains, and Gene Ambroson, former Director of Corporate Communications for IBP, helped me understand cattle-raising and the livestock industry.

Jon Long, Make Heynes, and Barb Anderson of BNSF in Sioux City, Iowa, cooperated greatly and answered my many questions.

I wish to acknowledge the help of many of my colleagues at Western Iowa Tech. John Scott gave me information about buffalo in the nineteenth century, and Jerry Forbes answered many questions about electronics and electric motors. Robert Friend and Charles LeMaster found many obscure books for me through interlibrary loan. Douglas Kanaly made several suggestions, and Charlene Balmer actually initiated the project. Dr. Duane Letcher, Executive Vice President, made the contract arrangements, and Dr. Robert Dunker, President, presented the project to the WIT Board of Directors.

I wish to thank the WIT board members individually: Eldon Schroder, Earl Pickens, John Elkins, Larry Hansen, Cathy Egan-Jackson, John Q. Harris, Jean Sandman, Gary Thies, and Derrick Frank.

Throughout the undertaking of the project, I have enjoyed the encouragement of the Western Iowa Tech College community. I am grateful to the board of directors and the college administration for funding clerical and graphic support which helped me immensely in completing the project. I am solely responsible for any error and all opinions stated in this book. Western Iowa Tech Community College is not held responsible for any of the same.

A number of people proofread and offered editorial comments on the manuscript. Barbara Pittman of Sioux City pointed out a number of areas that needed explanation. Bill Podrazik, Instructor in Railroad Operations Technology at Johnson County Community College/National Academy of Railroad Sciences in Overland Park, Kansas, made a number of editorial suggestions. In fact, Bill helped a great deal throughout the project, and provided materials on environmental legislation and the Federal Railroad Administration. Warren Scholl, Manager: Technical Training and Rules for BNSF at Oakland Park, Kansas, offered consultation on the steam and locomotive sections. Curtis Judd of Fort Worth, Texas, gave suggestions for the chapter on the Civil War. Marilyn D. Sommerdorf of the California State Railroad Museum offered many suggestions, particularly on the construction of the Central Pacific and Union Pacific.

Marilyn Mayer, Adjunct Instructor of English at Western Iowa Tech, functioned as editor for the initial manuscript. I am indebted to her for her many creative suggestions and for her final proofreading of the draft. I would also like to thank Joyce Dawson for her help with the final proofreading. Enid Peterson of Western Iowa Tech proofread for the second edition.

Randee Small turned my unintelligible lines into fine graphics. I am most indebted to Christy DuBois who spent many hours deciphering my handwriting and typing the draft onto the computer. Christy exhibited incredible patience as I made many changes before the book went to print. Jana Turner typed some late revisions.

I am grateful to Frank Wilner, Chief of Staff of the U.S. Surface Transportation Board, for his encouragement and suggestions. I appreciate his willingness and that of Thomas White of the Association of American Railroads to write Forewords to the book. I am grateful to Roger Cameron, General Manager, Public Affairs of the Railway Association of Canada, for doing so, too, as well as for making many corrections and editorial suggestions. The same for Johnathan Hanna of the Canadian Pacific Railway.

INTRODUCTION

*It welded the nation together, creating an American outlook,
an American point of view.*
— George Douglas

American railroads developed the United States and actually created the nation of Canada. Their achievements are more than the construction of thousands of miles of track. Railroads were the cause of the Industrial Revolution in North America as well as the biggest impetus for people to migrate to the continent from Europe and Asia in the nineteenth century. Railroad financing spurred the growth of stock markets and prompted the labor movement in the United States. The railroads were also the first industry to come under government regulation. For over a century they were leaders in scientific development and technology.

The railroads heralded a new age. They changed the nature of warfare, and their military use during the U.S. Civil War is still the model for the movement of supplies and personnel (logistics) at the beginning of the twenty-first century. Perhaps their greatest accomplishments were the development of the modern sense of time and space, creating the American character, and furthering the idea of freedom.

From 1828, until just before World War I, railroads constructed track across the continent. During the first thirty years, rails formed a web from the Atlantic Ocean to the Mississippi River. Railroads linked east-coast cities with farms and towns along interior water routes of the trans-Allegheny west. After the Civil War, transcontinental railroads had to create towns and cities along their tracks in building to California and the Pacific Northwest. They made agricultural and metallurgical communities possible in an area previously devoid of European settlement.

When railroad construction began in earnest during the 1840s, the U.S. companies needed iron — and later steel — to build rails, wheels, and locomotives. Rather than import expensive iron rail from England, they encouraged the start of the gigantic iron and coal industries on this continent. They transported the ores to furnaces and carried away finished products to markets all over the nation. The railroads, too, were these industries' largest customers. By the 1850s, the railroads were also the largest consumers of cloth, printed matter, and kerosene, among many other commodities. This web of "all weather" transportation was, by the time of the Civil War, the only means of adequate transportation. The United States profited from the inexpensive construction of track rather than more expensive road grading. Moreover, the railroad provided nearly instantaneous communication among towns and communities with its accompanying telegraph. In short, railroads provided an inexpensive means to transport products from factory and farm to market.

Although Canadian Railroads received their supplies from England, they, too, encouraged the growth of industry. The railroads were important in transporting finished and unfinished products in winter when water routes were frozen and the few roads were impassable. By the late nineteenth century, Canada had a significant rail network to assist the development of its own industrial base independent of England.

A huge continent as well as the great potential for industrial growth needed an increasing population to work in its factories and to till its fields. At first the Irish came to American shores to escape political oppression and famine. They found work constructing the Baltimore & Ohio Railroad. Other railroads quickly encouraged the Irish to immigrate. From the Erie Railroad to the lengthy transcontinentals, Irish, Germans, Scandinavians, and Chinese, among others came to build track and settle in the New World. Some railroads sent agents across the Atlantic to encourage Europeans to come. These immigrants lived on farms that turned the Great Plains into an agricultural center and provided the labor to extract ores from the western mountain ranges. Canada also used the railroads to populate its vast interior with immigrants. During the late nineteenth century, the Canadians attracted immigrants to build their railroads. Along with Chinese, many of Canada's immigrants came from eastern Europe. In both the United States and Canada, immigrants laid track and worked on farms and in factories to build two great industrial giants. If the Statue of Liberty in New York Harbor beckoned "the tired, poor, and hungry" to America's shores, it was the railroads that gave these people a new lease on life, the opportunity to make a living, and the capacity to grow food for themselves and others.

Sometime during the late 1700s, people began to sit on the wall of a Manhattan street to sell stock. When railroads came into being in the 1830s, people flocked there to buy stock in the new invention. By the 1840s, the nation caught "railroad fever," and people gambled, speculated, and sold stock in railroads and related industries. Movements in the stock market sometimes caused booms and busts in the nation's economy. The fierce and large volume of trading brought about the construction of large, permanent investment buildings on Wall Street, and caused New York to become the financial capital of the world today.

English investment played an early and strong role in Canadian railway construction. There is no doubt that initial funding was done for the benefit of the mother country. By the end of the nineteenth century, however, Canadians had established their own financial markets, and the railroads played a dominant role in them.

While investors made — and lost — fortunes on stock deals, railroad workers and the nation suffered the brunt of sporadic economic busts. Reductions in pay and layoffs prompted railroad workers to form unions and to strike. United States railroad employees set the model for court cases, labor legislation, and benefits for the entire working world. Modern laborers owe their safety, working conditions, and contract agreements to their forerunners in the railroad industry over a century ago.

Introduction

Federal and state agencies today regulate many industries and influence almost everyone through some form of legislation or code. This practice began in the railroad industry. During the early nineteenth century the states chartered railroads. As this procedure proved cumbersome, railroads fell under corporate or company law. Following the Civil War, however, farmers in the Midwest pressured both the state and federal government to regulate the railroads. By 1900, the U.S. railroads were the first industry to fall under specific regulatory legislation. By the end of World War I, almost all aspects of railroading fell under some federal guideline. Canadians also passed regulatory legislation. After World War I, however, the Canadian government created and owned a national railway system in direct competition with a private company.

Railroads are responsible for the invention of safety devices and articles of convenience that are in use today. By the late nineteenth century some set up laboratories to invent new products to use on trains and test them for durability. They were able to use these inventions to increase train speed and make passengers more comfortable. They stimulated the development and manufacturing of products that eventually would be used by almost everyone. For example, railroads devised the modern system of steam heat for warmth in winter and air conditioning for comfort in summer. Their system of air for stopping trains is also used on large trucks and busses. And to everyone's delight, a railroad chef invented Bisquick!

From the very first trains in the 1830s, railroads proved that they could move people and goods faster and in larger numbers on land than anything else. Both sides during the U.S. Civil War used the railroad for the first time to move soldiers and equipment into battle. Large numbers of men — thousands — could arrive from hundreds of miles away ready to fight the moment they disembarked. A movement of troops that had taken months in 1800 could be done in a matter of hours by 1860. This speed made warfare more bloody and battles more frequent. The railroads changed the nature of warfare, and the principles they created in rapid deployment of large numbers of people are an integral part of military strategy today.

American railroads experienced their finest hour during World War II. The railroads had already created the world's largest industrial giant in the United States by 1940. During the early days of World War II, Nazi Germany and the Empire of Japan had conquered almost all the other industrial countries in the world. In addition, German submarines had cut England off from the resources it desperately needed from overseas. The U.S. and Canadian railroads were able to keep American industry at full pace and deliver the goods and personnel to defeat the Asian and European dictators. Without the industrial might and efficient delivery system American rails created, the outcome of World War II would have been very different . . . .

American railroads gave the world its modern mentality as well as its sense of space and time. The first train rides of the 1830s fascinated people. Riding on rails at almost 20 miles per hour, people had two experiences that were impossible earlier. They were moved, i.e., pulled, by a mechanism thoroughly independent of nature. In other words, they did not depend on wind, animal, or their own feet to move on land. As they rolled along, they became observers of nature rather than people constantly reacting to it. They did not have to look out for ruts and holes in the road or the overgrowth of tree limbs in the path. There was no horse to stumble or to throw them. They could simply enjoy the ride and observe nature as they rolled by. In 1830, this sense was new, and it began the mentality that humans could master nature and not necessarily remain just a part of it, subject to its whims.

By the 1880s, trains moved hundreds of people at one time over hundreds of miles in just a few hours. Traveling on fast trains over long distances caused problems for people adjusting to the exact time from one locality to another. Each town set its own hour by a local sundial. Each railroad set its own train schedules by the clock at its head office — possibly hundreds of miles away. The convenience of rapid travel now brought about a sense of chaos for the modern traveler and the nation.

The U.S. railroad industry solved this problem and gave the world its modern perspective of time. The railroads created time zones across the United States, and declared that all railroad companies would begin the hour at the same second throughout the same zone. They then proclaimed that each zone would be an hour earlier going from east to west. Canadian railroads quickly recognized this pattern too. Very soon, all business in the United States and Canada followed "railroad time." The last vestige of local isolation vanished. Americans very soon perceived themselves as having the same time-mentality and all activity became synchronized according to the railroad time pattern. Canadians took this idea to England where British mariners adopted the American railroad time system for the entire world and set the International Date Line!

The railroads were an essential part of the formation of the U.S. political character. Americans have a unique sense of freedom; the federal government protects the citizen even against itself. Unlike other central authorities throughout history, the U.S. federal government had no compelling need to force its authority on others to form a nation. The railroads, as private enterprises, did it for Washington, D.C. The railroads created a sense of nation by providing relative ease of travel, the delivery of mail, and the linking of every small-town newspaper with daily events happening throughout the country by telegraph. In other words, the railroads formed the skeleton of the nation while permitting each locality to develop its own sense of politics and freedom separate from Washington, D.C. Given the several secessionist movements before 1861, it was the railroads as nongovernment enterprises that provided the means for the formation of the United States into a true nation without trampling upon local or individual liberties.

This nation-forming role of the railroads was noted from their inception. On July 4, 1828, Charles Carroll of Carrollton lifted the first shovelful of earth for the construction of the Baltimore & Ohio Railroad — the first rail common carrier in North America. Carroll was the last surviving signer of the Declaration of Independence, and he served in the first senate under the constitution. He was also no stranger to economics, as many considered him the wealthiest person in America at that time. On this July 4, the fifty-second anniversary of the Declaration of Independence, Carroll linked the two events. After putting down his shovel, Carroll turned to a friend and said: "I consider this among the most important acts of my life, second only to my signing of the Declaration of Independence, if even it be second to that." Charles Carroll of Carrollton recognized that the railroad had the potential to mold the new American political idea into a strong nation. He was so right.

More than just preserving a unique sense of freedom, the railroads were the first instruments that created an identifiable American character and society. Railroads were the first means of mass transportation. By the 1850s, large numbers of people moved freely by rail throughout the eastern portion of the United States. This movement brought about the first large-scale mixture of ethnic groups — more than in any other geographic area on the planet. Different ethnic groups mingled in coaches, and later the dining car was the first truly integrated workplace in the nation.

Railroads created Canada. When the Canadian Confederation was proposed in the 1860s, the Maritime Provinces demanded rail connections with Montreal and Quebec before they would join. British Columbia became a member in 1871, only after a transcontinental rail line was promised. It was not practical for British Columbia or the Maritime Provinces to become members without rapid transit and instantaneous communications with the capital. At the same time, the entire central plains and western mountain areas remained unclaimed. Each province could have become an independent country. The railroad created Canada and opened its interior to additional population.

The railroad developed two nations on the North American continent. Trains made them what they are today. The history of American railroads is in every way the story of the greatness of the United States and Canada.

PART I

Coal, Iron, and Steam

Historical Survey

European settlement of North America began with the Age of Discovery during the late 1400s. The Spanish settled in the southern portion and sought gold and other precious metals. England and France explored north of the Spanish possessions looking for a water route to the orient. They eventually formed colonies to gather the wealth of the new world.

Canada is derived from the Huron-Iroquois *kanata,* meaning a village or settlement. Jacques Cartier first explored the Montreal area in 1535. Newfoundland, which is part of Canada, was discovered by John Cabot in 1497. Samuel de Champlain explored the St. Lawrence River area for France and founded the city of Quebec in 1608. In 1642, he established Montreal as a missionary outpost. By 1663, King Louis XIV proclaimed Canada a French province. Many French were engaged in the profitable fur industry.

The British won Canada from France after the French and Indian War (1763). The English renamed the area Province of Quebec and encouraged people from England to migrate there to become the dominant population. There was early resentment between the two nationalities. To bring about some reconciliation, the English granted recognition of French civil law in Canada.

From its beginnings with English settlement in Jamestown in 1609 and in New England in 1620, the colonies that became the United States attracted people from all over Europe. Settlers first came to explore for gold, but soon settled down to farm and live a better life. Some explorers hoped to find a water route through the continent to reach Asia.

The population grew quickly, and the English colonists soon began to develop an economy and attitude distinct from that of their mother country. When England began to levy a series of taxes on the colonists to pay for wars fought in Europe, the Americans rebelled. The revolt led to revolution in 1776, and the Declaration of Independence.

During the revolution, many English loyalists fled to British North America. They lived chiefly in New Brunswick and Nova Scotia, and a few in Prince Edward Island. By that time Canada was divided into two regions: Lower Canada came to be known as Canada East and Upper Canada as Canada West in 1841. Lower Canada was the St. Lawrence area and Upper Canada was above the Great Lakes. Each area had its own governor, assemblies, and its own separate relations with England.

Canada continued to expand into the western Great Lakes area with traders seeking animal furs and hides. Two major companies merged into the Hudson's Bay Company, which became the largest fur-trading company in the world. The Hudson's Bay Company virtually controlled central Canada.

During their war for independence, the thirteen colonies, under the direction of George Washington, joined themselves into a United States of America. The fledgling nation began an experiment in democracy with a government that had limited authority and recognized every man, except slaves, as equal under the law. They committed themselves further by making a stronger union under a constitution in 1789 that gave a guarantee of rights to the individual citizen.

The United States held a special position among nations. Here almost anyone could own land if he were willing to work it. Moreover, court decisions were friendly to commerce, and almost anyone could start a business at will. The nation was young, and it wanted to grow.

President Thomas Jefferson purchased territory to the west, called Louisiana, from Napoleon of France. Neither he nor anyone else knew the extent of the land. In 1803, Jefferson commissioned the Lewis and Clark Expedition to explore the extent of the new territory. Expeditions of Zebulon Pike into present-day Colorado and Thomas Freeman into present-day Oklahoma followed.

During the first decade of the nineteenth century, the English in Canada began to funnel into U.S. western areas. The War of 1812 was fought between the two countries. Canada held off an invasion from the United States with assistance from the British. In the years following the war, the United States prospered, and more people from Europe fled to its shores.

When both founding fathers John Adams and Thomas Jefferson died on July 4, 1826, many citizens took it as an omen that God looked upon the new country with special favor. The United States was destined to grow and prosper. Moreover, by the 1830s a new generation took over the leadership of the nation. Such figures as Senators Daniel Webster of Massachusetts, John C. Calhoun of South Carolina, Henry Clay of Kentucky, and later Thomas Hart Benton of Missouri saw an almost unlimited potential in the nation and both inspired and legislated westward expansion. The land was almost limitless, and it needed people to grow with it.

The First Railroads and the Industrial Revolution

Railroads were the natural outgrowth of a historical movement called the Industrial Revolution. The Industrial Revolution, in simplest terms, was the beginning of using machines to make things formerly made by hand. The movement began in England sometime near the end of the 1600s through the next century. The first machines were used to weave wool and then cotton. Later, the iron industry was mechanized. In short, the Industrial Revolution began the use of labor-saving devices to make goods more efficiently.

The Industrial Revolution changed the economic landscape very quickly. It ended one handicraft trade after another. In the time it took an individual to make the cloth for one coat by hand, one machine could make thousands. This increase of production called for acquiring more resources to make a larger quantity of goods, and the larger quantity of goods demanded a larger market than the local population for their sale.

This process brought forth other changes. Since machines were located in one place, people had to move near the factory to seek employment. Therefore, England experienced a rapid growth in towns and cities. In other words, people left farms and relocated to urban areas to work for wages. With this growth in population, cities and towns took on an economic life of their own rather than their former roles as just administrative centers or markets for local agricultural products.

— The First Factories —

The building of factories and purchasing of machines demanded a new class of people who were willing to invest, perhaps gamble, on an industry. Some would invest their own savings or obtain loans from banks in the hope that their factory would turn a profit and make them rich. Just as quickly, financial institutions were willing to back some "risk takers" for a return through interest rates. At the same time, these banks took on a new role as clearinghouses for business transactions. As the more fortunate gained wealth on their original investment, they would often invest again by expanding their share in the business or by starting new ones. Thereby, shares of stock were sold in the various businesses. This was the beginning of the modern corporation: People owned a part of a business and reaped profits according to the shares they held in the enterprise.

A growing market was available for the increased amount of goods, especially clothing, produced by machines. By the early 1700s, the many plagues that had passed throughout Europe for centuries ended. There was also a series of good harvests throughout the 1700s which meant that there was a better supply of food. Such labor-saving devices as Tull's Drill helped plant crops and increased farm production. These changes in the agricultural economy encouraged many to migrate to cities to seek employment.

As the Industrial Revolution continued, newer and larger machines were able to increase production. Some people began to specialize in constructing and improving equipment. Although much was based on the "trial and error" method, it was the beginning of industrial engineering, or the application of science to make machines. They soon learned that the more iron used in the machine, the more durable it was.

England had sufficient sources of iron ore and coal to meet the needs of its early industry. At the same time, coal was an efficient fuel for heating and cooking in the homes of its growing cities. In order to meet demands, coal and iron mines needed a way to remove the water which accumulated in the shafts. Many mines in the 1700s used a crude version of the steam engine attached to a pump to remove the water. These engines were the only means, next to humans, of providing the on-site power that was needed over a long period of time.

— The Steam Engine —

By the mid-1700s the Scottish inventor, James Watt, improved on these early devices. Watt's design forced the steam to push the piston in both directions and exhaust on the opposite sides of the cylinder on the return stroke. He also attached the cranking arm to a "fly wheel" to steady the engine and to provide a consistent rhythm. Watt's engine was used to remove water from mines which in turn provided greater quantities of iron ore and coal.

Soon after, Watt's steam engine was applied to move machinery in factories. Formerly, factories had to be located near rapidly moving water to turn a wheel which, attached to gears, moved the machinery. They were always subject to droughts and floods. The steam engine provided more consistent movement and made it possible for a factory to be built anywhere — not necessarily next to a river. At the same time, the steam engine was more powerful, which meant even more machinery could be added in the factory.

— The Transportation Revolution —

An increase of production demanded the expansion of the market area, or the places where goods could be sold. Moreover, towns began to specialize in the manufacturing of one product or style of a particular product. People from one part of England wanted or desired products produced in another part of the country. While roads already existed, it was not cost effective to cart large quantities of a product or bulk materials such as coal and iron ore from mine to factory. A series of canals were dug linking cities with mines and/or other places of production. Large numbers of men, called "navvies," were employed for these projects. While canals were most efficient in carrying goods, they needed to be dredged from time to time and they were susceptible to low water levels and freezing. Moreover, canals were limited to relatively level terrain. England needed a better means to move commodities — and people — from one place to another. The solution was wheels on rails powered by the steam engine.

— How a Steam Engine Works —

The steam engine as designed by James Watt is a fairly simple device. Water is heated in a boiler to 100 degrees centigrade. The water at that temperature turns into steam. Steam is very expansive, and it needs a larger area. By confining steam to a relatively small area, it builds up a tremendous amount of pressure.

The steam is then released in controlled amounts into a pipe which opens into a cylinder. The cylinder contains a piston which can be pushed back and forth by the pressure of the entering steam. As the steam pushes the piston in one direction, an open valve behind it closes. When the piston reaches its greatest extension, steam enters again and pushes the piston in the opposite direction. The back valve then closes and the forward valve opens. When the piston reaches its greatest length, steam enters again to continuously repeat the motion.

The piston has an extending rod which is attached to a wheel. The wheel steadies the back and forth motion of the piston and provides power to machinery and, of course, steam locomotives. Boilers and pistons or locomotives had to undergo some changes from those that powered stationary machinery. These adaptations helped increase both power and energy savings.

Boiler explosions are always a danger with steam engines. It is possible that the boiler has built up so much steam pressure that it literally blows apart. The more common danger occurs when the water level drops below the topmost part of the area containing the fire (fire box). The metal then becomes extremely hot and weakens. The steam rushes downward into the fire exploding and literally propelling the whole boiler forward. Therefore, engineers must be always on guard to keep the boiler adequately filled with water.

— The First Rails —

Wheels on or in some type of runner had been used in European mine shafts since the late Middle Ages; i.e., from the 1200s onward. The shafts were usually cramped for space and in many cases had an incline toward the entrance. The ore or coal was quite heavy, and the use of conventional wagons would form ruts. The miners learned that by placing the wagon wheels on or in a runner helped overcome resistance

and kept the wagons from jerking from side to side. In other words, they were easier and safer to pull. This practice was well established in England by the 1700s. The rails were often extended beyond the mine entrance to loading areas at that time. It was a short leap from the use of railed carts in mines to trains on the surface and the steam railroad.

— The First Trains —

The first railcars were pulled by horses or other types of draft animals as they had been in the mines. While inventors in many places in Europe attempted to build some kind of contraption powered by steam, the first successful ones were in England.

Credit goes to Richard Trevithick of Cornwall. Around 1800, Trevithick attached a Watt design steam engine to a wagon. While it moved the wagon successfully, it became apparent that it was too awkward to be used on roads and streets. In 1804, he connected his engine to a four-car train. With runners guiding the wheels, his device became much easier to operate, and it was able to move more easily and even increased in speed. At one time, he used his steam tram or wheels-on-rails device to pull five wagonloads of iron ore for a total of ten tons and carried seventy men in its trailing carts. It is reported that Trevithick's first steam train achieved a speed of five miles per hour.

Trevithick continued to improve on his design. He was able to increase the pressure of the steam, and he set the cylinders in a horizontal rather than in a vertical position. He then used the exhaust steam from the cylinders to help draft the fire. Trevithick thereby created the general principle of steam locomotives which remained in use for over a century. This drafting mechanism created the chugging sound which is characteristic of moving steam locomotives. The new design increased both the efficiency and power of his engine.

In 1808, Trevithick constructed a circular track in London to demonstrate his new invention. According to some accounts, his train went ten miles per hour, and he named his engine *Catch-Me-Who-Can.* While his engine went faster than most people could run on foot, it tended to derail too easily. Proper ways to stabilize the wheels had yet to be developed.

John Blenkinsop used cogs to give both traction and stability to his "steam wagon" in 1812. While this idea provided the best traction and greater balance on a rail, its ride proved to be choppy at best. Even so, Blenkinsop's idea is still used by "cog railways" where the incline is too steep for regular traction.

Other inventors tried applying steam to pull railcars at this time. One notable example was William Hedley. In 1813, Hedley used his *Puffing Billy* steam engine to pull freight in what would be called a "regular service" on a tram line. While Hedley's device contained nothing new from an engineering standpoint, he did promise a practical application of steam to move cars consistently on rails. Nevertheless, it was George Stephenson who developed the steam locomotive as we know it today.

Stephenson built a number of successful steam wagons. His first attempt, the *Blucher,* gave him the reputation and experience to be recognized as a master builder. When a railroad was constructed between the cities of Stockton and Darlington, Stephenson was asked to equip it with both locomotives

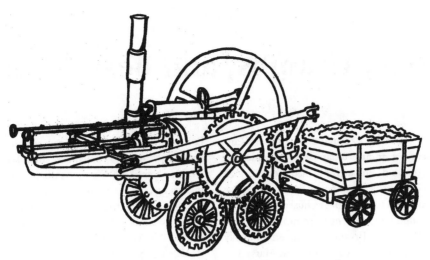

Trevithick's Steam Engine, 1804

and wagons. When the Stockton and Darlington Railway was opened for public business in 1825, both people and goods were pulled by Stephenson's steam wagon, the *Locomotion.* Of course, this is the origin of the term "locomotive" which we still use today.

Other railway companies quickly began to form. In 1828, the Liverpool and Manchester Railway wanted to use steam exclusively for all of its hauling. They offered a contest for the design of the most dependable and fastest locomotive. George Stephenson entered the race with his locomotive, *Rocket.* His new engine had a multiple tube boiler which produced steam more quickly. Moreover, the Liverpool and Manchester used iron fish-bellied rails. These runners were more stable and could carry heavier weights. They had a wide bottom with a crown on top. Stephenson's *Rocket* won the race, and the age of steam was securely founded. Stephenson also planned the placing of road beds in England and designed a type of running gear which remained the prototype until the end of the century. Just as important, there were American observers at the Liverpool and Manchester race. They quickly realized the possibilities of both railroads and the steam locomotive for their new country. The observers were also present at Rainhill where all forms of rail motive power were tested.

The English answered their economic needs by constructing their railways between cities or from mines to wharves on the coasts. They linked industries and towns which were already in existence and where markets had already been established. The use of steam locomotives was encouraged, because there was a shortage of horses due to the long war with Napoleon in the early 1800s. Horses were used for cavalry and to pull cannon and military supplies. Given the limited power of the earliest locomotives, railways sacrificed the shortest route for one with the least incline and the most gradual curves. The English also settled the problem of track gauges or the distance between the two rails.

— Early Track Gauge —

The setting of the rails at 4 feet 8½ inches became common during the first decades of railroading in England. As far as can be determined, it was the axle length or wheel width of the Roman chariots in England. It was a comfortable distance for hitching two horses to pull a carriage or wagon. Since the first wagons and carriages on the railways were converted from existing road vehicles, the spacing was convenient and natural. Another explanation is that England's most prominent locomotive builder, George Stephenson, tested his engines on a 4 foot 8½ inch colliery track. In 1846, Parliament passed a law establishing 4 feet 8½ inches as the standard gauge. This measurement became common in most of Europe and eventually Canada and the United States by the late nineteenth century.

Railroads quickly spread throughout Europe. In 1827, France constructed tracks between St-Etienne and Andrezieux. It started using steam in 1832. In the German states, a railroad was constructed between the cities of Nuremberg and Furth. Russia had a horse-drawn railroad in 1836, but any major construction did not occur until the 1840s. The English soon invested in rails in Canada, beginning with the Grand Trunk Railway.

Mail bag set-up and Railway Post Office car with hook on side. The hook snapped the bag at speed.

Lions, Thumbs, and Best Friends

Even before studying the Stockton and Darlington Railway, Americans were not totally unfamiliar with moving things by rail. Boston and Philadelphia had horse-drawn trams. During the 1790s, carts on runners were used to move dirt from Beacon Hill to build the Massachusetts capitol in Boston. In order to build a monument to commemorate the battle of Bunker Hill, Gridley Bryant constructed a railway to carry granite block from a quarry near Quincy, Massachusetts. Bryant developed the prototypes of switches and sidings as well as wagons which had eight instead of four wheels. The extra wheels added stability and distributed the weight of the heavy granite more easily. Bryant's "Granite Railway" was chartered in 1826.

The Province of Quebec's earliest railway was constructed in 1830 to build a fortress. It used a stationary steam engine to pull granite blocks up an incline.

There were theoretical developments that preceded the English. As early as 1755, Oliver Evans envisioned a railroad pulled by the new Watt-type steam engine. Later, John Stevens constructed a steam engine in his backyard in Hoboken, New Jersey. Stevens used his train for recreational purposes only. He did, however, apply to the state of New Jersey to build a completely functional railroad. He never followed through on the venture.

— The Stourbridge Lion —

Real developments in America occurred after the "Rainhill Trials" in October 1828, where different forms of propulsion competed against each other. Horatio Allen of the Delaware and Hudson Canal Company as well as Johnathan Knight, Maj. George W. Whistler, Ross Winans, and George Brown, later of the Baltimore & Ohio Railroad, observed the early steam experiments. Each observer would play an important role in U.S. railroad development. Allen was so impressed by the English steam locomotives that he ordered one for the canal company from the firm of Foster and Rastrick of Stourbridge. The locomotive, known as the *Stourbridge Lion,* weighed over seven tons. When Allen tried to operate it over the company's eleven-mile track near Carbondale, Pennsylvania, it was too heavy and actually sank a trestle into the soft ground. After a second trial which also proved unsuccessful, Allen had to give up, and the *Lion* was placed in storage. More important, however, Allen understood that a steam railway would permit the canal company to transport goods even during the winter months. He later took his expertise to the Charleston and Hamburg Railroad, which was starting to undergo construction.

Charleston, South Carolina, and Baltimore, Maryland became rivals in building the first railroad in America. Charleston wanted to form a link with Hamburg to increase its exports.

Baltimore, however, had a larger vision. With the Erie Canal completed in 1825, Baltimore could see that its commercial rivals of New York City and Albany had a great advantage in increasing business with the interior of the nation. With a port at Buffalo, the entire area of the Great Lakes would funnel its products to New York and vice versa. Baltimore had to look to the Ohio River Valley for a similar venture.

During the 1820s Baltimore boasted a population of over 60,000 people. As the third largest city in the United States, it had a newly constructed cathedral and a theater. Baltimore's one geographic advantage over New York and Philadelphia was that it was hundreds of miles closer to the Ohio River. The Ohio River Valley was already growing in population, and its connections with the east-coast cities was through the Mississippi River and the port of New Orleans. Traveling on the road to Wheeling (now West Virginia) took over three days by fastest coach under optimum conditions, and it was not suitable for carrying goods or produce in any quantity.

— The Baltimore & Ohio —

Some believed that Baltimore's only hope was to construct a canal through several hundred miles to the Ohio River. By late 1826, the merchant Philip Thomas and others from the Chesapeake and Ohio Canal Company realized that a canal through the Alleghenies would be prohibitive, considering the costs and the numerous locks that would have to be constructed. It was at that point that Evan Thomas, Philip's brother, suggested that a railroad might be the answer. Evan Thomas had visited England and had seen the Stockton and Darlington Railway in operation. Within a few months, the Thomas brothers developed a plan and went about convincing their fellow citizens of Baltimore to invest in building a railroad across the Alleghenies.

On February 28, 1827, the state of Maryland issued a charter for the Baltimore & Ohio Railroad. The new company was formed in April and released its first issue of 15,000 shares of stock. Other issues of stock soon followed. Philip Thomas was its first president and George Brown its treasurer. Some important board members were Alexander Brown, William Paterson, and Charles Carroll of Carrollton. The board appointed Johnathan Knight chief engineer and Col. Stephen H. Long and Maj. George W. Whistler to survey and plot the road. Both Knight and Whistler knew English railroading techniques first hand.

Construction began with a huge ceremony on July 4, 1828. Thousands attended as it is estimated that most of Baltimore had purchased at least one share of stock in the new company. The Grand Lodge of Masons of the State of Maryland officiated over the activities. The celebration included parades and speeches and toasts. A copy of the company charter

The B&O Station in Ellicott City was the first structure built as a railroad station in the United States. Courtesy B&O Railroad Museum.

The *Tom Thumb*. Courtesy B&O Railroad Museum.

and the day's newspapers were placed in the first stone. Ninety-two-year-old Charles Carroll of Carrollton, a board member and sole surviving signer of the Declaration of Independence, lifted the first shovelful of earth. He then looked to a friend and said: "I consider this among the most important acts of my life, second only to my signing of the Declaration of Independence, if even it be second to that." Indeed, Charles Carroll's vision for the new nation was just as accurate and prophetic in 1828 as it was in 1776.

Three days later, construction engineers began to survey the roadbed for a distance of 13 miles to Ellicott's Mills. Construction bids were taken over the remainder of the summer, and work began in October. Within a year, the railroad graded 25 miles, and by December there was enough track to provide rides for important guests in a coach pulled by a horse. Due to public demand, the first revenue runs began on January 7, 1830. By that spring, the Baltimore & Ohio Railroad had built the "world's first" railroad station and extended its revenue service to Ellicott's Mills. It expanded to Washington, D.C., in 1835. By the late 1850s the B&O reached St. Louis. It gained direct access to Chicago in the 1880s.

The Baltimore & Ohio set construction examples which led the way for U.S. railroads. They built their bridges to accommodate weights which were not yet realized in the 1830s. Its Carrollton and Thomas viaducts are still in use today. They actually paid for the passage of immigrants, particularly Irish, who escaped famine and political oppression to work on the road. These men were in a sense indentured servants as they had to pay for their travel by working for the railroad. Temporary shelters and even the earliest bunk cars were set up at the end of track for living quarters. At first the Baltimore & Ohio used granite for their tracksills, but this proved too expensive. They soon turned to using wood ties which gave a smoother ride and were cheaper.

— The Tom Thumb —

The Baltimore & Ohio is also responsible for the first important story in American railroad folklore. In 1829, Peter Cooper, a glue maker and real estate speculator, built an experimental steam engine called the *Tom Thumb*. Ross Winans, a horse dealer who knew about English steam engines, assisted. Cooper actually used old musket barrels for his boiler tubes and pulled carriages of dignitaries on the railroad from time to time.

There were still many people who believed that the horse was superior to the "steam contraption." A race took place between the *Tom Thumb* and a horse called "Lightning" along the double track between Baltimore and Ellicott's Mills. Cooper's *Tom Thumb* maintained the lead until the belt slipped off the drafting blower. The engine slowed down, and the horse passed it handily. Although the horse won the race, the steam engine made a strong and convincing impression of its capabilities.

The *Tom Thumb*, however, was an experimental engine. In 1831, the Baltimore & Ohio offered a $4,000 prize to the builder of a commercially successful steam locomotive. Phineas Davis of York, Pennsylvania won. He called his winning locomotive the *York*. By 1835, the B&O operated seven steam locomotives. It had 44 passenger cars and over 1,000 freight cars, called "burthen" or "burden" cars, in use.

During the 1830s a number of railroads received charters and/or began construction. In 1831, the Mohawk and Hudson ran a steam locomotive, the *De Witt Clinton*, over 12 miles of track. In 1833, the New York and Harlem opened for business, and the following year the state of Pennsylvania had 81 miles of track in use for its Philadelphia & Columbia Railroad, the origin of the future Pennsylvania Railroad. Others were the Central Railroad and Canal Company of Georgia, the Petersburg Railroad, the Boston & Worcester, and Boston & Lowell, just to name a few.

— Canada's Firsts —

The Champlain and St. Lawrence Railroad has claim to be the first railroad north of the U.S. border. A group of Montreal businesspeople understood the advantages of a railroad and eagerly kept themselves informed of developments in the United States and in England. In 1832, they formed the Company of

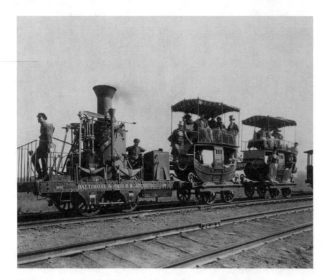

First coaches on the Centennial Celebration of the B&O.
Courtesy B&O Railroad Museum.

Proprietors to invest and begin construction. In July 1836, they staged a huge celebration to witness the official opening of the railroad. Lord Gosford, the governor general of British North America, and Louis-Joseph Papineau, a representative of the French-speaking population, were among the first to ride.

The line was barely ten miles long and ran between Montreal on the St. Lawrence River and St. Johns (Saint-Jean) on the Richelieu River. It was a means to overcome the rapids of the Richelieu on the last portion of a road from New York City. In short, it was a "portage" between the St. Lawrence River and Lake Champlain.

Its first locomotive, the *Dorchester*, was imported from England. The *Dorchester* ran the length of the road in less than an hour, thereby cutting the usual stagecoach running time to one-third. The line was profitable as many used it for both passenger and commodity service. By 1850, five other railways had laid track including one in Nova Scotia and the Montreal and Lachine.

— The Best Friend of Charleston —

While many of the early railroads would develop into or become part of much larger systems, the Charleston and Hamburg Railroad became a prototype of the southern system and the earliest rival of the Baltimore & Ohio. Chartered in 1828, for the South Carolina Canal & Railroad Company, the Charleston and Hamburg followed the banks of the Savannah River. Instead of trying to develop the interior per se, the motive was to make a direct connection with Hamburg for the exportation of agricultural products. It built tracks to a 5-foot gauge which would remain the "southern standard" until the 1880s.

The Charleston and Hamburg can claim several firsts. It ordered and used one of the earliest commercially built American locomotives, the Best Friend of Charleston. Also, during one of its early runs, the Army actually moved troops by rail for its exercises and shot a cannon from the moving train. It was the first railroad to offer regularly scheduled passenger trains in 1830.

The *Best Friend* was destroyed when its boiler exploded — probably the first on a North American railroad. While it was being turned and prepared on a turntable, the fireman sat on the safety valve to stop the constant and apparently angering hissing noise. The boiler exploded, killing the fireman and injuring several onlookers. When another locomotive was ordered from the West Point Foundry, the safety valve was placed on top of the boiler, well out of reach. The Charleston and Hamburg also placed a "barrier car" with bales of hay between the engine and the passengers for safety.

— Early Technical Developments —

During the 1830s and early 1840s the railroads experienced many technological and business developments. First and foremost, the railroads became "common carriers" for the general public. The owners determined at the outset that people and goods had to use or occupy railroad property only. The public could not use their own, private conveyances on tracks the way they used wagons and coaches on roads and turnpikes. This "single entry" practice permitted the railroads to become huge economic enterprises and to make improvements in a somewhat orderly manner.

If increasing the motive power to pull a train was a problem, finding ways to stop it consistently was an even bigger one. Since the movement of wheels on rails overcame resistance to a great degree, it was and still is difficult to stop a train quickly. The first attempts used the idea then in practice with stagecoaches. The brakeman wedged a club against a wheel to cause resistance. In fact, the early brakeman could be easily recognized with his club in hand at almost all times. Usually he was placed at the back of the tender, and he had to keep a sharp lookout for the engineer to hoist a white flag — his signal to stop the train.

By the mid 1830s, trains became too heavy and long for a simple club to stop them; by the early 1840s almost all railroads were using a shoe type brake which was attached to a chain and geared to a wheel. A number of brakemen would turn the top wheel to tighten the shoe against the rail wheel. As closed boxcars developed, the wheels were located on the top of the vehicle. The brakemen would then have to hop from car to car of the moving train to apply the brakes. This was an extremely dangerous task under the best of conditions. Nevertheless, they had to stop the train in any kind of weather: rain, snow, or sleet, as well as the heat of summer. Sometimes the brake was frozen, and worse, sometimes the chain would snap, injuring or killing the brakeman. Many were injured or killed by falling from the moving train. It was a most dangerous profession.

With longer trains, different cars, and a number of brakemen, the flag-brake signal would no longer work. Engineers then used the newly invented steam whistle to signal the brakemen to apply or release the brakes. Credit for inventing the whistle goes to Maj. George W. Whistler when he was chief design engineer at the Lowell Locomotive Works in Massachusetts in the mid to late 1830s. After surveying for the Baltimore & Ohio Railroad, Whistler resigned from the military and worked at the Lowell Locomotive Works. He also surveyed the Boston and Providence Railroad and

Consolidated Code of Operating Rules

The rules herein set forth govern the railroads operated as listed. They take effect June 1, 1967, superseding all previous rules and instructions inconsistent therewith.
Special instructions may be issued by proper authority.

ENGINE WHISTLE SIGNALS

15. The whistle must be sounded where required by rule or law. In case of whistle failure, speed of train must be reduced and the bell rung continuously when approaching and passing through stations, yards, over public crossings and around curves.

The unnecessary use of the whistle is prohibited and it must not be sounded while passing or being passed by a passenger train, except where required by rule or law, or in case of an emergency.

When two or more engines are coupled together, the leading engine only will sound the whistle signals.

The signals prescribed are illustrated by "o" for short sounds; "—" for longer sounds.

Sound	Indication
(a) —	When standing, air brakes applied.
(b) — —	Release brakes. Proceed.
(c) — o o o	Protect rear of train.
(d) — — — —	Flagman may return from west or south, as prescribed by Rule 99.**
(e) — — — — —	Flagman may return from east or north, as prescribed by Rule 99.**
(f) o o o —	Protect front of train.
(g) o o	Answer to 15 (k) or any signal not otherwise provided for.
(h) o o o	When standing, back. Answer to 8 (d) † and 16 (c). †† When running, answer to 16 (d). †††
(j) o o o o	Call for signals.
(k) — o o	SINGLE TRACK—To call attention of engine and train crews of trains of the same class, inferior trains and yard engines, and of trains at train order meeting points to signals displayed for a following section. If not answered by a train, the train displaying signals must stop, notify them and ascertain the cause, except in CTC territory, the train displaying signals will not stop. DOUBLE OR THREE OR MORE TRACKS—To call attention of engine and train crews of trains of the same class and inferior trains moving in the same direction and yard engines to signals displayed for a following section. Note. — Where single track is in use with portions of double or three or more tracks, this signal will also be given to trains in the opposite direction.
(l) — — o —	Approaching public crossings at grade. Standard sign will designate point at which signal must begin, to be prolonged or repeated until crossing is occupied by engine or cars. This signal must also be used frequently to warn trackmen and other employees when view is restricted by weather, curves, or other unusual conditions, and when approaching tunnels and snow sheds, also as alarm for persons or livestock on the track.
(m) ————————————	Approaching stations, junctions, railroad crossings at grade and drawbridges.
(n) — — o	Approaching meeting or waiting points. Answer to 16 (l). See Rule S-90.*
(o) o —	Inspect train for air leak or for brakes sticking.
(p) Succession of short sounds	When an emergency exists and it is necessary to use engine whistle to call for brakes to be applied on moving train or cars,

(continued)

Sound	Indication

or when necessary to use engine whistle to signal some other movement to stop.

(q) — o   When running against the current of traffic:

(1) Approaching stations, curves, or other points where view may be obscured.

(2) Approaching passenger or freight trains and when passing freight trains.

(3) Preceding the signals prescribed by 15 *(d)* and 15 *(e)*.

Note. — Where there are two main tracks on which movements are made in both directions by signal indications, trains on left track will sound this signal preceding 15 *(d)* and 15 *(e)*.

(r) — — — — — o   Flagman may return from east or north on 3 track or diverging line, as prescribed by Rule 99.**

(s) — — — — o   Flagman may return from west or south on 3 track or diverging line, as prescribed by Rule 99.**

(t) — — — — — o o   Flagman may return from east or north on 4 track, as prescribed by Rule 99.**

(u) — — — — o o   Flagman may return from west or south on 4 track, as prescribed by Rule 99.**

(z) o — o   Transfer of air brake control.

†Rule 8 *(d)*: Hand, flag, and lantern signal: Swung in a circle at right angle to the track—Indication: Back
††Rule 16 *(c)*: Three sounds: When standing: Back
†††Rule 16 *(d)*: Three sounds: When running: stop at next passenger station

*Rule S-90: On trains equipped with communicating signal systems, the conductor must give signal 16 *(l)* to the engineer immediately after passing the last station but not less than one mile preceding a scheduled meeting point with a superior train or a point where by train order it is restricted for an opposing train. The engineer will immediately reply with signal 15 *(n)*. If the engineer fails to answer by signal 15 *(n)*, the conductor must take immediate action to stop the train.

On other trains, the engineer will give signal 15 *(n)* at least one mile before reaching a meeting or waiting point.

Radio communication may be used instead of communicating signal and engine whistle signal, when so used an understanding of the conditions must be reached.

**Rule 99: When a train is moving under circumstances in which it may be overtaken by another train, a member of the crew must drop lighted fusees at proper intervals and take such other action as may be necessary to insure full protection.

When a train stops under circumstances in which it may be overtaken by another train, or when other conditions require flag protection, a member of the crew must go out immediately a sufficient distance to insure full protection, placing two torpedoes, and when necessary, in addition, displaying lighted fusees.

When a train is seen or heard approaching before a flagman has reached a sufficient distance, he must immediately place torpedoes and continue toward the approaching train, giving stop signals.

The front of the train must be protected in the same way when necessary.

When recalled, and safety of the train will permit, the flagman may return and when conditions require, he will leave a lighted fusee and torpedoes.

When a train requires protection the engineer must immediately sound signal 15 *(c)* or 15 *(f)*. Inability to hear these signals does not relieve members of the crew from protecting the train.

The conductor and engineer are responsible for protection of their train.

FLAGMAN'S SIGNALS

Day signals—A red flag, not less than ten torpedoes and six red fusees.
Night signals—A white light, not less than ten torpedoes and six red fusees.

Note. — When the rear of the train is protected by a continuous ABS System, protection against following trains on the same track is not required. This provision does not apply to any unit of equipment which does not actuate the block or cab signals or to a work extra.

(continued)

99 (A). When a train has been flagged, flagman must inform the engineer why the train has been flagged and engineer must be governed by conditions.

99 (B). When a train is unable to proceed against the right or schedule of another train, the conductor may send a flagman to hold that train. Flagman must be given written instructions to show to engineer of train on which he is sent and also to be shown to the engineer of the train to be held. Flagman must ride on the engine and engineer must stop and let him off at first switch at station to which he is sent. Conductor will retain a copy of flagging instructions.

BUTTE, ANACONDA AND PACIFIC RAILWAY COMPANY
W. F. Conroy, President and General Manager

CHICAGO, BURLINGTON AND QUINCY RAILROAD COMPANY
COLORADO SOUTHERN RAILWAY COMPANY
FORT WORTH AND DENVER RAILWAY COMPANY
I. C. Ethington, Vice President Operations

CHICAGO, MILWAUKEE, ST. PAUL AND PACIFIC RAILROAD COMPANY
F. G. McGinn, Vice President Operations

CHICAGO AND NORTH WESTERN RAILWAY COMPANY AND AFFILIATED LINES
S. C. Jones, Vice President Operations

DAVENPORT, ROCK ISLAND AND NORTH WESTERN RAILWAY COMPANY
J. E. Cary, General Manager

DES MOINES UNION RAILWAY COMPANY
F. E. Devlin, General Manager

DULUTH, MISSABE AND IRON RANGE RAILWAY COMPANY
D. B. Shank, Vice President and General Manager

GREAT NORTHERN RAILWAY COMPANY AND AFFILIATED LINES
J. L. Robson, Vice President Operations

MINNEAPOLIS, NORTHFIELD AND SOUTHERN RAILWAY COMPANY
B. N. Howery, Vice President and General Manager

SOO LINE RAILROAD COMPANY
T. R. Klingel, Senior Vice President

MINNESOTA TRANSFER RAILWAY COMPANY
ST. PAUL UNION DEPOT COMPANY
W. F. Bannon, Vice President and General Manager

NORTHERN PACIFIC RAILWAY COMPANY AND AFFILIATED LINES
F. L. Steinbright, Vice President Operations

PORTLAND TERMINAL RAILROAD COMPANY
J. H. Jones, Manager

SPOKANE INTERNATIONAL RAILROAD COMPANY
G. H. Baker, General Manager

SPOKANE, PORTLAND AND SEATTLE RAILWAY COMPANY
AND AFFILIATED LINES
N. S. Westergard, Vice President and General Manager

UNION PACIFIC RAILROAD COMPANY
OREGON DIVISION
G. H. Baker, General Manager

later went to Russia as chief construction engineer for the building of the railroad between St. Petersburg and Moscow. His son, James Abbott McNeill Whistler, however, became more famous for painting his mother and George W.'s wife: *Whistler's Mother*.

Railroad cars or "rolling stock" underwent great changes in the 1830s and early 1840s. The first cars were simply stagecoaches or carts fitted with flanges on the wheels. They were connected together by chains. Later on, cars were made specifically for use on the railroads. The Boston & Hamburg, later known as the South Carolina Railroad, used cars in the shape of barrels mounted on wheels. They became known as "Hacker's hogs head cars," named after Hacker, the builder.

Ross Winans of the Baltimore & Ohio pioneered several ideas which are still used today on rail cars worldwide. Winans placed the wheel flange on the inside of the rail. This placement gave the car greater stability and helped prevent tipping on curves. He also attached to and had the axle turn with both wheels. He then placed the bearing on the outside of the wheel itself. The moveable axle decreased wear on the wheel hub, and the outside bearing made it easier to grease and repair.

The Philadelphia, Germantown, and Norristown Railroad has claim for using the first four-wheeled swivel trucks or "bogies." These trucks gave a smoother ride, distributed the car weight over more track, and took curves more easily. The Baltimore & Ohio quickly adopted this idea and built passenger cars thirty feet long with benches on the sides. These cars had windows (which could not be opened), entry at ends, and even candles and a stove. Leaf springs attached to the trucks gave a smoother ride. By the mid 1840s, this type of car became the standard on U.S. railroads.

Boys heating stones for sale to train passengers. Sketch by Dee Dee Tymkowicz.

— Bumpers —

The first rail cars were stagecoaches with flanged wheels held together with three links of chain. When the train started, each coach jolted its passengers out of their seats as the chain became taut. There was always a jolt when the train stopped and the coaches banged into each other. Then too, there were jolts from time to time as each coach rolled faster or slower than the next.

During the 1830s, John T. Clark had the idea of placing a fence rail between the coaches to keep the chain taut. This bumper greatly lessened the jolts. The modern coupler functions as a bumper much in the same manner as Clark's fence post.

— Early Passenger Accommodations —

The early railroads stopped anywhere along the tracks to pick up passengers or freight. Nevertheless, most people gathered at the nearest way house along the track and waited for the train. Innkeepers were hired by the railroad to sell passage on the train. They would note passenger names in a book as they paid and carry it to the conductor as people boarded the train. The innkeeper-agent also had to keep a lookout for

the approaching train, and attic windows were often added to the building to give a clearer view of the clouds of smoke on the horizon. At the same time, it was hazardous to have a wood building close to the tracks. Many caught fire from the ashes spewing from the locomotives. Nevertheless, businesses wanted to locate as close to the inn-station as possible. The train station or depot quickly became the center of all the town's activities.

The inn-station was one of the few conveniences of early train travel. As distances increased, the train would often stop for passengers to gulp down a quick meal. Sometimes only 20 minutes were allowed. Passengers often stayed overnight at one of these inns during a long trip. There are accounts of people not only sharing a room, but also two or three to a bed. While sleeping cars and diners were still in the future, by the late 1830s the Cumberland Railroad did use a car that had wooden planks on ropes for people to rest or sleep. The railroad served a mining area of Pennsylvania, and it provided a way for the men to keep some kind of sleep schedule while underway. Last but not least, a few railroads had cars designated specifically for ladies. These cars had wash basins and changing rooms by the early 1840s.

Children took advantage of the early inconveniences of rail travel. During winter they would heat stones near the tracks and sell them to passengers to warm their hands and feet. Some carried water, snacks, and a local newspaper to the people. By the 1840s, they would travel on the trains themselves and were welcomed by the crew.

— The Steam Locomotive —

The steam locomotive is a Watt-type steam engine adapted to moving a train on rails. A fire heats water in a boiler to a temperature to turn it into steam. The steam gathers in the upper portion of the boiler, and as it does so, it builds up pressure. When the engineer opens the throttle, the steam shoots into a "dry pipe" to make its way to the cylinders. In locomotives manufactured after 1900, the steam runs once again through the boiler in dry pipes. As it does so, it becomes heated again to a higher temperature. This arrangement is called the "superheater." Superheated steam permits the locomotive to operate more efficiently.

When the steam enters the cylinder, it pushes a piston in one direction. When the piston reaches its furthest point, steam enters again at the opposite end to push the cylinder back. As the piston is pushed in one direction, the steam exhausts from the front of the piston into the "smokebox." The smokebox is located next to and above the cylinders at the front of the locomotive.

When the exhausted steam enters the smokebox, it creates a partial vacuum which draws air from flues through the boiler. Air enters the flues from grates located beneath the fire in the firebox. This drawing process causes a draft on the fire which makes it burn hotter and more cleanly. The sound of the drawn air entering from the flues and exiting through the smokestack causes the familiar "chugging" noise of the steam locomotive.

As the water boils into steam, the water level of the boiler is constantly dropping. Since the 1860s, the Nathan injector system replaced water into the boiler without losing much steam pressure. The water is stored in the tender which is coupled to the locomotive; it usually surrounds the coal or open area of the car. It is fed to the boiler from a hose connection. The fireman must be certain to maintain an adequate water level in the boiler at all times. If the water level drops below the "crown sheet" or top of the boiler, there will be an explosion which is almost always fatal for the engineer and fireman.

The boiler completely surrounds the sides of the firebox. If the engine is not used for some time or the water is not clean, sediment builds up which decreases the locomotive's efficiency. The fireman must "blow out" the water from the bottom of the boiler from time to time to prevent the accumulation of sediment.

Three types of fuel are used in the firebox to heat the water: wood, coal, and oil. The firebox of a wood-burning locomotive has a "V" form bottom. The angular bottom helps the wood burn more efficiently. Wood-burning locomotives have large "diamond shape" smoke stacks. The large opening contains a screen to prevent burning wood cinders from exiting and starting fires. The coal burning locomotive has flatter grates with an ash pan underneath to catch falling cinders. Its grates can also be moved back and forth or "rocked" for the dead ashes to fall into the pan. If the pan is not emptied periodically, it could crack the "rocker" panel.

After the 1900s, many larger locomotives had automatic coal feeders. An "Archimedes screw" brought coal from the tender directly into the firebox. The automatic feeder required smaller chunks of coal to operate effectively. Some locomotives in the Middle Atlantic States burned anthracite or "hard coal." These locomotives needed a wider grate to burn very small pieces of coal called "culm." Culm could not be used in furnaces or for commercial purposes. The larger grate area was known as the "Wooten firebox."

Oil-burning locomotives were developed around the turn of the century. Oil took less room in the tender and was less expensive to use in some parts of the country. Oil also permitted the "cab forward" locomotives. In these the engineer and fireman were placed at the front of the locomotive instead of at the rear near the tender.

The piston of a steam locomotive was attached to large wheels called "driving wheels" or "drivers." These wheels had matching "counter-weights" opposite the place where the driving rod was attached. The counter-weights permitted a smoother turning of the wheel. The driving wheels had an outer rim called a "tire" which had to be replaced every so many thousand miles. These tires protected the actual wheel. There could be two or more sets of driving wheels on a locomotive. A Mallet type of locomotive had two separate sets of six or eight driving wheels each. The first set was able to swivel or turn independently of the other wheels on the locomotive. Otherwise, the large number of driving wheels would not be able to negotiate curves. All types of non-switching locomotives had two or four smaller swiveling guide wheels on the front. This swiveling front wheel truck guided all types of locomotives to take curves more easily.

The piston and driver were attached to a "Johnson bar" in the locomotive cab. The Johnson bar determined the forward and reverse direction of the locomotive. In a center position, the gears were in neutral, and the locomotive did not move. The Johnson bar also regulated the amount of steam that entered the cylinder; the engine moved more efficiently using the expansion power of the steam rather than the amount. The less steam used to keep the locomotive moving meant greater fuel savings — and made the fireman's job much easier!

The steam locomotive had other mechanical devices. All were equipped with air compressors to operate the train's brakes. After 1900, most had steam-driven generators to provide electricity for the headlight and side marker lights. They also had a blower and blower ring in the smokebox to draft the firebox when the locomotive was not moving. Last but not least — after 1900, most locomotives had automatic lubricators. These used steam to push grease into the necessary assemblies while the engine was running down the track.

— The First Train Crews —

By the late 1830s, rails were a booming business, and the trains had to have some type of system to operate safely. The crew functioned in many ways similar to those running the new steamboats on the rivers. The men who ran and stoked the boiler below deck could not steer the craft. They could not see, and running the boiler took all of their attention. The captain ran the ship and was in charge of passengers and cargo as well as the ship itself. The same organization was applied to the train, although with some modification. The conductor was responsible for people and goods, and he ultimately decided where and when the train would stop, for how long, and who or what was permitted to board. The engineer and fireman were in charge of the boiler and running the engine. In contrast to the boat, however, they had to be constantly vigilant for any danger along the track as well as judging speed for safety. They were also responsible for alerting brakemen to stop the train. Conductors, engineers, firemen, or brakemen, the train crews quickly became heroes to everyone with whom they came in contact. In the public's mind, they were in charge of the marvelous contraption that changed wood and water into

motion and that ran faster and longer than anything seen up to that time. The phrase "All Aboard" applies equally to boat and train.

— Train Operation —

If a railroad had only one locomotive and a few wagons, there would be little chance of a collision on the rails. By 1840, there were almost 600 locomotives in the United States and thousands of cars riding on 2,800 miles of track. A signal system developed rather quickly to avoid incidents and determine which train should proceed first. The Baltimore & Ohio began a crude system using flags and lanterns in 1829. A better procedure began on the Newcastle and Frenchtown Railroad several years later. The Newcastle and Frenchtown used poles set approximately three miles apart. Large white and black balls were raised on them as signals. When a white ball was on top, the track was clear to the next pole, and the train could proceed. A black ball on top meant the train had to stop. The term "high ball" is still used today to indicate "clear track ahead."

Many railroads tried to keep an account of their trains by using a time schedule. Trains moved with the expectation that others would be at a certain place at a certain time. De-

Steam Locomotive

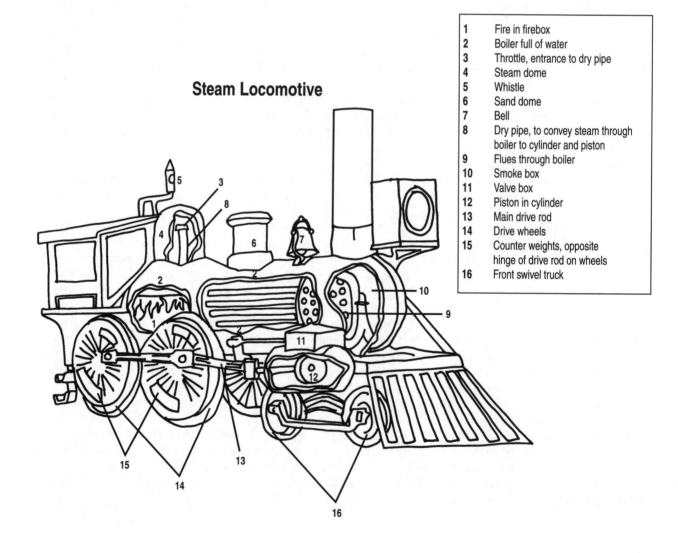

1	Fire in firebox
2	Boiler full of water
3	Throttle, entrance to dry pipe
4	Steam dome
5	Whistle
6	Sand dome
7	Bell
8	Dry pipe, to convey steam through boiler to cylinder and piston
9	Flues through boiler
10	Smoke box
11	Valve box
12	Piston in cylinder
13	Main drive rod
14	Drive wheels
15	Counter weights, opposite hinge of drive rod on wheels
16	Front swivel truck

The *John Bull* is an example of an early locomotive. It has a non-swivel front truck to guide it into curves.
Courtesy Railroad Museum of Pennsylvania, 039925.

lays, of course, almost always occurred. For passengers, the railroad companies posted the departure and arrival times of trains at the various stations. They sometimes published the "schedule of trains" in the local newspapers. The modern timetable was yet in the future.

Locomotives also underwent evaluations for consistent improvement. Ross Winans of the Baltimore & Ohio came up with a number of experiments. Some were called Crabs and Camels, because their appearance resembled those animals. For example, the cab of the Camel was centered in the middle of the boiler; it looked like the hump on a camel's back. Very quickly the horizontal or "Bury boiler" won over vertical designs. The most famous locomotive builder, however, was Matthias Baldwin.

— The Baldwin Locomotive Works —

In 1831, Baldwin built a steam engine to pull a train around a museum for recreational purposes, and sometime later he built a 5½ ton locomotive for the Philadelphia, Germantown, and Norristown Railroad. Baldwin used wooden wheels with iron strips around his *Old Ironsides*. This locomotive was able to achieve a speed of 30 miles per hour, but it lost power quickly on steep grades. He made several adjustments to overcome the problem, and used iron instead of wood for wheels. He increased the steam pressure from 60 to 120 pounds per square inch, and designed tubing capable of delivering that compression to the cylinders. His new locomotive not only had the power to climb steep grades, but his first model was recorded at a speed of 60 miles per

hour! By 1840, Baldwin had built ten of these locomotives, and by the end of the Civil War, his factory had produced over 1,500 locomotives! Baldwin became one of the largest manufacturers of locomotives in the world by the twentieth century.

— Locomotive Improvements —

In 1831, Isaac Dripps designed the first forward truck for a locomotive, the *John Bull*. He placed two wheels ahead of the boiler, which gave greater balance to the locomotive and guided it on curves. Since the driving wheels, by their nature, must keep a straight trajectory, they have a tendency to "climb the track" and derail on a curve. The forward truck helped prevent derailments. In 1832, John B. Jervis placed a four-wheel swivel truck on the locomotive *Experiment*. The swivel front wheels negotiated tight curves with ease and permitted railroad construction through mountain terrain.

Dripps also invented the "cow catcher" which became a standard on steam locomotives almost to their end. His first cow catcher was a series of iron spikes mounted on the front truck of the locomotive. Since it literally impaled roving cows or bulls, it was more of a problem than a solution; Dripps changed it to a less harmful series of downward sloping bars of iron which would push a bovine from the tracks. He designed these devices for the Camden and Amboy Railroad.

Soon an "American Design" locomotive emerged with 4 driving wheels and a swiveling four wheel truck and no trailing wheels. Steam locomotive styles are commonly described by wheel arrangements. The American Design would then be

Early rails were fastened to granite stone "sills." The practice proved too expensive, and wood ties became common.

DEVELOPMENT OF RAIL CROSS-SECTIONS
(Conventional measure — pounds per yard)

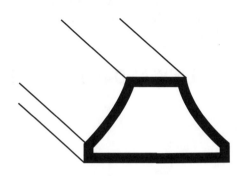

Fishbelly
1830s (England)

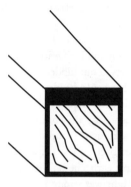

Strap iron on wood
1830s

60 lb
1860s — T rail

85 lb
1880s — T rail

130 lb
1940s — T rail

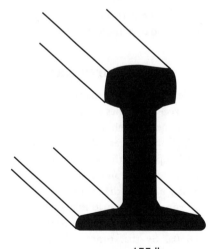

155 lb
1980s — T rail

4-4-0, describing the number of wheels from front to back. Steamers are often described the same way by diagram: oo00. This pattern means it has 4 front wheels, 4 driving wheels, and no trailing wheels. Henry Campbell and James Brooks used this wheel configuration in their *Blackhawk*. Nevertheless, Thomas Rogers is credited with producing what has become the "American classic," and the design lasted until the turn of the century.

Unlike the horse on the road, the locomotive could pull wagons in any kind of weather, day or night. People did not have to worry about hidden tree stumps in a river or holes in the road that could break an axle or the horse's leg. When railroads first ran trains at night, they kept a bonfire lit on a flat car pushed by the engine. By the late 1830s, railroads mounted a kerosene lamp on the locomotive's front with a reflector in back of the flame. By 1840, the familiar box-shaped light with a better-designed reflector was in common use. The light was strong enough for the engineer and fireman to see clearly down the track at night.

During the 1840s, the bell was added to warn people of an oncoming train, and the first known use of sand for traction was in 1836. When a plague of grasshoppers crossed tracks in front of a locomotive in Pennsylvania, someone had the idea of filling a box with sand which emptied through a tube to the tracks in front of the driving wheels. From that point on, a "sand dome" was added to locomotives. The engineer controlled the sand release with a lever in the cab.

Early locomotives burned both wood and coal. The railroads, however, favored wood, because it was both inexpensive and plentiful. As tenders came into common use by the late 1830s, locomotives began to use two firemen: One handed the wood, and another tossed it into the firebox. If they ran short of supply, it was common to stop and chop down a tree or two. For a while, Canada experimented with peat for fuel. The same went for water. Many times both crew and passengers had to carry water from a nearby creek or well to fill the boiler and reserve barrels. Locomotives often lost power when water was added to the boiler. The additional water was cooler in temperature which in turn temporarily lessened the amount of boiling water and steam. In colder climates the water often froze in its leather hose. It was a skillful crew who could thaw the leather hose without having it catch fire!

— Early Rails —

While there were not many collisions, since most trains did not exceed 18 miles an hour, there were numerous derailments and "snakeheads." Unlike England which used iron rails from the start, American railroads used wooden "runners" topped with a strip of iron. The strip was often at least ¼ inch thick and up to 2½ inches wide. The wood was mostly oak, and the iron strips had mitered ends. The rails or "runners" were held in place by stone at first. As this proved too costly, wooden ties became commonplace by the mid-1830s. By that time, railroads learned they could greatly increase the use of the wood by soaking it in certain solutions.

Snakeheads were hazardous and frightening. Quite often the end of an iron strip would spring upward through the car floor, injuring people. Sledgehammers were kept nearby to pound the strip back onto the wooden stringer. Trains often kept more tools in a rear wagon which soon became known as a "caboose," a name derived from the "cookshack" on steamboats. When a train derailed, which was not uncommon, everyone, including the passengers, had to help place it back on the rails.

LINK-AND-PIN COUPLER

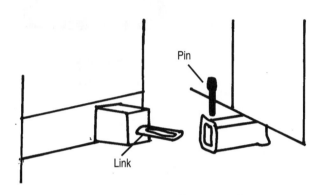

— Early Couplers —

At first, cars were attached to each other and the locomotive by chains. By 1840, passenger cars and freight wagons were being held together by a device called the "link-and-pin." A large iron rounded rectangular loop slipped into a housing on another car. An iron pin was dropped in a hole to fasten the two cars securely. The link-and-pin was a vast improvement over chains and other holding bars. It prevented cars from colliding into each other and provided somewhat smoother starts. It was dangerous, however, to couple and uncouple cars. Railroaders often lost fingers, hands, feet, and lives in the process.

— Mail and Express —

The U.S. government soon realized the potential for railroads to carry the mail. The first mail carry of record was in 1834. Four years later, in 1838, Congress declared all railroads "postal routes."

There were others who wanted a more direct or rapid way of carrying a package than by the usual teamster or freight possibility. In the early 1830s, William Frederick Harnden, a conductor on the Boston & Worcester Railroad, began carrying packages between the two cities during his work schedule. In 1834, the Earle Brothers set up an "express" business between Providence and Worcester by using the railroads. By 1839, Harnden advertised in newspapers as the Harnden Express Company. A year later he staffed an office on Wall Street in New York to facilitate sending small packages by boat and rail.

— The Celestial Railroad —

In 1843, the famous American author Nathaniel Hawthorne wrote a short story called "The Celestial Railroad." It is a take-off of John Bunyan's *Pilgrim's Progress,* except this time the hero, Christian, rides a train with baggage personnel who learned their trade from Prince Beelzebub.

Christian is accompanied by Mr. Smooth-It-Away who is a major stockholder and a member of Celestial Railroad's board of directors. Mr. Smooth-It-Away calms Christian when the tracks become rough and when they have to travel over a rickety trestle. When they arrive at Vanity Fair, Christian discovers that the rails do not reach the Celestial City; they must take a ferryboat to complete their journey. At that point, Christian wakes up and realizes that the entire trip was a dream.

Little more than a decade since the first train rode on American rails, locomotion became such a force that it was an integral part of mainstream literature. While Hawthorne may have been critical of train service, rail travel was already far superior to any other form of land transportation at that time.

— The Traveling Public —

By 1840, the business called the "Forwarding House" came into existence. The Forwarding House would purchase in advance large numbers of railroad and stagecoach seats to a number of destinations. It would then sell a traveler a "package" which included vouchers for rail and stagecoach connections. Many of these early forms of travel agencies were quite unscrupulous and left passengers stranded with invalid vouchers. Nevertheless, the railroads fostered the earliest "travel industry," and, as the railroad grew into more places, it forced the stagecoach and teamsters to move their business into new areas.

People liked to travel by train right from the beginning. They were fascinated by the new technology; in fact, it probably was the first truly technological device most people had ever seen. As they rode on the train, they were in awe of the speed, and some even experimented to see if they could write a letter or do ordinary tasks on a moving train. Perhaps more important, the train brought about a different relationship between people and the land. They became observers of the landscape; they were able to converse with each other very easily as the rivers and hills passed by. The journey became a matter of leaving one place and arriving at another rather than the difficulties and discomforts of the trip itself. In short, it gave people a great advantage in the struggle with nature.

The traveling public and the railroad builders still had a "canal and wagon" mentality in the 1830s. After all, water and horse had been conveyances for all of human history. Also, canal construction methods were used at first by the early builders. Running at night and during inclement weather were the first indications that the railroad truly changed people's perception of travel. The owners, too, realized that the steam locomotive did not need the rest stops required by the horse, and that it could achieve unheard-of speeds by an engineer moving certain levers. It was a matter of mechanics and technology rather than horse breeding.

The new technology carried with it a military attitude right from the beginning. For one thing, the planning and design engineers were for the most part West Point graduates who held military commissions. During the first quarter of the nineteenth century, only the United States Military Academy had formal courses in engineering. Also the similarity of running a train and sailing a steamboat required a well-defined hierarchical chain of command. Everyone had to perform certain tasks at a precise moment. A mistake could bring about problems or even a disaster. Then too, the early managers and engineers had to keep order among the construction brigades. The military structure was the best way to control hundreds of men and keep them on task.

More than ease of travel, right from the outset the railroads helped the country grow in a number of ways and set patterns for that development through the middle of the twentieth century. It helped the nation grow by facilitating the carrying of goods and people to more places much more securely and quickly. The sixteen-day journey by stagecoach or wagon now became hours.

Railroads also encouraged immigration to Canada and the United States. The new creation held out both political hope and economic opportunity to those who were adventurous enough to take advantage of it. The railroads played a large role in encouraging new people to come to America right into the twentieth century. Last but not least, by 1840 the railroads became a stimulus for the iron industry. The railroads' demand for iron encouraged the United States to begin an iron industry in earnest in order to be free of its dependence on English manufacturing. The early railroads were the leaders in North American economic development.

A few Americans in the 1830s — indeed, Charles Carroll of Carrollton — had a hint of the full potential of railroads. As early as 1835 the U.S. Senate discussed surveying the west to build a transcontinental railroad! While there was much interest, the bill failed. Moreover, railroad technology had not yet developed strong enough motive power to cross the mountainous west. That great feat was left to the next generation of railroaders.

Railroad Fever

Historical Survey

During the 1840s the New York journalist John L. O'Sullivan coined the expression "Manifest Destiny" to explain the growth of the United States. O'Sullivan argued that the country had a right, a God-given destiny, to expand from the Atlantic to the Pacific Oceans and to govern all the land in between. In a sense, O'Sullivan was putting into words a movement which was just beginning. During that time many people caught "Oregon Fever." They would travel to St. Louis, Missouri, where they would purchase horses and a "prairie schooner." They would then join with others to form a wagon train to cross the remainder of the continent to Oregon. Soon others branched off to California which was originally held by Mexico. Still others began to populate Texas.

These adventurous citizens declared Texas independent of Mexico and annexed it to the United States. By the late 1840s, others invaded the Sacramento River Valley and soon California became independent of Mexico. These settlers annexed California to the United States just before the news of the discovery of gold at Sutter's Mill spread. The Treaty of Guadalupe Hidalgo established the Rio Grande River as the boundary between Mexico and the United States. In 1853, the United States bought an additional 29,000 square miles from Mexico, called the Gadsden Purchase.

The admission of California as a state only heightened the slavery issue. From the birth of the United States, the southern portion had permitted the ownership of African Americans as slaves to do agricultural work. The northern states, particularly in the northeast, were becoming industrialized. For example, the one town of Lowell, Massachusetts, had more spinning factories than the entire South. In fact, the North made 85 percent of the manufactured goods in the United States. An anti-slavery or abolitionist movement began in that region. As the United States grew westward and new territories became states, both North and South competed for these regions to be designated "slave" or "free."

During the 1850s, the Republican Party was formed to prevent the expansion of slavery into new territories. The Republicans wanted to assure that any state admitted to the Union from the West would be considered "free." At the same time, they sponsored the building of a transcontinental railroad to aid the population growth in the West.

On the eve of the Civil War in 1862, the northern states were determined to prevent the expansion of slavery and to prohibit the southern states from leaving the Union. The southern states believed they had a right to leave the United States and to form their own country. They preferred to have a less strong central authority. During the Civil War, the South was correct that, if it could prevent the North from invading, the Confederacy would win the war and its independence. The North realized that it had to invade and conquer the South in order to win. The election of Abraham Lincoln, Republican presidential candidate, was the signal for the war to begin. The Civil War began with the Confederacy firing on Fort Sumter in April 1861, and ended with the surrender of the South at Appomattox Court House, Virginia, in April 1865.

During the 1820s and 1830s, England became alarmed that the growth and success of the United States would tempt the Canadians to follow that example. Lord Durham made an extensive study of the situation and recommended that Canada be permitted self-governance. He also recommended that Upper and Lower Canada be combined into a single province with each area having equal representation in an assembly. Such a confederation would permit both English and French subjects to have a large control of their respective affairs. In 1849, Vancouver Island was officially colonized and the Province of British Columbia formed in 1857.

In 1864, the new Canadian Confederation was planned at Charlottetown and later at a conference in Quebec. Those who formulated the documents became known as the "Fathers of Confederation." In 1867, the British North America Act formed Upper Canada into the Province of Ontario and Lower Canada into Quebec, along with New Brunswick and Nova Scotia. Vancouver Island merged with British Columbia in 1866, and British Columbia joined the Confederation in 1871. Manitoba joined in 1870. Prince Edward Island joined in 1873, Alberta and Saskatchewan in 1905, and Newfoundland in 1949. By the mid 1860s, Canada had a population of 3½ million people with only approximately 100,000 non-natives living west of the Great Lakes. Most of the population lived in a 200-mile strip north of the U.S. border.

Run to Goshen. . . .

Following a panic, or depression, in 1837, railroad construction went into a short slump. Nevertheless, for the next two decades, track mileage grew to over 30,000 miles, most in the northern states. Canada would have about 1900 miles of track by 1860. Steam engines became mostly the "American Type" and pulled longer trains. There were more conveniences for passengers, and the first sleeping cars came on the scene. By the time of the Civil War, the railroads altered the perceptions of distance and time for most Americans.

This spectacular growth, however, did not come without opposition. When the canal operators saw the loss of revenue to the rails, many argued that the new form of transportation was ruining forests, harming nature, and was generally against the "Almighty's handiwork." They were quick to point out that their canals were "God's Own Highway." Also, a number of ministers protested against the running of trains on Sunday. Their protests were in vain when the Civil War began. The owners of the Erie Canal, however, did get some retribution: the New York State legislature required the railroads running near the canal to pay tolls as if they were using the waterway. Thereby, the canal received revenue for goods and passengers it never hauled!

— The Courts —

Both federal and state governments became encouraging if not outright friendly to railroads and other industries. During the 1830s, states chartered railroads by individual legislative act as well as granting monopolies as they had in canal construction. By the 1840s, many states permitted the formation of railroad companies by the simple act of public incorporation. It was then much easier to incorporate, and there was the possibility of competition. In fact, the U.S. Supreme Court ruled in 1837 that state charters did not have the power to grant railroad monopolies.

American law helped the railroads by supporting the idea of eminent domain. In other words, the courts backed a railroad's right to take land legitimately owned by someone, reasoning that it could put it to better public use. In the area of "torts" or the ability to bring lawsuit, the courts ruled in favor of the railroads. Courts decided that the plaintiff had to demonstrate negligence on the part of the railroads to win a settlement. In short, court and legislative acts favored the financing and growth of the railroad industry. With this legal encouragement, from the 1830s to the Civil War period, a number of railroad companies started and expanded into a network that linked the major cities of the United States and Canada east of the Mississippi River.

The United States definitely caught "railroad fever" in the 1840s. The South, in wishing to remain a predominantly agricultural society, constructed railroads to haul its products to ports for overseas export. At the same time, given a milder climate, the South did not need the all-weather transport. Horses and wagons sufficed since roads were not blocked long by snow and ice. The North's railroads expanded rapidly, because it had to link together its growing manufacturing centers with resources as well as both urban and rural areas. With the outbreak of the Crimean War between England, France, and Russia in the 1850s, Europe purchased grain from the United States, and the railroads were able to transport the products from the midwestern states to the coast for shipment. At the same time, there was the need to increase the population of the plains states to provide greater production and westward expansion.

The Baltimore & Ohio Railroad, for example, did not stop its tracks at Wheeling, (West) Virginia, in 1853. Plans had been already underway to create an "American Central Line" of linkages with railroads in Ohio to expand further west. By 1857, the Baltimore & Ohio reached St. Louis. Competition from railroads in the North prompted the rapid growth.

— The Erie —

The New York & Erie Railroad, more commonly referred to as the Erie, was the earliest challenger to form a single company operating tracks from New York to the Great Lakes. The idea of constructing such a line belonged to William Redfield, who envisioned branches to the Mississippi River as early as the 1830s. He conceived the route from the Hudson River, above New York City, following south of the Erie Canal to Dunkirk on the shores of Lake Erie. He formed a company in 1833.

The New York & Erie Railroad was different from others starting at the time. For one thing, it chose to use all iron rails instead of wooden runners, and it constructed its tracks exclusively on trestles several feet above the ground. There were several good arguments for the elevation. For one thing, it avoided both people and cows on the tracks from interfering with train movement. It also permitted the train to ride above snow drifts and flooding.

The Erie engineers chose a 6-foot gauge. They believed that not being interchangeable with any other railroad would give them a monopoly on trade. In order to accommodate such a wide spacing, their ties had to be nine feet long and of the hardest wood — not to mention the trestle supports. They had to import the iron rails at first from England, but by the 1840s they were using American products. In fact, the Erie was one of the more important reasons for the growth of an iron industry in the United States.

The "Horseshoe Curve" on the Pennsylvania Railroad. Courtesy Railroad Museum of Pennsylvania. #26361.

During the Panic of 1837, the Erie, as with many railroads, fell into debt. Nevertheless, it continued to construct nearly 100 miles of its trestle tracks while bankrupt. When a large fire broke out in New York City and destroyed much of its records and property, the Erie had to abandon the project.

The New York & Erie Railroad was resurrected, however, in 1845, when the New York State legislature forgave its debts. A new president, Benjamin Loder, took over the company. While Loder kept the use of iron rails, he abandoned the idea of trestles, and constructed the tracks on the ground. He was also more fortunate, because a large number of Irish were migrating to the United States seeking work. The Irish were excellent workers, but from time to time they became quite rowdy. On one occasion when fighting broke out among a number of them, the railroad had to get the Army to stop the fracas. In fact, the soldiers had to use artillery against the fighting workers.

Farmers also caused some difficulties. Some opposed the railroad and accused it of destroying their land. A minor war ensued. Farmers took it upon themselves to destroy railroad property, grease the rails, and charge absurd amounts for use of water. They even placed already dead cows on the tracks and then sued the railroad for killing livestock.

The New York & Erie became known for engineering huge, extremely strong viaducts over rivers and valleys. Its management also created a number of railroad "firsts." It was the first railroad to issue a "train order" by telegraph. In other words, a message was sent from one train to another by telegraph from one station to another to tell it to stop or proceed.

It also innovated the "ticket punch." Even when the issuance of tickets was still fairly new, conductors realized that passengers were using them two or more times. The "punched ticket" kept passengers from using them again. Soon conductors had their own design, and at least 100 different punch holes came about. The Erie also institutionalized the "news butcher." The news butcher was an adolescent boy or young man in his twenties who sold newspapers, candy, and water on the trains. Railroad personnel welcomed them because of the convenience they brought the passengers.

There is some truth to the claim that the Erie invented the first "refrigerator car." During summer, the milk brought to New York City often arrived spoiled. Sometime during this early period, a railway worker had the idea of placing tubes of ice in the milk containers. Thereby, the milk was kept from spoiling before it arrived in the city. The Erie almost captured a monopoly in milk delivery because of this idea. Also, the train would arrive early in the morning in order to avoid the hottest time of day. This very early morning train came to be known as the "milk run" on other railroads throughout the country.

Another first led to the building of the huge iron and steel industry in the United States. During construction of the railroad, its directors sought cheaper sources of iron rails. One Erie director, William E. Dodge, loaned the Scranton brothers money to build an iron plant (at present-day Scranton, Pennsylvania) to produce rails. The Scranton enterprise started, and the Erie obtained cheaper rail. More importantly, the U.S. iron and steel industry was born.

The Erie Railroad opened all the way to Dunkirk on Lake Erie in spring 1851. The first train to cross the 450 miles carried dignitaries such as U.S. president Millard Fillmore and his secretary of state, Daniel Webster. Webster sat in a chair on an open flatcar, sipping his favorite rum which he claimed soothed his throat. . . .

Just prior to the Civil War, the Erie fell upon hard times. During the 1860s it revived and became a dominant player in New York to Chicago trade in succeeding years. In fact, three of its directors, Drew, Fisk, and Gould, were symbols of high finance chicanery. Nevertheless, the New York & Erie Railroad lived up to its title, "The Work of the Age." At almost the same time the Baltimore & Ohio built to Wheeling, the Erie opened up the Great Lakes water system with a railroad link to New York City.

— Captain Conductor —

Captain Ayers was one of the first conductors on the Erie Railroad. From time to time he had to remove an unruly passenger from the train. Since he did not want to wait until arrival at the next station to do the eviction, he rigged a device to signal the engineer to stop. Ayers strung a rope from the coach to the locomotive cab at the engineer's seat. When the conductor wanted to stop, he pulled the rope which lifted a stick attached to the rope's end in front of the engineer's eyes.

The first time Ayers pulled on the rope, the engineer, Abe Hammil, just kept on going. He had removed the stick. When they reached the next station, Ayers ran to the locomotive's cab and boxed the engineer on the side of the head; Hammil fell to the ground. The next time the signal was given, the engineer stopped the train. Other railroads adopted the idea, although some replaced the stick with a bell or gong. The conductor's authority over the engineer was thus established for all time.

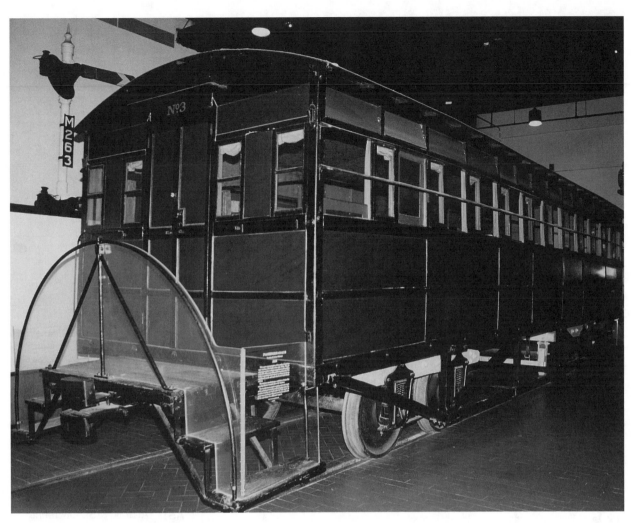

Exterior of Camden and Amboy coach — 1840s. Photographed at the Smithsonian Institution, Washington, D.C.

— The Pennsylvania —

Even before the Baltimore & Ohio reached Wheeling, the railroad petitioned the state of Pennsylvania to grant it a charter for trackage to Pittsburgh. Concerned businesspeople in Philadelphia realized that they too had to construct a railroad to the west. Without a railroad, Philadelphia would lose out commercially while both New York and Baltimore would grow. They convinced the Pennsylvania legislature to grant the Baltimore & Ohio entrance to Pittsburgh only if Philadelphia did not build a railroad itself.

Building a railroad across the Pennsylvania Allegheny Mountains was a formidable task. The mountain summits were much higher than in Virginia. A number of short lines already existed in the state on a Philadelphia–Pittsburgh latitude. What was soon to become known as the Pennsylvania Railroad was the creation of John Edgar Thompson.

Thompson had studied railroads in England, and served as chief engineer of the Georgia Railroad. He began his line by constructing a road from Harrisburg to Pittsburgh. He used inclined planes to haul traffic up the steeper grades. He then purchased the Philadelphia & Columbia Railroad to connect the eastern city with Harrisburg. Heavy construction began in 1847 and was completed in 1852.

Two years later, in 1854, the Gallitsin Tunnel was opened to traffic. The railroad could then cross the Alleghenies west of Altoona, climbing almost a thousand feet in 12 miles. The Gallitsin Tunnel and the Horseshoe Curve were marvels of pre–Civil War engineering. The 3,750-foot tunnel was constructed with only hand tools and gunpowder.

By 1857, the Pennsylvania had a one-company line from Philadelphia to Pittsburgh. It then secured a series of agreements to carry passengers and cargo all the way to Chicago in one system. This access to the area south of Lake Michigan gave the Pennsylvania a great advantage in the Midwest and was an important logistical factor during the Civil War. The Pennsylvania was built to a 4-foot 9-inch gauge.

— New York Central —

The New York Central System and the Pennsylvania Railroads remained archenemies throughout their existence. The New York Central originated with the merging of a number of short lines near the Erie Canal. Some had been constructed to bring people and cargo to the canal site, so they were not seen as competition. By the 1850s, the canal could no longer prevent the state from issuing charters for railroad construction in its vicinity anyway. The amalgamation in 1853 consisted of the following railroads: The Mohawk and Hudson,

25

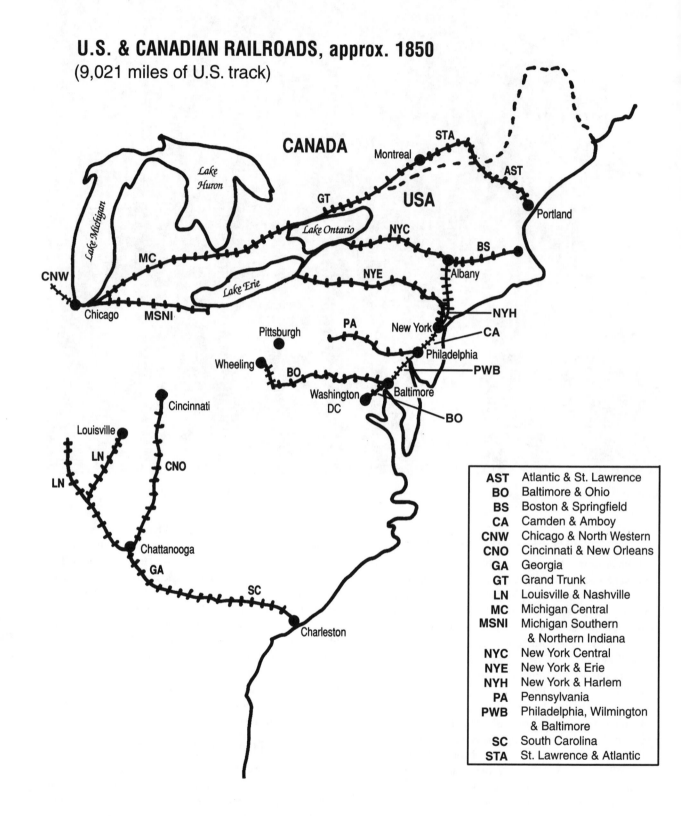

U.S. & CANADIAN RAILROADS, approx. 1850
(9,021 miles of U.S. track)

AST	Atlantic & St. Lawrence
BO	Baltimore & Ohio
BS	Boston & Springfield
CA	Camden & Amboy
CNW	Chicago & North Western
CNO	Cincinnati & New Orleans
GA	Georgia
GT	Grand Trunk
LN	Louisville & Nashville
MC	Michigan Central
MSNI	Michigan Southern & Northern Indiana
NYC	New York Central
NYE	New York & Erie
NYH	New York & Harlem
PA	Pennsylvania
PWB	Philadelphia, Wilmington & Baltimore
SC	South Carolina
STA	St. Lawrence & Atlantic

the Utica and Schenectady, the Syracuse and Utica, the Auburn & Syracuse, the Auburn & Rochester, the Tonawanda, the Attica and Buffalo, the Lockport & Niagara Falls, the Rochester Lockport & Niagara Falls, and the Schenectady and Troy Railroads. The Central used English standard gauge of 4 feet 8½ inches.

It had the advantage of not having to dig any tunnels or scale any steep inclines. It linked Albany with Buffalo, the two end points of the Erie Canal, and had the envious position of almost a monopoly of trade between those cities during the winter months. It was also able to link up with railroads in Ohio, most importantly the Lake Shore, which had a 4-foot 10-inch gauge. It had connections with New York City by the New York and Harlem Railroad.

Through keen business deals by its president, Erastus Corning, the New York Central had access to Detroit by means of the Great Western of Canada and the Michigan Central, which later acquired some small lines in Indiana and Illinois. Nevertheless, it did not control trackage to Chicago until 1872. It was relieved of paying toll charges to the Erie Canal in 1851.

The New York Central was not the only railroad to have association with lines from the northern provinces. Canadians were able to build a number of short lines, the longest being the Erie and Ontario Railway, which was only thirteen miles of track, to go around Niagara Falls. The most ambitious project, however, was initiated by a U.S. citizen, John Alfred Poor.

— St. Lawrence and Atlantic —

Poor wanted Portland, Maine, to become New England's principal port instead of Boston. He set out to convince the Montreal business community that there was an advantage to building a railway to the U.S. border. For one thing, a boundary dispute between the United States and Canada had recently been settled by the Webster-Ashburton Treaty in 1842. Then, too, the Montrealers knew that they lost commercial opportunities during the winter months when the St. Lawrence River was frozen. The St. Lawrence and Atlantic Rail Company was started in Montreal with some political maneuvering by Poor. He then started the Atlantic and St. Lawrence Railroad to meet with its northern counterpart. The United States's portion had to build through some of the most rugged landscape in New Hampshire. Ground was broken in 1846.

The 292-mile railroad was constructed at a 5-foot 6-inch gauge in order to inhibit competition. The Montrealers finally had an ice-free port at Portland, Maine, in 1853, and Portland was able to compete with Boston. Poor also had a vision of extending the line through Upper Canada to eventually connect with Chicago and the trade of the upper Midwest. The Montrealers received governmental financial assistance to complete their portion in 1849. Incidentally, John Alfred's brother, Henry Poor, edited the celebrated Poor's *Railroad Manual*, one of the most respected works of early railroading.

— The Great Western —

The Great Western Railway was organized in 1834. With governmental assistance, it began construction out of Hamil-

ton, Ontario, in the direction of London and another line to Niagara Falls. In 1855, it built a suspension bridge just below Niagara Falls over 200 yards long. It was regarded as an engineering masterpiece of its time. The Great Western Railway operated over 500 miles of track between Toronto, Windsor, Sarnia, and Niagara Falls by 1858.

— The Grand Trunk —

The Grand Trunk Railway was a more ambitious project. With its main office in London, the Grand Trunk built track from east of Quebec City, through Montreal west to Sarnia. In 1859, it opened the Victoria Bridge, which was over a mile and a half long, and spanned the St. Lawrence River at Montreal. It was known as the "eighth wonder of the world," and built as sturdily as any structure in North America. When the line opened from Montreal to Toronto, a spectacular party was held for over 4,000 guests! It connected with the Michigan Central at Sarnia.

Nova Scotia constructed a railway linking the port of Halifax with Windsor. Its track was most unusual; it was "double headed." As the crown wore on one side, it was simply turned over to use the bottom. The Nova Scotia Railway also carried farmers' products to market in horse carts placed on flat cars. When the train arrived at the station, they merely pulled the cart off the car and rolled it to the market. This may be the first consistent "piggyback" operation in North America. In 1859, a railway was built in New Brunswick to connect the Bay of Funday with the Northumberland Strait.

The various Canadian Railroads hoped to be able to siphon off commerce from the midwestern United States. It was important, therefore, to reach Chicago, the fastest-growing city on Lake Michigan. Chicago's growth in the second half of the nineteenth century is owed to a shrewd railroad policy.

— Mobile & Ohio —

The southern states regarded railroads as transportation for agricultural products rather than an industry in itself. In 1850, the Mobile & Ohio Railroad received a federal land grant and built as far as Citronelle in Alabama. By 1861, it built through Kentucky to meet the newly constructed Illinois Central at Cairo, Illinois. Also by 1861, the Louisville & Nashville connected with Western & Atlantic, the Georgia Railroad, and the South Carolina, to provide service from Charleston, through Chattanooga, and westward to Memphis. This southern east–west connection played an important role for both the Union and the Confederacy during the Civil War. The connection with the Illinois Central at Cairo, for example, gave the South railroad access to Chicago.

— The Illinois Central —

Even though the Mobile & Ohio and the Tallahassee Railroads received some federal funding, the Illinois Central became the model for the land grants given the transcontinentals. During the 1840s, the state of Illinois experienced an economic slump and out-migration. It needed something to encourage population growth and an economic stimulus. In 1851, the Illinois Central Railroad Company was created with a federal land grant of 2½ million acres. The grant was in cooperation with the state of Illinois and superseded all claims to properties. It was the first large land grant in history. The Illinois Central had to build 700 miles of track in six years. Cairo, Illinois, at the juncture of the Mississippi and Ohio Rivers, was its southern terminus. It had to repay the state with 7 percent of its gross income and agreed to haul all federal supplies and personnel free. The railroad had to sell the land to pay back its construction bonds. The land was located on alternate sides of the track in sections of 6 square miles — similar to a checkerboard design. The land originally sold for $2.50 per acre.

Like the New York & Erie, the Illinois Central had a rocky beginning. Its first president, Robert Schuiler, was forced to resign because of involvement in an embezzlement scheme. Nevertheless, construction began in 1852. The original plan was to build to the Indiana border on the south shore of Lake Michigan, but Chicago had its U.S. senator Stephen Douglas lead a protest. The Illinois Central entered Chicago proper.

There were many construction difficulties. The Illinois Central had to import iron rails from England. It had an advertising campaign in New York to hire laborers, but it eventually had to go to Europe to find workers. It hired as many as 10,000 men from Germany, Holland, and Ireland. The railroad offered an attractive wage and payment of all transportation. Many also came from New England. A good number settled along the tracks after the railroad was completed.

The Illinois Central's advertisements became famous for their exaggeration. There were scenes of beautiful landscapes and descriptions of Illinois as the "garden state of the west." The land, of course, had yet to be cultivated, and living conditions among the workers were primitive. Diseases spread quickly, and many workers left the site. In spite of these difficulties, by 1860, the Illinois Central sold 1½ million acres of land and was a huge factor in the state's doubling its population to almost a million.

By 1861, the Illinois Central had the longest track mileage under the direction of a single company. It also discovered coal near its line and was able to take advantage of it for fuel. The railroad sponsored county fairs to help farmers improve productivity — which of course meant more to ship by rail. It engaged in philanthropic work and contributed the founding money for Augustana College in Rock Island, Illinois. Both President Abraham Lincoln and George B. McClellan worked for the Illinois Central. McClellan was Vice President of Operations, and Lincoln, as an attorney, defended the railroad in a number of important court cases. After the Civil War the Illinois Central expanded southward to New Orleans and westward to Sioux City and Council Bluffs, Iowa.

— Chicago —

Chicago very quickly became the railway center of the United States and a southwest goal for the growth of the Canadian railway system. In reaching Chicago, the eastern railroads were now seeking a link with a midwestern urban, industrial, and commercial center rather than a lake or river. By the time of the Civil War, Chicago's railroad connections were far more valuable than its water routes.

The "Windy City," however, did not embrace "railroad

fever" as quickly as other places. In fact, some members of the Chicago business community wanted to keep the railroads out. Chicago became the nation's rail center as a result of efforts by William Butler Ogden. When Ogden arrived in Chicago from New York in the 1840s, he was an outspoken advocate of railroads and of the New York & Erie in particular. He suggested a railroad be built to the prosperous lead-mining town of Galena, located in a hilly area to the northwest. In the 1840s, many believed that Galena would soon become the largest city in Illinois. The Chicago business community was very skeptical. Their economy was then based on lake traffic and nearby farmers. Moreover, Chicago charged tolls on wagons entering the city, and the teamsters protested the arrival of a railroad.

— The Chicago & North Western —

Ogden did not give up. He spoke with farmers between Galena and Chicago and convinced them to invest in his railroad project. When Chicagoans learned of Ogden's activities, they refused to permit him to construct a depot or let his trains enter the city. He, therefore, built a station at the Des Plaines River outside the city limits in 1848. When his first train pulled into the station with 30 carloads of wheat, attitudes changed quickly. Chicago businesses realized they would grow faster as a railroad town.

Ogden extended his railroad toward Galena and eventually joined with other railroads in Wisconsin. The farmers became very enthusiastic about Ogden's scheme as soon as they received their dividend checks. In 1857, Ogden reorganized his railroad into the Chicago & North Western and expanded westward out of Chicago to Iowa and eventually joined with the Union Pacific at Council Bluffs. He allied with the Pennsylvania Railroad to get eastern connections and later became president of the Union Pacific.

With growth of the Chicago & North Western and later the Illinois Central, Chicago became a rail center. As more eastern and local lines were building into the area, Chicagoans realized that almost all the lines would converge on the southwestern shore of Lake Michigan. It was feared that a new town would spring up there, grow, and eventually eclipse Chicago. In order to prevent that from happening, Chicago passed an ordinance forcing each railroad to construct its own tracks into the city. Therefore, the railroads could not share tracks and there was less need to join together at the same spot.

Chicago was no longer dependent on the seasonal lake traffic for its economy. With the many railroads entering the city, it became a rail hub and a national location to process arriving resources and send manufactured products anywhere in the United States and Canada. In other words, it was a natural "break of bulk" point for all products. If "all roads led to Rome" in ancient times, all American railroads led to Chicago in the second half of the nineteenth century.

— Passenger Accommodations —

Passengers traveling by train in the 1840s and 1850s experienced a few improvements in accommodations. Most cars held between forty and fifty passengers. Seats were along the side with stiff-backed benches. Windows now could be opened, although there was always the chance of live ashes burning

Interior of a typical railroad coach of the 1840s. Courtesy the Smithsonian Institution. #P-65799.

clothing or getting in the eyes. These plain cars became known as "Accommodation Cars." There were also "Best Cars" with plush seats and even curtains. Many had ornately painted ceilings. In both cars winter travel still posed more inconveniences. If one sat near the stove at the end of the car, he or she baked, but if the passenger sat in the middle, he or she froze.

Some claim that the first vestibuled car was used in New England by the late 1850s. Vestibules are platforms usually at both ends of passenger cars. They are separated from the seating area by a wall and door. This open area helped make boarding and leaving the car easier. Enclosed vestibules, however, did not become common until the turn of the century.

— The Sleeping Car —

The first sleeping cars came into use at this time. In 1843, the New York & Erie took two coaches which they modified into the first true sleeping cars, using seat cushions to turn the benches into rudimentary couches. No linens or blankets were furnished. It did use candles to keep the cars lit at night. Passengers clamored to ride in these cars, but the Erie had to remove them from service, because they added too much weight and made the train slow down.

Just before the Civil War, Webster Wagner of the New

York Central built a number of cars which had berths rather than seats and restrooms at each end. These sleepers became immediately popular with travelers, and the New York Central as well as other railroads requested more. During the Civil War, Wagner established the Wagner Palace Car Company and in a few decades there were over 300 Wagner sleepers in use on American railroads. He also built "parlor cars" with large, comfortable chairs that could be moved from place to place.

— George Pullman —

The Pullman Company, however, became synonymous with railroad sleeping accommodations and luxury. George Mortimer Pullman was a cabinetmaker from New York. When he moved to Chicago, he first became involved in building construction, but that changed very quickly. In 1855, Pullman approached the Chicago and Alton Railroad with the idea of building a luxurious sleeping car. The railroad gave him two coaches with which to experiment.

Pullman hired the best German-American cabinetmakers in Chicago and set to work to transform the coaches. In 1858, he built the *Pioneer*. This car was the most luxurious ever built at that time. It had a black walnut interior with English royal velvet cushioned seats. It had an ornate chandelier for lighting and carpeting on the floor. The night curtains were of silk and it even had mirrors on the walls. The two washrooms had marble basins as well as toilets.

The *Pioneer* was a first for other reasons. The ten "bunks" were easily made into seats for day-time travel. Pullman made the bottom bed on hinges so it could be folded up or down. The upper berth was held by ropes and pulleys. During the daytime, the upper bunk could be pulled out of the way to the ceiling and also became a "closet" for the bedding. The Pullman sleeper furnished blankets for its patrons and had strict rules that passengers had to remove their boots before lying down on a bed.

Pullman's *Pioneer* quickly became the talk of railroaders. It is claimed that Abraham Lincoln rode the *Pioneer* to Chicago. According to tradition, he had to sleep on a couch at the end of the car since he was too tall to fit in a berth. Mary Todd Lincoln was so impressed by the car that she requested that it carry her late husband's remains from Chicago to Springfield for burial.

Pullman quickly improved on his car design. Subsequent sleepers had the upper bunk swing into the ceiling on hinges rather than ropes. They were easier to use and saved space. Understandably, there was competition between Pullman and Wagner for the sleeping car business. Pullman had an advantage with his association with Chicago railroads, and for yet another reason: Pullman's cars were at least a foot wider than those in common use at the time. Travelers relished the extra space, and railroads quickly followed the Chicago and Alton in restructuring bridges and station platforms to accomodate the larger cars. Pullman's sleepers set the width of passenger cars which is still the standard today.

Most travelers did not experience the sleeper until well after the Civil War. As railroad mileage increased, stations, restaurants, and inns were built to accommodate the still new mode of travel. There was little improvement over the lunch or dinner stop, and sleeping rooms at inns were still rather crude. The "news butcher" was a railroad institution by 1850. In fact, Horatio Alger immortalized him in the *Erie Train Boy* in which the hero goes literally from "rags to riches." It is also interesting to note that the great inventor Thomas A. Edison was a "news butcher" during his formative years.

— The "Call Boy" —

By the 1840s, youngsters also had the opportunity to work for the railroads as "call boys." The call boy had to run throughout the town to gather train crews. The call boy had to know where all the workers lived and, perhaps just as important, to be familiar with all their favorite taverns. Many times the call boy had to guide engineers and firemen to the station, because of their lack of sobriety.

— Safety —

Consumption of alcohol was a problem for some railroad workers even from the earliest use of trains. There were, however, few accidents other than "snakeheads" or derailments. Trains seldom ran over 20 miles per hour even though locomotives became stronger and faster. Running about 40 miles per hour became more common just before the Civil War.

Moreover, railroad travel did become safer, as many states outlawed the use of wooden iron-strip rails. Almost all railroad construction used iron rails in the 1850s, and the Pennsylvania Railroad experimented in some places with steel just before the 1860s. By the Civil War, boilers were being made of steel (see below).

— Technology —

There were other technological improvements in railroading. A Frenchman, Eugene Bourdon, invented the first accurate boiler pressure gauge. It was quickly adopted in the United States and Canada in the 1850s. By 1860, the Nathan steam water injector was used to force water into the boiler. The device saved time and gave greater assurance against boiler explosion. It was far easier than the earlier pumps which were operated off the drive wheels. If the train stopped for any length of time, the crew had to uncouple it and run it on the track to refill the boiler. Boiler pressure of over 100 pounds per square inch became common. The driving mechanism was also improved. The English-designed Stephenson Link Gear meant greater ease in placing the engine in forward and reverse and permitted higher speeds.

With the invention of the swiveling front truck, the American-type steam locomotive began to take shape. The cold weather of New England led to the first engine cabs to be made of canvas. By the 1850s all locomotives had wooden cabs and a tender. The "bonnet" or large diamond-shaped smokestack contained a "spark arrester" for wood-burning engines.

The straight stack usually meant a coal-fired locomotive. Some eastern railroads such as the Lehigh Valley, Delaware & Hudson, and Lackawanna & Western burned anthracite or hard coal by the 1850s. Anthracite provided a more intense heat and burned much cleaner.

Tracks themselves improved. During the 1840s, the U.S. iron industry grew in earnest. Foundries at Mount Savage, Maryland, and Danville and Scranton, Pennsylvania, furnished rails and other iron products. The T-rail, which is still used today, and the hooked spike were introduced on the Camden and Amboy Railroad, and by 1845, a mill at Montour, Pennsylvania, already had them in production. The railroads actually hauled the coal and iron ore for the products they

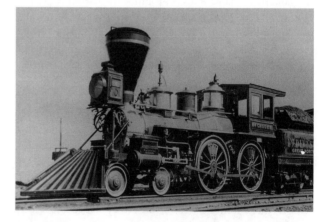

Great Northern's locomotive *William Crooks* is a good example of the American Type 4-4-0 Woodburner. Courtesy BNSF.

eventually purchased and consumed. The rapid growth of the railroad industry provided the stimulus for the U.S. iron and steel production. By the late 1850s, a small steel plant began making rails near Gary, Indiana. While steel production was both costly and slow, it did furnish enough rails for switchyards. In those heavy traffic areas, iron rails would wear out in less than a year.

— Telegraph —

Railroad safety and efficiency were greatly increased by the telegraph. Samuel F. B. Morse invented a way to transmit and interpret electrical impulses over wire. In May of 1844, he sent the first message, "What hath God wrought," over a line strung along the Baltimore & Ohio Railroad right-of-way between Baltimore and Washington, D.C. Before that time, the quickest common means to get information or anything else from one place to another was by train. Only the carrier pigeon could transmit information more quickly.

A crucial problem in controlling train movements was that it was impossible to inform people more quickly about what was happening down the track. If the Baltimore & Ohio did not know what advantage it had with the telegraph at arm's reach, Charles Minot of the New York & Erie certainly did.

Minot was an ideal railroad manager. He had experience working on railroads in New England and had studied law for a while. He also took a liking to the new telegraph and actually prepared himself to be an operator at one point. When inspecting Erie trackage under construction, he noticed someone stringing telegraph poles along a nearby road. Minot saw his opportunity and suggested that the line be strung alongside the tracks. The railroad right-of-way was an ideal place to set up telegraph poles. Minot bought stock in the company, and through his influence, it became known as the New York and Western Union Telegraph Company. Later it would be known throughout the nation simply as Western Union.

It is possible that Minot originally intended to use the telegraph to regulate train movements. He did so for the first time on September 22, 1851. Minot was riding a westbound train and was determined to keep to his schedule. Suspecting that an eastbound train was late, he asked the telegrapher at Harriman, New York, to contact the station at Goshen, fourteen miles away. He found out that the eastbound had not yet reached there. He then telegraphed Goshen and told the stationmaster: HOLD EASTBOUND TILL FURTHER ORDERS. He turned to his conductor and said: "Run to Goshen regardless of the opposing train."

When the engineer refused to obey the conductor's orders, Minot took over the controls himself and ran the train westward. The eastbound was not at Goshen when Minot arrived. So, he again telegraphed over the line to ask if the train had passed the next station, Middletown. The eastbound had not arrived there. Minot gave the same order to the Middletown station agent and proceeded westward.

Minot later printed forms for this type of regulation called a "train order." The telegraph could also keep an account of all train activities on a line. In many areas the railroad sta-

tion agent and telegrapher were the same person. People could go to any station and telegraph by Western Union a message to anyone else wherever a railroad reached. By combining the telegraph with the train, railroads would gain a near-monopoly on both transportation and almost instantaneous information through the United States and Canada. Along with sending and receiving express packages and mail, the railroad station became everyone's link to the nation and the world.

— The Train Crew —

The train crew's tasks became more standardized. Usually the engineer and firemen worked as a team and were assigned to a specific engine. The engineer was responsible for repairs and everything below the cab floor. The firemen were in charge of the boiler and everything above the cab floor. Two firemen were necessary on wood-burning locomotives, whereas one was expected to shovel more than a ton of coal an hour on coal burners. Both had to look down the track and watch for signals. The conductor, sometimes referred to as the "Captain," began to wear a uniform on most railroads by the 1850s. Now that tickets came into common use, the conductor punched them to ensure they could not be used again. He often placed a white piece of cardboard in the hat of someone traveling for free on a pass. The wearer quickly became known as having a "chalked hat." The conductor had access to each car through the front and rear entrances.

Railroads were major employers by the middle of the nineteenth century. There were numerous positions for trainmen who worked in the fast growing switchyards. Hostlers had to prepare locomotives for their work in roundhouses and repair shops. By the time of the Civil War, there were over 9,000 locomotives in the United States. Canadian railways were major manufacturers of locomotives and rolling stock for their own requirements. There were also attendants who had to prepare the coaches along with numerous clerks. In fact, the railroad industry was the first to see the need to keep accurate records of purchases and work production.

— The Caboose —

Conductors often sought an empty coach seat or an area in the baggage car to do paperwork. On freight trains such spare seats did not exist. According to tradition, sometime during the 1840s, on the Auburn & Syracuse Railroad, conductor Nat Williams would couple an empty boxcar to his freight train and use it for an office. He also used it to store lanterns and other tools. This conductor's car quickly became known as "the caboose." The concept grew quickly as the Auburn & Syracuse merged shortly afterwards with the New York Central System.

The name "caboose" supposedly came from a corruption of the Dutch *kabuis* or German *kabuus* which referred to the galley or cook shack on a ship during the eighteenth century. This explanation is possible since the Auburn & Syracuse area of New York State had a significant Dutch population. Chairs and a table were soon added, along with a stove. Later, a hole was cut into the roof so that the conductor could look out toward the front of the train.

— Express Companies —

Express companies also had to keep accurate accounts and waybills. A waybill is a piece of paper that accompanies a freight shipment giving details of goods, route, and charges. In 1845, the Adams Company bought out Harnden Express. Two agents, George Pomeroy and Henry Wells, expanded the business to Buffalo. Their success was so great that the U.S. Post Office complained about the competition. Congress later lowered postal rates to recapture business, but Pomeroy often used "fast horses" for delivery beyond the railway station — the beginning of the Pony Express.

After some changes, the company became known as Western Express, for the new agent at Buffalo, William C. Fargo, expanded business into the Midwest. The new company carried packages by rail whenever possible; in 1850, it became known as the American Express Company. Fargo had agents as far west as Minneapolis. As the company expanded to the Pacific with the railroad, it became known as Wells Fargo and Company. Another, also called the Adams Company, served primarily the South. By 1859, it served as far west as Galveston and Houston. During the 1850s, both companies required employees to wear uniforms and used their own systems of waybills to account for packages. Their quick letter-service delivery waned wherever a station with telegraph was installed. Then, too, whenever the railroad built in a new location, the stagecoach had to move on.

— Abraham Lincoln and the *Effie Afton* —

In February 1854, the first railroad reached the banks of the Mississippi in western Illinois. Two years later, the Chicago, Rock Island, and Pacific bridged the river to Davenport, Iowa. Within three weeks, however, the bridge was struck by the riverboat *Effie Afton*, caught fire, and was destroyed. The riverboat owners brought suit against the railroad for obstructing traffic. Although the Rock Island rebuilt the bridge, no new ones could be built for ten years until the case was settled by the Supreme Court. The Rock Island hired an experienced railroad attorney who later became one of the greatest U.S. presidents.

When the *Effie Afton* struck the bridge, its stove overturned. Both the boat and the bridge caught fire. The steamboat owners argued that the bridge obstructed the river channel and the Rock Island was responsible for the accident. Abraham Lincoln examined the scene, and, according to legend, questioned a boy who was on the riverbank about the water currents. He was able to argue that the currents at the bridge site did not pose any special navigation problem. If the captain had been vigilant, he could easily have missed the bridge. (There are some who argued that the boat hit the bridge on purpose.) In his summation to the jury, Lincoln argued a point more important than currents or vigilance. He based his case on the premise that one had as much right to cross a river as another has a right to go up- or downstream. He said that if railroads could not build bridges over the Mississippi, the development of the West would be hindered for years! Four years later, Lincoln's election to the presidency guaranteed a railroad across the continent and the development of the Trans-Mississippi West. And the Rock Island would be the first company to connect with the first transcontinental.

The *Effie Afton* case was one of Lincoln's many legal associations with railroads. When Stephen Douglas argued for a land grant for the Illinois Central, Lincoln traveled to Washington to lobby for the railroad. In the early 1850s he defended the Illinois Central from a property tax claim brought by McLean County. The county wanted to tax the railroad's property that went through its jurisdiction. Lincoln worked with Illinois Central's vice president, George B. McClellan. Lincoln won the case and charged the railroad $2,000. McClellan would not pay what he considered an exorbitant fee, so Lincoln raised it to $5,000 and took it to court! The court decided in Lincoln's favor. The judge who decided the McLean case was elevated to the U.S. Supreme Court in 1862. One humorous anecdote: Lincoln and McClellan had worked on other cases together, and, at times, they had to share sleeping quarters. McClellan would often complain that Lincoln would stay up at night telling ridiculous stories.

Lincoln had other financial dealings with railroads. He owned stock in the Seton & Sangamon, and he purchased a parcel of land from a colleague, Norman B. Judd, who had received the land when he worked for the Rock Island. The parcel was in Council Bluffs, Iowa, a frontier town of 1,500 people. In 1859, Lincoln went there to inspect his property and by chance met a railroad scout, Grenville Dodge. The two had a lengthy discussion about the best way to build a railroad to the Pacific. Afterwards, Dodge commented that he told Lincoln all the "company secrets."

— The Pacific Railroad —

The idea of building a railroad to the Pacific Ocean was not new in the 1850s, but there were a number of impediments. For one thing, the explorer Stephen Long, who led an expedition into the south Rocky Mountains, reported that the area was so inhospitable that no one could live there. He called the region from the Missouri River to the Pacific "the Great American Desert," and people referred to it as such for decades. That did not stop Congress from discussing the project, however, in the 1830s.

The first concrete proposal came from John Plumbe, Jr. In 1838, he actually received $2,000 from the federal government to undertake a survey from Milwaukee to Sinipee, Wisconsin, for a "National Railroad" to the Pacific. In 1839, he prepared a map of the line. Asa Whitney, a wealthy New York businessman, is often given the credit for giving the "Pacific Railroad" project its real impetus. He saw such a line as attracting trade from both Europe and the Orient by having the cargo pass through America on a railroad. Following Whitney's proposal in 1845, railroads included the word "Pacific" in their name in the hope of extending to the west coast.

There were several political events that encouraged the building of a transcontinental railroad. After a war with Mexico, the Treaty of Guadalupe Hidalgo (1848) recognized a vast tract of land from Texas to the Pacific Northwest as belonging to the United States. Only days before, gold had been discovered at Sutter's Mill in California. Now the huge numbers of Americans seeking gold would traverse U.S. territory as they sought their fortunes along the 35th parallel. In 1853, the United States bought a portion of land from Mexico, the Gadsden Purchase. A border dispute concerning the area of present-day British Columbia was resolved in 1846, which opened up more opportunities for Pacific Coast settlement. Furthermore, in favor of Asa Whitney's interests, the United States concluded trade treaties with China in 1844 and Japan in 1854.

The first attempt to build a transcontinental line was the Pacific Railroad of Missouri. Because of the California gold rush, the explorer and politician John C. Fremont received a charter from Congress to build a railroad from St. Louis to the Kansas border and beyond. At the same time, California's population swelled, and it became a state in 1850. Incidentally, Fremont was able to get support for the plan as his father-in-law was Senator Thomas Hart Benton of Missouri. Even though the project failed, due to financial problems, the charter was later received by the St. Louis & San Francisco Railroad and eventually used by the Santa Fe to reach the Pacific Coast.

Fremont did not give up the idea of a Pacific railroad. In 1856, he became the first presidential candidate of the newly formed Republican Party. During the campaign, the "Pathfinder," as he was called, proposed the construction of a transcontinental as one of his political promises. Even though he lost the election, his idea did not fall on deaf ears. Lincoln was interested in the Pacific Railroad of Missouri, and the Republican Party saw it as an important issue along with the prevention of extending slavery into the new western territories. When the Republican Convention met in Chicago in 1860 to nominate "the Railsplitter," Abraham Lincoln, for president, Plank 16 of its platform called for the building of the Pacific railroad "in the interest of the whole country." The platform also called for the federal government to aid its construction and stipulated that the line haul mail between the two coasts.

Such a declaration was not just a whim nor merely wishful thinking. After 1854, a series of explorations of the "Great American Desert" took place to find the easiest way to cross the Rocky and Sierra Nevada Mountains. The parties trekked along the following parallels of latitude: 32nd, 35th, 41st, and between the 47th and 49th degrees. The project was organized by Jefferson Davis, secretary of war, and there was some influence by the Chicago, Rock Island, and Pacific Railroad.

The line following the 32nd degree would originate from Shreveport, Louisiana, and the one following the 35th would start from Memphis, Tennessee. There was only an unofficial report stating that the 41st degree line would start where the Platte joins the Missouri River in Nebraska, and pass in the vicinity of the Great Salt Lake. The northernmost line would begin at St. Paul, Minnesota, and extend to present-day Great Falls, Montana, and on to the Columbia Lava Plateau.

The survey was done in very general terms. No specific mountain passages were found. Jefferson Davis and the southern members of Congress championed the 32nd and 35th parallel routes, while the northerners preferred the 41st and 47th–49th. Stephen Douglas led a campaign to make sure the transcontinental came as close to Chicago as possible. Eventually there were railroads constructed along all four parallels, and Chicago became a focal point for three of them and indirectly for the fourth.

The nation's fulfillment of its Manifest Destiny or expansion into and inhabiting of the land to the Pacific Coast by rail would have to be postponed until after the Civil War. In the meantime, the railroads increased the population of the United States east of the Mississippi and created a burgeoning economy with its rapid transporting of goods to and from the larger east-coast cities. Moreover, wherever the railroads went, the telegraph was alongside. Even towns on the Mississippi River could receive messages and information for their newspapers from the east almost instantaneously.

The Canadians also experienced changes. Even though railroads were still in the earliest stages, they did stimulate the economy, and Canadians were able to get an ice-free port and connections with its own and the United States's midwestern region. By the 1850s, the Canadians still had to look toward England for railroad investment, but they purchased locomotives from U.S. manufacturers.

Following the Civil War, the railroads made it possible for expansion into the Trans-Mississippi West to the Pacific Ocean. It would have been extremely difficult, if not impossible, to encourage people to move into this region without the ties of the railroads. People in the area were assured there was a way to get their products to market, and to receive information and manufactured goods to make their work and lives easier. In the second half of the nineteenth century, the railroads melded the vast land into a nation by creating dependable economic, social, and communication unity.

North vs. South:
The First Railroad War

The U.S. Civil War or War Between the States (1861–1865) was the first conflict in which railroads played an important role. Before that time, soldiers had ridden and had fired a cannon from a rail car for practice on the Charleston and Hamburg a generation earlier. Also, a few soldiers led by a young Col. Robert E. Lee arrived by train at Harper's Ferry, in October 1859, to end John Brown's famous raid. Those activities aside, it was the Civil War which became a blueprint for warfare until the mid-twentieth century. It is no accident that England and Prussia sent observers to study the new way to wage war.

— North and South Compared —

The Union had a great advantage in its industrialization; the South, by choice, placed emphasis on agriculture. For example, there was more cloth weaving in the town of Lowell, Massachusetts, than the entire South — where cotton was king. Even from an agricultural viewpoint, the Union was self-sufficient in food production with the opening up of areas in the Mississippi Valley and beyond to feed the rising numbers of industrial workers in the east. The Civil War proved conclusively that modern industry wins wars; the brave sharpshooter could not function without communication and supplies no matter how loyal to a cause.

Even if the South had adequate ammunition and supplies, it did not have an efficient rail system for delivery. Most trackage ran east and west; north–south routes were not direct. There were numerous track gauges, and many times stations at transfer points were a mile or so apart. The Union not only had more trackage; by 1861, several railroad companies had formed systems for the smooth transfer of passengers and freight. Some systems extended for several hundred miles without interruption. At the same time, the Union had a web of tracks to carry agricultural products from the Midwest to its large east-coast cities.

The Union had all the railroad advantages in 1861, and throughout the war. It had over 21,000 miles of track compared to the South's 7,000 miles. The North had well over 1,000 telegraph stations whereas the South had fewer than 200. There were more locomotives running on one line between Philadelphia and Pittsburgh in 1861 than in the whole Commonwealth of Virginia, which had by far the most miles of track in the Confederacy. The South had depended on railroad supplies from northern cities: whale oil for lamps, grease for running gear, and locomotives themselves. There had been only one locomotive manufacturing plant in the South, and it had ceased operation by 1861. After the outbreak of the war, all but one of its few repair facilities manufactured ordnance rather than railroad supplies. Moreover, southern railroads never stockpiled spare parts.

Even before the beginning of the Civil War, Confederate trains rarely ran faster than 25 miles per hour. This limitation was due to track conditions rather than locomotive power. While many southern railroads had installed iron T-rail, others were using earlier, lighter versions. In fact, some still used wood and strap-iron on main lines. Even where heavier rail was used, the South never ballasted the track. Its railroads saw little need to do so since they did not experience the frost problems of the northern climate. After 1861, not one yard of rail was manufactured in the Confederacy. To repair tracks, the South had to rip up rails from lesser-used existing lines. By the end of the war, the fastest Southern trains ran at a mere 10 miles per hour.

The North had no problem replacing rail and manufacturing locomotives. Most of the railroad companies were in acceptable to good condition to meet the Union's transportation needs. Maryland's decision to remain in the Union brought with it the Baltimore & Ohio Railroad. The Baltimore & Ohio was important strategically since it ran just north of the Confederacy. Moreover, it had the best-maintained roadbed and the most powerful and fastest locomotives. Its engineer, Ross Winans, had designed a locomotive with most of its boiler weight and side-mounted cab over the drive wheels to give it greater traction. This "Camelback" locomotive hauled heavy freight cars easily up mountain grades. It weighed 55,000 pounds and had 60-inch drive wheels. The Camelback could pull a 40-car train at 60 miles per hour on a level surface.

— The Civil War Begins —

On April 15, 1861, when South Carolina seceded from the Union and Ft. Sumter was fired upon, President Lincoln declared a "State of Rebellion." Secretary of War Simon Cameron immediately telegraphed the governor of Massachusetts to send a military regiment to protect the District of Columbia. The Sixth Massachusetts Regiment of 2,000 soldiers left Boston by train on April 17th. They arrived in Baltimore, Maryland, by noon the next day.

Even though Maryland remained in the Union, many of its citizens were sympathetic to the South. They planned to interrupt the regiment's progress to Washington. The soldiers arrived on the Philadelphia, Wilmington, and Baltimore Railroad. Their cars had to be pulled individually through town by horses to the tracks of the Washington branch of the B&O. The first cars got through without incident. Then the crowd set up barricades and began to hurl rocks at the soldiers. At that point, soldiers fired their rifles into the crowd, and a dozen

Baltimore & Ohio shops at Martinsburg before destruction by Confederate army. "Iron Pot" coal cars in foreground and "Camelback" locomotives in background. Courtesy Virginia Museum of Transportation.

civilians were killed. The regiment continued on to Washington, and thousands more traveled over this route without further problems.

— Harper's Ferry —

While the first Northern soldiers arrived in Washington, D.C., Thomas "Stonewall" Jackson arrived at Harper's Ferry with a militia. Jackson complained along with local residents to B&O officials that train whistles were making people and horses nervous and were keeping them from sleeping. After a series of complaints, the B&O agreed to send trains through Harper's Ferry during one short period of set, daylight hours. This reduction in schedule caused a large backup of trains each day.

At an ideal time, Jackson and his men attacked the railroad and confiscated 40 locomotives and over 300 freight cars! They dragged and pushed them by horse wagon to Confederate lines. They also tore up 100 miles of track, carried back over 30 miles of rail, and destroyed the bridge over the Potomac. Jackson's raid stopped east–west traffic on the B&O for nine months. In fact, during the next four years, the Harper's Ferry Bridge was destroyed nine times. Jackson would go on to destroy 23 railroad bridges during the war.

— The First Rail and Telegraph Maneuvers —

Union General George B. McClellan gave the first order for a military maneuver by telegraph. McClellan was no stranger to railroads, and Lincoln appointed him Commander of the Union Army for that very reason. On July 12, 1861, McClellan's army had nearly surrounded some Confederate troops. In order to cut them off completely, he telegraphed his generals to meet him at Oakland, Maryland, the next day to plan the action. The message, however, did not reach his generals in time due to human — not mechanical — error. Although the Confederates escaped, the telegraph would soon prove to be an important factor in war communications.

The Confederacy would be more successful with its initial railroad maneuvers. The first pitched battle of the Civil War occurred within two weeks of McClellan's ill-fated telegram. On July 21, Confederate and Union armies met at Manassas Junction, Virginia. Sightseers from Washington stood on a hill to watch the battle take place. They expected a Union victory and a quick end to the war.

The Union had the upper hand early in the conflict. The Confederacy telegraphed for reserves stationed in the Shenan-

CIVIL WAR RAILROADS — 1862

AF	Alabama & Florida RR		**NAS**	New Albany & Salem RR
ANC	Atlantic & North Carolina RR		**NYC**	New York Central RR
AWP	Atlantic & West Point RR		**NYE**	New York & Erie RR
BO	Baltimore & Ohio RR		**NYPB**	New York, Providence & Boston RR
BW	Boston & Worcester RR		**NC**	North Central RR
BM	Burlington & Missouri RR		**NCr**	North Carolina RR
CAS	Chicago, Aetna & St. Louis RR		**NP**	Norfolk & Petersburg RR
CA	Camden & Amboy RR		**NO**	New Orleans, Jackson & Great Northern RR
CO	Central of Ohio RR		**NW**	North Western RR
CBQ	Chicago, Burlington & Quincy RR		**OM**	Ohio & Mississippi RR
CHP	Cincinnati, Hillsborough & Parkersburg RR		**OA**	Orange and Alexandria RR
CNW	Chicago & North Western RW		**PC**	Pennsylvania Central RR
CRI	Chicago & Rock Island RR		**PhC**	Philadelphia & Columbia RR
CPA	Cleveland, Painesville & Ashtabula RR		**PFwC**	Pittsburgh, Fort Wayne & Chicago RR
CV	Cumberland Valley RR		**Pi**	Pacific RR
ETG	East Tennessee & Georgia RR		**PL**	Petersburg & Lynchburg RR
F	Florida RR		**PR**	Philadelphia & Reading RR
G	Georgia RR		**PS**	Pittsburgh & Steubenville RR
GC	Georgia Central RR		**PWB**	Philadelphia, Wilmington & Baltimore RR
GT	Grand Trunk RR		**RG**	Raleigh & Gaston RR
Gu	Gulf RR		**RD**	Richmond & Danville RR
InC	Indiana Central RR		**RFP**	Richmond, Fredricksburg & Potomac RR
JGN	Jackson & Great Northern RR		**RP**	Richmond & Petersburg RR
LN	Louisville & Nashville RR		**RY**	Richmond & York RR
MiA	Mississippi & Atlantic RR		**SC**	Savannah & Charleston RR
MC	Michigan Central RR		**SLAC**	St. Louis, Alton & Chicago RR
MCh	Memphis & Charleston RR		**VC**	Virginia Central RR
MCN	Mississippi Central RR		**VJ**	Vicksburg & Jackson RR
ME	Montgomery & Eufala RR		**VT**	Virginia & Tennessee RR
MG	Manassas Gap RR		**W**	Western RR
MO	Memphis & Ohio RR		**WA**	Western & Atlantic RR
MSNI	Michigan Southern & Northern Indiana RR		**Wd**	Weldon RR
NaCh	Nashville & Chattanooga RR		**WM**	Wilmington & Manchester RR
			WW	Wilmington & Weldon RR

MAJOR U.S. CIVIL WAR RAILROADS — 1862
32,120 miles of U.S. track

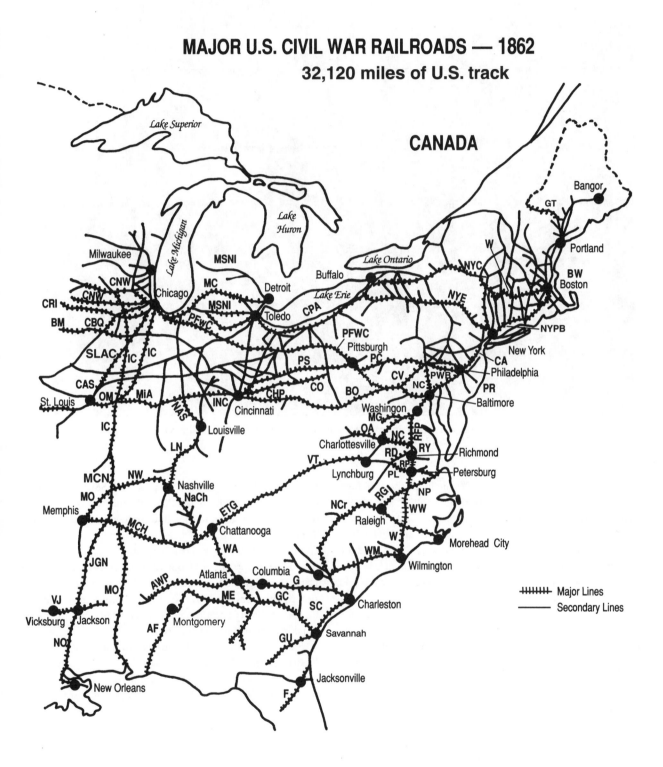

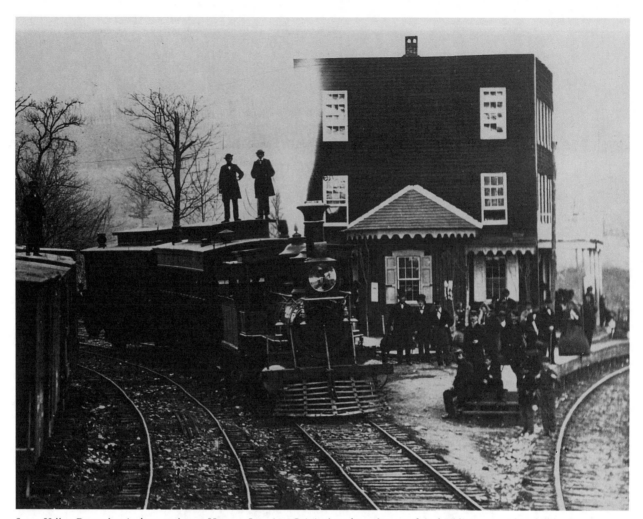

Seven Valley, Pennsylvania, known then as Hanover Junction. Original tracks and some of the buildings are said to still be there. Lincoln in center (c. 1863). Courtesy Virginia Museum of Transportation.

doah Valley to come to assistance. Within hours these soldiers made the trip, immediately joined the conflict, and won a great victory for the South.

Prior to the railroad and telegraph, it would have taken hours for the swiftest messenger to send word of the need for reinforcements the 25 or so miles to the Shenandoah Valley. Just as important, it would have taken two days for the soldiers and animals to make the trip and rest enough to be effective in battle. The railroad changed military strategies for all time. It permitted an almost instantaneous summoning and very rapid concentration of troops in any one place. The railroads gave birth to modern military tactics.

— The U.S. Military Railroad —

Lincoln signed the Railroad Act of February 1862 to create the U.S. Military Railroad (USMR). He gave his new secretary of war, Edwin M. Stanton, complete control over military train movements. Stanton was familiar with railroads as he, too, had been an attorney for the Illinois Central. Within a week, Stanton appointed D. C. McCallum Director and Superintendent of the USMR, with orders to report directly to the Secretary of War himself. On April 22, Stanton wired Herman Haupt in Boston to request that he come to Washing-

ton and to take over the operations of the USMR. Haupt had been a superintendent for the Pennsylvania Railroad, and had resigned that position in the 1850s to help build the Hoosac Tunnel in New England. The Hoosac Tunnel was the longest and most difficult to construct at that time. In May, President Lincoln appointed Haupt Chief of Construction in the Department of the Rappahanouck which gave him permission to repair and build tracks. Haupt's orders gave him the highest authority pertaining to railroad affairs. Haupt would quickly demonstrate his genius.

Stanton's first order to Haupt was to put the Richmond, Fredricksburg, and Potomac Railroad in working order. He proved his worth by building a bridge over Ackakuk Creek in less than a week. Then he built a bridge 400 feet long and 100 feet high in twelve days using untrained soldiers. He realized, however, that work would proceed even faster with a specially trained construction brigade.

Haupt centered his construction activities at Alexandria, Virginia. There he warehoused the necessary tools and equipment for his track crews. By mid-June he ordered all military trains to work only by strict timetables, because Confederate raiders were intercepting telegraph messages. The enemy could too easily learn of rail movements and sabotage troop and supply trains. He then organized a permanent construction brigade to repair tracks and bridges.

When some of his railroad orders were disregarded by General Pope, Haupt resigned in protest. Within a month Stanton issued a "general order" to Haupt to return to Washington and to resume his work. Haupt was promoted to Brigadier General. By early 1863, he had a crack construction crew of over 300 men and was prefabricating railroad trestles at

— The Underground Railroad —

The "Underground Railroad" was a term used to describe the way slaves were secretly brought north to freedom during the Civil War. It was not actually a railroad. The term was coined by a slave owner who was chasing his escaped slave. When he lost sight of the trail, the slave owner said, "He must have gone down an underground road." As railroads were the best means of transportation, those who helped slaves escape used the new terminology that was becoming common. Slave owners were known as "agents." Former slaves were hidden at "stations," and those who led them to freedom were "conductors." The slaves themselves were "passengers." Sometimes the freed slaves were sent north on trains hidden in crates, although the majority walked or rode in horse-drawn wagons.

Alexandria. Haupt eventually gained almost complete control of USMR train movements.

— Southern Difficulties —

In contrast with the Union, the Confederacy was unable to organize its railroads into a permanent arm of its military. Besides lack of rolling stock, locomotives, and poor rails, the habit of overloading trains caused equipment to deteriorate at a faster pace. In early 1862, railroad officials suggested a plan to encourage privateers to run the Union blockade and bring equipment from England. The Confederate government turned down the plan, because it did not want to directly assist private industry.

Confederate railroads remained local in character. For the most part, military movement by rail was under the authority of a local commander. The first attempt at organization occurred in April 1861. Confederate postmaster general John H. Reagan called a conference of railroad managers in Montgomery, Alabama. At the meeting, the railroads agreed to carry troops at 2¢ per mile and military freight at half fare. Mail service was organized by route and compensation by amount of traffic. The railroad would receive payment in Confederate bonds when cash was not available. Further postal meetings were held without many results.

In July 1861, Confederate president Jefferson Davis commissioned William S. Ashe a major and appointed him Assistant Quartermaster. Ashe had no authority to organize train movements, and by fall rail traffic bottlenecked throughout

Freight cars at Nashville, Tennessee. The yard is being restored after a raid. Courtesy Virginia Museum of Transportation.

Manassas Junction, Virginia, March 1862, after the Confederates had evacuated. It was here that the Orange and Alexandria Railroad joined the Manassas Gap Railroad. Courtesy Virginia Museum of Transportation.

Virginia and other places. Ashe requested legislation giving President Davis control of rail operations and authority to take over rail companies which would not cooperate. The proposal died in the legislature.

The rail situation grew worse in 1862, and Abraham C. Meyers replaced Ashe as Quartermaster General. Meyers issued directives which would govern military transport, but they carried no weight for local railroad managers. Probably due to Meyers's influence, the Confederate Congress introduced a bill to create a "Military Chief of Railroad Transportation" with the rank of lieutenant colonel. The bill also called for the appointment of district military superintendents and gave all railroad officials military rank and responsibilities. It demanded that through schedules be established as well as the interchange of freight cars. The bill would solve a great deal of the South's rail problems, but it was reduced to the calling of "consultations" between the secretary of war and railroad officials.

In December 1862, William Wadley was appointed colonel and Assistant Adjutant General to take over supervision of the railroads. Wadley called a railroad conference in March 1863. He hoped that the managers themselves could come to some understanding on train schedules and build a system of freight car interchange. When the delegates met, however, they refused to discuss those issues and spent their time working on tariff regulations. When Wadley introduced his plan, it

was quickly rejected. Wadley was dismissed a few weeks later.

In June 1863, Captain Fredrick W. Sims succeeded Wadley and created a "Railroad Bureau." The Bureau had little authority, and it was not until the end of the war that the Confederacy was prepared to deal with the railroad issue straight on. On January 11, 1865, the House Military Affairs Committee recommended that the Confederate government take over important railroads, seize rolling stock, and begin an organized construction program. President Davis signed the bill on March 9, just weeks before the surrender at Appomattox Court House.

The Confederate Congress's and Davis's reluctance to control or to take over the railroads is understandable from a philosophical point of view: The Confederacy was created on the issue that the individual states have a greater authority on matters within their borders than the central government. For Davis or for a Confederate agency to control railroads would be in violation of the very reason that the South seceded from the Union. In spite of their many shortcomings, southern railroads were capable of transporting large numbers of troops a great distance from time to time.

— Martinsburg —

General Robert E. Lee understood the strategic value of railroads and carried out his own raids on Union tracks. In

June 1862, he made his first invasion into Maryland. With his army he destroyed B&O tracks west of Harper's Ferry, tore down 90 miles of telegraph line, and burned the bridge over the Little Cacapan River.

In October, Lee raided the railroad center of Martinsburg. Lee and his soldiers destroyed the huge polygon engine house, repair shop, station, a warehouse, company hotel, and coal storage bins as well as other structures. They also damaged water storage facilities, and heated rails over fires to twist them around tree trunks. This twisting became common practice on both sides to make rail unusable. The twisted rails became known as "Union Bow Ties."

The Confederacy had to content itself with raiding border railroads for the most part. After Martinsburg, one group, called "Quantrill's Raiders," became famous for their daring exploits in Union territory. The future famous outlaw and train robber Jesse James was a member of Quantrill's Raiders.

— Gettysburg —

General Lee believed a surprise, large-scale invasion of the North would bring the war to an end. There was growing discontent in the Union's eastern cities, and some Northern politicians were in favor of a negotiated peace. Lee thought that if he could cut off the food supply from the Midwest, the peace movement would gain strength.

In early summer 1863, Lee marched his army of 65,000 soldiers northward out of the Shenandoah Valley into Pennsylvania. Along the way they destroyed the Northern Central Railroad, an important link between Harrisburg and Baltimore. The area around Gettysburg was attractive to Lee and his army. There were seven railroads nearby: The Cumberland, Hanover, Penn-Central, Baltimore & Ohio, Hampshire, and Western Maryland. The Penn-Central was a major artery of midwestern food to east-coast cities. Also, there was a shoe

— Pyramid Journalism —

The Civil War and the famous Gettysburg Address brought about modern journalistic style. During the early days of the conflict, newspapers often received incomplete stories from reporters, because telegraph wires would be cut. To overcome this problem, newspapers developed the style known as "pyramid journalism." A story begins with the most important information and continues in degrees to the least. If telegraph wires were cut in the middle of a report, newspapers and readers would still have the main points of the story.

Union locomotives stored in Washington, D.C., to protect them from Confederate Raiders (1863). The U.S. Capitol is in the background. Courtesy Virginia Museum of Transportation.

factory in the region, and Lee's army was desperate for footwear.

Herman Haupt was aware that the Confederates would attempt an invasion of the North. Earlier that spring he instructed telegraphers, linemen, and other Penn-Central Railroad employees to be on the lookout for Confederate activity. On the first of July, an off-duty telegrapher spotted a Confederate brigade advancing in search of the shoe factory. He alerted the Union command under General Meade as the Confederates occupied the town of Gettysburg.

Within 24 hours, Haupt arranged for the transport of provisions to Gettysburg and the evacuation of the wounded by rail. He moved the trains in convoy fashion in groups of five, spaced at eight-hour intervals. Each train had to be unloaded of supplies immediately upon arrival and reloaded with wounded before the next convoy got underway. Haupt was able to deliver 1,500 tons of supplies in 24 hours and evacuated 20,000 wounded. The arrival of the wounded at hospitals in Baltimore and Philadelphia within hours saved countless Union lives.

Lee had to retreat to Virginia carrying his wounded on wagons and on horseback. The march took days, and it was impossible to attend to the wounded while underway. The lack of railroad availability greatly increased the mortality rate.

In November 1863, President Lincoln and others gathered at Gettysburg to dedicate a cemetery for those who died in the conflict. Edward Everett, the principal speaker, in the long-winded fashion of the time, lasted for what some felt was an eternity. Lincoln wanted to contrast his address by being brief. Perhaps even more important, he wanted the newspapers to have his remarks promptly should the Confederates cut the wires after he began speaking. Tradition has it that Lincoln made revisions to the most famous speech in U.S. history when he was traveling to Gettysburg on a train.

— *The General* —

The most famous locomotive of the Civil War was not a new model nor one that broke speed records. A daring theft of the Confederate locomotive, *The General,* by Union soldiers, became a legend in its own time.

When guarding Nashville, General Mitchell wanted to take Chattanooga. His problem was to hold the city until reinforcements could arrive. He feared that the Confederates could bring up 15,000 or more soldiers to retake Chattanooga.

Mitchell asked the quinine peddler and Union spy James J. Andrews to reenter the South and burn railroad bridges over the Chickamauga River to prevent Confederate reinforcements from arriving quickly by train. In April 1862, Andrews recruited volunteers. They traveled into the South and met in Marietta, Georgia. Andrews posed as an official of the Western and Atlantic Railroad on a special mission for General Beauregard. When the train stopped for breakfast at Big Shanty, Georgia, Andrews and his band stole *The General* and several boxcars. The train's conductor, Mr. William Fuller, followed in pursuit. Acquiring other locomotives, Fuller and others chased *The General* at a distance to prevent the Union "engine thieves" from burning bridges

and destroying track. Andrews and his men did manage to cut telegraph wires and destroy some tracks, but they were unable to burn the all-important bridges. After days of soaking rain, the wooden bridges were too waterlogged to catch on fire.

The Andrews band ran out of wood and water for their engine, and they were taken prisoner. Andrews and seven others were hanged as spies. Eight escaped prison, and six others returned north during a prisoner exchange about a year later.

Andrews's raiders were the first to receive the Congressional Medal of Honor. Secretary of War Stanton presented the honor to the survivors in his office. They later met with President Lincoln. The others were granted the award posthumously.

There are some questions as to the value of the Andrews raid. Even though they failed to burn the railroad bridges, the Confederates had to set up sentries along the Western and Atlantic line. With a shortage of manpower, these men were prevented from taking part in more important military endeavors. There is no doubt that the theft of *The General* was a psychological blow to the South and a boost for the North. President Lincoln needed favorable war news, and the raid proved both timely and thrilling. It quickly became part of railroad folklore as well as U.S. history.

— **The Bragg Initiative** —

Confederate General Braxton Bragg initiated the first of a series of three point-to-point troop movements by rail in 1862. In order to counter the westward movement of the Union army, the Confederacy decided to reinforce Chattanooga. It moved 3,000 men by rail over 700 miles through Atlanta. Seeing the possibilities of rail transport, General Bragg moved 25,000 of his Army of the Tennessee from Tupelo, Mississippi, through Mobile, and up to Chattanooga. With only one short portage, the army ran on six different railroads fully equipped with ammunition and seven days of cooked rations to eliminate stopovers and foraging. Officers were stationed at junctions to prevent desertions and unnecessary delays.

Bragg held on to Chattanooga until September. He was forced to evacuate the city when the Union Army of the Cumberland under General Rosecrans moved into the area. Bragg called for reinforcements and took position at Chickamauga Creek.

With the help of Fredrick Sims, General James Longstreet moved the First Corps of the Army of the Potomac to reinforce Bragg. Longstreet moved his 12,000 soldiers by rail from Hanover, Virginia, to Chickamauga by first going through Atlanta. Sims routed the troops over 14 different railroads, and they arrived at Chickamauga in seven days and ten hours after traveling 843 miles.

Conditions were tight on the trains. Men were packed into boxcars and even assigned positions on the roofs. In many cars, there was not enough room to sit down. Some had to sleep under the wheels of their cannons. Well-wishers gave the soldiers food as well as liquor. Soldiers often piled sand on boxcar floors so that they could build fires safely to cook their rations. The day after the reinforcements arrived, Bragg began

The 17,000-pound mortar *The Dictator*. It had a 13-inch bore and shot a 200-pound shell which contained 20 pounds of gunpowder. It was used by the Union at the Battle of Petersburg. The small, wood-burning locomotive in background was used by General Grant. Courtesy Virginia Museum of Transportation.

his attack. Rosecrans was forced back to Chattanooga with only two weeks of supplies and enough ammunition to hold off for a two-day fight. He requested immediate supplies and reinforcements.

— An Armada to Chattanooga —

Secretary of War Stanton received the telegram of Rosecrans's request for help at 9:45 P.M. on September 23. Stanton immediately called a meeting of the war cabinet with President Lincoln. They simply could not permit the surrender of the Army of the Cumberland. The best estimate, however, would take three months to move enough troops and supplies to relieve Rosecrans. At that point T. T. Eckert, Chief of the Army Telegraph Corps, suggested moving the reinforcements by train. After some discussion, Eckert argued it could be done in three weeks. Others reduced the movement to days.

President Lincoln reluctantly agreed. He appointed General "Fighting Joe" Hooker to take the Eleventh and Twelfth Corps of Meade's Army of the Potomac to ride the rails to Tennessee to relieve Rosecrans. The Army of the Potomac was still recuperating from Gettysburg and was encamped near Washington, D.C. Early on the morning of the 25th, the first trains passed through the Union capital. By 10 A.M., the first cars

reached Martinsburg. Shortly after noon on the 28th, all troops had passed through Washington.

The first trains arrived at Bridgeport, just outside Chattanooga, on September 30, in 5½ days. The entire troop movement was completed on October 8. In 14 days, 25,000 men were moved 1,233 miles. The armada consisted of 30 trains with over 600 cars. It included ten batteries of artillery. They arrived in time to relieve Rosecrans.

Much in contrast with Longstreet's soldiers, the Union troops had seats in converted boxcars. Officers rode up front in regular coaches. Soldiers often climbed on the roof to get a better look at the scenery while others took away side boards for better ventilation. Food was provided at stopovers, and supporters gave the men the usual liquor and other treats. Some soldiers painted slogans and drawings on the sides of their car, similar to the airplane "nose art" of World War II. From a soldier's point of view, each turn of the flanged wheel meant not having to walk for three or more months. One soldier quipped: "From now on I do my marchin' on wheels" and another: "Why didn't Joe Hooker think of this before!"

— Sherman's March —

With the election of 1864 approaching, President Lincoln needed a decisive military triumph. General William Tecum-

U.S. Military Railroad locomotive *Fred Leach* (1864). Courtesy Virginia Transportation Museum.

seh Sherman provided that victory with a whirlwind march through Georgia. Much of the attention goes to destruction, and the scene of a burning Atlanta is fixed in people's minds from the movie *Gone with the Wind*. The real military feat, however, was to supply Sherman's 100,000 soldiers and 300,000 animals.

As Sherman marched forward, the Confederates destroyed railroad tracks. As the Union kept pace making repairs, the Confederates destroyed them behind the lines from time to time. At the Chattahoochie River, General E. C. Smead had to repair a bridge 780 feet long and 90 feet high. General Grenville Dodge was in charge of repairs on the "Sherman Road." He had a construction crew of 8,000 men. At one point Dodge's men repaired 182 miles of railroad with 182 bridges in 40 days!

The swiftness of Sherman's march is what made it even more devastating. Given track repairs, trains were never more than a day behind Sherman's army. As supplies arrived, wounded were placed on the cars for the trip back to Chattanooga. When Sherman reached Atlanta, the supply line extended 314 miles along the now Union-controlled Western and Atlantic Railroad. In one month alone over 32,000 freight cars were loaded and unloaded. It has been estimated that if Sherman's troops were supplied without the railroad, it would have taken 36,800 wagons pulled by six mules each averaging 20 miles per day. The railroad quickly made other forms of military land transportation obsolete.

Sherman's march brought about a huge psychological defeat for the Confederacy. He was able to go through the heart of Dixie. More important, however, was the March's strategic value. The Union now controlled several important Confederate rail links. For all practical purposes, Sherman cut off Lee's armies in the north from direct food supply lines in the south, in addition to dividing the interior rail lines of the Confederacy. With deteriorating conditions and without an adequate food supply by rail, the Confederacy's days were numbered.

— Petersburg —

The siege of Petersburg, Virginia, began on June 20, 1864. Petersburg was an important rail junction which controlled trains approaching Richmond from the southwest. If the Union could halt train movements at Petersburg, it could prevent supplies from reaching Lee's army. The Confederacy had to keep those lines open at all costs.

The Union brought up a 17,000-pound mortar with a 13-inch bore to shoot at Confederate positions. Called the "Dictator," the mortar could fire a 200-pound exploding shell which rained havoc onto Confederate lines. It was brought to location by a train called *The Petersburg Express*. The "Dictator" was not as effective at night, because its lit fuse easily traced its line of fire. The siege of Petersburg lasted until the surrender at Appomattox Court House. It predicted the trench warfare of World War I in France, where supplies and reinforcements could be brought up to a fixed front by rail.

— Appomattox Court House Surrender —

General Robert E. Lee surrendered the Confederacy to Union General Ulysses S. Grant at Appomattox Court House, Virginia on April 9, 1865. Lee's army was without rations, but he held out that long in anticipation of the arrival of four supply trains from Lynchburg.

The supply trains stopped at Appomattox Court House which was a railroad siding with a farmhouse nearby. When the Confederate troops arrived to unload the trains, General Sheridan's cavalry swooped down on them. The Union soldiers burned one of the trains and took the remaining three behind their lines. Lee realized that without the supply trains, it was useless to hold out any longer.

Wearing his finest attire, General Lee surrendered to Grant in the farmhouse near the Appomattox Court House railroad siding. In contrast, Grant borrowed a private's coat to receive Lee's sword. After the formal surrender, Lee asked Grant for two considerations. Lee requested rations for his men and that they could take their horses home with them. Grant gave Lee his requests.

The Union General then ordered the captured Confederate trains to be brought forward and rations distributed to the defeated soldiers. It's quite an irony that, at the end of the war, Lee had his own supplies delivered to him by rail. Grant was more than gracious when he permitted the southerners to keep their horses. From earliest times the horse was a weapon of war. Whether it pulled a chariot, carried a knight, or was drafted in the cavalry, the horse was just as important as a sword. The Civil War proved that a new age had dawned in warfare. The steam locomotive, a.k.a. the "iron horse," was more important for modern victory than a country's stable of trusty steeds.

— The Railroad as a War Machine —

Confederate railroads made an extraordinary effort considering their handicaps. There simply was not enough track mileage to strategic points. Even where junctions existed, there were gaps between railroad companies as well as different track gauges. Last but not least, the railroads were not able to replace parts and tracks. The railroad owners, too, were not willing to make the sacrifices necessary for victory. They wanted to retain autonomy. At the same time, the Confederate government was unwilling to impose a transportation policy on private companies.

Through the efforts of Stanton, McCallum, and Haupt, the Union welded its railroads into a true fighting force, while the U.S. Military Railroad functioned as a repair, construction, and supply unit. By the end of the war, the USMR had over 400 locomotives, 6,330 cars, and 21,783 tons of rail. It

Interior of a Baltimore & Ohio coach during the Civil War. Note the oil lamps. Courtesy Virginia Museum of Transportation.

moved millions of soldiers over a total of 75 railroads. In addition, nineteen railroads held a meeting in 1863 to discuss through ticketing. Overall, the Union railroads earned large profits during the war years. Even the Erie's ledger was in the black by 1865.

— The Military Train —

The typical Union military train consisted of the following: nine stock cars for horses or mules, five flat cars for artillery, and six boxcars and coaches to carry troops and supplies. Later they made windows in the boxcars to carry soldiers when there were not enough coaches. During the war they placed huge pots on flat cars to carry coal or gravel. They also used gondola cars and the first "tank cars" to carry liquids. Coaches carried 40 to 50 soldiers and were heated by stoves. Kerosene lamps had replaced candles for night lighting by the late 1850s. Before the end of the war, roofs were placed on stock cars. A military train did not have a caboose. They usually traveled about 40 miles per hour, but some were known to reach 60 miles per hour on some railroads.

A word must be said about the Civil War railroad workers. The USMR ran very few trains themselves. Both the Union and the Confederacy depended almost totally on civilian railroad employees. The engineers and firemen not only had to keep a sharp lookout for torn up track and to outrun occasional sharpshooters, they had to bring trains right up to the front lines many times. Their lives were in as much jeopardy as the soldiers in the field.

— The Hospital Train —

After the Battle of Wilson's Creek, the Union army placed the wounded in boxcars for transport to a hospital in St. Louis, Missouri, at a distance of over 100 miles. The car floor was strewn with hay. Later, wounded were placed on bed sacks after other battles.

The Army experimented with hanging stretchers from ropes in railcars which it believed would give the wounded a smoother ride. Permanent bunks and posts with loops to hold stretchers were also tried. Some coaches were modified to carry stretchers above the seats. Those who could sit erect traveled in regular coaches. The Philadelphia, Wilmington, and Baltimore Railroad designed an early version of an assigned hospital car. This car carried its own water supply and had removable berths as well as seats for physicians and nurses.

Early in the war, the U.S. Sanitary Commission was established to oversee the cleanliness of military accommodations. Dr. Erlish Harris of the commission refitted a baggage car with berths to remove wounded along the Louisville & Nashville Railroad line. By the end of 1863, Harris designed and ordered the construction of ten cars specifically to carry wounded soldiers. These cars had double springs, copper boilers, water tanks, and room for 24 removable stretchers. The car also had variable gauge axles so it could travel on different gauge tracks. The Commission ordered more such cars by the end of the war.

The typical Union hospital train consisted of five ward cars, a dispensary car, surgeon's car, kitchen, and conductor's car. With its kitchen car, these hospital trains had the first dining cars on the rails. A large red cross was painted on the locomotive smokestack, and the cars were labeled as hospital cars. Confederate raiders never attacked a hospital train. There is record that they stopped one's progress, but did not harm the wounded. The South also used railroads to transport wounded whenever possible. There are no indications or records that they developed specific cars for the purpose, however.

— Lincoln's Special Car —

President Lincoln often visited troops in the field and in the hospitals. He usually traveled in a boxcar, and there were times when he had to wait for a troop or supply train to go through. The USMR built a special car for him, but he never used it when he was alive. According to legend, Lincoln designed it himself, and it was armor-plated. Neither was true, however. It carried his body from Baltimore to Chicago after his assassination on April 14, 1865. From Chicago to Springfield, at the request of his wife, Mary Todd Lincoln, he was carried in Pullman's *Pioneer*. Lincoln's funeral trip was the last formal action of the U.S. Military Railroad.

— Technology —

There were several technological developments during the first half of the 1860s. Engine cabs were made of metal, and some Northern locomotives had windows cut in an oval shape to provide some protection against Confederate sharpshooters. The engines lost a lot of their brass ornamentation and bright colors. The wartime black locomotive would last on most railroads until the end of steam power. Herman Haupt

himself invented a levered device which twisted Confederate rails so that they were no longer useful. Union soldiers would also shoot a cannonball through the boiler to disable the locomotive. When the USMR had difficulty burning southern trestles in rainy weather, Haupt and his assistants designed a torpedo to blast the structure from safe distances.

Steam water injectors came into more common use on Union locomotives, and the Pennsylvania Railroad pioneered the *Consolidation*. This locomotive had a larger boiler and became more commonplace during the war. Locomotives, however, shot up in price. A typical new steam engine increased almost 300 percent in cost by 1865.

Sometimes armies unknowingly sabotaged their own locomotives. Whenever soldiers camped near tracks, they bathed in the railroad water towers and washed clothes in nearby streams. Many times, locomotives' boilers were clogged with soapsuds, turning them into disabled hulks.

Another change was the increased use of coal instead of wood to fire Union locomotives. Before the war, a few railroad companies began to use coal for fuel. The Central Railroad of New Jersey consistently burned coal since 1857. By 1863, other companies turned to coal as an economic measure. Overall, it was cheaper than wood, easier to handle, and far more efficient. Coal lasted as the most common steam locomotive fuel until dieselization. There is no record of coal-burning engines in the South during the Civil War.

— Passenger Comforts —

While soldiers at times traveled in modified boxcars, simply not having to march long distances was an accommodation. For civilian travel, newer passenger cars were larger and more comfortable. The latest models were 50 feet long and 10 feet wide. The ceilings reached 10 feet and had a second, clerestory roof for ventilation. These new cars could accommodate up to 60 passengers. Some stoves had ducts to help distribute heat more evenly throughout the car in winter, and a few companies experimented with gas instead of kerosene for lighting.

Sleeping cars came into common use on several lines. Sleepers were regularly scheduled between Boston and New York, Philadelphia and Pittsburgh, and Cleveland to Chicago. In the South, two sleeping cars ran under franchise on the Memphis & Charleston. Two others were added to the connecting Mississippi Central. Sleeping cars were immensely popular wherever they were introduced.

— The Block Signal —

The block signal was another technological innovation that came out of the war. Given the increased volume of traffic, regulating train traffic from one railroad station to another was not efficient enough. On busy lines the long distances could cause delays, and the telegraph message was often intercepted or sabotaged during the war. When a troop train was rear-ended in New Jersey, many soldiers were killed. To prevent another such accident, railroads placed towers at measured intervals or "blocks" where an operator worked a semaphore to permit movement or to halt a train. These block signals became more commonplace over the next two decades. The first went into operation on the New Brunswick, New Jersey, and Philadelphia Railroad (Pennsylvania) in 1865.

Though not a technological advance in itself, the rapid movement of supplies and personnel forced the railroads to interchange freight cars as track gauges permitted. They developed a rental system based on mileage.

— The Railroads and Warfare —

If the army engineers who built the first tracks gave them a military character, the railroads in turn changed the character of warfare. The American Civil War began a pattern of military strategy which lasted until the twenty-first century. The railroads linked factory and city directly with the battlefield. Troop movements that would have taken weeks or months were now done in a matter of hours. Since the railroad was an all-weather and all-season form of transportation, battles could be fought and last throughout the winter months. Moreover,

the railroad delivered soldiers "fresh" to the battle line, and generals no longer had to wait to regroup or rest their men and animals before sending them into action.

Supplies no longer "followed" an army. Food and all equipment traveled with the soldiers during this first "railroad war." Previously, as an army traveled away from its home base, soldiers had to scout the countryside and take food (forage) however they could. The search for provisions lost time and caused greater destruction of the countryside. It also caused loss of discipline. As the soldiers freely spread out over a wide area, they were away from their main corps. By keeping regiments together at all times, the railroads gave the officers greater control over the men.

Battles also became more frequent and far more intense. Armies could be moved swiftly from one place to another. Artillery mounted on flatcars was moved from battle to battle with ease. The military no longer needed teams of horses to pull a cannon hundreds of miles, and then be delayed because it got stuck in the mud. This ease of movement permitted larger cannons. Huge mortars were mounted on their own rail cars. A short, instantaneous telegraph message could set a bat-

Men work along tracks of the Orange and Alexandria Railroad at Deveraux Station near Bull Run, probably in 1863. Courtesy Virginia Museum of Transportation.

tle in motion within hours, whereas it would have taken months before the advent of the railroads!

The U.S. Military Railroad did an incredible job repairing tracks and adjusting train movements. Just as important, both the Union and Confederacy avoided any attempt of the government to take over the railroads. In other words, the railroad industry could respond to war needs without an excessive bureaucracy and possible conflicting chain of command. It worked particularly well in the North, where profit was the main motive.

The Northern railroads charged the government two cents per mile to haul each soldier, and the highest rates possible for supplies. The costs mounted quickly, and some became shocked by the huge outflow of money. In 1862, Congress formed a committee to investigate costs and other factors. Rumors of graft and corruption were rampant.

Much of the profit went into purchasing locomotives, rolling stock, and other supplies; it stimulated the iron industry and the infant steel industry. By the end of 1862, the Union was able to out-produce Confederate destruction of rails with ease. In supplying the Union Army, railroads formed a cohesive system which was not as much required of them before the war. They brought grain and meat from the midwestern states to soldiers stationed everywhere along the border of the Confederacy. By 1863, Chicago became the largest meat and grain market in the world. With tracks funneling into the city from all points of the nation, it became a natural "break of bulk" for processing foods. On the average, 90 trains left Chicago each day to supply the Union Army alone!

When the Civil War began, the Union feared that some midwestern states would join the Confederacy. (There were a significant number of southern sympathizers in Illinois and Iowa.) However, with the railroads firmly tying their economies to the North, they remained steadfastly in the Union. California, however, remained a problem: Many in the Union feared that the Confederacy would be attracted to it because of gold. A railroad across the continent linking California to the cities of the northeast would calm any such concerns. The Union planned the construction of a transcontinental railroad during the first years of the war.

— The Pacific Railroad —

With the Civil War raging, the North could discount the southern rail routes to the Pacific that were proposed in the 1850s. The Republican Party had championed such a railroad since its inception. In 1860, the Iowa delegation introduced a bill in Congress for the building of the "Pacific Railroad," but it failed. In July of 1861, Lincoln called a special session of Congress, and the bill was passed. Given California's gold and strategic advantage, the Civil War hastened the effort to build a "Pacific" railroad.

In 1862, the Pacific Railroad was chartered as: "An Act To Aid In The Construction Of A Railroad And Telegraph Line From The Missouri River To The Pacific Ocean, And To Secure To The Government The Use Of The Same For Postal, Military, And Other Purposes." The law gave President Lincoln the authority to decide the transcontinental's eastern ter-

minus and approximate mountain crossings with a variance of 300 miles. He also would decide the track gauge. With the Civil War in its early stages, the Pacific Railroad was now a Union project. Hence the name, Union Pacific Railroad.

Construction began during the war, but it was hampered due to lack of men and supplies. Nevertheless, the Union Pacific was on Lincoln's mind throughout his presidency. In the spring of 1863, General Grenville Dodge reported to Lincoln that the Union Pacific should follow the Platte River Valley through Nebraska. He argued that such a route gave them 600 miles of flat land from the Missouri River to the Rocky Mountains. He believed that the mountain summits were lowest in that line. Neither he nor Lincoln ever considered building the line further north. The Platte River route also had the advantage of attracting the Iowa railroads to build to Omaha at their own expense.

On November 17, Lincoln set the eastern Union Pacific terminus at Omaha, and on March 7, 1864, he decided that Council Bluffs would be the meeting point of the Iowa railroads. He thereby changed the original plans, which had different companies' tracks join the Union Pacific at the 100th Meridian (North Platte, Nebraska). Those railroads were originally to come from four places: Council Bluffs and Sioux City, Iowa, Atchison, Kansas, and Kansas City, Missouri.

Lincoln realized he was inviting charges of profiteering with the Council Bluffs decision. He said as much to others. The parcel of land he owned in Council Bluffs was within a few blocks of the proposed Chicago, Rock Island, and Pacific depot.

There is an element of mystery surrounding Lincoln's establishing the transcontinental's gauge. Lincoln issued a directive on January 21, 1863, fixing the gauge at an even five feet. Immediately, there was a series of arguments over the issue. The California delegation argued in its favor, but Oregon, which also wanted a railroad, demanded 4 feet 8½ inches. The 5-foot gauge would obviously favor the South whenever the war ended, so a number of the North and Midwest railroad executives demanded the 4 feet 8½ inches. Everyone realized that the gauge of the transcontinental would become the national standard. In spring Lincoln relented, and the 4-foot 8½-inch gauge was affirmed by Congress on March 3rd of the same year.

Some say Lincoln simply preferred the 5-foot gauge while others contend he secretly wanted the 4 feet 8½ inches all along. The Illinois Central had a 4-foot 8½-inch track to Cairo, but when it expanded further into the South, it was at five feet. Lincoln, of course, was most familiar with that railroad. Could the first decision have been a conciliatory gesture to the South — "with malice toward none"? There's another possibility: all the connecting railroads to Chicago through Iowa had gauges of 4 feet 8½ inches. In the mid-1850s, the Iowa legislature mandated standard gauge to qualify for future construction grants. There is much room for speculation. After the war, the reunited nation was poised to undertake one of the most daring and grandest construction projects the world has seen since the Egyptian Pyramids, Roman aqueducts, and the Chinese Great Wall. The United States built a railroad all the way to the Pacific Ocean.

PART III

The Glory Years

Historical Survey

Following the Civil War, the United States entered a period of extensive economic and population growth. Industrialization increased, along with food production. The government encouraged settlement of the vast area between the Missouri River and California.

Until the mid-1870s, the United States undertook a "reconstruction" of the southern states. It had to rebuild due to the devastation of the Civil War. New agencies were created to help the freed slaves, and southerners had to adjust to the formation of revised state governments. Some states began programs to industrialize.

The construction of the Union Pacific and Central Pacific Railroads right after the Civil War made settlement in the huge area between Omaha and San Francisco possible. The government encouraged its population by offering 160 acres free to anyone who wanted to live on the land. In 1873, Congress doubled the initial allotment. In 1877, Congress passed the Desert Land Act that granted 640 acres of land in relatively dry areas at a price of $1.25 per acre. This allotment was designed to increase settlement in the southwest. The relatively dry land could be used to graze cattle. At best estimates, only 300,000 Native Americans occupied the vast area.

The California gold rush and subsequent smaller rushes in Colorado, Idaho, and South Dakota also helped populate the area. The railroads made habitation of the land reasonably easy and were a practical means to build the economy. Farmers could sell their products to the growing cities hundreds — even thousands — of miles away and purchase goods from the factories on the east coast. The migration to the trans-Missouri West was one of the greatest movements in history. The historian Frederick Jackson Turner considered the availability of the cheap land a "safety valve." It was an outlet for the overpopulation on the east coast.

Many immigrants came from Europe and populated east-coast cities. These people provided cheap labor to work in the growing factories. City politics became corrupt, and "political machines" emerged in the larger municipalities. Efforts were made at reform. On the federal level, efforts were made to establish a "civil service" system whereby government positions were filled by examination rather than political appointment.

Both cities and the federal government prospered with the great industrial growth. The discovery of oil in Pennsylvania just prior to the Civil War permitted inexpensive lighting by kerosene lamp for even greater activity to take place at night. The mining of coal and iron increased, and Pittsburgh, Penn-

sylvania, became the center of a burgeoning iron and steel industry. The railroads made the carrying of the bulk materials to the mills easy, and themselves became major consumers of the products for rails, engines, and cars.

With industrialization came a labor movement. Working conditions in the factories were poor if not outright dangerous. There were long hours and no insurances or other benefits. In 1868, the Knights of Labor became the first union. Shortly afterwards, the American Federation of Labor was formed. The early unions struck the railroads and later almost all industrial sectors. Many of the issues, including the legal right to organize, would be settled in the early twentieth century.

The growing population and the high production in factories generated much commerce. Department stores opened in the larger cities, and mail-order houses sent products to the remotest areas by the railroad. The cattle industry supplied beef to cities thousands of miles away. Such economic prosperity created a "Gilded Age" for the United States.

The economy, however, went in cycles. Sometimes it turned down, and there was vast unemployment and a lack of production. These "panics" were often started with the failure of a major company. There were large downturns in the economic cycles (or depressions) in the 1870s and 1890s. In 1893, the failure of the Philadelphia & Reading Railroad triggered a huge depression where unemployment was estimated at over 25 percent.

The downturns in the economy also affected the new farm population in the Midwest. As farm production increased, prices declined. Moreover, farmers believed that the railroads were charging unfair rates. They banded together through a fraternal organization called the Grange. Eventually the farmers convinced the government to pass laws regulating the railroads. The Populist Political Party developed to represent farmers' interests.

Government regulations spread to other industries. A movement called "progressivism" grew by the end of the nineteenth century. The Progressives brought about legislation to ensure the quality of meat and drugs. They also caused further regulatory acts on the railroad industry. They were responsible for the introduction of the federal income tax and alcohol consumption prohibition in the early twentieth century.

Around 1900, the United States became a major world power. It began construction of the Panama Canal, and President Theodore Roosevelt sent a large naval fleet around the world to demonstrate the nation's military might. Even though President Woodrow Wilson campaigned to keep the United States out of World War I, the government declared war on Germany in April 1917. The federal government drafted men into the army, and began a program to control the national economy. The government took over the railroads for a specific period of time.

Similar to the United States, the Canadian government began plans to populate the large area west of the original provinces. After British Columbia joined the Canadian Confederation, there was the need to join the provinces together. Canada, however, had greater urgency for doing so.

Around 1870, the Metis, a people part French-Canadian and part Indian descent, began a rebellion to establish their own country independent of the Confederation. Under the leadership of Louis Riel, the Metis carried on a virtual revolutionary war. At the same time, Canada was suspicious that the United States might also make a claim on the interior area, as a significant number of U.S. citizens were moving into the territory.

In the years before World War I, Canada encouraged railroad construction to link its Atlantic and Pacific coasts. It encouraged immigration to populate the area. As with the Union Pacific–Central Pacific, the railroad was the means to encourage population growth in the region. Moreover, the transcontinental railroad was a condition for British Columbia to join the Confederation.

Canada entered World War I in conjunction with England in 1914. It made important contributions in both men and material to the war effort. It won a place for itself at the Versailles Peace Conference and became a member of an international League of Nations to prevent future wars. Although the United States played a large role in winning the war and helped negotiate the Versailles Peace Treaty, the U.S. Senate refused to ratify the treaty to join the League.

Harnessing the Elephant

From the Civil War until World War I, the United States and Canada embarked on building railroads to the Pacific Coast. The United States eventually constructed tracks along each of the previously suggested routes and had train and telegraph service along both its northern and southern border regions. Canada concentrated its projects within its southern tier. Both countries saw the railroads as a means of populating their vast interiors.

The building of the first transcontinental — the Central Pacific and Union Pacific — was unique among the others. Not only was it the first in a series, but it was the last grand project completed before the use of mechanized tools. Except for the use of black powder, the workers used the same techniques as the Egyptian pyramid builders or those who put up the Great Wall in China. They placed the track wherever convenient. The area was unexplored; and unpopulated, other than by Europeans in Salt Lake City — and Native Americans on the Great Plains.

— Theodore Dehone Judah —

The project was part of the Republican Party platform, and was seen as a Civil War necessity at first. President Lincoln gave it his personal approval. The real impetus for its beginning, however, belongs to Theodore Dehone Judah. Judah had previously constructed bridges and trestles for various railroads in New England. He later went to California to build its first railroad, a line from Sacramento to the mining town of Folsom. When the railroad was finished, he remained in California to convince others to invest in a transcontinental line. He could hardly meet anyone without bringing up the topic, and soon people would hide the moment they caught sight of him. He quickly gained the title "crazy Judah." He even ran a small railroad museum in the nation's capital in the hope of bringing public officials to his cause.

He was so convinced of his project's worth that in 1860 he set out alone to explore the Sierra Nevada Mountains. With only a notebook and riding a horse, he discovered a series of ridges that led directly to the summit. Having the experience of being a bridge engineer, he mapped out the route and decided tracks could be built successfully over the mountains. When he returned to Sacramento he was even more invigorated to make his dream become reality. At that point he won the attention of Charles Crocker, a dry goods merchant; Leland Stanford, a grocer; and Mark Hopkins and Collis P. Huntington who were partners in a hardware store.

All four were members of the recently formed Republican Party. They saw both business and political opportunities with the construction of the railroad. Huntington had traveled across the Isthmus of Panama and knew firsthand how a railroad would capture business from the east. At the same time they could control the gold wealth of California and also the

Comstock lode which was recently discovered in Nevada. Along with Judah, the Pacific Railway Convention drew up the "Articles of Association of the Central Pacific Railroad Association" in 1859. The company was chartered by the State of California. The Central Pacific Railroad was incorporated in 1861.

— Construction Terms —

Judah afterwards left for Washington, D.C., to lobby Congress and President Lincoln for support. When the Pacific Railway Act was passed in 1862, Judah informed his partners: "We have drawn the elephant. Now let us see if we can harness him." He then returned to Sacramento to organize construction from the West. They had to build 40 miles of track before they could qualify for financial support. The Union Pacific had to build from Omaha to the 100th meridian for its funding to go into effect. Since the Central Pacific had been chartered already by California, the Railway Act did not have to incorporate them again.

The Act gave the railroads a 130-yard-wide right-of-way. They also received 6,000 acres per mile divided into six sections on both sides of the track. The sections formed a checkerboard pattern. They were sold as collateral for the railroads' having received the federal grant. Congress later increased the amount to 12,000 acres in ten alternate sections. They also received $16,000 per mile for track construction on level land and $48,000 per mile in the mountains. There were three important restrictions: no grade was to exceed 2.2 percent (116 feet per mile), curves had to have a radius of at least 400 feet, and the railroads had to complete the work within 12 years.

The railroads formed separate companies to do the actual construction. Even though the railroads and construction companies had some of the same members on both boards, the separate firms provided greater flexibility and two investment opportunities. The famous but scandal-ridden Crédit Mobilier of the Union Pacific was chartered in 1863. It let out construction contracts and arranged for the purchase of materials.

The Central Pacific broke ground on January 8, 1863, in Sacramento, and the Union Pacific turned its first shovel of earth in Omaha, Nebraska, on December 2 of the same year. Progress was gradual until after the Civil War when manpower became available. Both also had the problem of getting materials to their respective sites. The Central Pacific had to bring rails, locomotives and everything iron 18,000 miles from the east coast of the country around South America. California had an abundance of wood for ties and trestles. Although the Union Pacific's distance was less, it was also troublesome. Railroads had not yet been completed across Iowa.

Therefore, material had to be floated down the Ohio River to St. Louis, then up the Missouri River to St. Joseph. From there it was floated or carted, depending upon the season, up to Omaha.

As construction progressed in California, there was a falling-out between Judah and the other four. Judah took issue with what he considered substandard construction practices. He also opposed their categorizing certain miles of land as "mountainous" to get the extra money from the government. The Big Four bought out Judah's shares for $100,000. Judah took the money and left for the east coast to raise funds to buy them out! He contracted yellow fever when crossing the Isthmus of Panama, and died in New York City. He never saw the "elephant" he drew and had tried to harness.

After Judah left the group, they appointed a new acting chief engineer, Samuel Montague. Stanford remained president of the Central Pacific, Huntington vice president, and Mark Hopkins treasurer.

The Union Pacific found it difficult to find workers because of the Civil War. In California, whenever the Central Pacific hired men, they left in droves to seek gold. They would have the railroad transport them to the nearest location where gold was found. Then they would leave to seek the precious metal. Crocker and his chief engineer James Strobridge first tried to hire Mexicans. Then Crocker suggested hiring Chinese. His argument was that they had built the Great Wall in China; therefore, they could build the railroad.

— The Chinese and the Central Pacific —

Crocker first tried 2,000 Chinese. He wanted to test them at work given their shorter stature and lesser weight compared to Caucasians. They worked superbly well. He then hired over 12,000 Chinese in all and even sent recruiters to Asia. The Chinese camped apart from the others and brought their own chefs to cook their food. They tended to work independently in groups of 30. The Caucasians resented them and the Chinese were soon labeled "Crocker's Pets." They attempted to strike, however, in the summer of 1862 to gain more money. They returned to work when Crocker threatened to fire them.

The Chinese did the most daring work. Some were killed during the excavations. According to legend, when widening ledges, they made their own baskets, lowered themselves down cliffs, and used hand drills to make holes for black powder charges. They also constructed 13 tunnels. The tunnel at Donner Summit was the most difficult. The men worked from both ends and from a shaft in the center outward. The mountain was solid granite, and progress was less than a foot per day. They worked in 8-hour shifts, and it took more than a day to drill deep enough to set a black powder charge. They did try using nitroglycerin at one point, but it was too unstable and dangerous. Dynamite had just been invented, but it was not commercially available until after the transcontinental was completed. The Summit Tunnel was 1,650 feet long.

Cold and snow were also inhibiting factors. During the winter of 1866–67, 44 snow storms occurred with an accumulation of over 15 feet. At one time it took 5,000 workers

to clear the tracks for the supply trains. The men often had to live in their recently constructed tunnels. One time an avalanche covered a complete camp of workers. They were found in the spring when the snow melted. It soon became apparent that snow would delay trains once the railroad was constructed. According to tradition, Stanford suggested the building of "snowsheds." They built wooden "tunnels" where the most snow accumulated. Between snow sheds and mountain tunnels, 34 miles of Central Pacific track was covered or encased in one way or another. One worker commented that it was a "railroad in a barn." Once the Central Pacific left the Sierra Nevada Mountains, its pace of construction quickened.

— The Union Pacific —

Until it reached the Rocky Mountains, the Union Pacific followed the fairly level grade of the Platte River Valley. It hired former Union and Confederate soldiers as well as a good number of immigrants, mostly from Ireland and Scandinavia. Some of the veterans were experienced railroad workers from the U.S. Military Railroad. Unlike the camps of the Central Pacific, the Union Pacific workers lived in dormitory cars. They also had their kitchens on wheels and even "arsenal cars" for weapons to fight hostile Indians.

The Union Pacific's organization copied the structure and chain of command of the military. President John Dix and vice president Thomas C. Durant had the foresight and good fortune to replace their first chief engineer, Peter Day, with General Grenville Dodge. Dodge not only had an engineering background, he had the reputation for the fastest laying of track during the Civil War. He also knew how to organize and lead men. Dodge's first goal was to reach the 100th meridian to qualify for federal funding to go into effect. He then had to find the easiest route through the Rocky Mountains.

Construction across the prairie had its own difficulties. Workers had to cart wood for ties over the treeless plain. Once they left the Platte River area, they had to carry water from sources of over 50 miles away. Dust storms in summer and snow in winter made life difficult. The Union Pacific also had to defend against Indian attacks.

— Indian Raids —

The Cheyenne and Sioux tribes in particular fought to prevent the railroad from invading the land. These tribes often let wagon trains through unscathed, because these people were moving on to the Pacific Coast. They left only their wheel ruts behind. The railroad, however, left not only its track on the earth, but also stations, watering towers, and settlements. Moreover, the train brought hunters who killed the buffalo in ever increasing numbers. Some shot buffalo just for sport, and others sought the hide which was used for machinery belting for industry in the east.

The Indians realized that their way of life would end with the disappearance of the buffalo as well as the settlement of the plains. They attacked trains and destroyed railroad property as much as possible. During one attack in 1867, they derailed a train and scalped the people. A survivor, William Thompson, walked four miles to Plum Creek to report the event. Newspapers picked up the story and sensationalized it.

Thompson became a hero, and the whole country became even more interested in the construction of the transcontinental.

The Central Pacific did not have as many difficulties with their Indian tribes. For one thing the Shoshoni and Payutes were not as warlike. Also, the Central Pacific gave passes to the chiefs to ride in coaches and permitted braves to ride on freights for free. They also gave them liquor from time to time.

Much has been written about the demise of the buffalo. The argument has been that hunters, arriving in large numbers by the railroad, killed off the herds. There is another theory that has some validity. The Union Pacific purchased cattle from Texas, and drove them north. The cattle followed the tracks westward as food for the workers. In fact, the workers referred to the drovers as "cowboys" and the term quickly spread throughout the country. The Texas Longhorns may have spread diseases, including brucellosis, to the buffalo. The diseases then spread like wildfire throughout the buffalo herd, as they could not be quarantined. Within a short time the once huge "thundering herds" of buffalo no longer roamed the plains, and the Indians had to accept the new technology which invaded their homeland.

— Construction —

When the Union Pacific track reached the 100th meridian, Durant threw a huge party. Dignitaries arrived from the east to the new town of North Platte. Even the senator from Ohio and future president Rutherford B. Hayes was among them.

— Hell on Wheels —

The workers had their own form of recreation. They had Sundays off from construction, and they made use of it many times in rowdy behavior. A group of saloons, gambling houses, and places of "ill repute" followed the workers to "end of track." As construction moved westward, so did the entertainment. It soon became known as "hell on wheels." Grenville Dodge eventually hired the brothers Daniel and John (Jack) Casement to establish law and order. "Hell on wheels" caused delays, injuries, and even deaths among the workers. In fact, for every accidental death through construction, there were four murders. At one point, the Casement brothers had to hang six of the most difficult troublemakers. Whether it was justice or not, the Casements were the law of the prairie without any challengers.

Grenville Dodge discovered the all-important pass through the Rocky Mountains by accident. A group of Indians chased his surveying party one day. To elude the warriors, Dodge and his men ran quickly in the opposite direction into what later became known as Sherman Pass. It provided them an ideal access along their line to Salt Lake.

As virtually the only original settlement between Omaha and Sacramento, Salt Lake City became a natural goal for both railroads. With the Railroad Act amended, the Central Pacific exceeded its original agreement by driving tracks eastward

of the California–Nevada border. A race was on between the two railroads: the more mileage, the more funds from the government, and the greater possibilities of earnings from nearby settlements. By the spring of 1869, the railroads had surveyed or graded over 200 miles past each other, and laid over 100 miles in excess rail. In fact, at times the tracks were in sight of each other, and "raiding parties" from each railroad harassed each other and destroyed property. It took a Congressional meeting to settle upon Promontory, Utah, as the place to join the rails.

After the Union Pacific reportedly set eight miles of track in one day, Crocker and Durant made a wager. Crocker bet Durant that his crew could lay ten miles of track in one day. Durant took him on for $10,000. Crocker won. His teams graded and laid ten miles and 56 feet of track from dawn to dark. There is no record of Durant having paid off the bet.

Durant had the reputation, perhaps deservedly so, of being a scoundrel. Just before the meeting at Promontory, about 300 workers kidnapped him for a ransom of $50,000. The railroad wired eastern bankers and paid the sum. Durant was released, but there were persistent rumors that he staged the whole affair and received a 10 percent kickback from the would-be kidnappers! Given Durant's personality and reputation, the rumor could be true.

— Promontory: The Last Spike —

The meeting at Promontory was originally scheduled for May 8, 1869. A storm, however, washed out a Union Pacific trestle, and it took more than a day to make the repairs. The joining of the rails thus took place two days later, on May 10th. The whole nation awaited the event, and was able to hear it almost instantaneously by telegraph. There were also three photographers present. In spite of all the witnesses, there are conflicting accounts of the proceedings.

Leland Stanford, now governor of California, arrived in his train pulled by the locomotive *Jupiter.* He carried with him the last tie and last spike. The last tie was of California laurel banded in silver. The spike was of California gold and engraved with the names of the Central Pacific Board of Directors. There was also a silver spike. The tie had pre-drilled holes so the spikes would not be damaged when driven into the wood.

Durant arrived behind locomotive *No. 119.* He was in a particularly ugly mood and suffered from a headache (some claim it was a hangover.) There was a short dispute over procedure, but it was quickly resolved. A telegraph wire was attached to a silver hammer. As it hit the spike, a click would be heard at stations around the nation. Stanford had the honor of the first hit. He missed and hit the rail instead. Durant then tried and hit the rail too. The real final tapping of the spike was done by engineers Montague of the Central Pacific and Dodge of the Union Pacific. The telegraph then sent the word: *DONE.*

The *Jupiter* and *No. 119* were uncoupled and both ran over the final tie and spikes. Everyone then posed for a picture. East and West met in a desolate location north of the great Salt Lake in Utah—Promontory. A band played and speeches were made. After the ceremony, the Central Pacific and Union Pacific officials went to Stanford's private car for dinner and a party.

53

The meeting of East and West at Promontory, Utah, on May 10, 1869. This photo by A. J. Russell is probably the most famous in railroad history. Courtesy The Andrew J. Russell Collection, Oakland Museum of California.

President U. S. Grant received the first official telegram that the rails had been joined. The Liberty Bell rang in Philadelphia, and other bells rang throughout the country. Some cities had parades, and many well-to-do citizens held parties. Others gathered at railroad stations to hear the "click" of the hammer and spike which made Promontory the first electronic media event in history. (Some argue that Stanford and Durant were instructed to hit the rail instead of the spike. The iron rail would carry current whereas the gold spike was insulated by the wood tie.) Both the spikes and tie were replaced after the ceremony to prevent theft. During the next few months, the tie had to be replaced ten times, because souvenir hunters took chunks and splinters!

Within a week the first train ran from coast to coast. Both railroads had to replace large sections of track that had been hastily constructed — sometimes laid on the ground without adequate ballast! Later, the Union Pacific sold a section of its track to the Central Pacific and the meeting place was moved to Ogden. Dodge later built the Texas & Pacific Railroad, and Stanford, Huntington, Crocker, and Hopkins became wealthy. Durant died in poverty. John Casement worked the construction of the Northern Pacific Railroad and eventually became a representative in Congress for Wyoming.

In the 1930s, Cecil B. De Mille produced a movie about the construction of the first transcontinental called *Union Pacific.* It starred Barbara Stanwick and Joel McCrea. While remaining mostly true to the epic event, it did take some Hollywood licenses.

— The Meaning of the First Transcontinental —

The population of California decreased by 35,000 over the next five years, and the Crédit Mobilier erupted in a scandal of huge proportions in 1872. The Central Pacific and Union Pacific Railroads, as all businesses, suffered during the Panic of 1873. Nevertheless, from 1869 to 1873, the amount of U.S. railroad track doubled to over 70,000 miles, and the railroad industry became a dominant employer of the nation's workforce. Within the next generation more transcontinental lines would be constructed in both the United States and Canada. Not just the coasts, but all economically important areas would be joined to give the United States an integrated, unified economy and a true sense of nationhood. The railroads not only linked California with states in the east, they populated the interior as well.

Towns sprang up along the track around water and coaling stations for the locomotives. There were restaurants for passengers. Just as important, station spacings were at a convenient distance for farmers to bring their produce to the depot within one day's wagon ride from nearby farms. Moreover, the railroads sold the land at prices affordable to the average homesteader. Many times, the men who laid the tracks purchased property and settled down on farms. The railroads created a ready market for their service and helped populate land that otherwise was unreachable and economically unfeasible given the condition of roads and wagon travel of the nineteenth century.

September 8, 1883. Last spike of the Northern Pacific at Gold Creek, Montana Territory. Former President U. S. Grant and Henry Villard did the honors. Courtesy BNSF.

The Union Pacific began the practice of naming towns after the construction engineers and workers.

A controversy grew over the years about the large amount of government assistance the railroads received to build to the Pacific Coast. The amount has truly been exaggerated. While over 155 million acres were granted, the railroads used only 80 percent of the allotment. Some of the projected routes were never completed. Moreover, almost all of the acreage would have been useless without the services rendered by the railroads. Furthermore, government assistance helped build less than 19,000 miles of track. In other words, over 92 percent of railroad construction in the United States was done through private means.

Government loans to the six "Pacific Railroads" amounted to little more than $64.5 million. When the loans came due in the late 1890s, the government received the principal plus nearly $105 million in interest, for a sum of over $165 million. At the same time the railroads had to agree to carry all government personnel, both civilian and military, as well as all government freight, at one-half the prevailing rate. (No doubt, the government wanted to avoid the transportation costs incurred during the Civil War.) Within a few years, even the railroads that did not receive government help had to agree to the half-fare rate. By the twentieth century the railroads became a tax target from both the state and federal government. When the special, reduced rates were repealed in 1945, a Congressional committee concluded that the payments transferred to the federal government amounted to over $900 million. When these rates were calculated according to World War II traffic, the railroad's contribution rose to $1.25 billion — or ten times the original value of the land. In other words, the government reaped a profit of $1,124,000,000! At the same time, the railroads opened up huge areas of North America that would have remained virtually unpopulated and nonproductive. Through railroad development, these regions became a source of immense mineral wealth and the nation's "breadbasket." In short, the railroads paid back all government assistance many, many times over.

— Northern Pacific —

Right from the start, the federal government believed one Pacific railroad was not enough to develop the interior United States. In July 1864, President Lincoln signed a bill into law to charter the Northern Pacific Railroad. The line was to go from Lake Superior to Puget Sound following a route suggested by Edwin Johnson and Isaac Stevens in the 1850s. The Northern Pacific had a right-of-way of 200 feet, but it could not make loans or issue bonds on any of its property.

It soon became apparent that the Northern Pacific could not raise any funds without collateral. Congress then permitted the railroad to offer bonds. Groundbreaking began just west of Duluth, Minnesota, in February 1873, and eastward from Kalama, Washington, three years later. Most of the work force consisted of over 15,000 Chinese. Some were veterans of the Central Pacific construction while others emigrated from China. The roadbed reached Bismarck, North Dakota, in 1873. Further construction westward and a line to St. Paul were not completed at that time. The Northern Pacific, as many other industries, fell into bankruptcy and caused the Panic of the 1870s.

Frederick Billings reorganized the company in 1878, and extended the line into Montana by 1881. He used new steel rail imported from England and Belgium as the U.S. industry was not able to supply enough. The German immigrant Henry Villard completed the construction of the 1,900-mile line. It crossed the Rockies at two summits: Bosman and Mullan Passes. In 1888, Villard dug the Stampede Tunnel, 1.8 miles long, to eliminate a number of switchbacks. (A switchback is the zig-zag track up a mountainside.) The railroad greatly increased the population of the northern territories and was instrumental in North Dakota and Montana becoming states.

After the Northern Pacific fell again into bankruptcy during the Panic of 1893, but began anew, as the Northern Pacific Railway Company in 1896. James J. Hill of the Great Northern was eventually successful in taking over the railroad. Together with the Great Northern, the Northern Pacific constructed the Spokane, Portland, and Seattle Railroad in Oregon and Washington to gain advantage over Union Pacific and Southern Pacific competition in the Pacific Northwest.

— The Great Northern —

James J. Hill was instrumental in uniting three great railroads into an economic system empire which ranged from the orient to Chicago and the ore mines of Colorado. Hill was born near Rockwood, Ontario, and originally intended to become a physician. Because of blindness in one eye, he had to seek a different profession. He went to New York City and sought a job as a cabin boy on a freighter sailing for the orient. He later returned to the Midwest and in 1866, he became an agent for the St. Paul and Pacific Railroad. Shortly afterwards he formed his own freight company, Hill, Grips, & Company. In 1870, he met with Donald A. Smith, governor general of the Hudson's Bay Company, who interested him in building a railroad in Canada.

During the Panic of the 1870s, Smith and Hill were able to purchase the St. Paul and Pacific Railroad. Hill and Smith joined forces with George Stephen, president of the Bank of Montreal, and Norman Kittson of the Red River Transportation Company to extend the railroad northward to meet

James Hill's railroad and shipping empire. The world's largest cargo ships, *Minnesota* and *Dakota*, with the *Oriental Limited* in the foreground. Courtesy BNSF.

Laying track on the prairie for the Great Northern in 1887. Courtesy BNSF.

Women Round House Laborers, Great Northern Railway, Great Falls, Montana, WWI (c. 1919). Courtesy National Archives. #24010.

the planned Canadian Pacific at Pembina. Hill was then appointed director of the Canadian Pacific and encouraged them to build southward to Puget Sound. Even though the Canadian government refused permission to construct on U.S. soil, Hill did influence the railroad to use the strongest foundations for trestles and bridges as well as a solid roadbed. The railroad, however, approached closer to the U.S. border than actually planned. Hill resigned from the Canadian Pacific board in 1883. He then concentrated his activities on building his own railroad to the west coast.

In 1882, Hill became president of his original railroad which became known as the St. Paul, Minneapolis, and Manitoba Railway Company. He planned a construction project all the way to Puget Sound. He then acquired complete control of the St. Paul, Minneapolis, and Manitoba Railway Company. He later purchased the Minneapolis and St. Cloud Railroad, which had charter rights to the west coast, and expanded tracks into the Dakota territory. His railroad reached Minot in 1887, and Great Falls, Montana, later. He was most fortunate that his chief engineer, John F. Stevens, discovered Marias Pass through the Rocky Mountains. At just over 5,200 feet, it was one of the lowest crossings of the mountains. Construction happened quickly after crossing Marias Pass, and tracks reached Puget Sound in 1893. Hill changed the company's name to Great Northern Railway in 1890. Hill often showed up at a construction site and gave the workers suggestions on how to do some task more quickly or more easily.

Hill almost immediately made plans to take over the Northern Pacific Railway. Court decisions thwarted him twice, but he finally won out by buying shares and gaining

Final Spike Ceremony on the Great Northern near Scenic, Washington, January 6, 1893. Courtesy BNSF.

controlling interest in both the Northern Pacific and Chicago, Burlington, & Quincy Railroads. With these three railroads, he built an empire from the Great Plains to the Pacific Northwest. Hill looked further than the farmers along the tracks for his profits.

— Chicago, Burlington & Quincy —

The Chicago, Burlington, & Quincy provided Hill access to Chicago and westward all the way to Denver. The CB&Q railroad began as a commuter line out of Chicago. During the Civil War it had grown to 400 track miles, and was the first railroad to enter the Chicago stockyards. It reached Denver in 1882. During the 1870s it sold over 2 million acres to farmers along its line. The Chicago, Burlington, & Quincy had a vigorous education program for farmers. It actually had a touring exhibit of the most recent agricultural techniques and even introduced the crop of alfalfa into Nebraska. Even more important to Hill, the Chicago, Burlington, & Quincy hauled ore from Colorado and cotton from its connecting lines from the south.

Hill was able to keep trains full traveling both east and west with these connections. In 1896, he negotiated with the Nippon Yusen Kaisha Company to ship cotton from the south, flour from the midwest, and steel from the east to the orient. The return trains were loaded with lumber from the Pacific Northwest to the plains states for housing and other construction projects.

Hill was interested in populating the countryside along his tracks. He encouraged immigration, particularly from Scandinavia. He actually gave farmers cattle if they would live in the northern Great Lakes or Puget Sound areas. The railroad then offered prizes for the best cattle and crops. More important, Hill kept shipping rates for farmers exceptionally low. After he died in 1907, the Great Northern Railway named its most prestigious train *The Empire Builder* in his honor.

— Denver & Rio Grande —

The Chicago, Burlington, & Quincy had a good connection with the mines of Colorado through the Denver & Rio Grande Railroad. Former Union General William Jackson Palmer began constructing a 3-foot gauge line through the Rocky Mountains in Colorado. He planned to build southward to the Rio Grande River, but came into open conflict with another line, the Atchison, Topeka, & Santa Fe. After a court battle which Palmer won, he decided to build to the northwest to reach Salt Lake City in 1880. The Denver & Rio Grande narrow gauge permitted easier construction in the mountains, and it formed branch lines to the various mines in the area. It had the distinction of 4 percent grades and a summit of 10,000 feet.

The Denver & Rio Grande changed its main line to standard gauge in 1890. It still maintained a narrow gauge third rail on the main line, so that it could move the smaller cars over the entire system. The Denver & Rio Grande was a major supporter of the Western Pacific Railroad in the early 1900s. Connections were made with the Western Pacific at Salt Lake City and with the Chicago, Burlington, & Quincy at Denver to form another transcontinental system.

— Santa Fe —

In 1859, three years before the Pacific Railroad Act, Cyrus Holliday secured a charter to build a railroad along the Santa Fe Trail. Holliday was an attorney who had purchased some railroad stock when he lived in New England. After moving to Kansas, he saw the possibilities of moving cattle from New Mexico to Kansas City by rail. At that time the journey took over 80 days by wagon; the train reduced the time to hours and opened the southwest to further settlement.

Most of the investors lived in Atchison and Topeka and, therefore, the railroad was called the Atchison, Topeka, & Santa Fe. Holliday secured a government grant which gave the railroad 3 million acres to sell along a line from Newton, Kansas, to the Colorado border. From Newton to Emporia, the land was in a checkerboard pattern for 20 miles on each side of the strip. From Emporia to Kinsley, the strip narrowed to ten miles on each side. The railroad had to reach the Colorado border by March 1, 1873. The estimated cost for the 340 miles of track was $5 million.

The railroad made a short detour to Carbondale because coal was discovered in the region. J. D. (Pete) Criley engineered the railroad to the Colorado border. The crew averaged two miles per day, with only one mile on Mondays since the men had to recover from their weekend hangovers! Similar to the Central Pacific–Union Pacific, the Sante Fe had only pre-mechanized tools to work with. They had to break rails in making some curves and grade with horse-drawn scrapers. Here again the Irish played a large role in the hard construction work. They were called "Jerries," and all the other workers became known as "Dagos."

The crew had to make one huge, last effort in laying track within hours of the grant deadline. Just before March 1, they believed that they had already crossed into Colorado. The border, however, was not clearly marked, and government agents told them they had four miles yet to go. With a snowstorm coming out of the Rockies, the crew constructed the last miles within hours!

One group in particular played a prominent role in building the Santa Fe. The railroad recruited Mennonites from Russia. The Mennonites were sober, God-fearing people who brought other advantages with them. They had accumulated a large number of gold certificates and developed a strain of wheat which was both drought-resistant and immune to most diseases. They also carried seedlings of fruit trees: olive, mulberry, apricot, etcetera. After they settled down and farmed, they were responsible for Kansas becoming a major wheat-growing state. Wheat, then, became an important commodity for the Santa Fe to haul to markets throughout the country.

In general, the Santa Fe became known for its truthfulness in advertising. Holliday and others determined that it was useless to attract people to the area by giving them a false impression of the region. They would only leave after a short period of time. The settlement of the state was one of the most successful of the time. Between 1865 and 1877, the population of Kansas increased from 136,000 to over 700,000 people. The increase permitted a 25 percent decrease in individual taxes!

When the Santa Fe expanded into Colorado, it came into conflict with the Denver & Rio Grande. Both the Santa Fe and Rio Grande competed for a route through Raton Pass. Fighting broke out. They interrupted each other's telegrams, and the Santa Fe actually took over some Rio Grande stations at one point. They fought again over the Royal Gorge which was the best route to the town of Leadville, where silver had been discovered in 1877. Shootings occurred. The Santa Fe eventually hired a "private army" and the western hero Bat Masterson for its protection. It finally reached Denver in 1878, through marketing agreements with the Kansas Pacific and Union Pacific.

The Santa Fe began surveying a line through New Mexico and Arizona to build all the way to the Pacific Coast. In 1880, it bought controlling interest in the St. Louis & San Francisco Railroad, because it had a charter to build across the continent. They also began discussions with the Mexican dictator, Porfirio Diaz, to construct a line directly into Mexico. (At that time, there was even some speculation that the Mexican state of Sonora would break away and annex itself to the United States.) The line, however, was never built.

During the extension further into the southwest, the engineers had to make a decision whether to build to Santa Fe. The city of Santa Fe was not on the best route for construction. They also had to search out sources of soft water and to build windmills as close to the track as possible. They decided to bypass the city but connect it with a branch line. Therefore, the main tracks of the Atchison, Topeka, & Santa Fe never reached the town of its namesake. The railroad did reach the Pacific Coast in 1881, through a connection with the Southern Pacific at Deming, New Mexico.

While the Deming connection served its purpose at first, the Santa Fe eventually wanted its own tracks to California. It was able to do so through agreements with the city of San Diego. Until 1881, San Diego had not been able to attract a railroad. That year the city put up $25,000 in cash with an allotment of over 17,000 acres of land plus another 485 city lots. The Santa Fe's Joseph Osgood began building a line eastward from San Diego. He used steel rails throughout and connected with the main Santa Fe line in November 1885. Agreements were then made for Santa Fe to have trackage rights on the Southern Pacific to reach Los Angeles.

In 1887, the Santa Fe began building eastward to Chicago. With a crew of 7,000, the railroad refurbished or built over 350 miles of track in almost a straight line between Kansas City and the shores of Lake Michigan. In less than a year, the railroad built over nine miles of bridges. By April 1888, the first train left Chicago for the Pacific Coast going all the way on the tracks of the Atchison, Topeka, & Santa Fe.

Riding the train was itself quite an event. The Santa Fe claims that it had the first train with enclosed vestibule cars throughout. The cars also had plush seats, electric lights, and different kinds of inlaid oak and mahogany for wall and ceiling decor. Passengers also had the treat of the best dining on the railroad at that time in the Harvey Houses set up along the Santa Fe tracks. Cyrus Holliday's cattle railroad grew into a transcontinental which developed the land that Stephen Long had called "inhospitable" and gave its passengers some

of the most luxurious accommodations on the rails up to that time.

Following a practice started by the Union Pacific, the Santa Fe named most of the towns along its tracks after its engineers and construction crew members.

— Southern Pacific —

Even before the United States completely came out of the Panic of the 1870s, the new president of the Central Pacific, Collis P. Huntington, began to expand his railroad. He purchased all short lines in California and merged them into the Southern Pacific Railroad. He then raised rates on service to the mining communities 100 percent.

Huntington attracted a large number of farmers to the fertile San Joaquin Valley by promising to sell them land for $2.50 to $5.00 per acre as soon as they settled on it. As more and more farmers came to clear and work the land, he raised the price to $40–$50 an acre or higher to any bidder. The farmers then took action. They formed a Settlers' League to sue the Southern Pacific. Huntington in turn "hired" government agents to force the farmers off the land. There was a clash, and six were killed in a gunfight which became known as the Mussel Slough Tragedy.

The farmers may have gotten revenge. There were a series of Southern Pacific train robberies, and the farmers did not lift a hand to capture the crooks. The Mussel Slough incident and the farmers' plight were later fictionalized in Frank Norris's novel, *The Octopus*.

In expanding south and then eastward to New Orleans, the Southern Pacific tackled one of the steepest mountain grades and had to merge a number of already constructed short lines. The Southern Pacific had to build through the Tehachapi Mountains. Tracks had to rise 2,754 feet from Caliente to a pass at an elevation of 4,025 feet within 16 miles. The grade was prohibitive. William Hood designed a series of switchbacks, tunnels, and a loop which proved to be a solution to the problem. He was able to reduce the grade to a manageable 2.1 percent. Southern Pacific tracks entered the Mojave Desert in 1876.

The next year, 1877, the Southern Pacific joined the Texas & Pacific at Yuma, Arizona, and built on to Tucson in 1880. After building to El Paso, it joined with the following railroads on to New Orleans: Galveston, Harrisburg, & San Antonio; the Texas & New Orleans; the Louisiana Western; and Morgan's Louisiana & Texas Railroad and Steamship Company. This "Sunset Route" was completed in 1883. It began a steamship service, "a hundred golden miles at sea," from New Orleans to New York, which lasted until the beginning of World War II.

The Southern Pacific expanded northward to Oregon in the 1860s. The line went through 18 tunnels — one over 3,000 feet long — and crossed the Siskiyous Summit at over 4,000 feet. After the absorption of the Central Pacific in 1885, the Southern Pacific's last major construction project was the Lucin Cutoff, completed in 1903. The cutoff is a 32-mile line across the Great Salt Lake. Twelve miles of the cutoff is on trestle which had to be filled in from time to time due to a soft lakebed.

The Southern Pacific was a major U.S. railroad by the turn of the century. It eventually had four main passenger routes. The "Shasta" ran from San Francisco–Sacramento to Portland and Seattle. The "Overland" was the chief route from San Francisco to Ogden, then via Union Pacific and Chicago & Northwestern to Chicago. The "Golden State" ran from San Francisco to El Paso, Texas, then on to Tucumcari, then via Chicago, Rock Island and Pacific to Chicago. The "Sunset Route" went to New Orleans, then the "Washington-Sunset Route" on the Louisville & Nashville to Washington and New York, or by steamship to New York.

Quite strange at first glance, the Southern Pacific Company began as a holding company in the state of Kentucky in March 1884 — about 891 miles from its nearest tracks at New Orleans! Kentucky's laws of limited liability attracted the corporation. The company could also increase its stock without state regulation. It paid a nominal tax of $100,000 a year to the state well into the twentieth century. The Southern Pacific "absorbed" the Central Pacific officially through a leasing agreement from Kentucky in February 1885.

— The Milwaukee Road —

The Chicago, Milwaukee, St. Paul, & Pacific and the Western Pacific Railroads built their lines in response to competition from the other transcontinentals. They were more interested in trade at the ends of their lines than population development along the tracks. The Milwaukee Road wanted to have its own line to the Pacific Northwest, and the Western Pacific wanted to break the monopoly that the Southern Pacific held over the San Francisco area.

The Chicago, Milwaukee, St. Paul, & Pacific Railroad began as the Milwaukee & Mississippi Railroad in 1849. By 1871, it reached Chicago, and southward to Kansas City by 1887. In 1907, it expanded to Council Bluffs and Sioux City, Iowa, and on to Rapid City, South Dakota. At the beginning of the century, the Milwaukee Road recognized that further growth was dependent on James Hill's Great Northern, Northern Pacific and Chicago, Burlington, & Quincy Railroads. Hill could easily cut off the Milwaukee's connections with the west.

To keep its independence, in 1905, the Milwaukee's board of directors authorized construction of a line from the Missouri River in South Dakota to Seattle. The 1,400-mile line was completed in May 1909, with east and west construction

crews meeting at Garrison, Montana. Freight began to move within a week, but passenger traffic did not start until 1911.

Given the abundance of hydroelectricity in the mountainous area, the Milwaukee decided to electrify portions of the line in 1912. Electric motors would power the locomotive and make it climb the mountain grades more easily, and even feed current back into the line and hold down speeds when braking downhill. Moreover, electric locomotives completely solved the problem of smoke accumulation in tunnels. By 1913, the Milwaukee had electrified over 400 miles of track. A second electrification project was completed in 1917 and added another 200 miles under the wires called catenery.

While capital-intensive and costly at the outset, electrification was a long-term economical investment. Nevertheless, the transcontinental line never produced the expected profits. For one thing, the Panama Canal had been completed shortly after the Milwaukee's rails met in Montana. Also, the numerous government controls on the railroads around the turn of the century and after World War I took their toll, among other factors.

— The Western Pacific —

The Southern Pacific had a monopoly on the San Francisco traffic. When E. H. Harriman gained control of both the Southern Pacific and Union Pacific, he virtually shut off the Denver & Rio Grande's freight in and out of Ogden. In 1903, Walter Barnett and George Gould (Jay Gould's son) obtained franchises to build a railroad through the Feather River Canyon of the Sierra Nevada Mountains. The road not only passed through some of the most beautiful mountain scenery, but its summit was 2,000 feet lower than that of the Southern Pacific.

The Denver & Rio Grande supported the Western Pacific by underwriting $50 million in bonds. The Western Pacific thereby guaranteed the Denver & Rio Grande an outlet to the Pacific and West Coast trade. The last spike was driven on a trestle at Keddie, California, just weeks after the Milwaukee Road completed its construction.

The Western Pacific had virtually no branch lines and little development along its tracks. By 1915, both the Western Pacific and the Rio Grande entered bankruptcy proceedings. In 1916, the Western Pacific was sold and reorganized. Just before World War I, it took over a narrow-gauge line to compete with the Southern Pacific to Reno, Nevada.

Chapter 6.

Canada:
The Work Has Been Done Well
in Every Way

Railroad construction played a necessary role in the creation of Canada as a confederation. In the early 1860s, both the Maritime Provinces in the east and British Columbia in the west based their decision to join the new confederation on whether thay would have railroad connections with central Canada. When the leaders of the four Maritime Provinces met at Charlottetown and again at Quebec in 1864, New Brunswick and Nova Scotia said they would not join until provided with railroad connections. British Columbia joined in 1871, only on condition of a rail link with the east — or else it might become part of the United States. In fact, the Canadians feared that the central area of Manitoba–Northwest Territories might become part of the United States unless it could make a claim with a rail line. Last but not least, Prince Edward Island joined the confederation in 1873, but only when it needed money to complete its own railway project.

— The Intercolonial Railroad —

Canada's Act of Confederation directed the building of the Intercolonial Railroad. The line, when finished, ran from Halifax in Nova Scotia to Rivière-du-Loup in Quebec where it joined the Grand Trunk Railway. The Canadian Confederation stipulated that the Intercolonial Railroad be built entirely on Canadian soil, and not take a shorter route through Maine. It was more a political and defense issue than an economic one.

The civil engineer Sandford Fleming carried out the survey. Due to Fleming's insistence, the Intercolonial's Board of Commissioners adopted the policy of a solid construction of the line and the use of iron instead of wood for bridges and trestles. While more costly at the outset, it meant greater maintenance savings in the future. They chose the 5-foot 6-inch gauge which was common in Canada at the time. They also imported steel rail from England.

In 1874, the Intercolonial Railroad was placed directly under the Canadian Department of Public Works. It opened between Halifax and Rivière-du-Loup in 1876; the line was extended to Quebec in 1879, and received trackage rights to Chicago. It reached Montreal in 1889. The experience gained in its operation was invaluable when the government came to decide how the publicly owned, and much larger, Canadian National should be operated.

— The Canadian Pacific Railway —

There are several similarities between the building of the Union Pacific and the Canadian Pacific. Both had vast stretches of prairie and high mountainous areas to cross. If the Union Pacific was started to tie California with the North during the Civil War, the Canadian Pacific was part of an agreement for British Columbia to join the Canadian Confederation. Again, both had unexplored territory between the beginning and end points of track. The Union Pacific had to contend with Indians, and the Canadian Pacific helped to settle a Metis revolt which threatened to create a new nation in what later became known as the province of Manitoba. The Union Pacific was to provide a quicker means to transport passengers and cargo to and from the west coast compared to ships sailing to the Isthmus of Panama. The Canadian Pacific would be quicker for Canadians rather than making connections with U.S. railroads through Chicago. And most important for Canadians, it was entirely within the borders of Canada. It also named towns and settlements after its construction engineers and workers. In 1899, with an eastern connection all the way to the Atlantic, the Canadian Pacific could boast being the first truly ocean-to-ocean transcontinental railroad.

As early as 1834, Thomas Dalton suggested the possibility of a Canadian railroad all the way to the Pacific Ocean. Even though it was a year before the United States discussed its own possibility in Congress, Dalton's idea was more of a dream than anything practical. Canada had almost no real railroad at the time. There was also some enticement a bit later from William Francis Butler's book, *The Great Lone Land*. Unlike the "Great American Desert," Butler's work depicted the plains area of Canada as a vast fertile garden! While a gross exaggeration, it did encourage thought of settling the area.

In 1851, Allan Macdonnell seriously proposed the construction of a transcontinental. At that time, however, the Hudson's Bay Company controlled the interior, and it at first rejected the suggestion. The company believed that any settlement would interfere and diminish its fur industry in the region. Moreover, Macdonnell's plan seemed impractical at the time. There was the same response in 1862, when Sanford Fleming made the same proposal.

Within another decade, the political situation had changed, and the Pacific Railroad would become a reality. British Columbia wanted promises of a railroad to connect it with the east before it would join the new confederation. In 1870,

Prime Minister John A. Macdonald made an official proposal for the construction of a transcontinental railroad. Also, before 1869, the Metis leader, Louis Riel, began a revolt against Canada and declared the Red River region an independent nation. (The Metis were part French Canadian, Indian, and Roman Catholic.) The railroad eventually brought troops to quell a second revolt in 1885.

Some Americans quickly joined in the act and plans were made for the Canadian Transcontinental. A Philadelphia banker, George Cook, supported the effort, but only because he wanted the Canadian railroad to join the Northern Pacific in the United States. James J. Hill also wanted the railroad to meet his line at Pembina and connect to St. Paul, Minnesota. Hill had a strong influence on the Canadians. He encouraged a more permanent construction policy right from the start. He also suggested that William Cornelius Van Horne head the construction and a member of the Hudson's Bay Company become a director. If he hoped Van Horne would swing the railroad southward, Hill was mistaken. Van Horne built the Pacific entirely on Canadian soil. At that point, Hill decided to build his own line to the Pacific northwest, the Great Northern Railway.

In 1871, Walter Moberly explored the region and plotted a route to cross the Rocky Mountains at Eagle Pass, then follow the Fraser River to Burrard Inlet on the Pacific Coast. Sandford Fleming also did a preliminary survey that year. With the possibility of a mountain crossing in hand, Macdonald promised British Columbia that construction would start in two years. In 1873, however, Alexander Mackenzie became Prime Minister, and he was not in favor of such a railroad. Macdonald succeeded Mackenzie, returning to power in 1878, and the Canadian Pacific turned its first shovel of earth to the west coast in May 1881.

— Canadian Pacific Construction —

Construction took place simultaneously in three regions. The eastern portion ran 650 miles from Callander on Lake Nipissing to Lake Superior. The route followed close to the Lake Superior shoreline. The central portion, almost 900 miles long, ran through Winnipeg to the Rocky Mountains. The western region extended from the Pacific Coast eastward for 450 miles. The Pacific portion was slowest in construction because of the mountains.

There were four steps in the building process. First, the route to cross at Eagle Pass had to be surveyed. Second, the Canadian Pacific had to make a right-of-way of 60 feet on both sides of the track. Third, on the prairie, it had to keep the track four feet above the surface and dig 20-foot-wide drainage trenches on both sides to prevent flooding from melting snow. They tried to keep to a 2.2 percent grade in the mountains. Fourth, at Kicking Horse Pass, trackage was much steeper, reaching a ruling grade of 4.5 percent; they used switchbacks and had to build run-offs manned 24 hours a day should a train lose its brakes during a descent. In 1909, however, the grade was lowered by constructing tunnels under Cathedral Mountain and Mount Ogden. The tunnels were "figure eights" or spiral tunnels, and it took 10,000 workers two years to build them! The Canadian Pacific also built the highest wooden

bridge in North America over Stoney Creek — with a 228-foot wooden tower — 1,200 feet long and 275 feet above the stream.

The Canadian Pacific had some advantages in construction over the Union Pacific. It used steam drills to dig tunnels and had more powerful explosives. It used huge "scrapers" pulled by horses to do much of the grading. According to legend, Van Horne developed an early version of a track-laying machine. Rails, fish plates, ties, etcetera. were carried on a truck, and they would slide the items off the wagon as construction went along. This saved much time and energy in hand — carrying each item — particularly the rails. Moreover, they used steel rail imported from England and Germany.

The Canadian Pacific was determined to avoid a "hell on wheels" at the end of its tracks. It forbade the selling and consumption of whiskey. It then hired "whiskey detectives" to stand around the crews from time to time. The officials, however, had only marginal success. While they did prevent saloons from being built along the track, whiskey peddlers often hid in bushes and sold their goods to the workers as soon as the detectives walked away.

Many immigrants built the Canadian Pacific. Swedes, Finns, American Irish, and Mennonites were mostly in the eastern section, along with French Canadians. The railroad asked the Oblate Catholic missionary Father Albert Lacombe to be chaplain. He often celebrated mass in a box car. The director of the western region, Andrew Onderdonk, supplemented the workforce with Chinese. He imported over 6,000 from Hong Kong. The Chinese met with some resentment

Sir William C. Van Horne (c. 1882). Courtesy Canadian Pacific Archives. #8889.

Canadian Pacific "Last Spike," at Craigellachie, November 7, 1885. Donald A. Smith drives the spike with Sanford Fleming on the left (white beard) and William C. Van Horne (black beard). Further to the left, but not visible in this photograph, is Major A. B. Rogers. The youth just to the right of Smith formed his own express company and carried packages back and forth from the construction camps to the nearest town. Photo by Alexander J. Ross. Canadian Pacific Archives. #1960.

from the European population of British Columbia. The Chinese dug 24 tunnels and sometimes averaged only six feet per day.

Financial conditions were not the best. At times managers paid crews with checks in winter knowing they could not cash them for months. Winter weather was sometimes so severe that they could not work. Snow often accumulated to over 15 feet. In the Selkirk Mountains, over 8 feet of snow fell in one six-day period. At another point they recorded over 6 feet of snowfall in one day!

The railroad encouraged people to settle and farm along its tracks. About half of those who moved into the region left by the mid-1890s. A short growing season was one deciding factor. Population did increase after 1905, when Charles Saunders developed a fast-maturing wheat called Marquis.

— Financial Arrangements —

The Canadian Pacific had its share of scandals. Unlike the United States transcontinental construction, the Canadian Pacific managed its own finances, purchased all its materials, and did the construction itself. Materials purchased through Cooper, Fairman, & Company were greatly overpriced. To make matters worse, former Prime Minister Mackenzie's brother was one of its business partners. The railroad constructed a number of buildings along the line and eventually sold them at greatly exaggerated prices to the government. The Neebring Hotel, for example, was constructed shoddily and sold at 400 percent above cost. Perhaps more important however, the roadbed was well-constructed and saved the company money in the long run.

While the westward construction was more dramatic and captured the most attention, the Canadian Pacific also expanded eastward. Right from the start, it began to purchase already existing railroads. In 1881, it bought the Canada Central and in 1884, the St. Lawrence and Ottawa Railroad. The Canadian Pacific then had access to the capital, Ottawa. In 1883, it made connections with U.S. railroads on to Portland and Boston. With the purchase of the Northshore Railroad, it secured use of a portion of the Grand Trunk Railway on to Quebec. With these buy-outs and connections, the Canadian Pacific became the first single-company system running coast-to-coast or transcontinental in the complete sense of the term. It extended to St. John, New Brunswick. The Intercolonial rarely granted it running rights to Halifax. By World War I, the Canadian Pacific also owned a worldwide steamship line.

There is no doubt that William C. Van Horne was the driving force behind the Canadian Pacific. In 1884, he became its vice president, and was president from 1888 to 1899. He was chairman of the board from 1899 to 1910. He saw the railroad through both good and discouraging times.

— The Last Spike —

Some members of the construction crew, a few board members, and Van Horne witnessed the driving of the last spike. Prior to the ceremony, at 9:00 A.M. on November 7, 1885, the last rails were measured, cut, and put in place at Craigellachie in the Eagle Pass. The governor general, who carried a silver spike with him, had to return to Ottawa. Van Horne said a plain, iron one would do just as well. Donald A. Smith, the eldest director, had the honor of pounding the last spike into the plain tie. They posed twice for the one solitary photographer, and Canada was united by rails. Van Horne gave a one-sentence speech: "All I can say is that the work has been done well in every way."

Within minutes, the party boarded a train. On November 16, Louis Riel, whose uprising proved the necessity to build the railroad, was hanged at Regina.

Canada and the rest of the world suffered a depression in the mid-1870s and 1890s. At the same time, over 400,000 immigrants arrived from Europe, and the government wanted other railways to break the Canadian Pacific's monopolistic position on the prairie.

— The Canadian Northern —

Other railroads began construction to answer the nation's needs. In 1896, William Mackenzie and Donald Mann purchased the charter of the Lake Manitoba Railroad and Canal Company. They were able to acquire a subsidy of 6,500 acres per mile for the first 125 miles of track they could construct. By 1902, they connected Winnipeg with Lake Superior. In 1903, the new railroad, the Canadian Northern, absorbed the Great Northern Railway of Canada at Quebec and other short lines through Ottawa and Montreal. By the end of the year, the Canadian Northern had over 1,700 miles of track and connections in Nova Scotia.

In 1905, it began to build across the new provinces of Saskatchewan and Alberta. The Canadian Northern constructed its roadbed very hastily. From Edmonton, the Canadian Northern built on to Vancouver. After surveying a route in 1908, the railroad constructed near the also-expanding Grand Trunk Pacific. Both lines crossed the Rockies through Yellow Head Pass. The western portion and some branch lines were completed in 1915. The Canadian Northern secured subsidies from the government and had permission to issue bonds.

The Canadian Northern quickly gained the reputation as "the farmer's railway," as it served many isolated farmers. When a train was delayed for some time, a Canadian Northern conductor explained they were waiting for a woman to get a 24th egg from her chickens. The woman needed two dozen eggs to take to town, and she was waiting for the hen. So, the train waited for the hen too. . . . The Canadian Northern Railway never enjoyed economic prosperity. It did, however, help attract people to the interior of the nation.

— The Grand Trunk Pacific —

The Grand Trunk Railroad became alarmed by the competition from the Canadian Pacific. In fact, the Grand Trunk tried to halt Canadian Pacific's construction through political maneuvering. In 1902, it offered to purchase the Canadian Northern for its outlet on the west coast. When its offer was rejected, the Grand Trunk formed a new company, Grand Trunk Pacific, in 1903, to build from Winnipeg to the west coast.

The Grand Trunk Pacific had five years to complete its construction. Groundbreaking began in 1905 on both ends, and the rails met in 1909. The Canadian government built a

bridge for it across the St. Lawrence River at Quebec at no cost to the railroad. The cost overruns for the railroad in general amounted to at least 200 percent. In fact, a Royal Commission was established to investigate the situation. They found that most expenses were in labor and materials. The railroad borrowed huge sums from England, and it is estimated that the Canadian government in the end actually loaned the Grand Trunk Pacific money to cover 90 percent of its expansion costs!

Both the Grand Trunk Pacific and Canadian Northern lines were located about 180 miles or so north of the Canadian Pacific. The Grand Trunk Pacific crossed the Rockies through Yellow Head Pass and then went northward to Prince Rupert — about 500 miles north of Vancouver.

The Grand Trunk Pacific was intended to be a grain-hauling railroad. The officials built stations about seven miles apart so that farmers would find it more convenient to bring their wheat to the depot. Quite interestingly, they named their stations in alphabetical order from east to west. They chose the names of officials and workers. One vice president formed one town's name for his four daughters: He from Helen, Ma from Margaret, Ru from Ruth, and Ka from Kathleen: Hemaruka, Saskatchewan.

— The National Transcontinental Railway —

After the Grand Trunk Pacific expanded to the west coast, the Canadian government sponsored another railroad to build from Moncton, New Brunswick, westward to Winnipeg. The National Transcontinental Railway ran north of Montreal and Quebec. Surveying the route posed many problems, because it ran through swamps and between series of lakes. There were also no settlements in the region. It did eventually ship metal ores to farmers in Montreal and Quebec. Just like the Canadian Northern, the line was never financially successful.

— Expansion in the United States —

Besides building the transcontinentals, Canadian railroads expanded southward into the United States. In 1858, the Grand Trunk built the Chicago, Detroit, and Canada Grand Trunk Junction Railroad across the border. In the 1870s, Canada acquired trackage on the Vanderbilt roads to Chicago. When Vanderbilt raised his rates, the Grand Trunk bought the Chicago and Lake Huron Railroad in 1879, to gain access to "the Windy City." They later renamed it the Grand Trunk Western.

When the Central Vermont needed income in 1898, it permitted the Grand Trunk to purchase some shares. When flooding ruined over 25 percent of the Central Vermont's trackage in 1927, the then successor to Grand Trunk, the Canadian National, purchased it outright at auction.

By 1912, the Canadian Northern purchased the Duluth, Winnipeg, and Pacific which ran north from Duluth to the Canadian border. It reached to Thunder Bay, and, thereby, the Canadian Northern had access to two ports on Lake Superior and important trackage across the borders with Canada's neighbor to the south. The line was important for transportation of lumber and other industrial products.

— Overexpansion —

During World War I, the government took over the Canadian Northern and appointed D. B. Hanna to form a new board. In 1918, the Parliament granted the board authority over the Intercolonial, the National Transcontinental, and thirteen other, smaller lines. The formation of a nationalized system was only months away.

Canada was overly optimistic about its population growth and transportation needs in the first decade of the twentieth century. It could not sustain its system of over 29,000 miles of track on the eve of World War I. Moreover, Canada declared war on Germany in 1914 to assist Great Britain, and it no longer had funds for sustaining its large railway network, not to mention further construction. Also, the immigrants ceased to arrive from Europe. And, ironically, the Grand Trunk continued to favor sending cargo through Portland, Maine, instead of Canadian ports.

When the railroads shipped soldiers and material for the war, the government paid rates far below cost. All the companies except the Canadian Pacific were heavily in debt by 1917. In fact, the Army removed portions of rails from the Canadian Northern to send to Europe! After his election in 1911, Prime Minister Sir Robert Borden argued for the government to take over the railroads. Borden had advocated a nationalized transportation network as early as 1902. In 1918, a government decision to form a board with authority over Canada's weakest railroads had political as well as economic implications.

Grand Canyon Railway.

The Pullman Company

George M. Pullman built a veritable railroad empire following the U.S. Civil War — without constructing a mile of track. In 1867, he formed the Pullman Palace Car Company and moved his plant to Detroit. By 1868, he built the first full-sized dining car, the *Delmonico,* and he had already made over 40 sleeping cars. He far outdistanced his main competitor, Webster Wagner. Some sleeping cars and rudimentary dining cars, of course, existed earlier. Pullman simply improved upon them and made them in a grand style.

In 1870, Pullman furnished his luxurious cars for a transcontinental round-trip from Boston to San Francisco. The patrons were wealthy members of the Boston Board of Trade and their families. Most owned stock in various railroads. The special, most luxurious train, attracted the attention of the press. As with transporting Lincoln's body from Chicago to Springfield, the Pullman Hotel Express was another great marketing tool. Soon many railroads wanted Pullman cars, and the members of the Board of Trade were in a position to influence their purchase.

Pullman expanded his business very quickly. He made arrangements with the railroads to carry his cars on their passenger trains and to furnish light and heat. Pullman would provide all the other necessities and service. The name "Pullman" soon became synonymous with innovation as well as luxury. From steam heat to electric lights and all-steel, closed vestibule cars, the Pullman Palace Car Company was the first in comfort. He built "Hotel Cars" which were a combination diner, sleeper, and lounge car. He also designed "Parlor Cars" which had large, soft chairs which could be moved about for better viewing of passing scenery or turned for group conversation.

Pullman later expanded into building freight cars by absorbing bankrupt companies such as Haskell & Barker and Standard Steel Car, among others.

— Standardized Cars —

Pullman became known for standardization in both design and service. While there were many floor plans, most early cars had 12 double-berth sections and one drawing room. Each section had two seats which faced each other during the daytime. At night, the seats pulled together to form the lower berth. The upper swung down on hinges from the wall. The upper berth contained the blankets, linens, mattresses, and pillows for both beds. At first there were curtains between the sections and the aisle. They could be closed with buttons. Later the sections had wood walls between them with curtains only for the aisle side. There were two clothes hangers for each berth and a mesh hammock strung above for small articles needed at night. Suitcases were stored under the bottom berth. Manufacturers were quick to make suitcases called "Pullmans" which fitted the under-seat storage dimensions. Passengers

needed a ladder to access the upper berth, and only the lower berth patron could see out the window at night. Spacious washrooms were at both ends of the car. The lower berth cost more than the upper.

The drawing room was much larger and faced the aisle to one side of the car. Besides the berths, it had a lengthwise couch. It also had its own wash basin and toilet.

— Pullman Service —

Pullman also standardized its delivery of services. All Pullman porters were African-American, and all lounge attendants were Filipinos. Conductors were white, and diners had mixed crews. After the Civil War, Pullman recruited porters mostly from the Carolinas and Georgia. There was an inference that Abraham Lincoln asked Pullman to provide jobs for freed slaves when the Civil War ended.

— Porter Training —

Pullman porters went through thorough training. Eventually there was a 127-page manual, and the apprentice had to sign his signature to show that he understood each item as it was taught. The first instruction period lasted two weeks; then there were six months of training with two veteran porters. (Diner and lounge attendants learned food and drink preparations similarly.) Each towel had to be folded a certain way, and even the pillows were fluffed and positioned precisely according to rules. Nothing was left to chance. The company hired "spotters" who rode in the cars from time to time to make sure the porter performed all duties strictly to code.

— The Porter —

The Pullman porters wore a tailored, dark blue uniform. They greeted everyone with a "broad smile" as passengers boarded the train. They were not permitted to touch a woman when boarding or ascending to an upper berth unless she requested it. The porters usually had to awaken passengers in the middle of the night as the train approached the station. They could only rustle the curtain — never knock on the bunk. They had to remember the destination of each passenger. As the passenger left the train, the porters had to check the section to make sure he or she did not forget anything, and it was not uncommon to see a porter running after a patron with some article in hand. . . . They could not keep anything left behind; that was grounds for immediate dismissal.

If passengers took towels or ashtrays, the porter had to pay for these articles out of his own pocket. Furthermore, he shined patrons' shoes at his own expense in hope of a good tip.

Porters could recognize a good tipper. The groom on a honeymoon was always generous! Salesmen showed their appreciation for good service. College students, too, gave decent tips — but only after playing pranks on the porter. They had to be good sports for the jokes. Women traveling alone did not tip well at all. The Pullman conductor collected tickets and supervised the porters when there were two or more sleeping cars on a train. When there was only one sleeping car, or a hotel car, porters were responsible for collecting tickets.

Pullman regulations allowed the porter only three hours of sleep on the first night out, and none on subsequent nights. They had to sit on a stool at the end of the car to make sure people did not disturb others during the night. The company expected them to travel 11,000 miles or 400 hours before qualifying for overtime pay. Because of the heavy schedule, many were accused of "sleepwalking." They had to be on the lookout constantly for people trying to steal a ride.

Before a run, porters gathered at the "Porter House," to grab a quick meal and to find out the latest information from around the country. These meetings became known as the "Baker Heater League" since they sat around a Baker stove. They also had their own terms for railroad things. Conductors were "The Big O," the fireman, "Greaseball," and the engineer, "a Hogger." The sleeper was a "boxcar," and a "tin can" was the diner. They had signals to warn each other when a "spotter" was on board.

While the hours were long and the pay relatively short, Pullman porters were people of distinction in the African-American community. Their services were also appreciated by almost everyone who traveled the rails in a sleeper. The Pullman Company received special recognition for employing former slaves in 1893. President Grover Cleveland presented the company with an award at the Chicago World's Fair.

— Pullman, Illinois —

The Pullman Palace Car Company became so large and successful that George Pullman created his own community. In 1881, he moved his plant to Chicago and built a town, Pullman, Illinois, to house over 12,000 of his car builders. In this way they would be close to the factory. It was a model community with parks and churches, but no bars. Pullman rented housing to his employees, but he did not permit the porters to live in this town.

Pullman made arrangements with railroads to pull his cars along with their coaches. Pullman provided the service and maintenance. This arrangement assured his company a substantial profit.

When George Mortimer Pullman died in 1897, Robert Todd Lincoln, Abraham Lincoln's son, became president of the company. He changed the name to simply the Pullman Company.

The Canadian railroads operated their own sleeping cars. In fact, Canadian sleepers had higher ceilings and larger berths — an insistence of William C. Van Horne of the Canadian Pacific. Pullman cars entered Canada, but popular Canadian history has it that the first sleeping car in the world was designed and built in Hamilton, Ontario.

— Coach Accommodations —

Passenger cars became even more comfortable by the end of the century. In the 1870s and 1880s, however, prairie rail-

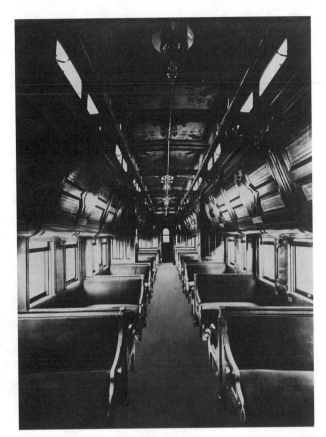

Interior of the *Pioneer*, Pullman's first sleeping car. Courtesy Virginia Museum of Transportation.

Interior of a luxurious 1880–1890s Pullman sleeping car. Courtesy California State Railroad Museum. Pullman 720.

roads offered very crude accommodations called "Immigrant Cars." There was minimal service and no luxury. Passengers, however, paid very little for travel, and the riders were more interested in finding a homestead than enjoying the journey. Within a generation, though, people who rode Immigrant Cars were traveling in Pullman Sleepers throughout the nation. Pullman became the U.S. institution which made people look forward to riding on the rails. The Pullman car and Pullman porter were synonymous with comfort, safety, and "home away from home."

Pullman builders' photo of Union and Central Pacific *Sybaris* for the *Golden State Special*. It is labeled a "Vestibule Library and Smoking Car." Courtesy California State Railroad Museum. Pullman 311.

Three "generations" of Pullman Porters. Courtesy California State Railroad Museum. Pullman 22194.

Glory Years Technology

Both the air brake and automatic coupler were lifesavers to railroad workers. George Westinghouse's air brake ended the need for brakemen to run on top of cars to twist wheels to stop the train. Many fell to their death when they slipped off the roof of boxcars, or the chain snapped back at them. The link-and-pin coupling unit required the worker to stand between cars when they were attached or released from the train. Many lost their fingers, hands, or toes in the process. In fact, it was generally accepted that brakemen and trainmen would lose fingers during their career. Major Eli Hamilton Janney's automatic coupler eliminated many of these accidents. It was Lorenzo Coffin, however, who got the railroads to apply both these lifesaving devices.

After serving for the Confederacy during the Civil War, Janney worked on models of a coupler that did not require a railroader to stand between the cars. To use the standard link-and-pin, the brakeman had to guide the link into a housing while the train was backing up. He then inserted the pin. This was obviously an accident-prone procedure. Janney devised a coupler whereby a "swing knuckle" closed and locked upon impact. Also, he devised a lever to open the coupler. The worker, therefore, did not have to stand between the cars when they were being attached.

The Miller Hook

Used on some passenger coaches prior to the Janney Coupler

While some roads had used a "Miller Hook" on passenger cars, the Janney Coupler proved far superior for more than safety reasons. It was far stronger and could withstand the pull of a long freight train. It was also far easier to use and more dependable.

— The Janney Coupler —

Janney worked on his coupler and first patented it in 1868. He perfected the device and acquired a second patent in 1873. The Pennsylvania Railroad tested the device shortly thereafter and began to make it standard equipment for all its cars in 1876. It took another six years for the Master Car-Builders Association to adopt his idea. The Master Car-Builders Association was created in 1867, with representatives from U.S.

and Canadian railroads, to help standardize the industry and permit greater interchangeability of parts.

1873 Janney Coupler

Even with the Master Car Builders' endorsement, there were 39 different varieties of the Janney Coupler in use by 1889. Most would not couple with each other! The Master Car Builders, by the early 1890s, reduced the number to 16, then later to 12 which worked with each other. By the mid 1890s railroads began to use the "Tower Coupler" which locked more strongly and placed the release lever handle outside the body of the car. Thereby, the railroad worker did not have to stand or reach between cars during the entire coupling and uncoupling process.

— The Air Brake —

The air brake was another lifesaving invention. George Westinghouse patented his air brake in 1869, when he was twenty-two years old. He had already invented a water meter and a railroad frog (a guide for switching tracks). He founded the Westinghouse Air Brake Company in Pittsburgh, Pennsylvania. He later bought a railroad signal system company and established the Union Switch & Signal Company.

Westinghouse's first air brake operated with a compressor on the locomotive filling an air reservoir. The air was released through a hose which forced shoes against the wheels of the car to slow down or stop the train. The device worked well on short trains. As cars were added, however, the third and following cars received less air pressure, and it took longer for their brakes to apply. In other words, the first cars of the train slowed down, and the rear cars plowed or pushed into them. Nevertheless, Westinghouse's concept did save lives when used to avoid hitting a horse and wagon on the Panhandle Division of the Pennsylvania Railroad in 1869. The air brake worked; it just had to be improved upon.

Westinghouse reworked his device from the opposite perspective. He placed air reservoirs on each car. He then devised a series of valves, which applied the brakes only when there was no air pressure coming from the locomotive. In other

A brakeman inserts a pole into the wheel spokes to gain leverage. Courtesy Canadian National.

Even after the invention of the air brake, railroad workers still operated brakes by hand for a time in rail yards. It was still a very dangerous practice on top of a swaying boxcar. Courtesy Canadian National.

words, to apply the brakes, the engineer released the pressure; to release the brakes, air pressure was resumed. Therefore, if cars separated or an air hose broke, the brakes were applied automatically throughout the train. This was a great safety factor as trains separating under load were not uncommon in the 1870s. Just as important, brakemen no longer had to run on top of cars to set the brakes.

The state of Iowa's railroad commissioner, Lorenzo Coffin, campaigned for the air brake. He convinced the Master Car Builders to test Westinghouse's device for general application on the railroad. In 1886, two days of testing ended in failure on long trains. In 1887, Coffin had Westinghouse observe the tests with him. At that point Westinghouse found a simple solution. He increased the diameter of the air hose and improved his valve mechanism.

The Master Car Builders held a third test that summer west of Burlington, Iowa, on the tracks of the Chicago, Burlington, & Quincy. The brakes were carried on a 50-boxcar freight train running at 40 miles per hour. When applied, the brakes stopped the train without any jarring and with less than a two-second lag from the first to the last car! The air brake would bring safety to railroaders, passengers, and the general public alike.

The railroads, however, were reluctant to install the automatic coupler and air brake even with all the apparent advantages. It took all the conviction and persuasiveness of Lorenzo Coffin to make them use these new inventions.

— Lorenzo Coffin —

Lorenzo Coffin had served as a chaplain for the Union Army during the Civil War and returned to farm near Fort Dodge,

Iowa, in the late 1860s. One day when he was waiting for his train to leave the station, he saw a railroader lose fingers while coupling a car with the link-and-pin. The incident affected him so much that he traveled the country talking with railroaders about their plight. Many told him about the air brake and Janney Coupler which were recently invented, and that the railroads refused to purchase them.

Coffin began a campaign from the halls of Congress to articles in farm magazines, while also speaking to any group that would listen to him. In 1883, at age 60, he was appointed railroad commissioner for the state of Iowa. While he had little legal power, the title gave him a respectable platform for his campaign. Through this position he was able to convince the Master Car Builders to test Westinghouse's air brakes. He also drafted the first Railroad Safety Appliance law requiring that all trains running in Iowa must have air brakes and automatic couplers. The railroads ignored the law, however, and he had no power to enforce it.

When the Interstate Commerce Commission was formed in 1888, Coffin rewrote his Railroad Safety Appliance Law to extend to the whole country. He addressed the commission about the dangers to railroad workers and passengers. While he made an impression, the commissioner did not act, and Coffin returned to his Iowa farm.

He continued to rework his law and submit it to Congress. Finally, it passed both houses, and President Benjamin Harrison signed the Railroad Safety Appliance Act in March 1893. All railroads operating in the United States had to use air brakes and automatic couplers. The application of these two devices reduced the accident rate for railroaders by 60 percent! Railroads, too, discovered that these inventions saved rather than cost money. They could now operate longer trains at higher speeds, and cars could be coupled more quickly. Safety soon became a concern and hallmark in railroading. Appropriately, President Harrison gave the signatory pen of the Railroad Safety Appliance Act to Lorenzo Coffin.

— Rule G —

Coffin still had more to offer the railroad industry. By the 1840s as train speeds and distances increased, the consumption of alcohol became a factor in accidents. Railroads tried to enforce a non-drinking policy known commonly as the "Rule G." (It was one of several safety rules — "G" on an alphabetized list.) Nevertheless, it was common for engineers, firemen, and brakemen to drink on the job. In fact, the call boys often had to rouse them from their favorite bars to tell them that their train was ready to run. Coffin formed the Railroad Temperance Association. He founded the society with his own money and traveled throughout the country giving white buttons to railroaders who promised to abstain from alcohol. It is claimed he gave out over 250,000 of these buttons. Coffin was also an instigator in founding the Home for Aged and Disabled Railroad Men in Chicago.

— Torpedoes, Flags, and Fusees —

During the nineteenth century, the railroad industry standardized a number of nonpermanent signals for safety reasons. They also developed a number of nonpermanent signal devices.

Railroad torpedoes are loud, noise-making devices placed on the tracks more than 100 feet apart. When a locomotive wheel hits one, it explodes, signaling the engineer to reduce to a speed of 20 m.p.h. or slower. The train cannot increase speed until it has passed a mile or more beyond the torpedo. Two torpedoes are used to ensure that the engineer hears the "bang."

Torpedoes are becoming obsolete. Today's soundproof locomotive cabs prevent the engineer from hearing them.

Flags are used as daytime signal indicators and lanterns at night. A red flag is a stop signal. A yellow flag indicates that the track ahead allows for a speed of only 10 miles an hour. A green flag means that the train has passed the yellow speed and restrictions have ended. A purple is also a stop signal, but as a light at night, it means that there are derails ahead. Derails are devices that purposefully cause a wheel to skip over a rail.

White flags on a locomotive mean that it is an "extra" or unscheduled train.

A blue flag alerts others that an inspector or a repair crew are working under or about a train. The train cannot move nor can cars be coupled to it or uncoupled from it. The workers who placed the blue flag are the only ones authorized to remove it. A blue lantern is used at night.

A hand-held flag or lantern can communicate orders to an engineer.

A fusee burns as a glowing fire alongside or between the tracks. The engineer must come to a complete stop to inquire about the problem. If no problem is found, the train may move

on at a speed not to exceed 20 m.p.h. for at least ½ mile. The engineer must be alert for any problem alongside or on the track.

— Block Signals —

The use of track blocks and signals spread quickly after the Civil War. Railroads set up towers linked by telegraph to control train entry into a segment of track. Once a train entered the block, the operator put out a red flag, and then telegraphed to the next tower to do the same. When the train completed its movement between the towers, the red flags were taken in and the track became clear for another train to enter.

— Automatic Block Signals —

Signal towers, however, disappeared within a few years. In 1872, Dr. William Robinson invented an electrical device to replace the operator and red flag. A low voltage direct current furnished by a battery passed through the rails. When a train now entered a block, its wheels and axles carried the electricity from one rail to another. In other words, it shorted the circuit. The shorted circuit "tripped" the mechanism to signal a stop to any other train approaching that block.

The stop position was the result of lack of current. Therefore, the mechanism was fail-safe should the battery run low or there was any debris on the track. In other words, any error or mechanism failure signaled a stop or nonentry into that block. More than a safety issue, these automatic block signals (ABS) permitted trains to control their own movements along the track. They, thereby, increased efficiency as well as safety.

It was not safe or efficient, however, for engineers to control their own entry onto tracks of another company. Switching and crossing tracks had to be controlled by one individual from one vantage point. Trains of rival companies often raced to a junction. In 1853, there was a serious accident when Illinois Central and Southern Michigan trains collided at a crossing south of Chicago. Afterwards, railroads agreed on a rule that trains must come to a complete stop before proceeding through a crossing. Within a short time, however, railroads set up towers with switches to control track crossings.

— The Switch Tower —

In 1856, John Saxby, an English engineer, invented a device that coordinated track switches with their appropriate signals. When a lever was thrown, it gave a signal for a train to enter the track or crossing. At the same time, it gave a stop signal and cut off the entry of any other train on that track or a cross track. The switches, therefore, were "interlocked" in their positions. In other words, the levers had to be moved at a certain sequence before a train could enter or cross another track. It also set "derails." If an engineer did not obey a stop signal, the train would be purposefully run off the track to prevent a collision with another. Saxby formed his own company, Saxby & Farmer, and marketed his device. By 1870, it was being installed in the United States and Canada. One operator in a tower would operate levers which moved

Hand, Flag, and Lantern Signals

Motion   **Indication**

Swung at right angle to the track.   **STOP**

Moved slowly with arm extended horizontally.   **REDUCE SPEED**

Raised and lowered vertically.   **PROCEED**

Swung in a circle at right angle to the track.   **BACK**

Swung slowly horizontally above the head.   **APPLY AIR BRAKES**

Held at arm's length above the head.   **RELEASE AIR BRAKES**

Any object waved violently by any person on or near the track is a signal to stop.

Signals (simplified): Aspects and Indications

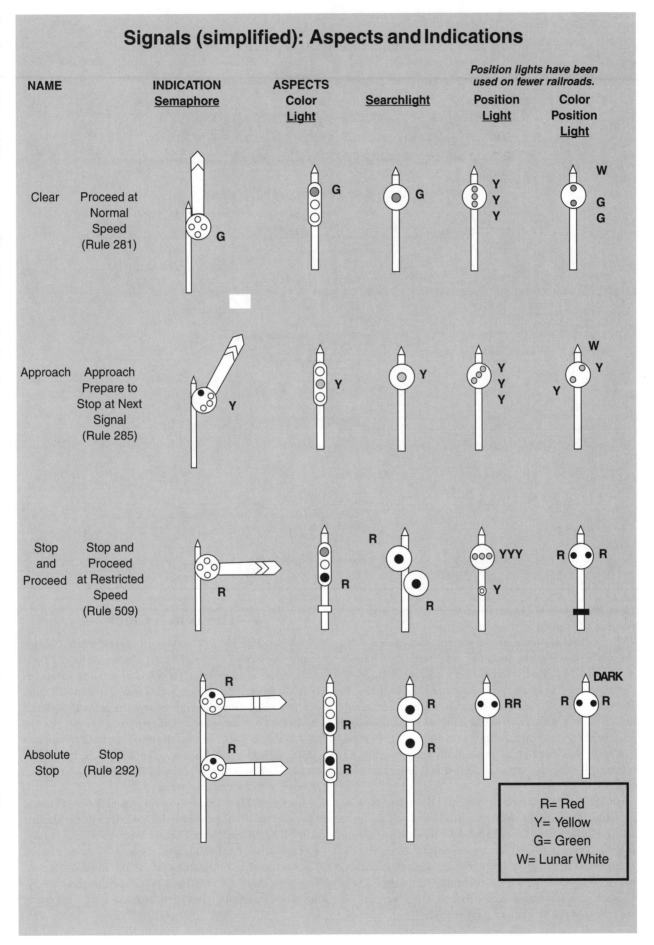

NAME	INDICATION <u>Semaphore</u>	ASPECTS Color <u>Light</u>	<u>Searchlight</u>	Position <u>Light</u>	Color Position <u>Light</u>

Position lights have been used on fewer railroads.

Clear — Proceed at Normal Speed (Rule 281)

Approach — Approach Prepare to Stop at Next Signal (Rule 285)

Stop and Proceed — Stop and Proceed at Restricted Speed (Rule 509)

Absolute Stop — Stop (Rule 292)

R= Red
Y= Yellow
G= Green
W= Lunar White

Communicating Signals

16. Each car of a passenger train must be connected with the engine by communicating signal appliance.

If the communicating signal fails, or an engine or car not so equipped is used on a passenger train, arrangements must be made for engineer to receive hand signal before passing stations. On passenger trains so equipped, radio or telephone may be used in place of hand signals.

When practicable, hand signals will be given in addition to 16 *(a)* and 16 *(c)*.

Number of Sounds	Indication
(a) two	When standing—start.
(b) two	When running—stop at once.
(c) three	When standing—back.
(d) three	When running—stop at next passenger station.
(f) four	When running—reduce speed.
(g) five	When standing—recall flagman.
(h) five	When running—increase speed.
(j) six	Increase train heat.
(k) seven	Shut off train heat.
(l) one long	When running—approaching meeting or waiting points as prescribed by Rule S-90; brakes sticking; look back for hand signals.
(m) one long	When standing—apply or release air brakes.

pipes, sometimes a thousand feet long, to open and close switches and signals for many tracks.

By the 1880s, electric circuits and compressed air assisted the muscle power in throwing switches; therefore, the tower operator could control switches even a mile away. By 1940, electric motors were used to operate and close switches. In 1883, the General Time Convention established a standardization of the signals, and two years later trains no longer had to come to a complete stop when approaching an intersection. The tower and interlocking mechanism, along with the automatic block signal, made railroading both safer and more efficient.

In 1887, Granville Woods developed the means for a locomotive to receive the electric signals inductively from the tracks. His discovery paved the way later for signals to appear in the locomotive cab and for an automatic "train stop" if the engineer ran a red signal. There was also some experimentation with a vacuum tube — a mechanical "train stop" in the 1880s. If a train entered an occupied block, a strut would break the tube, and the air brakes would be applied.

— The Dutch Clock —

All the safety devices in the world cannot protect people from recklessness. There was a great temptation for engineers and conductors to make up for delays by running a train beyond the speed limit. Freight trains were limited to 18 miles per hour until the twentieth century. The Santa Fe Railroad used a Dutch clock to keep their employees honest.

The Dutch clock recorded the speed of a freight train on a paper tape which could be inspected at any time by a superintendent. The company mounted it on the caboose. Other railroads soon adopted the device.

Crews quickly found a way to get around the Dutch clock. They uncoupled the caboose and the steam engine at the first siding they met underway. They then used the engine to crash the caboose into the standing train at exactly 18 miles per hour. The crash jammed the mechanism at the speed on impact. They then could run the freight at any speed without worrying about getting caught. The Dutch clock soon fell out of favor.

— Steel Rails —

Steel is far more desirable than other materials for rails and hardware. It is tough, flexible, and does not crack, splinter, or damage as iron does. Steel, however, was made in small quantities because of cost. There were some steel rails being manufactured near Chicago prior to the Civil War, but few railroads considered purchasing them. When they did so, it was for high traffic areas such as entrances to switchyards where iron rails had to be replaced yearly and in some cases every few months. Steel boilers on locomotives were commonplace by the Civil War. Steel car wheels came later in the century.

During the 1850s, Bessemer in England and Thomas in the United States developed similar methods to make steel from iron. By forcing blasts of cold air (blast furnace) over the molten iron, they were able to remove impurities. The result was steel, and the process became relatively inexpensive.

Railroads were both customers of and providers for the new industry. They were able to bring the coal, iron ore, and other necessary products from the mine to the furnace in large quantities and very cheaply. Pittsburgh became a steel-producing center with others in Indiana, Alabama, and Tennessee, to mention a few. Railroads brought iron ore from Minnesota and coal from the anthracite region of Pennsylvania. Just as important, freight trains conveniently carried the finished steel to destinations throughout the continent and the world. Here again, the railroads linked regions of the country which produced a product the best and most inexpensively. Then they carried the steel to consumers anywhere in the United States and Canada and to embarkation points for sale abroad.

The growth of the U.S. steel industry was phenomenal. In 1867, it produced only 2,600 tons of steel. Twelve years later, in 1879, production jumped to 930,000 tons. Right after the turn of the century, steel became America's second billion dollar industry after railroads.

Railroads were also a major consumer. Steel rails replaced iron throughout the 1870s and 1880s. It was not until the 1890s, however, that the industry could claim practically an all-steel network. At the turn of the century, steel railcars replaced wooden ones. New York City outlawed wooden cars in approach tunnels, which signaled the industry that steel would be the building product of necessity.

The steel rails permitted heavier cars which demanded yet heavier rails. Speed became important. By the turn of the century railroads attempted to set new speed records which were unheard-of during the iron rail era. New construction continued. During the 1880s, railroads built over 76,000 miles of new track which reached a total of 163,597 miles by 1890. By 1900, track mileage reached almost 200,000. There is no doubt that railroads were the major factor in the growth of the steel industry. And such incredible steel production made the United States a powerful nation in world politics by the twentieth century.

— Wheels —

Even after car wheels were made of steel, railroad workers used to keep a watch for "flat tires" and "hot boxes." Flat tires resulted when brakemen applied the brakes too tightly to stop a train. The brake shoe would completely stop the wheel from turning, and the wheel slid along the track creating a flat spot. Through further running and braking, the spot became larger. If not repaired, it could become large enough to cause a derailment. Some railroads threatened to deduct the repair charges of a flat wheel from the brakemen's wages. The rule was never strictly enforced and was done away with during the formation of railroad workers' unions.

Wheels also developed cracks from time to time. Again, if not discovered, the wheel could break and cause derailment. Carmen checked the wheels periodically by hitting the wheels with a steel bar; if the sound was dull, there was the high probability of a crack. These inspectors were commonly known as "car tonks." They also checked the air brakes and other aspects of the rail cars.

When a wheel journal became worn or defective, friction caused it to heat up the oil and eventually catch fire, thus the term "hot box." If not caught in time, these fires could cause an axle to break and cause a derailment. Railroaders soon developed an easy way to detect a "hot box." They placed oil-soaked wool in the box. When the wool started to burn, it smoked and let off a foul odor. Brakemen then could see and smell smoke coming from a wheel and stop the train. Even when almost cool, the odor lingered. In order to spot the smoke or any other problem on a freight train, cupolas were placed on the roof of cabooses. The conductor and brakemen had a higher vantage point. Some railroads used bay windows rather than cupolas on cabooses.

— Railroad Employment Organization —

The railroad employed many workers in various capacities. A military-like chain of command developed along the track and freight yards as well as on the train itself. Trainmasters and yardmasters had authority of train operation over conductors. The roadforeman oversaw locomotive movement on the line. Dispatchers were responsible for scheduling

Telegraph Key and Sounder.

trains. The telegraph operator made certain that messages were sent and received from the proper officials for safe movement of trains. Hostlers maintained locomotives and prepared them for the next run. They had authority over the locomotive from the roundhouse or repair facility to the outside track. Section gangs or track repair crews inspected and repaired up to 20 miles in their given area. They were often called "gandy dancers." When seeing them work from a distance, they looked as if they were doing an out-of-step dance along the track.

Conductors gained greater control over passenger-train movement on the track. A rope was strung throughout the cars to the engineer's cab. The conductor would pull on the rope to signal the engineer to stop or start the train. Other codes were developed. When air brakes became common, a second air hose went through the cars for the conductor to signal the engineer. The air hose was more dependable and was actually in use on some railroads into the 1960s.

— Finicky Finnigan —

Legend has it that there was an Illinois Central agent who had earned the nickname "Finicky." Finnigan worked in the Carbondale, Illinois, district many years. He was known for his efficiency, dedication, and punctuality. His only bad trait was writing lengthy derailment reports.

Finnigan's derailment reports included everything to the minutest detail. He described all the information he could whether it was pertinent or not. Then he would summarize it and write a summary of the summary. It got so that the head office dreaded receiving a derailment report from Agent Finnigan. Finally, the superintendant himself visited Finnigan and ordered him to write the briefest possible report — absolutely no unnecessary words — just the facts.

Following the superintendant's order, "Finicky" Finnigan used the following formula after listing the date and time of a derailment:

Off again, On again,
Gone again, Finnigan.

— Conductors and Brakemen —

Conductors and brakemen had other tasks on passenger trains. Brakemen were in charge of the stoves in the cars; they had to light them and feed them wood. Both conductors and brakemen had to help put out fires from hot cinders. During the summer, hot cinders would enter coaches through open windows. They often landed on clothing and upholstery and would begin to smolder or catch fire. Railway personnel also had to remove cinders from passengers' eyes from time to time. They formed a loop with horse hair to pull the cinder out. They also carried flaxseed to slip under the eyelid, which caused the eye to tear. After the turn of the century, using chewing gum became a popular method of cinder removal.

The superintendent's position differed from railroad to railroad. On some lines he was in charge of all activities in a given region. On others he supervised one particular activity along the entire railroad.

— The Telegrapher —

The telegrapher was the eyes, ears, and mouth of railroad operations. Throughout the second half of the nineteenth century and on through World War II, the telegrapher passed on information and directions for almost all train movements. The telegrapher was known to railroaders as the "brass pounder." His rapid writing while the key clicked dots and dashes became known as "telegrapher's fist."

Messages were often delivered to train crews without stopping. Stationmasters filled out "Form 19" and handed it to the engineer from a long pole with a hoop on the end. Sometimes they gave it to the conductor or brakeman on the caboose of a freight train. Direct telephone communication from a moving train to a station or tower was not introduced until the 1930s.

Railroads employed other craftsmen. From tinsmiths to carpenters, from accounting clerks to janitors, railroads were the second-largest industry in the United States by 1900. Only agriculture had more workers. In 1916, there were 1,700,000 people working on the railroad or roughly 4 percent of the entire population of the United States! This figure, however, still does not include railroad-related businesses such as locomotive manufacturing and other support services. By 1914, there were 253,000 miles of track. In 1865, gross operating funds were $300 million; on the eve of World War I, they grew to over $4,000 million. Railroad wealth was about 15 percent of the total wealth of the United States in 1900.

Railroad Financing

Even though the New York Stock Exchange began before the first rails were set in America, it owes its rapid financial success to railroads. When the nation caught "railroad fever" in the 1840s and 1850s, people purchased stocks in them. In fact, it was the first industry-wide stock-buying frenzy. After the Civil War, railroads were without doubt the primary growth industry. People wanted shares in railroads to make a fast fortune. The decoration on stock certificates looked like a mixture of locomotives running among the Greek gods and goddesses on Mount Olympus. Without any regulation, the stock market was the ultimate gamble. In fact, "fast lunch" restaurants originated in the Wall Street area of New York just so investors could return to the market quickly to keep an eye on their money.

— Crédit Mobilier —

Some of the railroad stock schemes were scandalous, and at times, illegal. The Crédit Mobilier which constructed the Union Pacific Railroad brought scandal to Congress and to the vice presidency. It was made up chiefly of Union Pacific stockholders that overcharged items. But that was not the only problem.

Oakes Ames was a representative to Congress from Massachusetts. He and his brother, Oliver, sold Crédit Mobilier stock to other representatives, even the future president of the United States, James Garfield. In fact, the seated vice president, Schuyler Colfax, purchased shares. Both Democrats and Republicans took part in this get-rich-quick scheme.

The stock deals became public in 1872, when Colfax and others were accused of "accepting bribes" from Union Pacific management. It also became known that congressmen bought stock at "discount prices." Oakes Ames and his fellow congressman James Brooks were impeached by the House. The Senate trial, however, cleared them of violating any law. Nevertheless, Oakes Ames was later censured by his colleagues.

Perhaps unethical at best, Oakes Ames did get congressional support and maintained its interest in the construction of the first transcontinental. Moreover, it was the first major stock venture by the general public in the United States.

— Commodore Vanderbilt —

Another more colorful scandal almost reached the U.S. presidency. It began in New York City shortly after the Civil War. Cornelius Vanderbilt, often called "Commodore" because of his earlier interest in riverboats, wanted to purchase the recently formed New York Central Railroad. He had earlier purchased its New York City link, the New York and Harlem Railroad.

During summers, the New York Central shipped its cargo to New York City on the Hudson River by boat. They used

Vanderbilt's railroad in winter. When Vanderbilt tried to purchase the Central, its directors refused. During the following winter, Vanderbilt dropped both passengers and Central-bound freight two miles out of their meeting place in Albany. The Central brought legal action against Vanderbilt and lost. Quite cagey, Vanderbilt had found an old law which prohibited railroads out of New York City from entering Albany proper. Afterwards, Vanderbilt simply bought out Central stock.

— The Erie Ring —

The Commodore then turned his attention to the Central's chief rival, the Erie. He began purchasing Erie stock to take over that road too. The chief officials of the Erie, however, learned of Vanderbilt's scheme and began their own plot. The infamous "Erie Ring" consisted of Jay Gould, James Fisk, and Daniel Drew. They banded together and simply printed more stock — illegally. As Vanderbilt purchased Erie stock, more would mysteriously appear.

At the same time, the New York Central and the Erie entered into rate competition. Vanderbilt lowered shipping rates to the point that the Central lost money for each cow transported. Drew and Fisk then purchased cattle and had their agents ship them on the Central to cause Vanderbilt to lose even more money! Drew actually took the cattle business a step further. While underway he had the cattle eat salt. Then, just before they were taken to market, the cattle consumed an incredible amount of water. When weighed and purchased at the market, the cattle carried a large amount of "water weight" — hence the origin of the term "watered stock."

When Vanderbilt learned of the Erie Ring's schemes, he had a court issue an order for their arrest. Drew, Fisk, and Gould hurriedly crossed the Hudson River to New Jersey with over $6 million of Vanderbilt's money. They then bribed the New York State Senate and several judges to "legalize" the fraudulent stock. Vanderbilt brought a series of lawsuits against the Erie Ring. When all the proceedings were over, Drew, Fisk, and Gould agreed to pay Vanderbilt over $4 million for the stock — realizing millions in profit.

In the meantime, the Ring attempted to corner the entire U.S. gold market with their "winnings." When the market reached a low point in September 1869, they bought all the available gold at a reduced price. They then attempted to keep President Ulysses S. Grant from releasing government gold reserves, so the gold would rise to a higher price. They bribed Grant's son-in-law to convince the president to keep the reserves closed. It did not work, however. Grant released $4 million worth of gold on the market. In one fifteen-minute period, the price dropped over $29 per ounce. Many speculators lost their shirts.

In the end Gould and Vanderbilt prospered. Drew and Fisk were ruined. Drew eventually lost all his money in the stock market, and Fisk was killed by his former mistress's new lover. Vanderbilt's fortune grew, and he left the New York Central to his son William. Gould remained as president of the Erie and gained a reputation as one of the most celebrated travelers of all times. He used three personal cars when on the rails: one for his personal physician, one baggage car for his favorite cow which produced milk with the exact butterfat content Gould wanted, and of course, a most luxurious one for himself. His chef became nationally famous for making "ladyfingers" which were Gould's favorite snack!

Rear parlor-lounge area of the business car *Shoshone*. It is in use by the president of the Union Pacific.

Many railroad owners had private cars and lived extravagantly. So did owners of most companies in the "Gilded Age." Many "Captains of Industry" amassed huge fortunes. Commodore Vanderbilt had a personal worth of $75 million, which, according to some, was the largest up to that time. His son, William, inherited the entire fortune along with the New York Central Railroad.

— "The Public Be Damned" —

William H. Vanderbilt, without malice or intent, was responsible for one of the worst railroad public relations messes of the age. After the New York Central reached Chicago, it began rate competition with the Pennsylvania. At one point, Vanderbilt had to lower the New York–Chicago passenger fare to $15, which was below the railroad's cost to carry. During a press interview, a reporter from the *Chicago Daily News* asked Vanderbilt if the fare was profitable. Vanderbilt answered "No." He explained that, if it were not for the competition with the Pennsylvania, he would "abandon it." The reporter followed up with another question: "But don't you run it for the public benefit?" And Vanderbilt answered: "The public be damned!"

The *Chicago Daily News* emphasized Vanderbilt's answer, and it resonated throughout the nation. Taken out of context, it seemed to give ammunition to the public's view of the railroads

in the 1870s. In all fairness, Vanderbilt's response meant that he could not run his trains indefinitely at such a low fare. The press and the public read it differently: Railroads ruled and controlled the public; they were not interested in delivering a service. Given the mood of the country, all railroads suffered from Vanderbilt's quote. It fueled the fire of public anger which led eventually to politicizing the Grange movement and the formation of the Interstate Commerce Commission.

— The Grange —

The Grange, known more formally as The Patrons of Husbandry, began in Washington, D.C., in 1867. Its founder, Oliver Hudson Kelly, had traveled for the federal government throughout the South after the Civil War. He was to report on farm conditions in preparation for Reconstruction for the Bureau of Agriculture. Kelly believed that farmers would benefit from belonging to some type of social organization. In contrast to Europe where farmers lived in towns and walked to their fields, their American counterparts lived on individual plots of land, sometimes miles from each other.

Kelly's Grange organization had seven "degrees" or ranks of membership. He founded the first Grange when he worked for the Post Office in Washington, D.C. He later traveled throughout the Midwest, principally his home state of Minnesota, then Iowa and Illinois. The movement grew quickly. As Kelly envisioned, it was an answer to the social needs of farmers scattered along the railroad tracks of the Midwest.

It was Ignatius Donnelly of Ninninger, Minnesota, however, who began the Grange's assault against the railroads. As the United States underwent rapid industrial growth following the Civil War, the railroads were indeed one of the leading economic sectors. Agriculture, however, by the 1870s was becoming less profitable. As the farm population increased due to large immigration, and new areas in the Midwest opened to planting by the railroads, more and more agricultural commodities were produced. As farm products increased, their prices went down.

A popular rhyme was:
>   Railroader — I Carry All
>   Soldier — I Fight for All
>   Doctor — I Prescribe for All
>   Statesman — I Legislate for All
>   Lawyer — I Plead for All
>   Merchant — I Trade for All
>   Preacher — I Pray for All
>   Farmer — I Pay for All

At the same time, farmers noticed the huge profits the railroads were making. More particularly, they were aware that railroads charged customers more to carry an item a short distance than if it traveled several hundred miles further. This complaint became known as the "Long Haul–Short Haul" controversy.

Farmers, under Donnelly's leadership, used the Grange to put political pressure on the railroads. By 1873, there were 20,000 Grange Lodges in the United States with over 800,000 members. The farmers, indeed, now had political power, and they wanted government regulation of railroad prices.

— Long Haul–Short Haul Argument —

The railroad price structure was governed only by competition. From that point of view, it made sense to charge proportionately more for a "short haul" than for a commodity going a longer distance. Short distance carrying was usually from a small farm town to a larger city. Most of these towns had only one railroad serving them; there was no competition. The farther a commodity traveled, from one large city to another, there could be two, three, or four choices of carriers, and those prices remained low due to competition. When railroads had a monopoly, they charged what the farmer could bear. Where there was competition, prices fell as low as possible. This argument, however, fell on deaf ears to farmers who were struggling for survival.

— The Interstate Commerce Commission —

The Grange at first turned to their state legislatures to regulate the railroads. By the mid 1870s, the Grange influenced the passing of many laws, but most of them were impossible to enforce. Many had to be repealed. They did influence the U.S. Congress to pass the Interstate Commerce Act in 1887. This act established the Interstate Commerce Commission (ICC) to oversee railroad activities.

The Supreme Court thwarted the power of the Interstate Commerce Commission during its first years. In 1906, however, the Supreme Court upheld that the ICC could set maximum rates for the hauling of both goods and people. This decision solved the "Long Haul–Short Haul" issue. In 1910, the Commission could actually suspend a railroad's rates upon further investigation. By the 1890s, railroad owners realized that competition was not their only problem. Government was becoming very quickly the deciding factor of the railroad industry.

— Government Regulation —

There was a movement to regulate industry in general around the turn of the century. Railroads, however, were a favorite target. In 1903, Congress passed the Elkins Act which outlawed rebates or "kickbacks" to certain shippers. The Hepburn Act of 1906 limited the use of free passes to clergy, charity cases, and railroad employees. Passes were often used to influence politicians or to bribe shippers. It also regulated sleeping car services and express shipments. The Mann-Elkins Act of 1910 gave the ICC authority to alter passenger and shipping charges on its own. It could also unilaterally suspend a new rate for up to ten months. In 1913, the Railroad Valuation Act further authorized the ICC to assess the value of each railroad. A railroad's gross worth became a factor in determining rates.

Taxes were also levied on the railroads. From 1900 to 1915, state and federal government increased taxes three-fold on the railroads. During those same years, railroad revenues doubled. In other words, the government tax rate increased far more than railroad revenue. Moreover, railroads fell on hard times just prior to World War I. One-sixth or 37,000 miles of road were in receivership by 1916. The St. Louis & San Francisco, the New Haven, the Rock Island, and the Wabash Railroads were in difficulty. The railroad industry had its economic ups and downs during the Panics of the 1870s and 1890s. The situation, however, was different in 1916 due to government regulation. The railroads also had to cope with difficulties among their own employees. Unionization and strikes now affected the way they could do business. Just prior to World War I, the Adamson Act of 1916 established the eight-hour work day for railroad engineers.

— Railroad Unions —

Railroad worker unionization began right after the Civil War. Early union formation was more in character with a fraternal club than a labor movement. In 1866, locomotive engineers formed the Brotherhood of the Footboard. Two years later, conductors formed their own brotherhood. In 1877, track workers founded their Maintenance of Way Brotherhood. That same year the Brotherhood of Locomotive Firemen and Enginemen came into existence, and the Brotherhood of Railroad Trainmen followed in 1883. The telegraphers established their own in 1886, and the switchmen in 1894. The Express and Station Employees Union began theirs in 1898, and signalmen formed their own in 1901. In 1912, African-American railroad workers established the Association of Colored Railway Trainmen and Locomotive Firemen. Porters, dining car employees, and the Brotherhood of Sleeping Car Porters organized during this time. With the threat of strikes, and fraternal groups becoming hard and fast labor unions, Congress passed a law in 1888 to create emergency boards to investigate labor disputes.

— Labor Disputes —

The first dispute that became almost a nationwide strike occurred in July 1877. The Panic or Depression of 1873 wore on for several years. In fact, it was caused by the failure of Northern Pacific stock.

Railroads are definitely at a disadvantage during a depression. As a capital-intensive industry with operating schedules that have to be met, they cannot adjust as easily as other economic sectors during hard times.

The railroads wanted to keep up the 8–10 percent dividends to stockholders throughout the Panic. In order to do so, the Pennsylvania announced a wage cut of 10 percent. The Baltimore & Ohio followed with the same in July 1877. By the Fourth of July, the Baltimore & Ohio laborers at Martinsburg, West Virginia, refused to work unless the wages were restored in full. They blocked the tracks with 70 trains. The railroad appealed to the governor to send the militia. Soon after, President Rutherford B. Hayes sent in federal troops to restore order and to move the trains. When the railroad began to hire non-brotherhood workers or "scabs" to move the trains, a mob gathered and hurled rocks. Soldiers fired upon the crowd, killing ten.

The strike spread to the Pennsylvania line. Along with its initial wage cut, the railroad announced doubling the length of freight trains. Protests occurred along the line. Over a thousand soldiers were dispatched to Philadelphia — with artillery. Twenty died and fifty were wounded, but not until others fired on the soldiers and killed three. Looting began and fires were set along the tracks. In Pittsburgh a mob of 10,000 stopped train movements, with similar actions in New York, Trenton, Reading, and St. Louis.

The strike spread to the Erie and the Chicago, Burlington, & Quincy. The New York Central, however, remained immune to the strikes. Vanderbilt issued a bonus of $100,000 to be divided among all nonstriking workers.

In the end, the railroad strike of 1877 was unsuccessful. A fireman on the Terre Haute and Indianapolis Railroad, Eugene V. Debs, realized that each brotherhood approached the strike differently. In other words, the strikers were not united in tactics, and it was not a coordinated movement. In 1893, Debs proposed the formation of the American Railway Union with himself as president. He wanted to unite all railroad workers into a single national union. By 1894, he listed 150,000 members, including Pullman car builders. His new union was successful in striking the Great Northern in the same year, and by summer, it backed the Pullman strike south of Chicago.

— The Pullman Strike —

The Panic of 1893 brought on the Pullman strike similarly to the way the Panic of 1873 initiated the strike on the Baltimore & Ohio. With a decline in revenues in 1894, the Pullman Company cut employee wages to maintain the 8 percent dividend on its stock. Workers who lived in the company town of Pullman, Illinois, expected a comparable decrease in their rent to offset the cut in wages. When rents remained the same, the Pullman car builders demanded the restoration of their salaries. In May, 2,500 walked off their jobs and formed a "grievance committee." The plant closed, and the new American Railway Union pledged support.

On June 26, the Union called a general strike on all Pullman cars and on the trains pulling the cars. Rioting began in Chicago, and federal troops were dispatched. Twenty were killed and others wounded during one incident. The strike was ended, and Debs was indicted on the charges of hindering interstate commerce. Other Union members were also arrested.

The Pullman strike demonstrated the growing power of labor and the union movement. In reaction, the railroad General Managers Association compiled a "blacklist" of strikers. Whenever a striker applied for a job with another railroad, management had a warning code. They used the watermark of a crane on recommendation stationery. If the crane's neck was broken, it was a signal to an employer not to hire the worker, no matter what was written on the paper. If the crane's neck was intact, the worker had not participated in the strike.

The code did not last long. Union organizers learned about the crane, and they obtained their own stationery with the neck intact and wrote their own letters of recommendation. Moreover, some managers were sympathetic toward the Union and hired former strikers anyway. Nevertheless, by the turn of the century, railroads were under pressure from both unionized employees and federal legislation. They had to find greater operating efficiency and attract more customers with attractive accommodations to make a profit.

Chapter 10.

Perfecting the Network

By the 1870s there were over 150 railroad companies, and many cities and towns were served by two or more lines. One transcontinental linked the coasts, and more cross-country lines were soon under construction. Other railroads traversed almost 1,000 miles linking major cities. All of the companies needed to run their trains along schedules as precisely as possible. The one big problem was when a passenger traveled long distances and had to make connections with several railroads.

Each railroad measured time by a sundial at its main office. Therefore, on the hour was "sun time" in one particular location. For example, noon in Philadelphia would be minutes later than New York, and would not occur in Cleveland for almost half an hour, and much later in Chicago. In large railroad stations, each railroad company would have its own clock which gave its particular time according to the sun at its headquarters. The system was confusing at best, especially since the railroads had speeded up travel from one part of the nation to another. One town or city was no longer an isolated economic and social unit unto itself. In little more than a generation, people and goods arrived in hours from distant places that could have taken months just forty years earlier. News was almost instantaneous with the telegraph. Moreover, the United States was becoming an industrialized nation, and the swift transportation and communication had already made one part of the country interdependent on others. The railroads quickly came upon a solution which united the country even more.

— Sunday, Noon, 18 November 1883 —

In 1872, railroad representatives met in St. Louis, Missouri, to discuss coordination of their time schedules. They elected William Frederick Allen to work on the project. More than working with schedules, Allen believed that the idea of "time zones," which had been bantered about in one form or another, would be a good solution. The railroads formed the General Time Convention in 1876, and appointed Allen its secretary. In 1883, he submitted his final plan for adoption.

He proposed the creation of four time zones across the United States. They were to run approximately along the 75th, 90th, 105th, and 120th meridians. The General Time Convention adopted his plan on October 11, 1883. Each zone represented an hour of time, and the top of the hour was the same throughout the distance from meridian to meridian. All railroads quickly adjusted their timetables to conform to the zones. These schedules went into effect at noon, Sunday, November 18, 1883.

Within a short period shippers and factories adjusted to the new time zones in order to meet railroad schedules. By the 1890s most people living in cities and towns scheduled almost all events according to "railroad time." Whenever anyone traveled or sent or received a package, it was according to the railroad time and timetable. The process definitely became a national practice during World War I.

With the large number of soldiers and materiel moved by the railroads during the first World War, "standard time" permeated even the remotest corner of the nation. In March 1918, Congress passed the Standard Time Act. The time zones of the railroad's General Time Convention became law throughout the nation — the government merely recognized a reality already created by the railroads almost a generation earlier.

Sandford Fleming convinced the Canadians to adopt the U.S. time zone organization during the construction of the Canadian Pacific. He was also instrumental in convening the International Prime Meridian Conference in Washington in 1884.

The General Time Convention was the beginning of the future Association of American Railroads.

— Railroad Pocket Watch —

The picture of a conductor and engineer checking their watches before a train departs is an icon of late nineteenth century railroading. The image brings to mind dependability, safety, and on-time performance. The railroad itself functioned with the precision of a fine-tuned watch.

Although the telegraph added a great deal of safety to train movements, running on time decreased the possibility of accidents. An accident near Aleary, Ohio, in April 1891 brought attention to the need of an accurate timepiece. Before that, conductors and engineers used any type of watch, even cheap alarm clocks.

When an eastbound train left Aleary, it had orders to permit a fast mail train to pass it at Cripton. The mail train left on time. It was assumed that the engineer's watch on the first train stopped for four minutes, and then restarted — unknown to him. The trains collided, and the engineer and ten other people were killed.

Two years later the railroads developed the General Railroad Timepiece Standards. Webb C. Ball established the criteria for an "official" railroad watch. The watch must be accurate to within 30 seconds in 7 to 14 days. It had to perform to this standard in any position. If not, it had to be repaired by an approved watchmaker. Very soon watchmakers set up shops near railroad depots.

A number of watch companies developed watches to conform to the railroad standard. Hamilton, Waltham, Illinois, and Elgin made watches especially for railroad workers. After World War I, Hamilton purchased the Illinois Watch Company. Elgin and Waltham manufactured over 50 million watches between them. The Hamilton #940 in 1902 brought that company to the forefront of the industry. The Hamilton #992 had the most respect among railroaders.

MAJOR AGRICULTURAL AND INDUSTRIAL SOURCES AND PRODUCTS 1880s

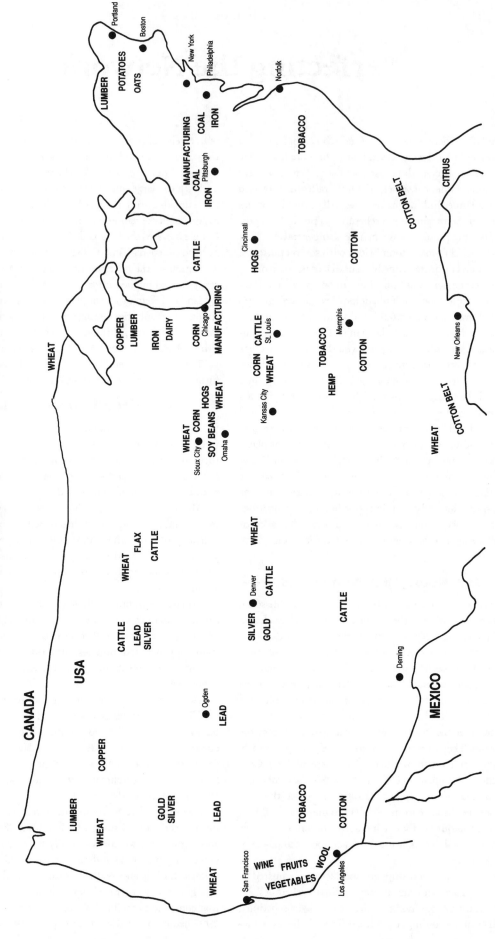

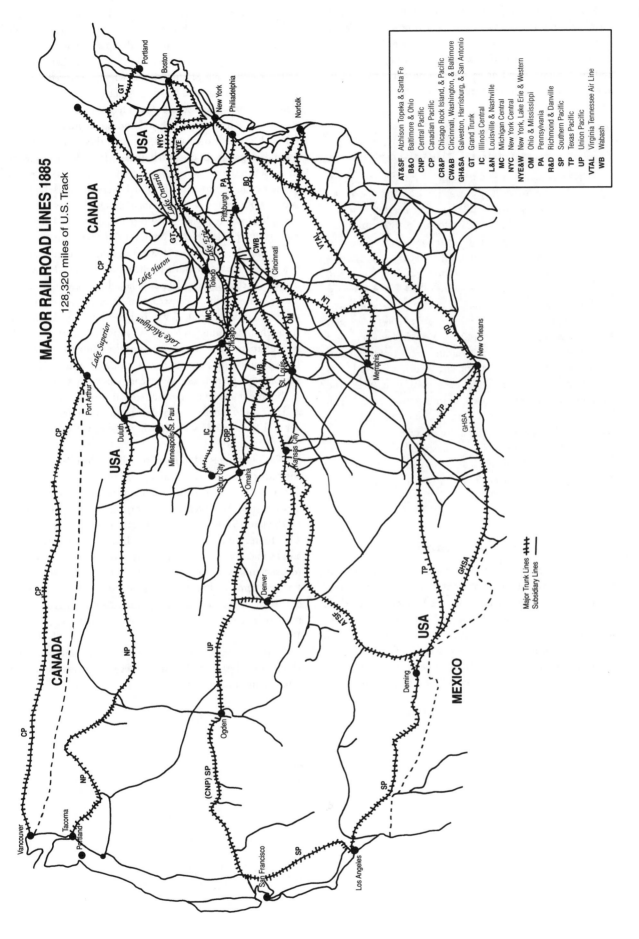

MAJOR RAILROAD LINES 1885

128,320 miles of U.S. Track

AT&SF	Atchison Topeka & Santa Fe	
B&O	Baltimore & Ohio	
CNP	Central Pacific	
CP	Canadian Pacific	
CR&P	Chicago Rock Island, & Pacific	
CW&B	Cincinnati, Washington, & Baltimore	
GH&SA	Galveston, Harrisburg, & San Antonio	
GT	Grand Trunk	
IC	Illinois Central	
L&N	Louisville & Nashville	
MC	Michigan Central	
NYC	New York Central	
NYE&W	New York, Lake Erie & Western	
OM	Ohio & Mississippi	
PA	Pennsylvania	
R&D	Richmond & Danville	
SP	Southern Pacific	
TP	Texas Pacific	
UP	Union Pacific	
VTAL	Virginia Tennessee Air Line	
WB	Wabash	

Major Trunk Lines ┼┼┼
Subsidiary Lines ───

Modern quartz watches are far more accurate than the spring-wound and geared items of a century ago. Wristwatches have replaced the chained and pocketed mechanism. Yet, on the threshold of the twenty-first-century, one can still find an Amtrak attendant gazing at a pocket watch (quartz movement) before the train pulls out of a station.

— The Bunn Special —

A jeweler in a midwestern city was the official watch inspector for the Milwaukee Road. He leased a clock from Western Union by which railroad pocket watches were calibrated. When the Illinois Watch Company went out of business, the jeweler purchased crates of the internal mechanisms without cases. He then purchased cases from another manufacturer, placed the approved mechanism in them, and prepared them for sale. They were called Bunn Specials.

Railroaders at first were reluctant to purchase the watch even though they were officially approved. So the jeweler had an idea to promote the product. A railroad worker could purchase the watch on an installment plan. The worker would pay $1 for the watch and also receive a free ticket to the movie theater across the street. The next week, the worker paid $2 and received another movie ticket. The amount doubled each succeeding week until the watch was paid for. (The railroader, of course, received a free movie ticket each time.) News of the plan spread quickly among workers on the Milwaukee Road. Both the jeweler and railroad employees were very happy with the Bunn Special.

— Standard Gauge —

When President Lincoln and Congress established a 4-foot 8½-inch gauge for the first transcontinental, it tacitly set that measurement as the "standard" for the U.S. railroads. It was the predominant gauge in the north. Nevertheless, the South still rebuilt their railroads to the 5-foot gauge, and several important railroads in Ohio were set at 4 feet 10 inches, known as the "Ohio Gauge." In fact, the New York Central, for a time, built what were known as "compromise cars" which had wheel widths especially cast to roll on both standard and Ohio gauge tracks. While they permitted a nonchanging of cars from New York to Chicago, they had a tendency to derail, particularly when crossing switches. The Central's cars rolled over the Lake Shore Railroad which measured the Ohio Gauge. New Jersey had a 4-feet 8-inch gauge track, and the Pennsylvania was constructed to 4 feet 9 inches.

During a four-month period ending in June, 1886, the railroads on their own accord, adjusted their tracks closer to a standard gauge. In the north it was 4 feet 8½ inches, while in the south the adjustment was to 4 feet 9 inches, since most of their connections with the North were through the Pennsylvania Railroad — the ½ inch difference was forgiving enough. It was really after 1896 that the precise 4-foot 8½-inch gauge predominated on almost all main line systems.

During the 1880s and 1890s, a significant number of narrow gauge lines were built in the United States. Many were owned by the larger railroads. The advantages of a narrow gauge were chiefly in construction. It permitted companies to build rails in rough, winding terrain, where blasting through mountains and gorges would be costly to make enough room for standard gauge tracks. Most narrow gauges linked lumbering, farming, and mining communities to a standard gauge railroad. Many companies added a third rail within the standard gauge track so that narrow gauge engines and cars could move place to place on the main line. The Denver and Rio Grande was probably the most famous for this type of operation.

Narrow gauges fell out of favor after World War I. With the growth of cars, trucks, and paved roads in the 1920s, the narrow gauge railroads were among the first to feel the new competition. Many fell into bankruptcy in the plains states by the late 1920s. The mountainous, ore-carrying lines did a bit better for a while. They still had some advantage over trucks in carrying heavy bulk materials. Nevertheless, they, too, succumbed to the new competition. The Newfoundland Railway remained narrow gauge until its relatively recent end. It was a model of efficiency when the Grand Trunk Railroad switched from provincial to standard gauge in the 1870s.

With time zones and movement to a standard gauge, the U.S. railroad system became a network which smoothly linked almost all parts of the nation.

Locomotive Evolution
and
the Creation of a Railroad Culture

New steam locomotive designs and increases in weight and length brought about greater speed and efficiency. Even though the 4-4-0 "American Type" was the dominant standard on almost all railroads, there were some variations from time to time. After the Civil War, however, there was a rapid growth in different styles, sizes, and wheel arrangements. Soon locomotive manufacturers began building locomotives to meet specific needs.

According to legend, Alexander Mitchell of the Lehigh Valley Railroad began the trend. He asked the Baldwin Locomotive Works to build a larger engine with eight driving wheels to pull longer coal trains over the mountains of eastern Pennsylvania. The Lehigh Valley called the new 2-8-0 the "Consolidation" in honor of the merger of several small lines into its system. Baldwin later added a set of wheels under the cab to make it a 2-8-2 and the style became known as the "Mikado" since a large number were sent to railroads in Japan.

— Anthracite Locomotives —

The Lehigh Valley, Lackawanna, Central Railroad of New Jersey, and Reading, among others burned and hauled anthracite or hard coal. Anthracite burned cleaner and gave off a more intense heat than bituminous or soft coal. By the 1890s, some of these railroads developed a way to burn the small bits of coal that fell around the breakers and storage areas. Although these small pieces, called "culm," could not be sold commercially, they could power a steam locomotive. In 1877, John Wooten of Philadelphia designed a grate which extended the entire width of the cab and burned enough culm to power a locomotive successfully. It was so wide that the engineer's cab and controls had to be mounted on the side of the boiler.

With the fireman's cab mounted on the opposite of the engineer's, these locomotives took a design from the early locomotives of Ross Winans and the Baltimore & Ohio. They became known by the old name of "Camelback." They were also called "Mother Hubbards." Both engineer and firemen experienced far greater heat next to the boiler in the summer. Passengers, however, enjoyed the anthracite burning locomotives; there were fewer cinders and less soot. In fact, the Lackawanna Railroad created the figure, "Phoebe Snow," who without worry could "dress all in white, because she rode the road of anthracite." Some of the Camelbacks were capable of speeds over 100 miles per hour. The Cambelback design was discontinued after World War I.

— Increasing Power and Speed —

There were other technical developments which increased the efficiency and speed of trains. In 1889, Samuel Vauclain invented a dual cylinder system. He pioneered one high pressure and another low pressure cylinder to give greater use of steam to power the drive wheels. With both cylinders working, he was also able to achieve better fuel efficiency. The dual cylinders were used on 2-10-2 locomotives built for the Santa Fe.

Other styles came into existence. In the 1890s, the "Atlantic" 4-4-2 became popular for passenger service, along with the 4-6-2 "Pacific" by 1902. The Pacific's driving wheels were 69 inches in diameter. With the larger drivers, these types of passenger locomotives became known as "high wheelers." When the New York Central's Engine #999 ran at 112.5 miles per hour in a stretch near Batavia, New York, in 1893, the race was on for all railroads, as managers and owners looked for new ways to increase speed safely.

Increasing boiler and driver size were the best means of pulling a train faster. At the same time, of course, the locomotive and its running gear became heavier. The Johnson or reverse bar became heavier and heavier to operate. Finally, in 1904, a steam pressure gear mechanism called the Walschaert was invented to assist the engineer in controlling the amount of steam in the cylinders. Automatic oiling systems also saved time on stops, and "piston type" steam valves increased efficiency.

— The Real McCoy —

After the Civil War there were a number of devices in use to lubricate moving parts of locomotives while running under steam. In 1872, an African-American, Elijah McCoy, invented a superior lubricator. Soon railroaders would not settle for any other lubricator than "the Real McCoy"! Within a few years, "the real McCoy" would describe the best of anything and something identifiable from poor imitations.

In 1897, Wilhelm Schmidt of Germany invented a way to increase temperature. He passed the steam through dry boiler flue pipes before sending it to the cylinders. His "superheater" made the steam hotter and drier. It could then expand more in the cylinders and cause less condensation. The process increased the engine's efficiency over 25 percent. The Canadians were first to adopt the invention. By World War I, all locomotives, except switchers, were built with superheaters.

— Articulated Locomotives —

During the early 1880s, some locomotive manufacturers experimented with two sets of cylinders and drive wheels.

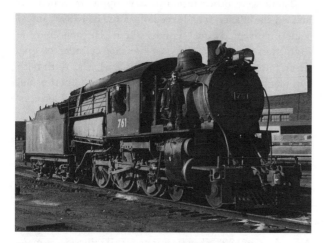

"Camelback" locomotive at Jersey Central's Communipaw Terminal. Courtesy Railroad Avenue Enterprises. #13349.

Steam from the first set of cylinders would exhaust at lower pressure into a second, larger set to increase power. This longer locomotive, however, could not negotiate tight curves. This problem was solved in 1888, when a Swiss engineer, Anatole Mallet, built a locomotive with a front set of drive wheels that could swivel.

In 1903, the American Locomotive Company built the first Mallet locomotive in the United States for the Baltimore and Ohio Railroad. Known as *Old Maude,* the OOO OOO locomotive could pull a heavy load up mountain grades with ease. It could not, however, run over 20 miles per hour without threatening to derail. Subsequent Mallets were manufactured with guide wheels which permitted safer, higher speeds. Using guide wheels, Baldwin Locomotive Works built thirty 2-6-6-2s for the Great Northern Railway in 1906 and 1907. Most railroads with significant mountain grades now ordered Mallet locomotives.

By the 1920s, the compound cylinder system was abandoned. Larger boilers were able to furnish high pressure steam to both sets of cylinders. These "simple articulateds" grew into behemoth-sized locomotives and could achieve relatively fast speeds as well. Some versions ran at 60 miles per hour. Although not precise, it is common practice to call all articulated locomotives "Mallets" in honor of their inventor.

— Automatic Stoker —

Other than relatively slow speeds at first, the Mallet had another drawback. It took two firemen to feed its huge firebox. In fact, the fireman's job had already become more demanding with the increase of locomotive size. In 1905, the Pennsylvania Railroad successfully developed a steam-powered "Archimedes screw" to move coal from the tender di-

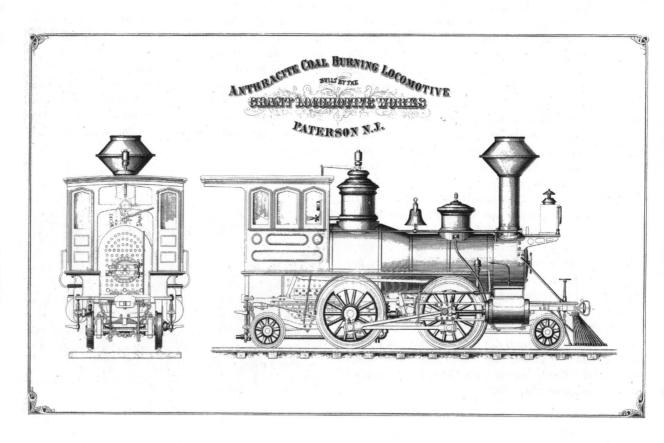

2-6-2	Prairie	

Front Swivel Truck   Driving Wheels   Trailing Wheels

Wheels	Common Name	Diagram
0-4-0	Switching	
2-6-0	Mogul	
2-6-2	Prairie	
2-8-0	Consolidation	
2-8-2	Mikado (MacArthur)	
2-8-4	Berkshire	
2-10-0	Decapod	
2-10-2	Santa Fe	
2-10-4	Texas	
0-6-6-0	(First U.S. Mallet)	
2-6-6-2		
2-6-6-4	Articulated	
2-8-8-0		
4-6-6-4	(Challenger)	
4-8-8-2	Cab-Forward	
4-8-8-4	Big Boy	
4-4-0	Standard	
4-4-2	Atlantic	
4-6-2	Pacific	
4-6-0	Ten Wheeler	
4-6-4	Hudson	
4-8-2	Mountain	
4-8-4	Northern	

rectly into the firebox. With this device, one fireman alone could automatically stoke the largest of boilers by moving levers. The automatic stokers, however, needed a smaller, standard size chunk of coal to work effectively.

— Oil for Fuel —

By the early 1900s, the Santa Fe, Great Northern, and Southern Pacific began using oil to fire their boilers. Oil contains much more energy per pound than coal, although it is a far greater pollutant. The oil-burning locomotive helped the Southern Pacific solve the problem of intense smoke in its Sierra Nevada Mountain tunnels. Southern Pacific designers were able to put the engineer's cab in front rather than at the rear of the locomotive. These Mallet-type locomotives became known as "Cab Forwards" and were a distinctive Southern Pacific feature.

— Smoke in Tunnels —

Other railroads had smoke problems in tunnels as well. More than just discomfort with sore eyes and coughing passengers, engineers at times were overcome by smoke inhalation. Railroads tried some ingenious devices. Some extended the smoke stack along the top of the boiler to open behind the cab. At times engineers wore a mask to protect their eyes and breathed air from the bottom of the cab. The last transcontinental railroad, the Milwaukee Road, used electric locomotives in tunnels to avoid the smoke problem.

— First Electric Engines —

Thomas A. Edison is credited with inventing the first electric "traction motor." Soon electric motors were used on streetcars. In 1895, the Baltimore & Ohio used an electric locomotive to pull trains through a 3½-mile tunnel in Baltimore. General Electric built these "steeple type" locomotives which took current from an overhead rail and an extending "hot shoe" or tongue which extended from the bottom to touch a third rail.

Electric motors or "mules" pulled trains for the Pennsylvania Railroad in its twin tunnels under the Hudson River into New York City in 1910. In 1913, the New York Cen-

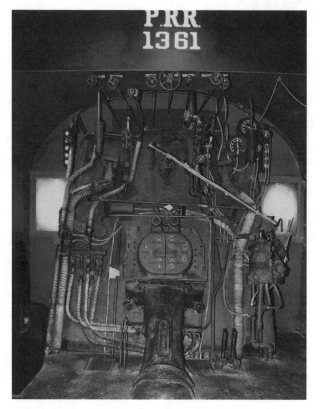

Boiler and controls of a K-4 Pacific steam locomotive. Photo taken at the Railroaders Memorial Museum, Altoona, Pennsylvania.

Pennsylvania 4-6-2 Pacific steam locomotive. Courtesy Railroad Museum of Pennsylvania.

tral used electricity into Grand Central Station, New York, from Harmon. The New York, Hartford, & New Haven also entered Grand Central electrically. Along with smoke problems, electric motive power in tunnels helped eliminate fire hazards.

— The True Legend —

The Chesapeake and Ohio Railroad began to use the "new-fangled" steam drill when they were constructing a tunnel in the early 1870s. One of the human steel drivers took issue with the new invention. John Henry claimed that he could drive a drill faster than the machine. According to the legend, he won, but died on the spot afterwards.

There were many variations of the story by the twentieth century. Many states claimed John Henry as their favorite son. Each ethnic group soon claimed him as their own. Some even said that he had only one arm. Others later argued that John Henry never existed. Whatever, he was the ideal symbol of human determination and accomplishment over the machine. By the end of the century the legend of John Henry was worldwide.

During the 1920s, university researchers began to study the John Henry legend. They concluded that John Henry was an African-American steel driver who worked on the Chesapeake and Ohio's Big Bend Tunnel. He was real. John Henry was a large man who weighed about 200 pounds. He played the banjo, was a jokester, and was known as the "stingiest" worker on the crew. More important, the steam drill had just come into use, and the C&O used it as an experiment on the Big Bend Tunnel when it was under construction from 1870 to 1873.

John Henry did challenge the steam drill. Both man and machine worked for 35 minutes. John Henry wielded two 20-pound hammers — one in each hand. The machine lost time when its drill was caught in a seam. At the finish, the steam drill made one hole 9 inches deep. John Henry drilled two holes 7 inches deep for a total of 14 inches. John Henry won!

The hero did not die on the spot. Several claim he was buried in a blast at one end of the tunnel. The legend, however, lives on. Even current Amtrak train guidebooks suggest that passengers listen closely when going through Big Bend Tunnel — John Henry's hammer-strikes still echo from the mountain!

— Repair Facilities —

With the huge increase in track mileage and number of locomotives and cars, railroads had to build repair and service facilities in various places. They were often located in an area that either had or promised to have a high economic value. For example, in the Midwest, cities that had large stockyards were sure to have a nearby service facility.

Servicing cars and particularly locomotives was very labor intensive. It has been estimated that it took eight workers to keep a steam locomotive running well. The railroad quickly became a major employer. A small town could become an important city very fast when a railroad chose to build a facility there.

— Train Wrecks —

Greater traffic brought about an increase of accidents and train crashes. One of the more famous occurred near Ashtabula, Ohio, in 1876. A bridge gave way. The cars plummeted downward, and some caught on fire from their stoves. Thirty-four died in the wreck. The Ashtabula accident called for safer bridge construction and maintenance. It also pointed out the need to eliminate open flames in the cars.

— Casey Jones —

Perhaps the most famous was the Casey Jones wreck. His real name was John Luther Jones. He took the nickname "Casey" from Cayce, Kentucky, where he grew up. Jones was known for running locomotives at high speeds. In 1900, when his "Cannonball Express" was two hours late, Casey believed he could make up the time during his portion of the run. He crashed into a freight train at Vaughn, Mississippi.

The crash is still a controversial matter. A freight train was being moved to a siding to clear the main line. Apparently, Casey did not hear the warning torpedo placed on the tracks. When he saw that he was going to crash, Jones told his fireman, Sym Webb, to jump. Jones placed the locomotive in reverse and remained at the throttle to lessen the impact and save passengers' lives.

Jones sacrificing his life grew into a legend — a hero's death. At the same time rumors spread that Jones's Cannonball Express accident was sabotage. Some said that the freight brakemen wanted to target Jones, because he would not join a union. Others claimed that he was under the influence of alcohol and broke Rule G. Sabotage or not, the rumors are not substantiated. Jones was a union member, and co-workers swear that he was a teetotaler. The most likely explanation for the crash was that an air hose broke in the freight train. The broken hose set the brakes on the cars which were still on the main line. The freight crew could not move them fast enough to avoid the accident.

— Other Accidents —

Perhaps one of the most tragic crashes happened near Ivanhoe, Indiana, in 1918. A train went through closed signals and plowed into the back of a stopped circus train in the middle of the night. Sixty-eight circus performers were killed and 147 were injured. The engineer of the speeding train had not slept for 24 hours and had taken "kidney pills" for a back ailment. Lack of sleep and the sedative effect of the pills caused the engineer to doze at the throttle and miss the signals.

At least one crash was planned. In 1896, G. W. Crush of the Kansas & Texas Railroad organized a head-on crash of two obsolete locomotives hurtling toward each other at full speed. Over 30,000 spectators came to see the event. The locomotives hit, and their boilers exploded immediately upon impact. Parts flew in all directions. Several spectators were killed and many were injured.

In spite of the deaths and injuries, the Texas train crash set in motion a series of such staged events through the 1930s.

Any state fair was sure to host a larger crowd by providing two locomotives hurtling toward each other at top speed. What was a nightmare for railroaders was a show for thrill seekers.

— Train Robberies —

Train robberies had great popular appeal. The first robbers of note were John Reno and his gang. Reno held up a baggage car on the Ohio & Mississippi Railroad in 1866. The

Early electric locomotive at end of tunnel under Baltimore, Md. Manufactured by General Electric, they used both overhead wires (catenery) and third rail "hot shoe." Courtesy B&O Railroad Museum.

New York Central 4-6-4 Streamlined Hudson by Dreyfus. *The Empire State Express,* 1941. Courtesy Railroad Museum of Pennsylvania. #20984.

New York Central T-Motor at Harmon, New York, 1950. These "electric mules" pulled trains in and out of Grand Central Station in New York. Courtesy Railroad Avenue Enterprises.

— The Kate Shelly Bridge —

It was a rainy summer in 1881, and by mid-July central Iowa had already experienced flooding. The Shelly house was near the railroad track and Honey Creek. On a dark and stormy night, Kate Shelly and her family saw Honey Creek fill and then flood. In the midst of the storm, they heard the whistle of a local switch engine.

Later during the storm, Kate heard a crash at the Honey Creek trestle. She ran out in the rain and saw the switch engine in the creek and two crewmen trying to escape. The trestle had washed away. Kate knew the railroad schedules and realized that the midnight passenger train was almost due. She had to warn the railroad station at Moingona!

Taking a roundabout route, she had to cross the Des Moines River Bridge. Years earlier, workers had removed some ties to discourage pedestrians from using it. With the storm raging anew, Kate crawled across the bridge along the rails. If the train arrived, she would be killed instantly, but it also would have plunged, taking hundreds of passengers to their deaths in Honey Creek. This thought pushed Kate across the bridge.

When she arrived at the Moingona Station, the crew listened to her story and stopped the passenger train in time. In appreciation, the Chicago & North Western Railroad and the State of Iowa honored Kate and gave her gifts. After attending college in 1903, Kate became the station agent at Moingona. She died in 1912. When the Chicago & North Western built a new bridge across the Des Moines River, they named it after their station agent hero — *Kate Shelly Bridge*.

railroad hired Allan Pinkerton and his sons, William and Robert, to capture the crooks and retrieve the stolen goods. The Pinkertons caught Reno and his gang, and became famous detectives in nineteenth century America. They tracked down and caught other criminals and established the form of identifying the hunted criminals and placing reward posters. Their motto was "The Eye That Never Sleeps" — the origin of the term "private eye."

— Jessie James —

Jessie James learned how to sabotage trains as a member of Quantrill's Raiders during the Civil War. Some claim his crime spree was to avenge the South's defeat rather than the desire for money. Frank and Jessie James and the Younger brothers staged the most famous heist in 1873. They stopped a Rock Island express near Adair, Iowa, and made off with the contents of the baggage car. The Pinkertons and other law enforcement officials made careers in tracking down the James and Younger brothers.

These and other train robberies made exciting reading. Stories of criminal bravado were a prime source of material for police magazines which became popular by the turn of the century. More than the thrill of holding up a train, many perceived the criminals as "latter day Robin Hoods," stealing from the greedy, rich railroads.

Trains were real robbery targets — as well as banks — in the second half of the nineteenth century. Railroads were the only way to transport anything — including gold and cash. There was a good chance of something valuable being transferred in a baggage car on any main line at that time. Of course, the railroads boasted the bravery of their baggage and express agents. Some incidents, like the James-Adair robbery, became part of railroad folklore.

— Express Companies —

Both the express companies and the U.S. Post Office used the rails almost exclusively to carry their items. From the Civil War until World War I, there were four express companies functioning in the United States. Without much competition within select regions, the Adams, Southern, American, and Wells Fargo were able to charge relatively high prices for carrying packages. In 1913, the U.S. Post Office introduced Parcel Post as an alternative to the private companies. Parcel Post was a response to increasing complaints about rates as well as a way of cashing in on a profitable business. Nevertheless, Parcel Post did not make a significant decrease in the use of the private companies. The Canadian railroads acted as their own "express companies." There was no outside or separate agency.

— The Railway Post Office —

Designated as "post roads" from the 1830s, railroads were the chief means of transporting mail throughout the United States. During the Civil War, when there was a significant increase in mail throughout the Union, George B. Armstrong,

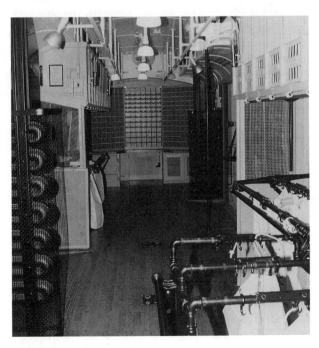

Interior of railway post office car.

Mail bag ready to be hooked into a Railway Post Office Car. The bag is held securely by flat springs on round bars (side view).

assistant postmaster in Chicago, came up with the idea of sorting mail while en route. In 1862, W. A. Davis of St. Joseph, Missouri, had the same idea. As an experiment, Davis sorted mail on the train between Quincy, Illinois, and St. Joseph, Missouri.

In July 1864, the Chicago & North Western Railway remodeled three of its cars to designs by Armstrong. The first official run using them was between Chicago, Illinois, and Clinton, Iowa. Shortly thereafter, the second run started between New York City and Washington, D.C. In 1869, Armstrong headed the entire system which officially came to be known as the Railway Mail Service. Armstrong also developed mail cranes and catcher arms to gather mail onto a moving train, as well as fast mail trains.

In 1871, George S. Banks succeeded Armstrong. Banks made promotions in the Railway Mail Service from within its ranks, which some believe was the prototype for the Civil Service System created in the 1880s. Banks also promoted the idea of fast mail trains in the 1870s. The New York Central pioneered a "fast mail" between New York and Chicago. The Pennsylvania, not to be outdone, inaugurated its own "limited mail" between Philadelphia and Chicago. Both guaranteed delivery between cities within 20 hours! By 1877, with congressional approval, the service was expanded to the Pacific Coast. In Canada, mail sorters were Post Office employees, and not of a Railway Post Office.

A school was started to train employees to sort mail on moving trains. In 1891, these special mail clerks formed the Railway Mail Association. The organization received government recognition in 1912. Virtually every city, town, and village with train service was served by the Railway Postal Service. Almost all through and local passenger trains carried the mail.

— Mail Order Houses —

The railroad was the only way that local merchants could receive goods from factories or wholesale houses until almost World War I. During the 1880s, however, Richard W. Sears was able to market goods directly to customers by using express companies and the mail. Sears was a station agent for the Minneapolis & St. Louis Railroad at North Redwood, Minnesota. When a jeweler refused to accept a shipment of watches, Sears bought the package himself instead of returning it to the wholesale house. He then sent out leaflets by mail to surrounding communities. Upon receipt of a money order, Sears would send a watch directly to a home by express. After selling out the original shipment, he ordered more watches and continued to sell by mail.

Sears found the practice profitable enough to quit the railroad position and move to Chicago in 1887. He then met Alvan C. Roebuck and expanded his mail order business. By 1902, Sears, Roebuck and Company occupied an entire city block with a nine-story building, and issued a catalogue of almost 1,200 pages for 50 cents. They sold everything from tea to tombstones, and carbines to baby carriages. The catalogue also included ten pages of different watch styles and movements.

During the 1890s, other dealers put together catalogues and sold items by mail. Sears and others were able to price their goods more cheaply because of volume ordering. Sears also refused C.O.D. purchases. By insisting on prepayment by postal or express money order, he experienced no losses. This form of marketing made purchasing from even the remotest settlement easy and practical. Sears claimed: "Shipping goods by express is an absolutely safe method of transportation and offers the advantage of quick service." Whether by post, freight, or express, the railroads were the only means that made catalogue direct marketing possible by the end of the nineteenth century.

— New Freight Cars —

The railroads moved everything. Larger freight cars carried more goods per load. Boxcars, gondolas, and tank cars carried agricultural and industrial products from one end of the country to the other. Nevertheless, cars specifically made to carry cattle and refrigerated products made a singularly great difference. Before the refrigerator car, called a "reefer," cattle had to be moved to the place of consumption to be slaughtered. Otherwise the meat would spoil if butchered a distance away. Even though the train trip was less stressful than a long cattle drive, many animals died due to lack of food and water. While there had been some attempts during the previous two decades to invent practical and more hospitable cattle cars, in 1877, the Boston-based American Humane Association offered a contest and the prize went to Alonzo C. Mather in 1883.

— The Humane Cattle Car —

Mather knew almost nothing about railroads and probably less about cattle. He was a Chicago clothing merchant. While on a trip east in 1881, his train was stopped due to an accident on the track ahead. He was kept awake all night when cattle in a car on a nearby siding made a horrendous racket. The next morning he discovered that a large steer had injured other cattle in searching for food and water. Mather then devoted his energy to remedying the situation.

After investing a fortune of his own money, Mather developed a way to keep food and water furnished to the animals in a car from outside doors and compartments. By 1895, his Mather's Palace Car Company operated 3,000 cars. Competition soon came about. The Street Company managed 9,000 cars by 1902. More than just more humane treatment to animals, these cars delivered cattle in much better condition to slaughterhouses.

— The Refrigerator Car —

Refrigerator cars permitted the economic efficiency of "break of bulk." It was far more economical to slaughter cattle near their place of origin than in the city of consumption. Quite plainly, a rail car could carry many more butchered carcasses than live cows. Moreover, the carcasses did not need food and water — just a cool temperature. Farmers in the West and Midwest could send their cattle to nearby cities for slaughter rather than to New York, Philadelphia, or Boston. The Chicago Union Stockyards opened in 1865; Kansas City and Cincinnati began production in 1871. Omaha, Sioux City, and Dubuque, among

others followed shortly afterwards. With the use of refrigerator cars, the Chicago stockyards changed from salted products to over 75,000 carloads of fresh meat a year by 1901.

There were a number of early attempts at making an ice-refrigerator car. In 1851, Jonas Wilder insulated the walls of four boxcars to carry butter. He had to restock ice en route. Wilder also used his cars to carry meat on the Rutland & Washington Railroad. In 1857, a gentleman by the name of Lyman carried beef, mutton, and poultry to New York City. Right after the Civil War, Parker Earle delivered fresh, cool strawberries to Chicago from Carbondale, Illinois. His cars carried ice in bunkers beneath the floor. George Hammond and William Davis patented a refrigerator car for carrying cattle carcasses in 1868.

Joel Tiffany, a Chicago lawyer, designed a car with a top or clerestory-type bunker which contained ice. The cooled air fell downward over the meat. Tiffany's cars were chartered by the National Dispatch Live to carry both carcasses and fresh fruit from Chicago to Boston. By 1883, Tiffany operated over 1,000 refrigerator cars.

James H. Wickes patented a car similar to Tiffany's in 1877. He used galvanized fins on his ice tanks to increase the

Interior of observation-parlor car around 1900. Courtesy Railroad Museum of Pennsylvania.

cooling surface and fans driven by the car axles. Armour and Swift, among others, built meat packing empires with the use of cattle and refrigerator cars. By 1887, Wickes operated over 2,000 cars and by 1898, almost 10,000 were carrying meat and fruit around the country. In June 1886, the Southern Pacific moved its first refrigerated cars of California fruit to Boston. In 1907, the Southern Pacific and Union Pacific created the Pacific Fruit Express. By 1913, the Pacific Fruit Express carried 70,000 cars of fruit and vegetables.

— Interchange of Freight Cars —

While railroads had rolled competing lines' cars over their rails since the Civil War, by the turn of the century tracking by mileage proved too difficult. After 1902, the railroads agreed to a per day charge. They began at twenty cents per day and increased it to one dollar by 1920. They also agreed to divide car repair costs. Per diem freight car charges helped to integrate the rail network and to make shipping more efficient.

With humane stock cars and refrigerator cars, railroads were able to deliver fruits, vegetables, and meat from farm to table anywhere in the country in only a matter of days. Trains permitted the American economy to make the most efficient use of "break of bulk." Moreover, small towns in even some of the remotest areas of the country could send and receive goods as easily as the largest cities.

— Caboose Cupolas —

For over a hundred years the caboose was the most distinctive car on a freight train. It was painted in its railroad's colors and had the company's name written on its sides. Some even had official slogans. The real reason for its standing out, however, was its cupola or little cabin above the roof.

During the summer of 1863, conductor T. B. Watson grew tired of climbing up to the roof hole to look at the train. He convinced some Chicago & Northwestern shop workers in Iowa to add a small enclosed area with windows above the hole and added a seat. He could then observe the train in relative comfort and freedom from the elements.

Watson's idea caught on. By the 1880s, people began to refer to the raised area as a cupola or lookout. Others expanded the covering, while a few companies went backward and placed seats on the roof without any covering. The traditional cupola, however, became standard before World War I. The Baltimore & Ohio Railroad built bay windows instead of cupolas. This idea spread to some other railroads. Porches were added to ease mounting and dismounting. Many included bunks and became known as "Drovers' Cars," as they were used by farmers who rode with the train crew in the caboose when accompanying their livestock to market.

— Passenger Accommodations —

Passengers found train travel more comfortable as well as faster by the end of the century. However, lighting coaches was a major problem. Kerosene lamps had replaced candles by the Civil War. While they provided better light, they were a fire hazard, dirty, and each had to be maintained as a separate unit. There was some experimentation with gas as early

as 1851 on the Hudson River Railroad between Albany and New York.

In 1860, the New Jersey Railroad and Transportation Company and the Philadelphia and Reading Railroads used coal-compressed gas. The Pennsylvania planned to use gas lighting in all its cars in 1871. Other railroads followed suit during the 1870s. Still a fire hazard, cars could not carry a sufficient supply of gas for a long journey.

A Berlin lampmaker, Julius Pintsch, invented a lamp which cleanly burned compressed petroleum gas. He marketed his lamp to European railroads, and his product was so successful, he began to sell it in the United States in 1861. His Pintsch gas lamps burned slowly so that refueling was not a problem. At the same time, their light was good enough to read a newspaper or book! In 1882, the Erie bought the first large order of Pintsch lamps. In 1887, George Pullman, Sidney Dillon, and T. C. Pratt established the Safety Car Heating and Lighting Company to market the product. By 1891, 2,000 railroad cars used Pintsch lamps. By 1908, over 32,000 cars had them.

— Electric Lighting —

While other gas systems were introduced by the turn of the century, all had the danger of burning flame. Although Pintsch gas lamps were available until the end of the 1920s, electricity had many advantages. Within a few years of Edison's inventing the incandescent light bulb, an English railroad used them on an experimental basis. In 1881, Pullman installed Edison electric lights in its parlor car, *Beatrice*. The Pennsylvania Railroad permanently used a car for electric lights with power furnished by a rechargeable battery. Later, the Pennsylvania used steam-driven generators in a baggage car to supply current. Other railroads soon used their own early version of "head-end power" or the energy came from a single source at the front of the train.

These early electric lighting set-ups were more for advertising value than practical use. During the 1880s Morris Moskowitz invented an axle-driven generator which provided current for both lights and battery as the car rolled down the track. The battery kept the lights lit when the car stopped for short intervals. After some experimentation in Germany, he installed a successful unit on cars of the Central Railroad Company of New Jersey in 1893. In 1902, the New York Central's Twentieth Century Limited used the Moskowitz system on its entire train. By 1912, almost 14,000 rail cars were lit by electric lights.

Electric lights began to replace the large box-like kerosene fixture on the top front of locomotives in 1883. The more powerful electric lights aided safer, faster speeds.

— Heating —

Another fire hazard was the stove. Stoves at both ends of the car provided uneven heat. Near the stove, the traveler roasted; in the middle of the car, passengers froze. Devices to vent the heated air to the center did not work well. In 1865, William C. Baker invented a hot water or Baker Heater stove. Baker ran a pipe filled with water and salt through a coal burning stove. The pipe circulated throughout the floor of the car and provided steady, even heat. In 1882, Baker, with the help of George Westinghouse, developed a steam version with an automatic coal feeder.

Steam heat from the locomotive was far safer than individual car stoves. After the invention of several devices, the locomotive boiler could heat cars from the front to the back of the train. Moreover, during the 1880s several states passed laws forbidding the use of stoves in train cars. By 1891, locomotive boiler steam heated over 9,000 cars. In 1893, the Pennsylvania Railroad prepared over half their fleet for steam heat. Electric lights and steam heat eliminated the open flame fire hazard in cars.

— Steel Cars —

The rail car itself went through several improvements. As usual, there were early experiments with closed vestibules or closed entry and passage ways. The Lake Shore Railroad had vestibules in their fast mail cars in 1875 to permit postal agents to pass easily. During the mid 1880s, Henry Sessions of the Pullman Company developed the first, true closed vestibule car. The Pennsylvania bought the first cars for its New York to Chicago express in 1887. The closed vestibules encouraged passengers to move from car to car and increased the use of the dining car. People could move from car to car without being exposed to the elements.

Steel cars were the last fire prevention development during the nineteenth century. While trade journals and the public asked for steel cars, railroads at first hesitated to adopt them. Steel cars were much more expensive, yet they would carry the same number of passengers as wooden ones. While some prototypes were built, the Pennsylvania Railroad placed the first significant order. The Pennsylvania needed the steel fireproof cars for passing through its Hudson River tunnels to New York City. The Pennsylvania cars had a concrete floor; the wood interiors were treated to resist flame; the wood roof was encased in copper. In 1907, the Pennsylvania improved the design for an 80-foot car to hold 88 passengers. Its only wood was the seat armrests. By 1912, the Pennsylvania had 2,800 steel cars in operation. Other railroads followed. The last wooden car was produced in the United States in 1913.

By the turn of the century, most rail cars carried their own water in tanks for drinking and washing purposes. Flush toilets were becoming common on first-class, distance trains. Many cars were ornate and had plush, heavy seats. Some trains had a small library in the parlor car.

— The Diner —

Dining on the rails has always been a special treat for travelers. Ever since Pullman created the *Delmonico* in 1867, railroads used the dining car as a showcase to the public. The Pullman Company's production of dining cars was rather slow. Individual railroads in turn operated their own diners for the most part. First used in the Midwest, the idea spread quickly throughout the country. By 1882, the Baltimore & Ohio and the Pennsylvania Railroads added their own diners. In fact, the Pennsylvania's New York–Chicago Express boasted a 125-bottle wine rack.

It was difficult for railroads to make money on dining cars. They tended to overstock items just so everything was available for all the passengers. Each road claimed some specialty. The Northern Pacific served potatoes of 20 ounces or more, along with seasonal game fish. Some served game fowl or other delicacies.

During the early 1880s, tables and benches were immovable. Later, alternate seatings of tables for four and two permitted more aisle and elbow room. Most cars seated about 30 people at one time. By the 1890s, dining cars grew to 80 feet in length.

On some railroads only the best china and silver were used. Diners had larger windows at table height so that people could look at the ever-changing landscape. By the 1890s the diner no longer had a vestibule. More space was then allotted to the kitchen and table area. The crew would number from twelve to fourteen. All members of the staff were well trained and emphasized service for the customers. Last, but not least, the diner's weight of up to 85 tons before World War I made it a very smooth riding car.

— The Harvey House —

One railroad held out the longest from using diners. In 1876, Frederick H. Harvey approached a Santa Fe superintendent with a plan. Harvey was very successful in operating hotels and restaurants. Harvey suggested that the Santa Fe help him establish restaurants along their line every hundred miles or so. He would then provide passengers with the best food and service possible. By the time of his death, Harvey was in charge of 47 restaurants, 15 hotels, and 30 dining cars as they were eventually added to the Santa Fe fleet.

Harvey set standard prices for his restaurants. He regulated the menu so that passengers could have a different meal for each stop. Travelers were never rushed. Coffee was always fresh; it was discarded when only two hours old. Orange juice had to be squeezed fresh for each glass. He always used fresh eggs—a practice unheard-of at the time.

Harvey hired young women for waitresses. They wore a uniform of black shoes, black stockings, a simple black dress

A switch tower. Courtesy Canadian National. #38679-2.

and with a black bow around an "Elsie collar." They could wear a white ribbon in their hair, tied neatly. Their starting wage was $1.50 per day with room and board. They were highly trained. They set tables perfectly and had to carry all items to the customers on trays. Many "Harvey Girls" were able to save good sums of money at these "Harvey Houses."

Even though Fred Harvey forbade his waitresses to marry during their first year of work, it was difficult to enforce the rule. Harvey himself often gave permission for them to marry earlier. In fact, it is estimated that over 5,000 Harvey Girls married through connections in the restaurant, many to railroad workers. Some claim that 4,000 babies were christened "Fred" or "Harvey" in honor of the famous restaurant owner.

Fred Harvey also took over concession sales on Santa Fe trains. He insisted that his "news butchers" sold only the best quality candy and the most wholesome literature. He forbade the sale of smut. He encouraged Indians to set up booths near stations and Harvey Houses to sell their rugs, jewelry, and other works of art.

Fred Harvey became synonymous with the best of food and the best of service. The "Harvey Girls" brought a distinct el-

ement of culture and graciousness to the wild west. Most certainly, the Harvey House became one of the strongest marketing tools for the Santa Fe Railroad. In fact, the Santa Fe enjoyed a large share of the Chicago–California trade due to Fred Harvey hospitality.

The Harvey House stops became fewer with the increased use of diners on the Santa Fe. Many, however, were reopened during World War II to serve the large number of sailors and soldiers who traveled by train.

— Luxury Trains —

Other railroads began to run luxury or "crack" trains. These trains maintained the tightest and fastest schedules between major cities. While it is impossible to include all of them, the New York Central's *Twentieth Century Limited* and the Pennsylvania's *Broadway Limited* became the most famous because of their archrivalry. George M. Daniels named the train for the New York Central. He was a former patent medicine salesman and had a keen sense of marketing. Daniels even had a U.S. postage stamp issued to carry an image of "The Greatest Train in the World." It began service on June 15, 1902.

The Pennsylvania's *Broadway Limited* was not to be outdone. It began its run one day after the *Twentieth Century* on June 16th. By 1912, both trains ran from New York to Chicago in 18 hours. It, too, had a luxurious diner, the best of service, and the most comfortable sleeping accommodations of the time.

— Railroad Resorts —

Only the wealthy could afford to ride the *Broadway Limited* or the *Twentieth Century Limited*. But the less wealthy, even the poor, were not forgotten. Other railroads provided excursions and trips to resorts. Many railroads out of New York City ran trains to mountain resorts for people to enjoy fresh air, sports, and fine food. The Chesapeake & Ohio Railroad created the Greenbriar luxury hotel at White Sulphur Spring, West Virginia. Railroads from smaller cities also provided excursions. The Milwaukee Road helped create a resort establishment in the lake district of northwest Iowa. A variety of these railroad resorts and parks catered to all classes of people.

One resort was at first only for the rich and famous. A wealthy Ohio businessman, Henry Flagler, took his wife to Florida hoping that the warmer climate would restore her health. At the time of her death in 1881, he recognized the potential of Florida as a winter resort area. He purchased a narrow-gauge railroad which ran from Jacksonville to St. Augustine. He changed it to standard gauge and extended it to the area of Miami in 1896. He built motels and developed it into a resort for the rich and famous. Soon luxury trains left northern cities during winter for patrons to enjoy the warm Florida climate.

Flagler extended his Florida East Coast Railway along the islands of the Florida Keys. He began construction in 1904. In 1907, workers completed two miles of concrete arches to Knights Key. Tracks reached Key West in 1912. Flagler wanted to use this extension to develop trade with Cuba. There is no doubt that Flagler's railroad was the chief factor for the development of Florida as a winter vacation mecca.

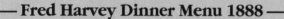

— Fred Harvey Dinner Menu 1888 —

Blue Points on Shell

English Pea, au Gritton

Fillet of Whitefish, Maderia Sauce
Potato Francaise

Young Capon, Hollandaise Sauce

Roast Sirloin of Beef, au Jus   Pork, with Apple Sauce
Turkey, Stuffed   Cranberry Sauce

Mashed Potatoes   *Boiled Sweet Potatoes*
Elgin Sugar Corn
Marrowfat Peas   *Asparagus Cream Sauce*

Salami of Duck, Queen Olives
Baked Veal Pie, English Style
Charlotte of Peaches, Cognac Sauce

Prairie Chicken, Currant Jelly

Sugar Cured Ham   Pickled Lamb's Tongue
Lobster Salad, au Mayonnaise

Celery   *Beets*   *French Slaw*

Apple Pie   Mince Pie
Cold Custard, a la Chantilly

New York Ice Cream   Assorted Cakes   Bananas
Oranges   Catawba Wine Jelly   Grapes

Edam and Roquefort Cheese
Bent's Water Crackers   French Coffee
Meals, 75 cents

— The Orphan Trains —

One type of passenger never traveled for pleasure. They were orphans found on east-coast city streets without parents, home, or protection. Just before the outbreak of the Civil War, Charles L. Brace had the idea of moving these children from the cities to the country to live with families. He worked through the Legal Aid Society to place the children on trains to the western part of the United States.

The children carried their lunches, and the railroads provided milk at various station stops. Posters were hung at stations to announce the arrival of the "orphan train." The children would stand on the station platform, usually of a county seat, as people — mostly farmers — looked them over. Upon choosing one, the couple signed "indenture papers." The child then lived with the couple and performed chores for his or her keep. Some were later adopted. An inspection system was organized; there were often reports of child cruelty. By the time the "orphan trains" ended, it is estimated that 300,000 children rode these trains to Louisiana, to Nebraska, and to other western parts of the country.

Sketch by Dee Dee Tymkowicz.

— Hobos —

Hobos were unwelcome train "passengers." This American institution began after the Civil War. Many former Union and Confederate soldiers let loose their roaming spirit by traveling almost aimlessly from town to town. The figure of an unshaven man wearing tattered clothes and carrying all his possessions in a bag, called a "bindle," became a common figure along the tracks. By the 1880s such characters as Weary Willie or Happy Hooligan were part of the American cultural

landscape. According to estimates, there were over 60,000 hobos riding the rails by the early twentieth century.

Some hobos paid conductors at least a portion of the fare. Others hid on trains. Riding the "bumper" between freight cars was a good place, but they could be easily spotted. Some tried to "ride the rods" by hanging onto the bracings under the cars. This was very dangerous since a jolt would cause a loss of grip and cause a fall onto the rails. Also, conductors and brakemen would drag a spike on a chain under the car to dislodge the hobo. Some would "deck" a passenger train and ride on top of the roof. Of course, it was best to "flip" into an empty boxcar.

Hobos were found near railroad tracks, particularly at the junction of two roads. A number would camp in what became known as a hobo jungle. The most famous hobo jungle was in Chicago. Some worked from time to time, while others "mooched" free food from people as often as possible. They had their own symbols to point the way to a "kind lady" who would give the next troop of hobos a free meal. Dr. Ben Reitman, who was an M.D., socialist, and former hobo, treated the entire Chicago hobo community to a banquet in 1907!

As colorful as they were, hobos were both a nuisance and danger to the railroads. Not only did they not pay for rides, they interfered with train activities from time to time. In winter they would start fires along the tracks and in boxcars. The fires often went out of control and burned railroad property and freight. The railroads hired detectives or "bulls" to keep hobos at a distance. Some bulls were known to throw hobos from moving trains.

A few hobos settled down and lived a regular life. The famous writer Jack London rode the rails as a hobo during his teenage years.

— Chapel Cars —

On a trip to Russia, Episcopal Bishop William D. Waller noticed people attending church services in a railroad car. When he returned to the U.S., Bishop Waller thought his church could use "chapel cars" to bring religious services to people in the American West. The Pullman Palace Car Com-

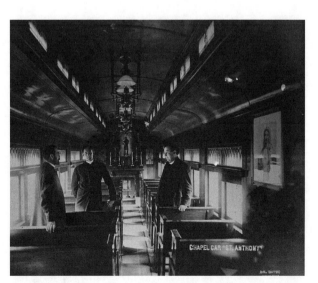

Interior of chapel car *Saint Anthony*. Courtesy Sioux City Public Museum, Sioux City, Iowa.

pany completed Bishop Waller's first "chapel" or "cathedral" car, *Church of Advent,* in 1890. The car brought Episcopal services to the people of Minnesota and North Dakota. A second car, known simply as "the Bishop's Chapel Car," was used chiefly along the shores of Lake Superior in upper Michigan.

At the same time that Bishop Waller was developing his "chapel car," Boston Smith had the same idea for creating a Baptist Gospel Tram. It was Colgate Hoyt, however, who formed the Baptist Car Syndicate to finance the project. The syndicate's *Evangel* also ran in the upper Midwest within months of Bishop Waller's car. Other Baptist cars soon followed: *Emmanuel, Glad Tidings, Goodwill, Messenger of Peace, Herald of Hope,* and *Amazing Grace.*

In 1904, a Roman Catholic priest, Fr. Francis Kelly, noticed one of the Baptist cars in Saint Louis, Missouri. The next year he formed the Catholic Extension Society and became its first president. The society refurbished a discarded Wagner car into its own "chapel car," the *Saint Anthony*. The *Saint Anthony* ran mostly in Kansas and South Dakota. The Society later ordered the *Saint Peter* and *Saint Paul* from the Barney & Smith Car Company. When the all-steel *Saint Peter* was constructed in 1912, it was considered the longest car on U.S. rails at 84 feet and 7⅝ inches.

Episcopal, Baptist, and Catholic "chapel cars" ran throughout the West wherever their particular denominations needed their services. Some lasted through the 1930s. Their usefulness ended as towns grew large enough to have their own churches, ministers, and priests.

— Railroad Empires —

Flagler's railroad construction in Florida was just a portion of the huge growth of trackage at the turn of the century. There was also a series of mergers which brought about the railroad map which would be familiar until the 1950s. Along with these mergers, some railroads were joined by ownership or marketing agreements. In 1906, there were 224,000 miles of track in the United States. More than half, or 138,000 miles, were controlled by seven people or empires:

— The Seven Empires —

- J. P. Morgan — Southern, New Haven — 18,000 miles
- Vanderbilt — New York Central, Chicago & Northwestern — 22,000 miles
- The Pennsylvania — Baltimore & Ohio, Chesapeake & Ohio — 20,000 miles
- Hill — Great Northern, Chicago, Burlington & Quincy, and Northern Pacific — 21,000 miles
- Harriman — Illinois Central, Union Pacific, and Southern Pacific — 25,000 miles
- Gould — Erie, and Missouri Pacific — 17,000 miles
- Rock Island — Its own line for 15,000 miles

James J. Hill, "The Empire Builder." Courtesy BSNF.

— Union Station —

Railroads built huge, magnificent stations to show their power to the public. Many stations were architectural monuments and works of art. Passengers who walked through their colossal halls and waiting rooms were aware of the railroads' power. A "union" station meant that two or more railroad companies used the facility. Constructed in 1894, the St. Louis Union Station served 18 different railroads. The famous Boston South Street Station was built in 1898. The present Washington, D.C., Union Station was completed in 1907, and stands just a few blocks from the Capitol. Pennsylvania Station in New York City received trains from the Hudson tunnels. Its two halls stood on 18 acres of prime New York real estate across the street from the post office. It had tunnels to the Long Island Railroad. Not to be outdone in 1913, the New York Central built its Grand Central Station. Its own tunnels, trackage, and halls were in every way comparable to the Pennsylvania. Chicago's Union Station was completed after World War I. The union station's main clock was often the choice meeting place.

— A Railroad Culture —

The railroad was a way of life for many people in the second half of the nineteenth century. It touched almost everyone. It is not surprising, then, that many songs were written about trains. One of the earliest, "Paddy Works on the Erie," spoke of the Irish immigrants who helped build and work on the longest railroad of the time. Track workers had their "Track Lining Song," and Casey Jones is celebrated in his own ballad. Even hobos had their own music with "The Gambler" and

Union Station, Washington, D.C. Amtrak headquarters are in right wing. Banner at entrance celebrates 25 years of Operation Lifesaver.

Depot at Wahoo, Nebr., on the Burlington Route. It was built in 1886, and an agent lived upstairs until 1970. Photo by Duane M. Miller.

Outside view of Union Station in Chicago.

The classical waiting room of Chicago's Union Station.

"You Wonder Why I'm a Hobo." The two most famous are the "Wabash Cannonball" and the all-time favorite "I've Been Working on the Railroad."

"I've Been Working on the Railroad"

I've been working on the railroad
All the livelong day.
I've been working on the railroad
To pass the time away.
Don't you hear de whistle blowing?
Rise up so early in de morn;
Don't you hear de captain shoutin'
"Dinah blow yo' horn."
Dinah won't you blow, Dinah won't you blow,
Dinah won't you blow your horn?
Dinah won't you blow, Dinah won't you blow,
Dinah won't you blow your horn?
Someone's in the kitchen with Dinah,
Someone's in the kitchen I know,
Someone's in the kitchen with Dinah,
Strumming on the old banjo,
Fe Fi Fiddely Aye Oh,
Fe Fi Fiddely Aye Oh, Oh, Oh, Oh
Fe Fi Fiddely Aye Oh,
Strumming on the old banjo.

— Reputation vs. Reality —

In 1916, railroads carried 98 percent of all passenger traffic service. Nevertheless, they fell on hard economic times. Taxes began to take their toll as well as government regulations. In fact, when President William Howard Taft signed the Mann-Elkins Act, he referred to the railroads as "monopolies" and as "lawless in spirit." Just before World War I, the St. Louis & San Francisco, the New Haven, the Rock Island, and the

99

Wabash were in serious financial difficulty. Thirty-seven thousand miles, or one-sixth of the U.S. railroad network, were operated by trustees or receivers.

In August 1916, workers threatened a general strike against the railroads. At that point, President Woodrow Wilson summoned the major railroad presidents to the White House. President Wilson argued in favor of the workers gaining an 8-hour workday. He was not willing, however, to give in to the demand for extra overtime pay. He also wanted to convene a special commission to investigate work conditions. The unions accepted President Wilson's suggestions, but the railroad companies would not.

President Wilson summoned the railroad presidents once again to Washington, D.C. He then went to Congress to get support to avoid a strike set for Labor Day, September 4, 1916. Upon Wilson's suggestion, William C. Adamson of Georgia sponsored the Adamson Act which legislated the 8-hour railroad workday effective January 1917. Wilson signed the Adamson Act into law while seated in a railroad car at Union Station.

The railroads challenged the Adamson Act in the courts, and the unions threatened again to strike in March 1917. On the 21st of March, in the case Wilson v. New, the Supreme Court upheld the constitutionality of the Adamson Act. This decision in effect gave Congress unquestionable authority over the railroads.

Nevertheless, on the eve of World War I, the railroads still seemed to be unbridled engines of greed and unlimited wealth. Their reputation by 1917 outlived the reality. The railroads had fallen on difficult times in the 1910s. Their ability to generate wealth was severely curtailed by government regulation, taxes, and union pressures.

The railroads had also lost their leadership. By 1910, the age of the Hills and Harrimans had passed. Bankers now ran the railroads. They were not as interested in improving trains as gaining profits in shrinking financial conditions. In 1900, railroad assets, however, were estimated at $12.5 billion or almost 14 percent of the entire wealth of the United States at that time. There were 193,346 route or point-to-point miles of track owned and 258,784 miles operated. It was both a high point and the beginning of almost a century of decline.

In the public's mind the railroads were still at the top of the "Robber Baron" list as they had been in the 1870s. In all fairness, the railroad owners were no better or worse than the heads of meat-packing companies, textile manufacturers, or owners of the steel mills. Railroads, however, touched everyone's life more directly than any other enterprise. Everyone traveled by train, news arrived by the station's telegraph, and so did packages and the U.S. and Canadian mail. In other words, the railroads were ever present in the minds of North Americans prior to World War I. They took the brunt of the excesses and criticism of the "Gilded Age." There is no doubt, however, that the railroads deserve the credit of developing the United States into the most modern and industrialized country in the world at the turn of the century.

Chapter 12.

Government Intervention

Canada and the United States entered World War I at different times. Canada's participation began with England's declaration of war in 1914. As a dominion, Canada contributed both men and materiel to the war effort. The United States joined England and France in the war in 1917. Earlier, it had used the railroads to move small numbers of men and supplies to stop Pancho Villa's raids from Mexico. Even so, President Wilson campaigned on the slogan "He kept us out of war." His administration, however, did make a few plans in the event of war in Europe. He involved the railroads as early as 1916 for defense preparations.

During the war, Canada's railroads had the task of carrying men and materials to east-coast ports for embarkation to England. When approaching the east coast, all supplies and personnel had to be switched from the Canadian Pacific to other railroads. Since the Canadian Pacific's tracks entered Maine, these items could not be sent through the United States, which remained neutral for almost three years. By 1915, it became apparent that the Grand Trunk Pacific and Canadian Northern were hard pressed. The predecessor to the Railway Association of Canada grew out of the cooperation of the railroads to handle the war traffic, and to get empty railcars back to Canada from the United States after 1917.

In spite of the war traffic or perhaps because of it, many Canadian lines were not able to sustain themselves. At that point Canadian Finance Minister Sir Thomas White suggested three possibilities: Simply let the weaker railroads die or go their own way; permit them to default, and the government would decide whether to take possession or not; and third, the government would give temporary financial assistance during the war and hope for better times afterward.

— Royal Railroad Commission —

In 1916, Parliament established a Royal Commission to investigate the railroad issue. The following year it reported the results. The Canadian Pacific was in good financial and operating condition. It needed no assistance. If the government helped the other railroads, it would be unfair to the well-run Canadian Pacific. They recommended, however, that the Grand Trunk Pacific, the Grand Trunk, and the Canadian Northern simply be "assumed by the people of Canada." At the same time they cautioned that such an assumption would bring political interference in the operation of the railroads.

— The "Dominion Railway" —

The Commission, therefore, recommended the creation of a "Dominion Railway" consisting of the Grand Trunk, Grand Trunk Pacific, and Canadian Northern. A board of five members would oversee its functions, thereby avoiding any direct political interference. They would also combine the Intercolonial and National Transcontinental eventually into this system. The government would pay the interest on the existing securities. The board would also acquire 600,000 shares of the Canadian Northern along with an outright gift of $25 million. By October, 1917, the remaining shares were purchased outright. They would then call for a "permanent board of experts" from business and labor to actually run the new system. They suggested track improvements as well as increasing the number of rolling stock and locomotives. They looked to the individual provinces to assist with the transition and finances.

In May 1918, the government offered the Grand Trunk $500 million for stock dividends and a promise of 2½ percent on futures. The Grand Trunk refused the offer. The railroad defaulted the following year. The government simply picked up the stock. A three-member Board of Arbiters determined the total value of the Grand Trunk and inspected its operating conditions. It did the same with the Grand Trunk Pacific. Former U.S. president William Howard Taft was one of the arbiters.

As for the individual railroads, even during the war years, the Grand Trunk Pacific carried less than half the traffic of the Canadian Pacific. Its outlet at Prince Rupert never generated the projected trade. In 1921, the head office of the Grand Trunk was moved from England to Montreal. This move made nationalization easier. The Grand Trunk was assimilated in January 1923.

— Canadian National —

The Canadian National Railway Company was officially born in January 1923. A fifteen-member board oversaw management and operations for the government. They had the power to issue securities based on track mileage. The Canadian National also included the Intercolonial, the Hudson Bay, and several other former short lines in the Maritime Provinces. The Canadian Pacific remained a private, separate railroad.

For operational purposes, Canadian National divided the railroad into four divisions: the Atlantic westward to Riviere du Loup; the Central to near Port Arthur; a Grand Trunk Western, from the Detroit River; and finally a fourth which went westward from Port Arthur to the Pacific Coast. The Canadian National's first task was to create a unified system from formerly rival roads. They had to eliminate duplicate trackage and determine on a priority basis which communities needed the most service. They also had to bring both the physical plant and equipment up to the standards of the privately owned Canadian Pacific. It was a huge task particularly since both Canada and the United States experienced an economic slump during the early 1920s.

CANADIAN NATIONAL'S PREDECESSOR LINES 1918

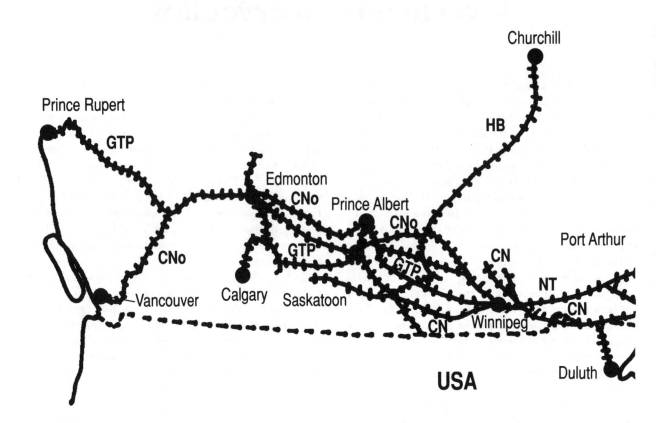

CNo	Canadian Northern
GTP	Grand Trunk Pacific
HB	Hudson Bay
IC	Intercolonial
NT	National Transcontinental

— U.S. Council of Defense —

The United States began some defense preparations during 1916. Along with the calling up of some National Guard units, Secretary of War Newton D. Baker recommended the passage of the Army Appropriation Act of August 1916. Congress thereby established a "Council of Defense" to coordinate the nation's natural resources and industries for purposes of national security. It established an advisory commission of business leaders. Daniel Willard, president of the Baltimore & Ohio Railroad, represented the railroad interests. The Appropriation Act permitted the president to take over all transportation should it be deemed necessary. The nation's railroads began to prepare for the possibility of war. In February 1917, the American Railroad Association enlarged its board from five to 18 members and appointed Fairfax Harriman of the Santa Fe chairman.

— Railroad War Board —

When the United States declared war on Germany in April 1917, Daniel Willard called together the presidents of the nation's 51 major lines. He asked them to cooperate as closely as possible. They planned to pool their resources and function as one "continental rail system." They set up the Railroad War Board chaired by Fairfax Harriman. The Board was to keep a smooth flow of boxcar traffic for the war effort. By May, however, Congress passed the Esch Car Service Act which gave the Interstate Commerce Commission authority to regulate traffic movement according to certain rules. Army and Navy agents thereby had the authority to issue "priority tags" on rail shipments. Chaos occurred. For one thing the railroads had a shortage of both boxcars and motive power to meet the demand. The designation "Priority" was much overused to the point it was meaningless. For example, gov-

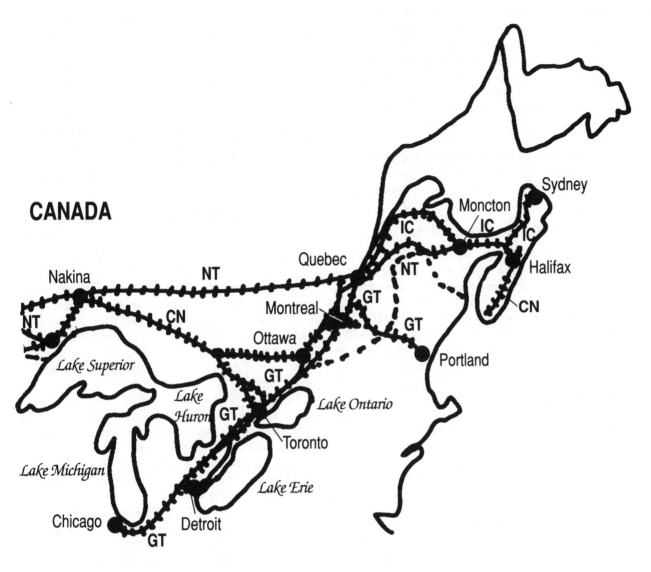

CANADA

ernment agents labeled 85 percent of rail cars in the Pennsylvania's Pittsburgh division "priority." Moreover, when the cars reached eastern ports, there were no unloading facilities. The government used the greatly needed equipment as a storage facility — sometimes for months. By November 1918, the government estimated the need for over 15,000 freight cars!

— Military Railway Service —

General Orders on May 14, 1917, called for the formation of Military Railway Service regiments. In total, 83,000 men participated under the direction of the Thirteenth Engineers in France. Former vice president of the Pennsylvania Railroad W. W. Atterbury was appointed Brigadier General to head the railway service.

The Military Railway Service personnel began activity in December 1917. They operated in an area from south of the Havre to Paris, on to Marseilles and the Rhone River Valley.

They also worked at the ports of St-Nazaire, Burt, LaPallise, and Bordeaux. In all, the Americans constructed 937 miles of track and hauled 3,430,000 gross tons.

The Military Railway Service fired Navy Battery guns from cars on special trains. They also operated a series of sixty-centimeter narrow-gauge lines leading to the trenches, along with 130 miles of light rail track behind the lines. There is no doubt that the United States Railway Service was the primary supply and transportation line for the United States Expeditionary Force in France.

— William McAdoo —

The winter of 1917 was one of the most severe in living memory. Trains were delayed throughout the country. The travel time of the average freight was reduced by almost 30 percent. With car shortages brought on by the government's own policies and increased delivery times, President Wilson declared the government "takeover" of the U.S. railroads as of Monday, December 28, 1917. Wilson formed the United States Railroad Administration (USRA) and appointed William McAdoo as director. McAdoo was secretary of the treasury and had run Wilson's 1912 presidential campaign. He was also Wilson's son-in-law. For the day-to-day running of the railroads, McAdoo created a board consisting of representatives from government, the unions, and the railroads. McAdoo and his staff represented the government; William S. Carter, president of the Brotherhood of Locomotive Firemen and Enginemen, spoke for the unions; and Walter Hines of the Santa Fe and Carl Grey of the Union Pacific gave the carrier's point of view.

— Railroad Control Act —

According to the Railroad Control Act of March 1918, all property would be returned to the private companies "in good repair" within 21 months from the signing of a peace treaty. McAdoo had originally suggested five years. The Interstate Commerce Commission would determine compensation to the railroads based upon a three-year average rate prior to June 1917. The railroads also could not pay any dividend in excess of those of the prior three years without presidential approval. Any other financial dealings also had to have government permission. The President had the authority to set rates through the Interstate Commerce Commission, and any monies derived during the control period would be considered property of the U.S. treasury.

— United States Railroad Administration —

The United States Railroad Administration divided the United States into three districts: East, South, and West. The East comprised all roads north of the Potomac and Ohio Rivers. The South was from the Mississippi and south of the Potomac and Ohio. The West consisted of everything west of the Mississippi. All freight shipments were planned along the shortest routes. Both duplicate freight and passenger services were eliminated wherever possible. The Administration took over Western Union as well as railroad telegraph operations. Except for the southwest portion of the Southern Express, the USRA combined the four major companies into the American Railway Express, Inc. and took over its operation.

The USRA ordered almost 2,000 new locomotives and 100,000 freight cars to meet shortages. It set standards and design for 12 types of steamers for the three leading manufacturers: American, Baldwin, and Lima. Switch engines had 0-6-0 and 0-8-0 wheel arrangements. For heavy mountain service USRA ordered 2-6-6-2 and 2-8-8-2 Mallet types. There were both light and heavy 4-4-2 (Atlantics), 4-6-2 (Pacifics), 2-8-2 (Mikados), then 2-8-2 and 2-10-2 designs. The Mikado freight locomotive was produced in the largest quantity — almost half of the government order. The USRA determined both the number produced and where assigned. While railroad workers claimed these "McAdoo Locomotives" did not fit certain districts' specific needs, many remained in service through the Second World War and on to the early diesel era.

Even though the USRA curtailed passenger service during 1917 and 1918, passenger traffic increased by 8 percent. The government regulated Pullman service and eliminated à la carte meals in dining cars. It determined that the customary large variety of dishes encouraged waste and were difficult to prepare. Passengers could choose from a few set menu "packages."

The government discouraged any unnecessary civilian travel. From the best estimates, American railroads from April 1917 through November 1918 hauled almost 6½ million military personnel. In 1918, the railroads accumulated 405 billion ton miles of freight and 42 billion passenger miles.

— Railroad Wage Commission —

War almost always brings economic dislocation. Besides shortages of certain goods and services, inflation became a problem. As prices rose throughout 1917, the railroad brotherhoods began making demands for increases in salaries. In January 1918, McAdoo, upon the advice of his friend Alfred E. Smith, appointed a Railroad Wage Commission to investigate working conditions and salaries. Some of the brotherhoods requested a 40 percent wage increase to keep up with inflation. During 1916 and 1917, salary increases rose less than 20 percent.

In its April 1918 report, the Railroad Wage Commission recommended increases on a sliding scale — retroactive to January. Those on the lowest salary rung received a 43 percent increase while those at the top received nothing at all. The increases went into effect that May. The Commission also established the 8-hour workday throughout the industry. Moreover, women employees were to receive "equal pay for equal work," and the same held true for African-American workers. The Commission defined almost all railroad positions in exact detail and set up new work rules.

The Railroad Wage Commission in effect established the first nondiscrimination work policy in the nation's history. At the same time, railroad owners had to manage the increase in salaries and the newly defined positions throughout most of the twentieth century. The effects were immediate. Railroad employee rosters increased from 1,732,000 in 1917 to 1,841,000 in 1918 and over 2,000,000 in 1920. Based on the Commission's judgments, wages increased from $1,782,000 in 1917 to $2,665,000 in 1918. By 1920, they increased over another 29 percent. In other words, in 1917, railroad workers' salaries were 27 percent more than the average U. S. factory workers'. By 1920, railroad workers received 33 percent more than his and her counterparts in manufacturing. While working for the railroad was always attractive, the Railroad Wage Commission made it a financially rewarding means of employment. The railroads themselves, however, had to carry the burden of payment.

— Financial Burdens —

More than just salaries, railroad management had to contend with rising prices. Coal and oil prices rose over 100 percent from 1916 to 1918. At the same time, freight traffic increased only 12 percent. In June 1918, McAdoo permitted an increase in passenger rates of 18 percent and freight charges at 28 percent. While these increases did help, they did not

Women locomotive mechanics, WWI (c. 1918). Courtesy National Archives. #14381.

offset expenses. Even with the increased revenues, the government's operation of the railroads cost taxpayers $2 million per day!

In its final report, the United States Railroad Administration declared a loss of over $900 million for the railroads. This figure, however, did not include an additional $200 million in claims for destroyed property due to negligence or disrepair. The railroads brought lawsuits against the government for $670 million, but they had to settle for an eventual $222 million final payment.

McAdoo himself resigned as Director of the USRA following the Armistice in 1918. He claimed personal financial loss as his reason. Rank-and-file railroad workers tried to encourage him to remain at the post. They even started a movement for each to contribute one dollar out of pocket for him to reconsider. (Such an amount would have made McAdoo a millionaire almost twice over.) McAdoo became so popular during the war that workers often chanted: "McAdoo's work is never McAdone."

The new USRA Director, Walter Hines, did his utmost not to increase railroad rates. His position, along with a coal strike in 1919, caused even more problems for railroad management.

— Nationalization Attempt —

With the war's end and time approaching for the return of the railroads to their owners, the brotherhoods began a movement toward "nationalization." Canada's nationalization then underway greatly encouraged them. The unions directed their chief legal counsel, Glen E. Plumb, to argue their case to the government. Plumb recommended that Congress create a 15-member board consisting of representatives from labor, management, and government. The government would simply buy out all the railroads through a bond issue and empower the board to run them. Unfortunately for the union and fortunately for the railroads, U.S. popular opinion was against nationalization. President Wilson personally was against such a venture, so the nationalization movement died.

— Esch-Cummins Act —

Congress returned the railroads to their owners well within the deadline of the Railroad Control Act of 1918. Senator Albert Cummins and Congressman John Esch drafted the Transportation (Esch-Cummins) Act of 1920. The Act returned the railroads to their owners as of March 1 of that year. At the same time it increased the Interstate Commerce Commission from nine to 15 members. The expanded Commission now had the authority to set both maximum and minimum passenger and freight rates throughout the nation. The Commission had the guideline of basing railroad profits upon a "fair rate of return." In other words, any profit above 6 percent or so was subject to recovery by the federal government. Congress also gave the Commission final approval over railroad securities as well as new construction and abandonment of track. No merger could take place without the Commission's approval. The Esch-Cummins Act also set up a nine-person Railroad Labor Board. This board had authority over wage increases and railroad working conditions.

The Esch-Cummins Act treated the railroads as a monopoly industry. Even before collective bargaining became law later on, railroad management had to contend with a government labor board. In fact, during the early 1920s the board granted workers a 22 percent wage increase. From a once highly competitive industry, by the 1920s the only differences among railroads were in schedules and dining car service. While such a situation brought about the utmost creativity from railroad management, it could not match changing conditions. Moreover, the railroads had to repair all the damage done during the USRA years.

The railroads attempted to minimize their reconstruction by suggesting to a merge into 19 large systems. The ICC rejected the proposal, and until post–World War II there were no major merger attempts.

Reputation lasts longer than reality. While many still viewed the railroads as unlimited sources of wealth, times had changed. Along with government regulation, railroads were now owned and run by bankers rather than the Hills, Harrimans, and Vanderbilts. These stockholders lacked the "railroad sense" of the leaders of a generation ago. Moreover, competition had already come about from other areas near the end of World War I.

— Growing Competition —

In 1916, Congress began the federal highway program. The federal government matched state appropriations for through road construction. By 1917, there were over 4½ million cars and about 400,000 trucks in the United States. By 1914, Henry Ford's assembly line was already producing 500,000 cars a year.

In May 1918, the Army flew the first plane carrying airmail between New York City and Washington, D.C. The pilot became lost, ran out of gas, and was forced to land. The mail sack was transferred to a train. . . . Nevertheless, by 1920, there was regular airmail service between those cities flown by civilian pilots. Passenger airlines were in the very near future.

In 1919, Army Chief of Staff General John J. Pershing ordered Colonel Dwight D. Eisenhower to carry out an experiment. Eisenhower took a convoy of men and materiel across the United States by truck. At times the trucks were bogged down in mud and at others they averaged only six MPH. They drove alongside railroad tracks at times. It took the convoy 50 days to cross the nation. Even though it would have taken them slightly more than 50 hours by train, the experiment proved a greater flexibility for the military and lessened the dependence upon the railroads. It foreshadowed a new means of transportation.

PART IV

The Golden Years

Historical Survey

The United States rejected the Treaty of Versailles and refused to join the League of Nations. The people wanted a "return to normalcy" and to avoid foreign entanglements. The economy began almost a decade of incredible growth. Chain stores were distributed throughout the country. Michigan became a center for the mass production of automobiles. Henry Ford's assembly-line car production made his "Model T" and "Model A" within reach of most family budgets.

Electric appliance inventions and sales increased enormously. Electric toasters, fans, heaters, and a host of labor-saving devices became commonplace in homes. Radio was transformed from an experimental signal device into a household entertainment center. For the first time human voices and dramas could be heard in thousands of homes simultaneously from a studio miles away. The radio opened up a whole industry as well as careers. Along with talking movies by the end of the decade, the whole entertainment industry developed by mass proportions.

People had more leisure time. Baseball became an "all American" sport. Baseball players made headlines, and cities built huge stadiums to hold spectators. With the prohibition of the sale of alcoholic beverages, many, known as "bootleggers," made their own booze and served it in illegal, secret clubs called "speakeasies." Young women, who had recently received the right to vote, began to smoke in public and wore boots that "flapped" as they walked. They became known as "flappers" and started many modern trends. Some felt that the country's morality was slipping.

The stock market made unprecedented growth in the 1920s. Some people borrowed money to invest in somewhat flimsy companies and gambled on a supposedly never-ending increase in dividend payments. In 1929, the stock market "crashed." Some who had been "millionaires" became penniless overnight. The nation plunged into a long economic depression. By the early 1930s the United States's gross national product was one-half of what it had been in 1929. Millions were unemployed.

Franklin Delano Roosevelt became president in 1933 and began a series of experiments to help the economy recover through federal projects. He called this "priming the pump." His administration became known as "the New Deal." He set up a number of administrative agencies to both encourage and to regulate the economy. The Agricultural Adjustment Act (AAA) regulated agriculture, and the Public Works Administration (PWA) funded the construction of public buildings. The National Labor Relations Board (NLRB) helped settle workers' disputes with management and helped the union movement. In spite of all these efforts, the depression became worse after 1936. The United States came out of its economic decline toward the end of 1938, when it began to produce war materiel.

Canada also suffered economically during the depression. In 1931, Canada became a voluntary member of the British Commonwealth of Nations. It was a member of the League of Nations in its own right. Canada came out of its economic difficulties in 1939, when it declared war on Germany along with England. In 1940, both Canada and the United States formed a "Permanent Joint Board of Defense" to guard both ocean coasts. The Board also oversaw the construction of the Alaska highway, linking the territory of Alaska with the 48 states.

"The Public Be Blessed. . . ."

Both Canadian and U.S. railroads met new challenges in the years after World War I. The formation of Canadian National Railways created a government-owned system in direct competition with the private Canadian Pacific. In the United States, the railroads, still in private hands, were regulated as a monopoly. Nevertheless, they had to compete among themselves and also with autos, busses, trucks and then the airplane. While the 1920s and 1930s were a "golden age" of railroad travel, individual companies found it difficult to meet budgets, particularly during the Great Depression.

The Canadian National (CN) inherited over 100,000 employees, about 190,000 cars, and over 3,200 locomotives from previous roads. Its telegraph division added 3,852 more people along with a similar number in its express department. It also inherited eight hotels worked by its dining car staff. With the amalgamation of the Grand Trunk Railway, CN added 4,775 miles of track and emerged as the largest single system in the world up to that time.

— Henry Thornton —

Due to soaring expenses and political problems, CN's first president, David Hanna, resigned. Henry W. Thornton was appointed president and chairman of the board in 1922. Thornton previously worked for the Pennsylvania Railroad, and climbed his way up to become manager of its Long Island subsidiary. He also headed troop train arrangements in England during the war.

Thornton immediately began the task of consolidating the tracks of the formerly competing railroads. Many sections needed maintenance, and he gave priority to serving farm communities. In fact, he traveled throughout the system to inspect conditions for himself.

In 1923, Thornton ordered new locomotives. Along with freight-hauling 2-8-2 Mikados he also ordered 2-8-2 fourteen-wheeler "Mountain type" engines. In 1927, he introduced the "Mastadon" 4-8-4 Northern Type (CN 6100 series) for both fast freight and passenger service.

The Canadian National had yet to prove itself. As an arm of the government, Thornton worked on reducing the debt. By 1926, he cut 9,000 employees. He created a Department of Colonization to attract emigrants from Scandinavia and East Europe. About 4,200 families responded to the invitation and settled in the Canadian interior. The CN built 3,000 miles of branch lines to give better service to the farming communities.

— The Radio Car —

Thornton also wanted to increase passenger ridership throughout the system. In July 1923, he inaugurated the "radio car." The CN installed ratio sets with both headphones and speakers in some of its cars. They then created broadcast stations in various cities along the line which sent music, hockey games, and other entertainment over the air. The gimmick was a success. The CN radio network was later sold separately to the government and was the genesis of today's CBC. Later the railway installed telephones in some passenger cars. The CN soon lived up to its slogan of "Courtesy and Service."

— Silk Trains —

Both Canadian Pacific and Canadian National took advantage of the demand for silk in North America. Since raw silk rots quickly, it was carried by the fastest ships from Japan to Vancouver. CN loaded bales into boxcars within 30 minutes, and the trains left for the mills at Hoboken, New Jersey, at speed. The 2,749-mile trip was accomplished in 91 hours. Ten minutes was the longest stop for fuel. CN operated over one hundred of these "silkers" from 1925 through 1931. Speed was also important to prevent theft. The average CN silker carried $2 million worth of the commodity. Synthetics, as well as the Great Depression, ended the demand for silk. CN, however, still had an excellent business in grain transport. By 1928, the CN was third in earnings among North American railroads.

— The Canadian Pacific —

The Canadian National and Canadian Pacific maintained an interesting relationship with each other. If the CN was Canada's largest deficit item at its beginning, the CPR was the nation's largest taxpayer. CPR's president, Edward W. Beatty, actually hoped for CN's success to reduce its own tax burden! In 1923, both railroads led the permanent formation of the Railway Association of Canada. At the same time, both railroads competed for business — particularly among the farmers of central Canada. They cooperated in the 1920s to build Toronto's huge Union Station.

— Brownie Points —

Railroad employees could be dismissed from their jobs for a number of rule infractions. Even when some were fired, they were rehired in a short time, because it was difficult to find people with certain skills. Discipline was difficult to maintain at times.

In the early twentieth century, G. R. Brown of the New

Canadian National "Radio Car" 1920s. Courtesy Canadian National. #32082.

York Central devised a system of granting and taking away points for anyone who did a good or bad deed. Good and bad points could negate each other. Sixty negative points could mean dismissal. This system of "Brownie Points" spread to both Canadian and U.S. railroads during the 1920s. Actually, it spread quickly to other industries and to the American school system. Students who did well in school were accused of getting "Brownie Points."

— The Depression —

The Great Depression hit both railroads. By 1931, CN's receipts dropped 40 percent. During 1933 CPR did not make a dividend to its stockholders and had a 40 percent payroll reduction from 1928. By 1935, grain shipments on both roads declined to less than 20 percent of what they were before 1928. By the mid 1930s, CN accounted for one-third of Canada's debt! Moreover, there were continuous allegations of corruption made against Thornton. He fell out of government favor, and some did not like his competing with CPR for passengers. He was forced to step down in 1932.

The agency which investigated Thornton suggested the possibility of an amalgamation between CN and CPR. The Select Committee on Railways and Shipping formed a Royal Commission to look into the matter. After much political jostling, under the advice of CN's vice president for law, Gerard Ruel, the Commission recommended against a merger.

CN and CPR, however, did cooperate in a number of areas. They switched each other's cars at some facilities, and pooled passenger service between major eastern cities. They also cleaned and readied each other's cars in some yards, and combined ticket sales and services at some stations. Both railroads assisted the running of such small provincial roads as the Northern Alberta Railway.

In one area they maintained a distinct mode of competition: the airline industry. By the late 1920s, it was becoming apparent that James Richardson's Canadian Airways would affect transcontinental travel in the near future. CN and CPR at first both bought shares in the airline. CPR eased

out by 1937 leaving CN the sole proprietor. CPR later formed its own company, Canadian Pacific Airlines. Both also owned ship lines. CN's traffic between the Maritime Provinces and the Caribbean, however, was beginning to lose out to the airplane by the start of World War II.

If some of Canada's railroad economies were made worse with constructing and maintaining little-used branch lines, those extra rail miles quickly became a necessity during the Second World War. Nevertheless, cooperation rather than amalgamation served the Canadian people during the bleak depression years.

Even though they were not nationalized, railroads in the United States found it difficult to make budget in the 1920s. During the Great Depression, many became bankrupt. While the 1920 Esch-Cummins Act returned the railroads to their owners on March 1st, they were severely restricted from performing. The Interstate Commerce Commission set passenger and freight rates according to the shortest rail distance between two points. Railroad costs increased, and, during the next two decades, railroad and Pullman workers gained the right of collective bargaining. Railroads had to repair property damaged during the United States Railway Administration, and purchase necessary new equipment. They also had to live with the many changes brought about during the war years.

The railroads averaged a 4½ percent rate of return for profit. Therefore, there was little need for interference by the Interstate Commerce Commission on that issue. While freight had a slow growth, passenger use began to decline before the 1929 stock market crash. Any financial successes of the 1920s quickly evaporated in the 1930s. Operating revenues declined a billion dollars per year from 1930 through 1933. Passenger revenue dropped 40 percent during those years alone. The rate of return on all operations averaged 2¼ percent during the decade. From 1928 to 1938, railroad employee rosters dropped from 1.7 million to 939,000 workers. Ridership dropped from 780 million in 1929 to 478 million in 1932. While industry experienced a painful decline during the 1930s, railroads were saddled with ICC regulations and a relatively inflexible plant. They could not easily or quickly respond to the decline in demand. Trackage decreased from 252,845 to 249,433 miles by 1930, and down to 231,971 by 1941, just before the Second World War.

— The Van Sweringens —

Many roads went bankrupt. Led by the Missouri Pacific, nearly one-third of railroad trackage was in receivership by the late 1930s. In fact, the last railroad empire, the Van Sweringen, succumbed to the depression. Just prior to World War I, two brothers, Oris Paxton and Mantis James Van Sweringen, turned from the real estate business to railroading. In order to operate a transit line to a new housing development in Shaker Heights near Cleveland, they had to purchase the Nickel Plate Road from the New York Central. The Buffalo to Chicago Nickel Plate Road did so well under their direction that the ICC approved the addition of the Toledo, St. Louis, & Western and the Lake Erie & Western into a 1700 mile system in 1923.

The "Vans," as they became known, then purchased the Chesapeake & Ohio, the Erie, and a major portion of the Pere Marquette. They later acquired the Missouri Pacific and the Chicago & Eastern Illinois. They also owned the Hocking Valley, Wheeling & Lake Erie, and the Buffalo, Rochester, & Pittsburgh. The Vans held their stock through a newly formed Allegheny Corporation. This holding company permitted the railroad to operate during bankruptcy without the owners having a lion's share liability.

As with many stock transactions in the late 1920s, the Vans purchased their interests with borrowed money. As the Great Depression worsened, the Vans encountered economic difficulty. Low traffic and growing fixed costs hurt their business. At first they shuffled their funds between the Allegheny Corporation and the individual roads. With the failure of the Missouri Pacific, they had to auction off a good share of their properties in 1935. After gaining new funds, they were able to repurchase a good portion of their former empire. Nevertheless, after Mantis James died of heart failure that same year, Oris Paxton was not able to keep his railroads afloat. In 1936, most of the trackage was in bankruptcy. Oris Paxton also died of a heart attack by the end of the year, and the last attempt at a railroad empire died with him.

The Van Sweringens and railroads were able to last longer than expected due to changes in bankruptcy law. In 1932, President Herbert Hoover signed the Federal Bankruptcy Act. Under Section 77, a bankrupt railroad could continue running under court-appointed trustees. The ICC had to oversee the transaction, and it was definitely in the government's interests to keep the railroads operating.

— The Alaska Railroad —

While track miles began to decline in the lower 48 states after 1916, they grew in leaps and bounds in Alaska. Just before World War I, the U.S. Congress funded the construction of a railroad from Seward to Fairbanks. It was the last new main line, beginning to end, constructed in the United States. Construction continued until July 1, 1923, when President Warren G. Harding drove the last, golden spike at Nenna.

The Alaska Railroad operated in deficit until 1938. It became an important route for U.S. Armed Forces during World War II when Japan occupied some of the Aleutian Islands. Due to more deficit years into the 1970s, the state of Alaska took over ownership and operation of the railroad in 1985.

In recent years the Alaska Railroad revived its passenger traffic (mostly tourist) and became a major hauler of petroleum products. Today it boasts of being the last full service railroad in the United States.

— Grin and "Bear" It —

Alaska railroaders often have to contend with large wildlife on their tracks. Moose, bears, and wolves often seek the cleared rails after a large snowfall. When the animals are particularly numerous, the railroad sends out a pilot car with special whistles before a train. Moose are a particular problem, because sometimes they just do not move. When a pilot car is not available, the procedure is to turn off the headlight and blast the horn within a few feet of the animal. Sometimes that scares it off the tracks. One time a large bull moose with antlers larger than track gauge actually lifted a locomotive from the rails. When a moose is struck, the crew notifies the dispatcher. The railroad quickly retrieves the carcass and distributes the meat to the needy.

One memorable time, a mamma grizzly bear with her three cubs were running before the train on the tracks. They would not run off to the left or right, and the train was gaining on them. All of a sudden she turned around and growled in defiance at the locomotive so loudly that the crew heard her in the cab. She then safely left the tracks with two of her cubs and the third was "thumped" to the side uninjured. Bears are tough. . . .

There's also the story of the wolf who became so angry at the trains that he died biting a rail. . . .

In recent years the Alaska Railroad has made every effort to preserve wildlife. When there is a particularly heavy snow, the railroad clears sizable areas off to the side of tracks for animals to seek refuge from passing trains.

— New Competitors —

The railroads were severely limited in making profits in the 1920s and absolutely unable to do so in the 1930s. Busses could compete successfully on short runs to smaller towns. In the 1920s, Americans wanted to drive their own automobiles. By 1929, U.S. auto makers were turning out five million cars a year. With the ability to provide door-to-door delivery, trucks made inroads into the freight business. They had another advantage: trucking was unregulated well into the 1930s. Moreover, both the federal and state governments constructed and maintained roads to towns and villages that had — and those that did not have — railroad stations. At the same time, the airplane became a scheduled passenger carrier. In fact, some U.S. railroads invested in the new airline industry.

The railroad industry met the challenge of the new competition in new ways. Each road stressed efficiency and speed. Each told the passenger that it had the most comfortable seating and the most convenient schedule. Each sought smart car and locomotive styling. Each railroad had its crack train or trains that meant comfort and even pampering of passengers. The industry developed clever advertisements to catch the public's eye.

With fares the same from city to city, and Pullman charges and accommodations also the same, differences were in coach seating, the diner, and lounge cars. The services of the valet, lady-in-waiting, barber, or secretary were charged as used.

111

Cantwell Section Gang, 1948: Valdez Tyone, Alice Norton, John Nicklie, Grace Secondchief, Yetta Stickivan (behind Grace), Lingo Nicklie, and Helen Stickivan. Courtesy Anchorage Museum of History and Art. #BL79.2.2565.

President Warren Gamaliel Harding driving in the golden spike of the Alaska Railroad at Nenana, July 15, 1923. Courtesy Anchorage Museum of History and Art. #B75.134.186.

These rates were not regulated. Only the well-off traveler, however, could afford these on the best luxury trains.

During the 1920s the railroads added 15,000 new steam locomotives to their rosters at a cost of $765,000,000. They also purchased 850,000 new freight cars. Heavier rail permitted longer trains that could carry more tonnage. Freight train speed increased by 20 percent. Stronger and faster locomotives and heavier rail were only a partial solution. The railroads needed a lighter, smaller vehicle to compete with the bussing industry.

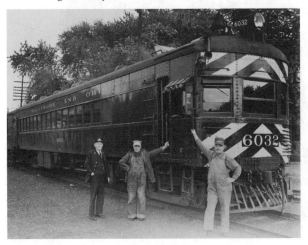

"Doodlebug" on the Baltimore & Ohio. Courtesy B&O Railroad Museum.

— The "Doodlebug" —

Some smaller steam-driven vehicles had appeared on the scene shortly before World War I. The Stanley Brothers, builders of the Stanley Steamer automobile, constructed a few single-unit "steam cars" for the Canadian National in 1922. The Boston & Maine also acquired a few. The Milwaukee Road experimented with some in the 1920s. The steam car was awkward and not as efficient as expected.

There was some experimentation with gasoline motor cars at the turn of the century. General Electric built a gasoline-electric vehicle prior to World War I. Credit goes to the Chicago, Burlington, & Quincy for creating the first practical "doodlebug." In 1922, the CB&Q put a bus-type compartment atop a Mack Truck chassis. The CB&Q eventually put 50 "doodlebugs" into service. During the early 1920s, the trolley car maker J. G. Brill sold a bus-type version to some railroads. At the same time, General Electric improved their gas-electric unit car for sale to railroads. General Motors (GM) produced a stronger version in 1926. In 1928, Westinghouse produced a yet more powerful diesel-electric version.

In 1929, the Chicago Great Western ran their "doodlebug" *Blue Bird* between Minneapolis, St. Paul, and Rochester, Minnesota. The *Blue Bird* had a "Pullman Section" aboard for invalids who traveled back and forth to the Mayo Clinic. The *Blue Bird* was a GM product.

Train load shipment.

President Franklin D. Roosevelt leaves the Union Pacific M-10000 after viewing its interior at Union Station, Washington, D.C. Courtesy Union Pacific.

Union Pacific Gas-Electric at Kearney, Nebraska, 1955. Courtesy Railroad Avenue Enterprises.

By 1930, some estimate there were about 1,000 "doodle-bugs" in revenue service throughout the United States. The Canadian National's C. E. "Ned" Brooks produced 14 diesel-electric cars to compete with busses on branch lines. Brooks's "doodlebug" gained much publicity with a 2,937-mile trans-continental run in 67 hours!

Even though the "doodlebug" is a colorful aspect of early twentieth-century railroading, and did compete to some degree with bus service, most were underpowered. They were also noisy and tended to sway as well as rattle quite a lot. Their interior was plain and almost uncomfortable. They were, how-ever, much more efficient than a steam locomotive and stan-dard passenger coaches on branchline service. In spite of their efficiencies, by 1929, railroads ordered only 132 from man-ufacturers. Only 11 were on order in 1933. As railroads de-creased 15,000 miles of branchline passenger service in the 1930s, the "doodlebug" need dried up.

— The Streamliners —

The "doodlebug," however, did inspire the lightweight, ar-ticulated streamliner of the Depression era. An aeronautical engineer, W. B. Stout, used lightweight materials and airplane design to fashion a 60-foot, 12½-ton railcar. In September 1932, his "Rail Plane" tested successfully and reached a speed of 90 miles per hour. This Pullman-sponsored vehicle went into service on the Gulf, Mobile, and Northern Railroad.

W. Averall Harriman, Chairman of the Board and Presi-dent of the Union Pacific Railroad, followed the "Rail Plane" progress. In 1933, Harriman assembled a team of Stout's, U.P.'s, and Pullman's engineering staff to produce a new type of train. He wanted a high-speed, articulated (two cars ride on and share the same 4-wheel truck), multi-car train for mainline service. In May 1933, UP placed an order for a three-car version of "Today's Train of Tomorrow."

— M-10000 —

Progress in lighter-weight, more powerful diesel engines and stronger traction motors by the early 1930s made Har-riman's dream possible. The UP's M-10000, as it was called, had a 600 horsepower distillate engine. The three-car body was 200 feet long, weighed a mere 85 tons, and was made of a special aluminum alloy. It rode the rails with a 9½-inch un-derside clearance and was 3 feet lower in height than a stan-dard train. The first car contained the engineer's controls, diesel engine, generator, traction motors, and a baggage com-partment. The last car was a lounge with snacks available.

In February 1934, the M-10000, better known as the *City of Salina* in revenue service, began a 22-state tour. President Franklin Delano Roosevelt visited the train in Washington, D.C. It then traveled to Pittsburgh, Omaha, and throughout California and the Pacific Northwest. Over 1.2 million people walked through the train and received an aluminum alloy coin to commemorate their visit.

Unlike the box-like "doodlebug," the *City of Salina,* with its brown and yellow casing and with a slight hump in the roof of the engineer's cab, looked more like a "caterpillar on wheels." UP workers often referred to it as "The Little Zip." In tests, the train reached a speed of well over 90 miles per

hour. Even before tests were completed, Harriman ordered larger streamliners with sleepers. They were named after the cities they serviced: *City of Portland, City of Los Angeles, City of San Francisco,* and the *City of Denver.* UP's largest consisted of ten cars and two engines. The Pullman Company produced one other streamliner, the *Green Diamond,* for the Illinois Cen-tral in 1936. This three-car version was made of steel instead of aluminum and contained complete kitchen facilities.

— The *Zephyr* —

Almost simultaneously with the Union Pacific's order, Ralph Budd, president of the Chicago Burlington & Quincy, sought a similar new train design. The CB&Q turned to a rel-atively new Philadelphia firm instead of Pullman to build the new train. The new company was formed in 1929, when an auto parts manufacturer, Edward G. Budd (no relation to Ralph Budd), joined forces with the French Michelin Com-pany to build motor rail cars. Some of their early products used pneumatic rubber tires with flanges to give a quieter and smoother ride. The vehicles, however, were unstable and tended to derail easily. In 1933, the Budd Company devel-oped an all-stainless-steel body, articulated three-car train powered by a 600 horsepower diesel engine.

The CB&Q's president, Ralph Budd, liked the sleek design and rounded nose with a scoop bottom. He named it the *Zephyr* in honor of the west wind of Greek mythology. The *Zephyr* was 196 feet long and could carry 72 passengers. The third or last car was a buffet and lounge. The train was an immediate suc-cess. The UP M-10000 gained fame by a multi-state tour, but Ralph Budd had another approach to publicity.

On May 26, 1934, the *Zephyr* left Denver at 5:05 A.M. and reached Chicago at 7:10 P.M. the same day. The train aver-aged a speed of over 77 miles an hour, with a fuel cost of un-der $15.00! The *Zephyr* became an immediate news story as it pulled into the Chicago World's Fair that very evening.

The spectacular Denver to Chicago trip, however, began with some irony. As the train was made ready, an armature bearing broke. The Union Pacific hurriedly shared a replace-ment bearing so that its competitor could make the historic run. When the technicians went to start the engine again, just before leaving, the electric starting cable was cut in two by accident. A most loyal Electro-Motive employee, Roy Baer, held both ends together so the train could get underway. The employee suffered burns in the process.

The *Pioneer Zephyr,* as it became known in service, soon be-came a movie star. Hollywood filmed *The Silver Streak* fea-turing the *Zephyr* doing heroic deeds for humanity. Scenes showed the engine and the plush passenger accommodations, as well as the train running at top speed. The entire country could "ride the *Zephyr*" at their local theater! The CB&Q or-dered more *Zephyr*s to serve the Twin Cities.

— *Rebel, Flying Yankee,* and *Royal Blue* —

The CB&Q *Zephyr* made the Budd Company a worthy competitor with Pullman in the 1930s. While both were de-signing new cars, the Goodyear-Zeppelin (blimp manufac-turer) joined with American Car and Foundry to produce a

1934. The first *Zephyr*. Courtesy BNSF.

Union Pacific Streamline M-10000. Courtesy Union Pacific.

Air-conditioned dining car, 1930s. The finest china, linens, and silverware. Courtesy Canadian National. #40561.

less luxurious version for the Gulf, Mobile, & Railroad. They produced a three-car non-articulated version with a compartment to carry the mail. The G, M, & N *Rebel* was both practical and economical to run.

Other railroads began to order streamliners. The Boston & Maine ran the *Flying Yankee* between Boston and Bangor, Maine. The Baltimore & Ohio began operation of its *Royal Blue* streamliner between Jersey City and Washington, D.C., in 1935. The New Haven *Comet* proved a success even though it was used on a local schedule.

The metamorphosis from the ugly "doodlebug" into the attractive, sleek streamliner served its purpose. The American public turned its attention again to the railroad. These new trains convinced the public once again to leave their cars at home and to travel by rail. Some of the "Zephyrs" and "Cities" actually had ridership waiting lists weeks long. Along with speed and styling, the streamliner had another most important feature: air conditioning.

— Air Conditioning —

Given the refrigeration technology of the time, the rail car was the only conveyance that could carry an air-conditioning unit. Travelers during the 1930s would much rather ride distances in air-conditioned comfort than swelter in a dust-filled car, bus, or airplane. For the railroads, air conditioning and closed windows solved the problem of a cinder occasionally entering a car. There is no doubt that air conditioning was a large factor in retaining ridership and in competing with the new forms of transportation.

Job A. Barry of Philadelphia designed and patented the first air-conditioned railroad car in 1855. While he never built the ice flow system, his ideas came of age in the early twentieth century. Just prior to World War I, the Santa Fe Railroad experimented with a water-spray-over-ice system in its dining cars. It proved awkward and did not substantially decrease the

temperature in the car. The Pullman Company also made an early attempt. In 1913, they asked Willis Carrier to design a cooling system for their cars. Given the means at hand, Carrier could not put together a satisfactory system. In 1927, Pullman tried a mechanical system, and did succeed in 1929 by blowing air over blocks of ice housed under the car.

That same summer, 1929, Carrier outfitted a Baltimore & Ohio coach with an experimental system. With its preliminary success the B&O had him install the device on its diner, the *Martha Washington.* The B&O, however, hired the York Ice Machine Company to install air conditioning devices in the other cars. Its *Columbian* became the first completely air-conditioned train.

Other railroads followed suit. The Santa Fe contracted for air conditioning in all of its diners in 1932. Even smaller lines, such as the Missouri-Kansas-Texas, installed air conditioning as soon as possible. Passengers would even take a longer route between cities if they could ride on air-conditioned trains. Records indicate that the Chesapeake & Ohio's passenger list immediately increased by 25 percent when it installed air conditioning. By 1932, eight different companies manufactured air conditioning systems for the railroads.

The Pullman Company also saw air conditioning as a boon for its business. In 1935, it began a drive to air condition its cars. By the end of 1936, Pullman owned 2,320 of the 5,800 air-conditioned cars in the United States. By 1940, there were over 12,000 air-conditioned cars in service.

There were three principal forms of railroad air conditioning. Many roads circulated air over 4,000-plus pounds of ice stored under the car. There were 3,900 of this type in use by 1939. Other railroads, for example the Santa Fe, used steam jets to turn a compressor-refrigeration unit. This device was bulky and consumed a large amount of steam. It was phased out when the diesel locomotive came into common use. The Pullman Company drove its compressor by the car's axle-

Chapter 13.

wheel rotation. It had an electric motor and outside hook-up should the car remain in one place for any length of time. Whatever the system, air conditioning helped the railroads compete with alternate modes of transportation. Air conditioning made the railroad passenger even more of a spectator to nature separated yet another level from the environment passing swiftly on the other side of the window.

From the 1939 New York Central
20th Century Limited dinner menu.

THE NEW 20TH CENTURY DINNER
$1.75
Chilled Celery Hearts
Spiced Pear   Radishes Rosette
Pimiento Olives   Ripe Olives

Pot-Au-Feu-Fermiere
Consomme Julienne or en Gelee
Clam Bouillon, Hot   Clam Juice Cocktail
Chilled Tomato Juice   Two-Tone Cocktail
Fresh Fruit Cup
Canape of Anchovy-Shrimp
Fresh Shrimp Cocktail Lorenzo

Broiled Lake Trout, Maitre d'Hotel
New Brussels Sprouts with Crumbs, Julienne Potatoes

Poached Eggs Benedict on Peanut Canape,
New Beets Fermiere, Argentine Potatoes

Planked Spring Lamb Steak, 20th Century,
Carrots and Peas

Broiled Shrewsbury Squab, Guava Jelly,
Timbale of Wild Rice,
Creamed Wax Beans, O'Brien Potatoes

Roast Prime Ribs of Beef, Au Jus
New Brussels Sprouts Polonaise, Lyonnaise Potatoes

LOBSTER NEWBURG, 20TH CENTURY,
New Wax Beans Fermiere, Julienne Potatoes
Served on this dinner $2.25

Romaine, Orange, and Avocado, N.Y.C. Dressing

Peanut Muffins   Assorted Rolls
Lemon Raisin Sticks

Individual Lemon Cream Pie
Plum Pudding, 20th Century Sauce
French Pancakes with Orange Marmalade
Hot Chocolate Fudge Sundae
N.Y.C. Baked Apple with Cream
Grape Fruit on Ice, Half
or
Cream Cheese with Toasted Rye Bread, Wild Grape Jelly
Roquefort, Camembert or Liederkranz Cheese
with Toasted Biscuits

Tea   Individual Milk   N.Y.C. Special Coffee

Guests will please write on check each item desired.

— The Dining Car —

Air conditioning was most important in the diner, and the diner, along with the lounge, was any railroad's showcase to its passengers. Weighing up to 90 tons, and measuring 80 feet in length, the diner was often the heaviest and longest car on the train. Depending on the degree of luxury, most diners seated 36 to over 40 passengers at a time. The usual arrangement placed four to a table on one side across from two at a table on the other An 8 x 30-foot kitchen could prepare up to 100 meals for one series of seatings. A full crew consisted of six waiters, three cooks, a steward, and a dishwasher.

On many first-class or crack passenger trains, the porter announced dinner seatings with musical chimes. Only the finest meals appeared on the tables covered with the very best silverware. Each railroad designed and labeled plates of the finest china available. Every passenger could look forward to a culinary delight and top service in the diner. During the 1920s, railroads served about 60,000 meals a day at a loss of $9 million per year. If a railroad did make a profit on dining, it was marginal. While buffet cars and soda fountain cars also attracted the public, there is much truth to the lyric that "nothing's finer than dinner in the diner."

— The Five-Minute Egg —

In 1926, a gentleman ordered a three-minute boiled egg on the Southern Pacific's *Overland Limited*. He explained that any boiling over three minutes spoiled the egg for him. The steward asked him where he lived. The gentleman answered San Francisco. The steward at that point underlined the *three-minute egg* on the order card.

The steward turned the order in to the chef. Three minutes went by . . . then four. The gentleman summoned the steward and began to complain that his egg was taking too long! After another minute the steward appeared with the egg. The gentleman growled that he did not want the egg, since it was boiled beyond the three minutes, and it was not edible.

The steward explained to the gentleman that when he ordered the egg, the *Overland Limited* was approaching an elevation of 7,018 feet. The train was now descending to about 6,800 feet. The steward continued by reminding the gentleman that he lived in San Francisco, at sea level, where water boils at 212 degrees Fahrenheit. When he ordered the egg, the train was at a higher elevation where the atmosphere is much thinner, and water boils at 199 degrees. Therefore, it takes longer here to boil an egg in the mountains to give it the same consistency of cooking it three minutes in San Francisco. Therefore, his three-minute egg took five minutes to cook at the mountain summit on the *Overland Limited*.

118

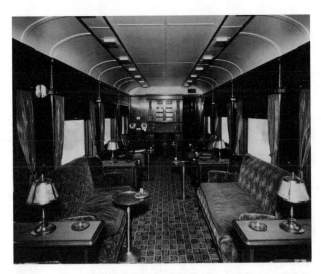

Interior of a lounge-library car in 1930s. Courtesy Canadian National. #42418.

— The Lounge Car —

The lounge car was another attraction. An attendant sold sandwiches, snacks, and various beverages. After Prohibition, wines, cocktails, and beer appeared on the card. The seats were more comfortable in the lounge car and were placed to encourage conversation. On longer distance trains the entire car served as a lounge facility. On shorter or one-night runs, it could be part lounge with one or two bedroom compartments. During the late 1920s and the 1930s, the lounge car featured a radio. The car would often offer a particular decor, art, and photos in tune with the particular railroad's service area. In short, the lounge car had a comfortable, club-like atmosphere.

Most long-distance trains ended with an observation car. The interior had comfortable chairs and sometimes a lounge-type service. Until the mid-1930s, the car had an open observation platform at the rear. Even though there is no record of anyone falling from it while the train was in motion, railroads began to adopt a closed-end version prior to World War II. Railroads displayed their heralds and/or the train's name on a "drumhead" just above the coupler.

— Sleepers —

No matter which overnight train or railroad, Pullman always represented the best of "Sleep in Safety and Comfort." During the 1920s, approximately 100,000 people slept every night and everywhere across the nation in a Pullman. The company kept to its open section cars as long as possible, but it had to give in to constructing private accommodations during the streamline era. Competition from Budd forced them into it. As the company built new sleepers, the older open-section Pullmans became "tourist cars" and were less expensive to ride.

In 1927, Pullman issued its first all-private-rooms sleeping car. It consisted of 14 rooms of 33 square feet. Each room had its own toilet and washstand. The fare was 25 percent above the regular train ticket. The company produced 45 of these "Night Series" cars. In 1933, it remodeled two baggage cars into bilevel duplex sleepers. The 16 compartments were on one side of the car and placed alternately at a three-step difference. They were not financially successful.

In June 1937, Pullman finished a new model consisting of eighteen separate accommodations. The roomettes had a washstand, toilet, and beds that folded down from the wall and ceiling. The company built 68 of these new cars and remodeled over 300 others to this new configuration before World War II. The roomettes were more comfortable because they were on one level. The main inconvenience was that the occupant had to lift the bed in order to use the toilet at night.

Pullman also experimented with lighter-weight sleepers in the 1930s. In 1933, the company made the *G. M. Pullman* which came close to being an all-aluminum car. Its underframe, roof, and hardware, as well as the outer shell was of the lightweight metal. In 1936, Pullman produced two cars, the *Advance* and the *Forward,* which were joined together and made of lighter Cor-Ten steel. Each car weighed 55 tons and had eight open sections, two compartments, and two double bedrooms.

During the 1930s, the Pullman Company operated a pool of 9,000 sleeping cars. This large number permitted the company to move them from one place to another to accommodate peak traffic situations. For example, more were needed on the New York and Chicago to Miami runs during January and February. During summers, numbers increased to New England. Most were painted "Pullman Green" and some claim the dark color hid dirt and grime. It also did not complement or favor most railroads' color schemes. There were some exceptions. Those riding on the Pennsylvania Railroad were Tuscan red. The Southern's *Crescent* were the crack train's gold and green, and the Milwaukee Road had orange and maroon Pullmans in their consists or line of cars.

If the sleeping car arrived at its destination in early morning, the company often permitted guests to sleep until a reasonable hour before leaving the car. Passengers could also board the train earlier, if it left the station during the wee hours of the morning. Sometimes this was not possible. Sometimes one hundred sleepers would arrive at the New York Central Grand Central Station in New York during the early morning. The porter then had to make certain the car was empty before moving it to make room for other arriving Pullmans. Regardless, passengers often enjoyed their overnight ride in the "hotel on wheels."

Some trains and railroading in general were celebrated in song. The Delaware, Lackawanna, & Western is laughed at in "Where do you work-a John?" "Tuxedo Junction" is where everyone met in Birmingham. Of course, the "Chattanooga Choo Choo" glorified the diner. Glenn Miller's version received the first "gold record" in history after selling over six million discs. Miller and his band featured the song in a movie, *Sun Valley Serenade,* starring Sonja Henie and John Payne. The Union Pacific built the Sun Valley winter resort in Idaho to stimulate ridership during what would normally be off-season months. UP technicians and engineers built a modern-design ski lift on the slopes as an added attraction.

1937 Pullman magazine advertisement.

In spite of their financial difficulties and competition from car, bus, and plane, passenger railroads were still at the forefront of American life.

Baths, barbers, and hairdressers were available on most luxury trains. Ladies-in-waiting helped women, and valets assisted men in dressing for dinner. A businessperson could dictate a letter to the on-board secretary, and some railroads, particularly the Union Pacific, had crews of registered nurses as hostesses. During the 1920s, lounge cars included libraries and writing desks, and a rear section could even be a "solarium." By the late 1930s a few trains bragged of having a radio in each master bedroom. Of course, the Pullman porter attended to every need. He often brought a passenger a last bucket of ice for a "nightcap."

Speed was also important. The Milwaukee Road's *Hiawathas* cruised between Chicago and the railroad's namesake city at well over 90 miles per hour. Otto Kuhler designed a distinctive shroud to streamline its Hiawatha Hudsons. The Milwaukee's F-7 version had 84-inch driving wheels which made speed easy. This Hudson earned its title, *The Queen of Steam.* In January 1935, the Chicago & North Western began its *400 Service* between Chicago and the Minneapolis. These trains averaged over 60 miles per hour, an almost 6½-hour schedule. By 1939, the CNW used diesels to pull a new, streamlined *400.*

— Luxury Trains —

Most railroads, including some short lines, had at least one crack passenger train as its "showtrain" to the public. This train would have the best equipment, best schedule, and the most attentive and proud staff. The roads named the trains either according to their herald or region of the country they traveled through. While it is impossible to name all of them, the listing of some will give an example from the era. A few of the names survived into the Amtrak period.

Railroad	Best or Crack Train
Atlantic Coast Line	*Florida Special, Silver Meteor Champion*
Baltimore & Ohio	*National Limited, Capitol Limited Royal Blue*
Boston & Maine	*The Gull*
Canadian National	*The Super Continental*
Canadian Pacific	*The Canadian*
Central of Georgia	*Nancy Hooks, Man O'War*
Central of New Jersey	*Blue Comet, Bullet*
Central Vermont	*Washington*
Chesapeake & Ohio	*George Washington*
Chicago & North Western	*400 Service*
Chicago, Burlington, & Quincy	*Denver Zephyr, California Zephyr, Twin Cities Zephyr*

Railroad	Best or Crack Train
Chicago, Rock Island, and Pacific	*Denver Zephyr Golden State Limited, Rockets*
Delaware, Lackawanna, & Western	*The Phoebe Snow*
Denver & Rio Grande	*The San Juan*
Erie	*Erie Limited*
Florida East Coast	*Havana Limited*
Great Northern	*The Empire Builder*
Gulf, Mobile, & Northern	*The Rebel*
Gulf, Mobile, & Ohio	*Abraham Lincoln, Ann Rutledge*
Illinois Central	*Panama Limited, City of Miami*
Kansas City Southern	*Southern Belle*
Lehigh Valley	*The Black Diamond*
Lackawanna	*Phoebe Snow*
Milwaukee Road	*Olympian, Olympian Hiawatha*
Missouri Pacific	*Eagle*
Monon	*Thoroughbred*
New York Central	*20th Century Limited, Commodore Vanderbilt, Empire State Express, James Whitcomb Riley*
New York, New Haven, & Hartford	*Merchants Limited, Yankee Clipper, Colonial*
Norfolk & Western	*Powhatan Arrow*
Northern Pacific	*North Coast Limited*
Pennsylvania	*Broadway Limited, The General, Spirit of St. Louis, The Congressional Crusader, Wall Street*
Reading	
St. Louis & San Francisco (Frisco)	*Texas Special, Meteor*
Santa Fe	*Chief, Super Chief*
Seaboard Air Line	*Orange Blossom Special*
Soo Line	*Winnipeger*
Southern	*Crescent*
Southern Pacific	*Sunset Limited, Golden State, Daylight*
Union Pacific	*Overland Limited, City of Los Angeles, City of San Francisco, The Portland Rose*
Wabash	*Blue Bird*
Western Pacific	*California Zephyr*

(Some name trains continued their journey on more than one railroad company.)

Two Milwaukee Road Hudson locomotives or "The Queens of Steam." The art-deco design was by Otto Kuhler. Courtesy Sioux City Public Museum.

Streamlined *Twentieth Century Limited*. Courtesy California State Railroad Museum. #26062.

The late-1930s streamlined *Broadway Limited*. Courtesy Railroad Museum of Pennsylvania.

Southern Pacific *Daylight* streamlined train running through Santa Susanna pass, California. Courtesy California State Railroad Museum. #26061.

— The *Twentieth Century* and the *Broadway* —

Perhaps the most famous luxury service was on the *Broadway* and *Twentieth Century Limited*s. Both railroads had been in perpetual rivalry since after the Civil War, and the 1920s and the Depression gave it every reason to become even more intense. When the *Twentieth Century* rolled out a "red carpet" for people to walk on to approach the train, the *Broadway*

announced its boarding with a bugle call at the doorway of Penn Station's Savarin Restaurant. The bugler sounded again at the train's gate, and Redcaps joined together and chorused, "*Broadway Limited* leaving at 5 P.M. from track twelve." Both trains raced to and from their respective stations in New York and Chicago.

Both railroads introduced new, streamlined equipment on the same day, June 15, 1938. Raymond Loewy designed the *Broadway,* and Henry Dreyfus the *Twentieth Century.* The

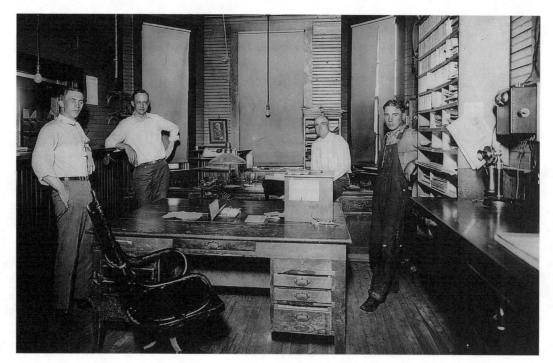

Typical railroad station interior at bay window. At Ihlen, Minnesota, in the mid-1920s on the Great Northern Railway. Shades drawn to permit use of flash photo. Photo of James J. Hill on wall. Courtesy Curtis Burge.

Broadway's sleeping cars consisted of master bedrooms, drawing rooms, compartments, double bedrooms, and roomettes. The open-section sleeper was eliminated. It had a two-car diner at the train's center, and refreshments were available in both lounge and observation cars. The colors were café-au-lait, burgundy, and gold. Table linens were a light tan. The lounge car had sofas and large murals of Chicago and New York scenes on the walls. Raymond Loewy also designed a streamlined K-4 Pacific and GG1 electrics which pulled the *Broadway Limited.*

Dreyfus gave the *Twentieth Century's* Hudson locomotive a more rounded, bullet-shaped nose. The sleeping compartments were also just as luxurious and private. Along with the same service, the observation car had models of famous New York Central landmarks for decoration. The dining car dimmed its lights after dinner, and rust-colored linens were placed on tables to create another lounge. Exterior colors were two tones of gray set off with light blue and silver stripes. Overall, the *Twentieth Century* carried more passengers than the *Broadway.* Sometimes it ran in multiple trains on the same schedule, as many as four or five at one time!

Hollywood made both trains nationally famous. In 1934, Ben Hecht's play *20th Century* was made into a movie starring John Barrymore and Carole Lombard. Most of the drama took place in compartments and the lounge car. In 1941, Hal Roach Studios, in cooperation with the Pennsylvania Railroad, released a light comedy, *The Broadway Limited,* starring Marjorie Woodworth and Dennis O'Keefe. Although the *Broadway's* drama did not receive the best reviews, the movie had many more train scenes to show off the streamliner's equipment. There is no doubt that these movies increased the prestige of both trains.

— Chicago Stations —

With 20 different railroads entering Chicago, *Broadway* and *Twentieth Century* passengers could choose a number of trains to continue their journey. Since there were seven different stations in the "Windy City," they may have had to travel from one to another. Even though there were some exceptions, passenger trains pulled into the following stations:

Union Station
(Canal and Jackson Streets)
Pennsylvania RR
Burlington Route
Gulf, Mobile, & Ohio
Milwaukee Road

C&NW Terminal
(½ mi. from Union Station)
Chicago & Northwestern

Grand Central Station
(½ mi. from Union Station)
Baltimore & Ohio
Chicago Great Western
Soo Line

Engelwood Station
(3 mi. from Union Station)
Pennsylvania RR
New York Central
Nickel Plate Road
Rock Island

Central Station
(1.6 mi. from Union Station)
Illinois Central
Michigan Central
South Shore Line

Dearborn Station
(1 mi. from Union Station)
Chicago & Eastern Illinois
Erie
Grand Trunk
Monon
Santa Fe
Wabash

La Salle Street Station
(.6 mi. from Union Station)
New York Central
Nickel Plate Road
Rock Island

The Parmalee Transfer System furnished rides between the stations. The company had a modest beginning in the nineteenth century, but in 1903, Frank Parmalee sold out to a syndicate headed by Marshall Field and John J. Mitchell, among others. In 1921, the Parmalee Company used only motorized vehicles.

The other east–west transfer point, St. Louis, did not have this problem. The St. Louis Union Station accommodated all of its 18 railroads on 32 tracks under an enormous train shed. Whether in Chicago or St. Louis, many passengers still had to change trains. Only a few Pullmans crossed the Mississippi River.

— Mary Ann's Story —

The first week of September 1934, my father put me on board a Pullman railway car. It was evening and we were at Union Station, Los Angeles, California. I was nine years old.

My mother had died that winter, and my father had made the very difficult decision to send me to Iowa to live with his parents in the little town of Bronson. He had found it impossible to financially maintain a household and to take care of me. It was very hard for me to leave my father after having lost my mother such a short time before.

On the trip, people would ask where I was going. My answer would always be "back East" as this was the reference I'd heard adults in California use when speaking of any place east of the Rocky Mountains. When people would persist and ask "Where back East?" I'd always answer "Oh, Iowa," being certain they had never heard of the place.

I don't remember how many days it took to get from Los Angeles to Sioux City. I do remember it was hot. The windows had to be open, and at times smoke from the coal-fired locomotive would blow in the window. The smoke was sooty and occasionally cinders blew our way.

The conductor was the man in charge. In my case he was in charge of me, making sure I was not wandering throughout the train. He would take me to the dining car at the correct times. I did not make it easy for him. When we arrived in Salt Lake City, Utah, we had a layover. I thought it would be a good thing to check out the big station. I remember buying a souvenir railroad lantern filled with candy. Then I decided to find the restroom before I reboarded the train. When I was ready to leave, the door of the stall wouldn't open. In the meantime, the conductor missed me and after looking in the station he asked one of the women in my car that knew me to check in the restroom. I don't know how they got me out and back on board, but I'd be willing to bet that the conductor was very upset with me. I'm sure he must have told me in no uncertain terms not to get off the train again.

Every Pullman car had a porter. It was his responsibility to make up the berths at night and fold them up in the

morning. It's so interesting to watch him at night, pulling the top berth down where it was stored above the seats over the windows during the day. He had to fasten curtains in front of each berth for privacy. All the bedding was stored during the day in the upper berth.

I had to change trains in Omaha, Nebraska, on the last night of my journey. The conductor took my hand and my suitcase and put me aboard a Pullman sleeper that would take me to Sioux City, Iowa. It was late in the evening, and he put me in a little room that had benches on each side. The porter occupied this room when he wasn't busy. I was tired, and there was no one around so I went looking for a bed. I crawled into the first unoccupied berth. It had a reading light, and seemed much newer and fancier than the one I had occupied before. But it wasn't long before the conductor found me and hustled me back to the little room with the benches, so I just curled up and went to sleep.

I must have looked a sight when I got off the train in Sioux City. That last morning I had put on my best dress; it was white! I wanted to look my very best when I met my family. It was late when I arrived in Sioux City and my white dress was sooty after wearing it all day and wrinkled after sleeping in it half the night. Most of the adults in my extended family were there to greet me, and I was so happy to see them all.

— Tickets and Fares —

Most tickets were purchased at windows in the station. Tickets could be purchased on the train from the conductor, but with an extra charge. Most people rode in the coach which was the cheapest fare.

Pullman tickets included coach fare plus the particular accommodation. People could purchase a Pullman berth or get an upgrade from the Pullman conductor on the train as available.

In 1929, a ride from Chicago to Omaha on the Rock Island Railroad cost $3.00 in coach. A Pullman lower berth was $4.50 and $3.60 for an upper. A compartment went for $12.75, and a drawing room cost $16.50. The coach fare between Chicago and New York on the Pennsylvania Railroad in 1932 was $32.70. An upper berth in a Pullman was an additional $7.20 and the lower $9.00. A compartment was another $25.50 and the drawing room $31.50. Travel on the *Broadway Limited* required a special service charge of an additional $10.00.

— Hobos —

It is an irony that hobos riding freights could travel across the country without worrying about a transfer. As far as any statistics can tell, there were about ½ million riding the rails during the Great Depression. Women and girls now rode dur-

MAJOR RAIL ROUTES, 1935

(241,822 miles of U.S. track)

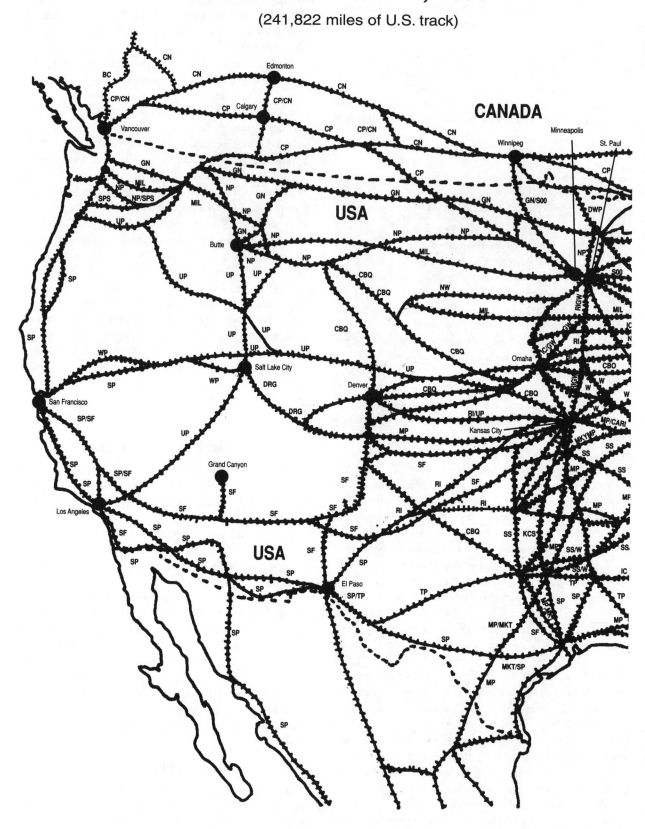

ACL	Atlantic Coast Line
BO	Baltimore & Ohio
BA	Bangor & Aroostook
BC	British Columbia
BM	Boston & Maine
CN	Canadian National
CP	Canadian Pacific
CO	Chesapeake & Ohio
CBQ	Chicago, Burlington, & Quincy
CEI	Chicago, Eastern Illinois
GW	Great Western
GN	Great Northern
CNW	Chicago & North Western
DH	Delaware & Hudson
DRG	Denver & Rio Grande
DWP	Duluth, Winnipeg, & Pacific
E	Erie
FEC	Florida East Coast
GT	Grand Trunk
IC	Illinois Central
LN	Louisville & Nashville
LV	Lehigh Valley
MC	Maine Central
MIL	Milwaukee Road
MP	Missouri Pacific
MKT	Missouri-Kansas-Texas
MO	Mobile & Ohio
NJC	New Jersey Central
NYC	New York Central
NW	Norfolk & Western
NP	Northern Pacific
PA	Pennsylvania
RI	Rock Island
SF	Santa Fe (Atchison, Topeka, & Santa Fe)
SAL	Seaboard Air Line
SOO	SOO
SOU	Southern
SS	South Shore
SPS	Spokane, Portland, & Seattle
TP	Texas & Pacific
UP	Union Pacific
W	Wabash
WP	Western Pacific

ing the 1930s. Many were subject to sexual harrassment, while others offered "favors" to conductors to get a more comfortable, free ride. The famous "Boxcar Bertha" was probably one of the most liberated women of her time. She did whatever

Hobo riding a boxcar. Sketch by Dee Dee Tymkowicz.

she wanted, whenever she wanted. Some say that a number of women take credit for the name "Boxcar Bertha." All in all, there were few women hobos.

Even though hobos could travel freights non-stop through or around Chicago, most did not. In fact, during the 1920s, the former hobo, Ben Reitman, M.D., started a genuine "hobo college" in the Windy City. He offered courses in everything from philosophy to medicine. At the end of the instructional program, certificates were given to participants. The movement caught on, and hobo colleges were started in several other major railroad junction cities.

During the 1920s and 1930s, many railroads waged all-out war against the hobos. Destruction of property rather than theft was the problem. Their police, known as Bulls or Cinder Dicks, beat hobos and even threw them from moving trains. The familiar hobo "flipping a train" disappeared after 1940. With the economy picking up prior to World War II, everyone had a "job to do." It was everyone's patriotic duty to work after Pearl Harbor in 1941!

— Reviving Business —

The railroads developed some new services to weather the bad economy. In 1933, the Baltimore & Ohio started the "Cooperative Traffic Program." B&O employees went about their communities encouraging merchants and factories to use their rails. It also began a "Less than Carload" service. A shipper could send small quantities by the B&O at a reduced rate. Of course, passenger ridership increased.

The Erie Railroad revised their schedules for more convenient on-line stops between New York and Chicago. It reduced coach fares, started an at-the-seat lunch service, and acted as its own tourist agency. It arranged vacation trips using all transportation modes — bus, boat, or airplane.

Other railroads tried different ideas. The Chicago, Burlington, & Quincy ran its own poultry farm to furnish the freshest chickens and eggs in its diners. It also operated bus service between branch-line cities. The Chicago & North Western and Milwaukee Road did the same. The Pennsylvania Railroad purchased interest in an airline. Its Transcontinental & Western Air, Inc., offered 36-hour service from coast to coast. (Transcontinental later became Trans World Airlines.) The Pennsylvania also linked with Associated British Airways for tours of England. Along with other railroads, by 1935 it offered free pick-up and delivery from homes or businesses for Less-than-Carload shipments.

Some railroads operated "economy trains." In 1934, the Union Pacific began its Chicago–Los Angeles *Challenger* service. The *Challenger* was an all-coach train. By 1938, busses were capturing 60 cents on every dollar of intercity passengers. At that point the Santa Fe began its all-coach *El Capitan* from Chicago to the Pacific Coast. The idea caught on. The *El Capitan* became a popular train, especially with young people. The atmosphere was informal, and after dinner, the tables were removed to permit dancing until 3 a.m.! It was a great way for young people to meet and to party.

A few months later, the Pennsylvania Railroad began its New York to Chicago all-coach *Trail Blazer* and the New York Central started its all coach *Pacemaker.* These trains kept al-

Chessie images are used with permission of CXS Transporation, Inc.

most as fast a schedule as the more luxurious ones. There were waiting lists for seats. It is quite an irony, but only the crew had berths on these trains.

The Chesapeake & Ohio Railroad started a public relations campaign in the mid 1930s, featuring a cat, Chessie and her kittens. Everyone wanted to sleep "as sound as a kitten" on the C&O line. Chessie's husband, Peake (Chessie-Peake), became a wounded "war hero" during the Second World War. Chessie was originally used to feature the availability of air conditioning on the Chesapeake & Ohio.

As a separate transportation institution, the Pullman Company, and especially the Pullman porters, became the railroads' best friend in the 1920s and 1930s. Whether traveling on the *Twentieth Century Limited* to New York City or the *Corn King*

— "Horses Be Blessed, Too" —

The railroads had to accommodate all types of passenger situations. During the 1930s, a Midwest chapter of a certain men's benevolent society was traveling by train to the Pacific Coast. This chapter was widely known for riding a particular type of all-white horses in parades. In order to do so, they outfitted a railway car to take their horses with them. They modified the car so that it could be attached to a coach, and they could enter it to attend to the animals en route.

The members used such occasions to have a party. During the height of one such festivity — in the wee hours of the morning and somewhere in Utah — one member decided he wanted to ride his horse. He got up, went to the horse car, mounted his steed, and proceeded to ride it the entire length of the coach! When the horse and rider reached the front end, they could not turn around. The horse also refused to walk backwards. Both the horse and the railroad conductor were near panic, and the rider's fellow society members both jeered and cheered him on. Soon the whole train was in an uproar. . . .

At that point the conductor signaled the engineer to stop the train. They conferred as to what to do. They decided to pull the train onto the next siding. They then uncoupled the horse car, and pulled it alongside the front coach where the horse was trapped. They put planks from door to door so the horse could move forward into its own car. With the horse safely in its proper car, the train got underway again, and the rider returned to his fellow chapter members to become the center of unwanted attention the rest of the way to California.

Needless to say, the story spread quickly among conductors, brakemen, and engineers all along the line — and even on other railroads! On the return trip, the conductor locked the doors to the horse car. Anyone wanting to enter had to get his permission, which was not easily granted.

to some rural whistle stop in the Midwest, passengers received the same efficient and courteous service. It was as if the railroads were saying: "The Public Be Blessed. . . ."

— The Pullman Porter —

By 1926, the Pullman Company employed over 9,000 porters; some were grandsons of those hired by George Pullman himself. The porters' duties were now defined even more strictly. Training was comprehensive. After being hired, the future porters underwent 14 days of general instruction, mostly in the rail yard. As a generation earlier, at each stage of instruction, a future porter had to sign on a form that he understood what had been explained to him. If he did not understand, the lesson was repeated.

After the general instruction, he then studied for some particular position. He took lessons in cooking, waiting tables, preparing cars, or the most familiar one of being a car attendant. Every towel was folded exactly the same way throughout the entire Pullman system. The future porter, again, learned everything down to the minutest detail. He had to be able to assemble a section from daytime chair use to sleeping berth in under three minutes. Only then could he enter a six-month probationary period of actually working on a sleeper as an apprentice to two veteran porters.

There are many stories that give an example of the Pullman porters' outstanding service. Reportedly, a diplomat traveling on the *Twentieth Century Limited* gave his trousers to the porter for pressing. The porter left them in the valet car which was switched from the *Century* to another train that night. Upon discovering the change, the porter arranged for the other train, going in the same direction, to catch up and run parallel to the *Century*. A porter then handed the trousers from the lounge window of his train to the *Century*'s porter standing on the observation platform. The next morning the diplomat received his freshly pressed trousers on time and none the wiser. Such remarkable service and cooperation with other railroad employees was all in a day's work for the Pullman porter.

The porter had to work 400 hours or 11,000 miles a month to qualify for overtime. In 1925, the average salary was $720 a year, tips excluded. Tipping, therefore, was important to the porter. There are many accounts to illustrate some passengers' generosity, but probably the best example includes the popular entertainers Bob Hope and Bing Crosby. On one occasion, when traveling on the Union Pacific's *City of Los Angeles*, they tipped three porters $1,300 each! It was their custom to tip the amount of their check — and then some!

Passengers often called the porter "George" no matter what his name really was. According to legend, the custom began when a boy was trying to open a window on a Santa Fe train. His mother stopped him from struggling and said "Let George do it!" The name stuck, and the phrase became a common expression. Some passengers believed the name "George" was out of respect for the company's founder, George Pullman. Some porters, however, resented the expression. A Midwest businessman, George M. Dulany, founded — tongue-in-cheek — the Society for the Prevention of Calling Pullman Porters George. With no dues to pay, Delaney claimed that his Society had over 10,000 members at one point! The practice of calling a porter "George" died out on its own after World War II.

Railroad workers and Pullman porters began a new chapter in U.S. history. Railroad employees were the first in the nation to have collective bargaining, and the Porters' union gained the same rights shortly afterward. They became the models of the labor movement across the nation. These rights were recognized in the Railway Labor Act of 1926.

— Railway Labor Act of 1926 —

During the nineteenth century most Americans were suspicious of or outright against unionization. In fact, the federal government used the Sherman Anti-trust Act of 1890 to

Make-up and rest area of a ladies' lounge in a 1940s "Pullman Style" railroad car. Courtesy Fremont Dinner Train.

prohibit such strike activities as picketing and boycotts. Attitudes changed, however, near the turn of the century. New legislation made it illegal for a railroad company to prevent an employee from joining a union. The Erdman Act of 1898 provided for mediation and for voluntary arbitration during which time current rules and salaries would remain in force. Shortly thereafter the railroad brotherhoods formed the earliest bargaining units. The Brotherhood of Locomotive Fire-

men and Enginemen demanded an 8-hour day which was recognized in the Adamson Act of 1916. In 1914, the Clayton Act gave the courts power to determine whether union activities were lawful or unlawful by means of jury trial.

Labor did receive a setback with the Esch-Cummins Transportation Act of 1920. The Act gave Interstate Commerce Commission the authority to regulate wages and working conditions for all railroads involved in interstate commerce. The

Left to Right: William Green, President of the American Federation of Labor; Asa P. Randolph, President of the Brotherhood of Sleeping Car Porters; and Milton P. Webster, First Vice President of the Brotherhood of Sleeping Car Porters. Courtesy of African American Museum and Library of Oakland.

U.S. attorney general had the power to obtain an injunction to keep trains moving during a strike. He also could prevent picketing. Such authority prevented a strike in 1922. In four years, the labor provisions of the Transportation Act were nullified.

The Railway Labor Act of 1926 ended the application of the Sherman Anti-trust Act to railroad strikes. It guaranteed employees the right to establish their own unions and to engage in collective bargaining through their own duly chosen representatives. The unions could now settle grievances and fight for wage increases and better working conditions. The law also created a mediation board which later evolved into the National Mediation Board to help resolve disputed issues. President Calvin Coolidge signed it into law that May.

The Railway Labor Act divided disputes into major and minor categories. Major disputes concern pay, rules, and working conditions. Minor disputes have to do with the interpretation or application of the previously agreed-upon pay rates, conditions, and rules. The National Mediation Board hears the major disputes. A National Railroad Adjustment Board hears minor disputes. The Adjustment Board consists of 34 members from the railroads, unions, and neutral parties.

In 1934 Congress passed the Norris-LaGuardia Act which specifically gave the unions the right to strike, to picket, and to boycott their employers. In other legislation, the railroads were forbidden to sponsor employee unions over which they would have undue influence. By 1938, Congress passed the Railroad Unemployment Insurance Act which permitted striking employees to collect unemployment benefits. Many of the rights defined in the Railway Labor Act and subsequent laws were extended to other industries in the National Industrial Recovery Act or Wagner Act of 1935.

Unlike other industries, railroad workers had additional bargaining leverage. Former union members headed the Bureau of Locomotive Safety. They could easily declare a particular railroad's locomotives "unsafe" should negotiations become too harsh. Overall, railroad employees fared much better than their counterparts in other industries. Their salaries placed them within the top 1 percent of wage workers of the entire nation.

The Pullman porter had a longer struggle to gain union recognition and justifiable wage increases. The average porter's salary in 1925 was $720 a year at a time when the U.S. Department of Labor established that $2,000 per year was needed to maintain the average family. The porter had to make up the difference in tips.

— Pullman Porters Unionize —

When the United States Railway Administration recommended that porters had a right to organize, the Pullman Company then established its own "Plan of Employee Representation." As a company-sponsored group, it did not have the porters' best interests as its chief goal. One porter, Ashley Totten, urged his fellow porters to form their own organization separate from the Pullman Company. When he was able to convince a few to join, he realized he had neither the time or skills to attract a large following.

Chapter 13.

At that point Totten attended a program at an athletic club where Asa Philip Randolph was the speaker. Randolph was a socialist and publisher of a radical magazine, the *Messenger.* More important to Totten, Randolph had already helped six unions to organize. After the program, Totten asked Randolph to help organize the Pullman porters. Randolph accepted the invitation — even though he knew nothing about railroads. The first organizational meeting of the Brotherhood of Sleeping Car Porters was held in Harlem, New York, in August 1925. The new brotherhood also organized its members' wives into an auxiliary for support by the end of the year.

The brotherhood's first goal was to gain the Pullman Company's recognition. They demanded a 240-hour work month and a salary increase to $150 a month. They also requested a pension plan. To help overcome work fatigue, they wanted a minimum of four hours of sleep on the first overnight of travel and six hours on subsequent nights on longer-distance trains.

As the new union grew in membership, the Pullman Company did what it could to break it. While the company had used spotters to check on employees, it now doubled its efforts. They hired spies to find out about union activities and did what they could to encourage employees to spy on each other during work. Those who reported to the company became known as "stool pigeons," because the porter often sat on a stool at the end of an open-section sleeper at night. At one point the company tried to bribe Randolph to cease his activities. It did not work.

The passing of the National Railway Labor Act of 1926 encouraged the porters in their efforts. Their membership increased and, in 1929, they called for their first national conference. In spite of the Pullman Company's attempts to break the new union, the porters held firm. In 1934, the American Federation of Labor voted to include the brotherhood with full membership. Later that year the Federal Mediation Board granted the organization union status and, by July 1935, it entered into negotiations with the Pullman Company.

The Brotherhood and the Pullman Company signed their first contract on August 25, 1937. The porters received a 100-hour work-month schedule with a salary of $175. They received job protection: no porter could be fired without a fair and im-

— The Diesel-Electric Locomotive —

Pullman service, streamliners, and air conditioning all helped retain passengers in light of competition from cars, busses, and airplanes. One other aid came about during the 1920s and 1930s: the diesel-powered locomotive. Diesel-electric power plants were already in use in "doodlebugs" and in the new streamliners. The problem was developing units which could haul long consists, or train make-up, of currently used standard passenger cars. More than efficiency and cost, the diesel, or more properly, diesel-electric locomotive, would bring about a revolution in the railroad industry.

The diesel engine ran on fuel oil, which in the 1920s and 1930s was readily available and relatively cheap energy. The engine ran a generator which created an electric current. The current passed through a rectifier to electric "traction" motors attached to the locomotive's wheel axles. It is the traction motors which actually provide the direct power to move the train. That power is limited to the size and capacity of the motors and the amount of electricity generated. The traction motors, with the engineer's turning of a switch, could be changed into "generators." In that capacity, they function as a "frictionless brake" to help slow down or stop the train. When they act as generators, their current is changed into heat energy, and the heat is exhausted through the top of the locomotive through a series of radiators and fans.

The entire process is cost effective. Diesel fuel is less bulky and more easily transported than coal. The diesel can travel much further without refueling. It also does not need large quantities of water. It ended ash pits, constant cleaning, and servicing. It completely eliminated the risk of "boiler explosion." The diesel eventually eliminated the fireman's position, and its dynamic braking saved both time and brake shoes.

Although the diesel could not achieve the speed of a fast steamer, it had other schedule advantages. For one, it was ready for service the moment the engine was started; it took up to 2 hours to develop a head of steam on a steam locomotive. Also, it did not require coaling or water during station stops, nor the constant bearing lubrications and inspections. Furthermore, dynamic braking kept better control of the train on a long descent, and it did not have to stop to keep brake shoes from smoldering. By the late 1930s, its exterior looked sleek and was in the style of the modern, streamline era.

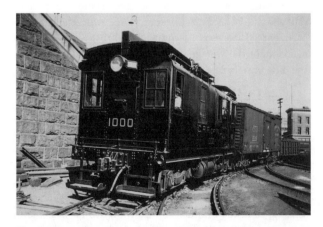

First long-standing diesel-electric switching locomotive. Central Railroad of New Jersey, #1000. Courtesy B&O Railroad Museum.

partial hearing. If a porter would be prevented from working during the hearing, the company had to reimburse him. In 1938, the Brotherhood of Redcaps was formed. Canadian porters, who were employed directly by the individual railways, organized in 1946. The Brotherhood of Sleeping Car Porters lasted longer than the Pullman Company itself. In 1978, it merged with the Brotherhood of Railway and Airline Clerks.

Diesel - Electric Locomotive

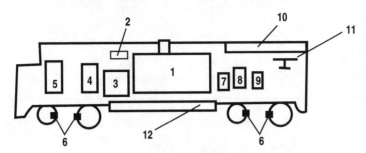

1. Diesel Engine (Prime Mover)
2. Rectifier
3. Alternator
4. Cooling Blower
5. Engineer's Controls
6. Traction Motors
7. Oil Reservoir — Lubricator
8. Air Filters
9. Air Pump (compressor)
10. Radiator
11. Fan
12. Fuel Tank

The Diesel-Electric Locomotive

Diesel-electric or diesel locomotives have a large diesel engine or "prime mover" which turns a generator. The current generated is fed through a rectifier to electric motors attached to the axle of the locomotive wheels. Older models produce DC or direct current. More recent diesel locomotives have alternators which produce alternating or AC current. The rectifier changes AC current to DC.

Diesels have a blower which cools the prime mover and generator. They also have a compressor for the air brake system. Diesel locomotive motors can produce "dynamic braking." The traction motors can be changed into an electric braking unit. When braking, the motor becomes a "generator." The electricity produced in the process is changed into heat energy which is released through a radiator and fan unit.

The axles and motors are usually classified by alphabet letters. A means that one axle, has a traction motor, B indicates that two axles have motors, and C means that three do. Almost all diesel locomotives today have motors attached to each axle. Older models may have a non-motored axles.

— Early Diesels —

While some railroads carried on experiments with some form of diesel power, the first successful attempt was the Central Railroad of New Jersey's Engine *1000* in 1925. The box-like unit functioned as a switcher in its Brooklyn, New York, freight yard. These diesel switchers had many advantages. They were always ready, and did not consume tons of coal and gallons of water while idle between operations. There was much less smoke pollution than a steamer, particularly when operating in a relatively confined area. The diesel's smaller wheels and flexible trucks were easier on the yard tracks.

Diesel manufacturers turned first to making switchers for several reasons. The yard switchers did not need the power or

speed of a long-distance freight or passenger locomotive. At the same time, given the rapid buildup of McAdoo locomotives during World War I, switchers wore out more quickly. It was easier to get a foothold in the yard market. Moreover, railroad management could more easily grasp the new engine's efficiency as a switching unit. At the same time, both management and employees still regarded the switcher's firemen as a necessity to help read a yard's intricate signal system for safety purposes. These early switchers proved to be very durable. The Central of New Jersey's *1000* continued to work well into the mid 1950s.

Road dieselization was a different matter. For one thing management and employees alike were insistent that steam would remain the chief, if not only, motive power for long-distance, heavy trains. Ned Brooks of the Canadian National, however, pioneered the first successful road unit in 1928. The

Cab of a switch locomotive.

Pre–World War II "Vulcan" chain-drive switch locomotive at a grain elevator.

Canadian Locomotive Company built a 2660-horsepower twin unit, the 9000, and assigned it to its International Limited. CN, however, did not continue further dieselization because of the Depression and Brooks's death in the early 1930s.

In 1918, General Electric produced North America's first diesel-electric locomotive. During the 1920s, it teamed with diesel manufacturer Ingersol-Rand to produce 300–600 horsepower switchers. GE then began a partnership with the American Locomotive Company to produce larger engines just prior to World War II. General Motors purchased the Winton Engine Company and a rail car manufacturer to form the Electro-Motive Company in 1930. GM then began to develop standard road passenger and freight diesel locomotives. Their locomotives soon became the prototype of the diesel-electric.

In 1935, the Electro-Motive Division of General Motors produced its first twin, 3600 horsepower, boxcar diesel-electric locomotive. Numbers 511 and 512 could run separately or as a locomotive team. In August, it built a similar single unit to power the Baltimore & Ohio's *Royal Blue* passenger train. The road diesel quickly proved itself. It accelerated faster than a steamer and took curves more easily. These locomotives became the prototype of what became known as the "E series" or "E units."

— The FT Diesel Locomotive —

In 1939, EMD introduced its freight model. Known as the FT, GM took it on a demonstration trip from Kansas City to Los Angeles pulling 66 freight cars. The tour was a success. The Santa Fe Railroad was the first to put in an order for these "F units." The freight diesels eliminated the need for costly water as Santa Fe tracks ran through hundreds of miles of desert. The railroad already oil-fired its steamers.

— Diesel Efficiencies —

The E units and F units were available in A and B sections. The A section contained the cab with the engineer's controls. The B section was a "slug" or just the diesel, generator, and traction motors. The B unit needed at least one attached A section to operate. The first locomotives had semi-permanent "draw bars" between the locomotives. EMD quickly changed the bars to standard couplers. Railroad management could then easily add or subtract units depending on the length and weight of the train. Two units coupled together approximated the pull of a heavy steam locomotive. Six units equaled three steamers and so on.

The real savings was in crew size. A freight train headed by three steam engines needed three complete crews of engineers, firemen, and brakemen. In other words, they needed nine employees. Six diesel units needed only one crew in the first diesel's cab. The savings were immediately apparent.

Diesels had other advantages for management. The diesel ran efficiently from start to full speed. In other words, it had a wide range of energy for pull with very little difference in oil consumed. The steam locomotive, however, ran efficiently only within a narrow margin. Its gear ratio was primarily the size of its driving wheels. While a "high wheeler" fast passenger steamer ran efficiently at 60 miles per hour, it was a coal and water hog at any other speed.

First successful road diesel-electric locomotives #9000 on the Canadian National. Courtesy Canadian National. #31545.

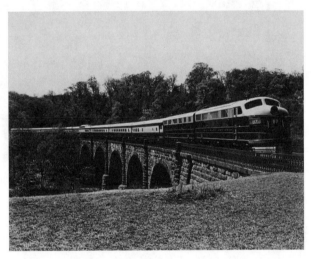

B&O E units pulling the *Columbian* over the Thomas Viaduct, 1949. Courtesy Railroad Museum of Pennsylvania. #35015.

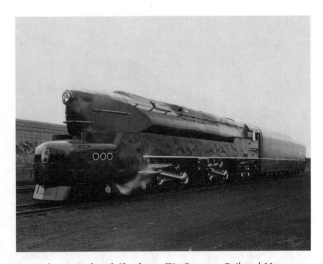

Pennsylvania Railroad *Sharknose* T1. Courtesy Railroad Museum of Pennsylvania.

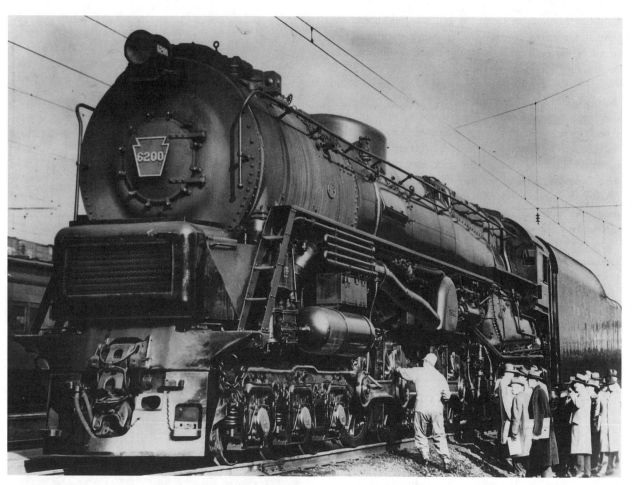

Pennsylvania Railroad turbine locomotive. Courtesy Railroad Museum of Pennsylvania.

Jersey Central 4-6-2 steam locomotive. Courtesy Railroad Avenue Enterprises. Photo by Bob Pennisi.

Union Pacific "Big Boy," the largest and strongest steam locomotive ever built. Courtesy Union Pacific.

Driving wheels of a Union Pacific "Big Boy." Notice the two sets of pistons, drive rods, and wheels of an articulated locomotive.

Steamers also need much more maintenance time than diesels. A platoon of repairmen were needed to keep the steam locomotive running. Boiler tubes had to be cleaned periodically of "scale" which attached to the walls and decreased efficiency. They had to inspect flues and change "tires" or outer rims of the driving wheels every so many thousands of miles. Many steamers, even of the same series, were slightly different. Therefore, replacement parts had to be tailor-made for each locomotive. In short, steam locomotives were extremely labor intensive both to operate and to repair.

General Motors applied the new technology of making automobiles to their locomotive manufacturing. Each series was made of interchangeable parts. There was no need for a "skilled craftman's art" to repair or fit any part. The repair time was also reduced. A diesel's truck with traction motor could be removed and replaced with a new one within hours. In fact, a complete overhaul could be accomplished in days rather than the weeks required with a steamer.

— Financing Diesel Purchases —

General Motors's Electro-Motive manufacturing concept at first seemed strange to railroad management. The railroads for generations had dictated to locomotive builders both design and function of the locomotive. General Motors now offered a one-design-fits-all. The only differences were a higher gear ratio on passenger locomotives for speed and a steam generator to heat the cars. General Motors's chief designer, Richard Dilworth, would not budge from his one-product offer. The diesel, however, cost twice as much to purchase as a steamer.

General Motors quickly won the railroads to their position. They created a design studio to paint an emblem on the diesels to match the railroads' color schemes and heralds. They began training facilities to teach railroad personnel how to operate and repair the new locomotives. Most important, General Motors overcame the higher price of its diesels by permitting the railroads to use the locomotive as its own security. In other words, General Motors could always retrieve the diesel, repaint it, and sell it to another road if necessary. Thereby, even a mar-

ginal railroad company could purchase a diesel locomotive and use its operational savings to pay General Motors.

With easy financing and colorful ornamentation, the diesel locomotive gave the railroads greater flexibility in assigning motive power. Steam locomotives, however, did not disappear overnight. Government restrictions on the manufacture of diesel and gasoline engines during World War II placed a temporary halt to their expansion.

— Steam Locomotive Developments —

With the new competition coming from diesels, steam locomotive manufacturers improved their product. They put roller bearings on the drive wheel axles, which decreased running maintenance by 60 percent. The Lima Locomotive Works designed a new boiler which increased efficiency. Just prior to World War II, manufacturers installed "poppet valves" on the steam cylinders. Poppet valves worked more quickly and exhausted all steam from the cylinder. In some cases, poppet valves added almost 700 horsepower to an older steam engine.

The Pennsylvania Railroad developed a new T1 class passenger steam locomotive. Designed by Raymond Loewy, the T1 could easily achieve a speed of 120 miles per hour with a complete passenger train. The Pennsylvania also began engineering a turbine drive S2 just as the United States entered World War II. The S2 had a 1,000-blade turbine and was a joint manufacturing project of the Pennsylvania Railroad, the Baldwin Locomotive Company, and Westinghouse. The turbine propelled a set of eight drive wheels and had 6,900-shaft horsepower. It could easily reach speeds of 100 miles per hour.

The Chesapeake & Ohio proposed its own steam turbine design in 1944. Baldwin and General Electric built three prototypes of these M-1 models. The M-1's steam turbine turned a generator which provided electricity to its traction motors. In other words, the locomotive was a "steam-electric." Coal was stored in the locomotive's nose with its boiler and tubes behind the cab. Its tender held only water and was designed to look like a passenger car. The M-1 was powerful enough to climb the Allegheny Mountain grades with ease, and it could

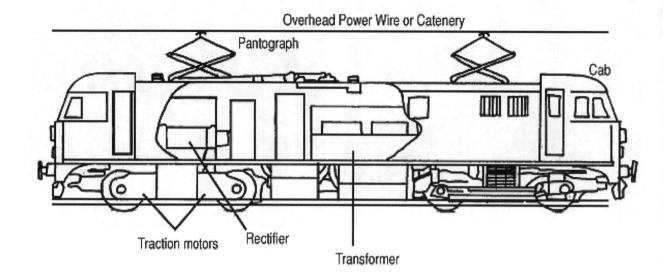

Overhead Power Wire or Catenery

Pantograph

Cab

Traction motors   Rectifier

Transformer

The Electric Locomotive

The electric locomotive draws its power from an overhead wire called "catenery" or from a "third rail" with a side-mounted tongue called a "hot shoe." The "pantograph" is the spring-like device which touches the overhead wire. The electric locomotive has traction motors and functions similar to a diesel-electric. It does not need a diesel and generator.

do 100 miles per hour on a flat surface. The intricate mechanism, however, was subject to frequent breakdowns. By the late 1940s, diesel-electric locomotives proved more efficient. The S2 and M-1 steam technology came too late to have any impact.

In 1936, Union Pacific developed its *Challenger* locomotive in cooperation with the American Locomotive Company (ALCO). This 4-6-6-4 locomotive had greater stability than earlier articulateds, because its boiler slid along a horizontal joint. With 69-inch drive wheels, the *Challenger*s were excellent for pulling heavy loads at high speeds. In 1942, ALCO used new technology to create an even more powerful and speedy "super" *Challenger*. Altogether, 105 *Challenger*s were built.

In 1941, Union Pacific began another steam project with ALCO. Twenty-five huge, 4-8-8-4 steam locomotives were produced. With 300 p.s.i. of boiler pressure and 6,000 horsepower, a *Big Boy* locomotive could pull a five-mile-long

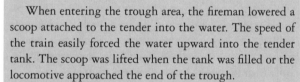

When entering the trough area, the fireman lowered a scoop attached to the tender into the water. The speed of the train easily forced the water upward into the tender tank. The scoop was lifted when the tank was filled or the locomotive approached the end of the trough.

While picking up water underway at speed saved time, the situation was accident prone. In colder climates workers had to keep the water from freezing. Any obstruction in the trough or the failure of a fireman to retract the scoop before the end could result in serious injury or death.

freight train at 60 miles per hour on a flat surface. *Big Boy*s were used primarily to haul 100-car freight trains over the Sherman Summit of the Continental Divide in Wyoming. They also pulled troop trains during World War II. An ALCO employee wrote "Big Boy" on the smokebox of the first production model. The name appropriately describes one of the most powerful locomotives ever built.

— Electric Locomotives —

Some railroads turned to electric power from overhead wires, called catenery, to power their traction motors. The Milwaukee Road used electrics even prior to World War I. The New Haven, Virginian Railway, and the Great Northern carried out electrification projects between the two World Wars.

— The Water Scoop —

Steam locomotives consumed large amounts of water when operating. In order to eliminate stops for long distances on fast passenger trains, some railroads developed a way to replenish the water supply as the train ran by. They placed water troughs, which extended for hundreds of yards, between the tracks.

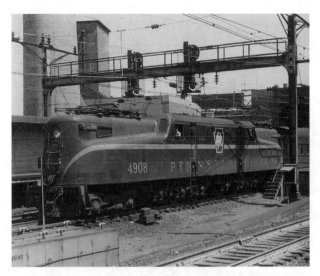

A GG1 Pennsylvania Railroad electric locomotive at Newark, N.J. Courtesy Railroad Avenue Enterprises. Photo by Bob Pennisi.

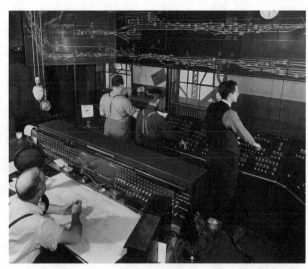

Early Centralized Traffic Control. Courtesy Candian National. #X30102.

During the depths of the Great Depression, the Pennsylvania Railroad began an electrification project for 2,677 miles of track or 40 percent of all electric railroads in the United States. Prior to 1930, it had electrified the entrance to Penn Station in New York City and an area from Trenton, New Jersey, to Wilmington, Delaware. By 1935, tracks from New York to Washington, D.C., were under catenery, and plans were underway to expand electricity all the way to Harrisburg.

— The *GG1* —

The Pennsylvania already had in use several types of electric locomotives. To inaugurate the huge electrification project, it headed a cooperative effort with General Electric, Westinghouse, and Baldwin Locomotive Works to create a new type of locomotive. Its own Raymond Loewy would finish the engine with an art-deco streamlined design. By August 1934, two prototypes of the *GG1* were developed.

The *GG1* lived up to all expectations. Not only was the design captivating, it proved versatile and had an extremely low breakdown and maintenance record. During its first test run, it accelerated from 0 to 100 miles per hour in less than a minute! It delivered a continuous 4,620 horsepower and could increase to over 8,000 for a short term. It had six pairs of traction motors or one for each of its 57-inch-diameter driving wheels. Pennsylvania employees simply referred to it as "the motor" and its engineer as a "motorman." The *GG1* lasted well into the Amtrak era pulling Metroliners at speeds of well over 100 miles an hour. The last *GG1* was retired in August 1983, just short of its golden anniversary under the wires.

— Signal Developments —

The railroad industry improved and developed new safety devices to move trains more efficiently. After World War I, many installed color searchlight signals whose filaments burned so intensely that an engineer could see them clearly even on the brightest day. During the early 1920s, the signal system was picked up inside the locomotive cab and lit a panel of lights simultaneously with the trackside signal. Both en-

gineer and fireman had their own set of lights, and they continuously checked with each other's readings en route. Trains could then run safely even on the foggiest of nights.

Also during the 1920s, the industry perfected the Absolute Permissive Block (APB) signal system. By using a complex electrical relay circuitry, APB closed all the blocks all the way to the next siding in line of an oncoming train. At the same time it permitted a second train running in the same direction to approach as close as two blocks behind. The APB system went a long way to avoiding head-on collisions and speeding traffic on its way.

In 1922, the Interstate Commerce Commission ordered the larger passenger roads to install Automatic Train Control (ATC) in at least one division. The ATC automatically stopped a train if the engineer failed to comply with a restricting signal.

— Centralized Traffic Control —

By 1930, electronics progressed to the point that a dispatcher at a switchboard could control miles of track. Centralized Traffic Control (CTC) was cost effective in high density traffic. The dispatcher could see the exact placement of all trains on a light board. He could then open or close switches on his control panel which corresponded to signals along the track. At the same time the circuitry prevented his making the mistake of causing two trains to collide on the same track. CTC increased track efficiency as much as 70 percent in some areas.

Just prior to World War II the Pennsylvania Railroad began experiments of using an inductive telephone system on its trains. The messages were carried electronically through the rails and telegraph wires alongside the tracks. The system permitted telephone communication between conductor and engineer and with towers within a limited distance on the line.

— Stronger Couplers and Brakes —

There were other on-train devices which increased safety and comfort. Shortly after World War I, railroads used a new "Type D" coupler. This "Type D" weighed 400 pounds and

Chesapeake & Ohio M-1 steam turbine locomotive pulling lightweight, streamline passenger cars of the *Chessie*. The *Chessie* never went into revenue service. The cars were assigned to other trains. The turbines were shortly replaced by diesel-electrics (Summer 1950). Courtesy Chesapeake & Ohio Historical Society.

Milwaukee "box" electric locomotive at Tacoma, Washington (1962). Courtesy Railroad Avenue Enterprises.

GG1 locomotive at speed with heavyweight passenger cars. Courtesy Railroad Museum of Pennsylvania.

New Haven electric locomotive. Courtesy Railroad Museum of Pennsylvania.

had twice the strength of all previous models. A stronger "Type E" was invented in 1931, which increased knuckle depth two more inches. Charles H. Tomlinson invented a "Tightlock" coupler which eliminated much of the play between knuckles on passenger equipment. Many railroads began installing the "Tightlocks" after 1936. They became an industry standard in the 1950s.

In addition to the diesel engine's dynamic braking, the freight train air brake system was improved by a new type of

1940s passenger coupler. Milwaukee Road Car on the Fremont Dinner Train. Note the steam heat connecting pipe.

valve system by the mid-1930s. The new valve system permitted the safer lengthening of freight trains. The Budd Company began marketing a disc brake for passenger cars. It did not become an industry standard, however, until the 1950s.

— Railway Express —

The American Railway Express, Inc., remained intact following its return to private enterprise after World War I. When its original contracts ran out in 1929, 86 of the U.S. railroads formed the Railway Express Agency to carry on the business. The railroads moved the cars and provided depot spaces. By contractual understanding, no single railroad or group of railroads could gain control over the agency. After expenses, the Railway Express Agency shared profits with member roads in proportion to traffic. By 1939, the Railway Express Agency could deliver a package overnight to any location within a radius of 2,500 miles! They used a combination of train, plane, and truck for an integrated delivery system.

— Railway Post Office —

The Railway Post Office used trains exclusively throughout the 1920s. Most passenger trains carried the mail between every city and village that had rails. During the 1930s, the U.S. Post Office began to use trucks and modified busses to deliver mail to smaller towns. The Railway Post Office also helped to introduce airmail service.

— Train Wrecks —

If advances in technology made passenger trains safer and almost eliminated head-on collisions, people still gathered together to watch train wrecks from time to time. A sure-fire

AUTOMATIC CAB SIGNAL SYSTEM RULES

ASPECTS
NAME — RESTRICTING

Indication — Proceed at restricted speed.

NAME - ADVANCE APPROACH

Indication — Proceed prepared to pass next signal at not exceeding 40 miles per hour.

NAME - CLEAR

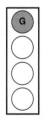

Indication — Proceed prepared to pass next signal at not exceeding 40 miles per hour.

way to attract a large crowd at a state fair during the 1920s and 1930s was to stage two steam engines racing toward each other on the same track. The practice died out, however, by World War II.

— Association of American Railroads —

At the end of World War I, the U.S. government requested that the various railroad professional organizations form into a single group. The American Railway Master Mechanics and the Master Car Builders became part of the American Railway Association. The Association of Railway Executives and several smaller groups merged into the current Association of American Railroads. Just before World War II in 1941, there were 231,971 miles of track between points (route miles) with 403,625 miles of all track operated in the United States.

— The Lionel Company —

Railroading held the fascination of the general public even after a century since its beginnings in the 1830s. In the years following World War I, a toy manufacturer, Lionel, built an empire making scale-model trains that ran on electricity. An owner could carry out all kinds of railroad operations, switching, loading, unloading, and running on an elaborate network of tracks through miniature towns and landscaping. It was even better than what the Central Traffic Control used on the real thing. It quickly became a tradition that more tracks, specialty cars, and scale towns were added each Christmas. Dad, of course, enjoyed assembling and "testing" the new equipment.

On the eve of World War II, both Canadian and U.S. railroads had made a substantial recovery from the Great Depression. Canada declared war on Germany in 1939. The United States declared war on Germany, Japan, and Italy in 1941, after the bombing of Pearl Harbor. The North American railroad system was prepared to move the necessary personnel and materials to win. It would prove to be the railroads' finest hour.

PART V

Their Finest Hour

Historical Survey

As war broke out in Europe in 1939, the people of the United States desired to keep out of the conflict. Franklin Roosevelt, having won an unprecedented third term as president in 1940, wished to help England. In 1940, Congress passed the first peacetime draft in its history, and the following year the United States issued $7 billion in loans to help friendly governments overseas.

On December 7, 1941, the Japanese bombed Pearl Harbor, Hawaii, Midway, Guam, Wake, and the Philippines without any forewarning. The United States was plunged into World War II. Declarations of war on Germany followed within days. The United States declared war on Italy later. The entire nation became one gigantic war machine. Unemployment ended, and soon there was a labor shortage. Women began to work in factory positions formerly occupied by men. Most commodities were rationed, and some items were no longer available. Automobile pleasure driving and manufacturing was postponed until after the war.

To coordinate military action, the allies formed the United Nations. Over 15 million U.S. men and women entered the Armed Forces. These soldiers, sailors, and marines eventually occupied almost every corner of the world. The Navy and Marines made their way to Japan by "island hopping" westward. The U.S. Army first saw conflict in North Africa and later invaded Italy. On June 6, 1944, the United States, along with other Allied forces, made a mass invasion of France. Germany surrendered in May 1945. Japan surrendered later that August, after the United States dropped atomic bombs on Hiroshima and Nagasaki. Both Japan and Germany surrendered unconditionally and were occupied for a time by United Nations forces.

The Canadian army of over 600,000 personnel aided England directly during the war. It also contributed over 700 ships and 100,000 sailors to fight against Hitler. When the war ended, both Canada and the United States wanted to bring home their military personnel as soon as possible.

"Together Again" by Charles E. Bracker. Chessie images are used with permission of CSX Transportation, Inc.

The Lifeline of the Nation

As Japan, Germany, and Italy began their programs of expansion and conquest during the late 1930s, the Canadian and U.S. railroads helped prepare North America for defense. The worldwide conflict began when Germany invaded Poland in 1939. England and France declared war on Germany immediately. War with Italy and Japan followed. As a Dominion in the British Empire, Canada joined immediately to help England.

Right after the declaration of war, the Canadian National ordered more locomotives and over 5,000 new freight cars to meet the task. The Canadian Pacific retooled their shops to produce naval guns and tanks. The Canadian National also built warships, merchantships, and trucks, as well as guns.

The Canadian National had two unique tasks during the war. Fearing an invasion by Nazi Germany, the Bank of England transferred all its gold and securities to Canada. The CN carried $7.5 billion of the Bank of England's property to vaults in Ottawa and Toronto. The CN also transported the first Canadian division of soldiers to Halifax for embarkation to England in December 1939. It took 25 troop trains to carry the personnel and supplies.

It soon became apparent that the Canadian National faced a huge bottleneck on its single track line to Halifax. It was both time-consuming and very expensive to lay a second set of tracks. Instead, the Canadians installed the U.S. Central Traffic Control (CTC) system in 1941, which solved the congestion problem.

— Canadian Statistics —

The Canadian railroads' performance statistics are very impressive. In 1939, the Canadian Pacific carried just over seven million passengers. From 1940 through 1945, it transported 86 million; most were military personnel. During the war years the Canadian Pacific's workforce grew from 48,689 to almost 71,000. Its shipline carried over 800,000 troops across the Atlantic, and its CP Air helped ferry planes to the beleaguered Soviet Air Force. By 1945, CP was able to increase its freight car utilization by 98 percent of what it was in 1939.

The Canadian National helped carry U.S. troops to Prince Rupert for easier travel to Alaska after 1941. It put together over 6,500 troop trains and moved 4,381,000 military personnel individually as well as in units. By 1944, CN employed a workforce of 102,000. CN moved 138 tons of freight every minute during the war years!

— Canadian Railways Overseas —

Both the Canadian National and Canadian Pacific sent personnel to England to help run its overworked railways. They also helped restore railroads on the European Continent after the invasion in June 1944. Even though Canadian railway workers were exempt from military service, 21,165 of the pre-

1939 CN workforce volunteered for military duty. Over 13,000 were wounded, and 842 died in service. Over 14,000 Canadian Pacific employees also volunteered and another 1,406 became members of the Canadian Reserve Army; 658 died in the war. Both railways employed women in various blue-collar jobs to help with the increase in traffic and to substitute for the men in the military.

— 2,800 Meals —

On a Canadian troop train between Halifax and Winnipeg, soldiers ate a total of 2,800 meals. The Canadian Pacific larders furnished 2,100 pounds of meat, 1,000 pounds of poultry, 3,600 eggs, 14 bags of potatoes, 365 loaves of bread, 100 pounds of butter, and 110 gallons of milk!

— The U.S. Railroads Prepare for War —

With war clouds gathering over Europe in 1939, the U.S. government began to consult with Ralph Budd, president of the Chicago, Burlington, & Quincy. In the event of conflict, Budd recommended the government not nationalize the railroads as it did during World War I. He suggested that they create a number of advisory agencies to guide the railroads under the general direction of the Office of Defense Transportation headed by Joseph B. Eastman. The government wisely followed Budd's advice.

When the Japanese bombed Pearl Harbor on December 7, 1941, the United States had 41,000 locomotives and two million freight cars. There were also approximately 7,500 Pullman sleepers readily available. The government immediately requested to have 65 percent of all passenger cars at its disposal. These numbers were 30 percent fewer than during World War I. The newer locomotives and freight cars, however, had a greater hauling capacity than those of 20 years earlier. Moreover, the greatest efficiency was assured by keeping the railroads in private hands. The overall coordination was accomplished by the Interstate Commerce Commission and especially the Association of American Railroads.

Unlike during World War I, the railroads did not move freight cars to a destination unless they were sure that they could be unloaded quickly. They took the shortest route and were certain to fill each car to capacity. These practices needed precise coordination. The military insisted that unloading be done as much as possible at night, especially at points of troop embarkation.

One incident can explain railroad cooperation and efficiency. Soon after the attack on Pearl Harbor, a few Army officers remembered they had assigned 42 railcars of crated airplanes for shipment to Sweden. They contacted the railroads to locate the shipment, if it had not already left the country. The railroads found the planes in New York. They quickly reloaded them onto the railcars on New Year's Day, 1942. The shipment arrived at the Army base at Oakland, California, early morning January 7, ready for service in the Pacific.

— Railroads Take on the Responsibility of Transportation —

The U.S. Railroads were truly "the lifeline of the nation" during the Second World War. Gasoline was rationed, and airplane transportation was severely limited. Cross-country trucking was out of the question. Coastal shipping of many products was restricted due to the threat of submarine warfare, and the Panama Canal was closed to the passage of certain materials. The railroads had to compensate for these difficulties.

The Southern Pacific Railroad took the heaviest burden during the early days of the war. With the United States no longer depending on the Panama Canal, the SP had to haul over 900,000 barrels of oil from California to the east coast. Moreover, most of the country's aircraft manufacturers were located on its line, not to mention all of the west-coast naval bases. Its traffic jumped a huge 136 percent from 1939 to 1942.

All the nation's railroads felt the pressures of increased traffic. By 1943, they had already transported 4½ times what they did during all of World War I. During 1944, they registered 96 billion passenger miles; almost anything that could move safely down the track was pressed into service to haul passengers or cargo. More than 2,500 troop trains moved soldiers from one place to another, and it was estimated that 100,000 service personnel traveled on some type of train during any given day.

— Military Travel Statistics —

The military ordered the construction of 1,200 "troop sleeping cars" and 400 "kitchen cars" for troop trains. These were the only new cars constructed during the war years. These "troop sleepers" were very crude and contained only the basic travel necessities. The government did require that any troop transfer lasting more than 12 hours provide sleeping accommodations. To save space, the Army put two men in the lower berth; the Navy held off this practice until November 1944. Pullmans carried 66 percent of all troop movements. They averaged 30,000 soldiers a night; the Pullman Company loaded a sleeping car every three minutes in 1944. The military also equipped and maintained a number of hospital trains to run to and from both coasts.

Along with the soldiers traveling as units attached to regularly scheduled trains, the military operated 113,891 special troop trains during the war. There were also over

Armored train during World War II. Courtesy Canadian National. #X19431.

300,000 coach trips. These figures do not include personnel traveling in small numbers under orders or those traveling during leave or furlough. The average division of 15,000 men and equipment needed 65 trains consisting of a total of 1,350 cars. An armored division took 75 trains of 28 to 45 cars each. According to Association of American Railroads' statistics, a troop train was filled and left a station every six minutes in 1943. Troop trains were often referred to as "Maines."

— Civilian Travel —

The railroads did their best to encourage civilians to keep travel to a necessary minimum. In advertisement after advertisement, they suggested that travelers "double up" on accommodations and be sure to cancel reservations immediately should travel plans change. Every seat and every berth was needed for military and defense travel, and, of course, for the soldier or sailor who wanted to visit home on furlough. The U.S. railroads carried 97 percent of all organized military personnel travel and 91 percent of all military freight during the war years. They handled an incredible 83 percent of all traffic, civilian or military, in the nation. In 1943, railroads accumulated 727 billion ton miles of freight and 87 billion passenger miles. These staggering numbers increased to 737 billion ton miles of freight and 95 billion passenger miles in 1944, the last full year of World War II.

— Financial Support —

The nation's railroads also financially supported the war effort. In 1943, the railroads paid over $1,850,000,000 in

Part of the 35th Division loading railroad cars leaving Camp Robinson, Arkansas, December 18, 1941. Courtesy Virginia Museum of Transportation, U.S. Army Signal Corps.

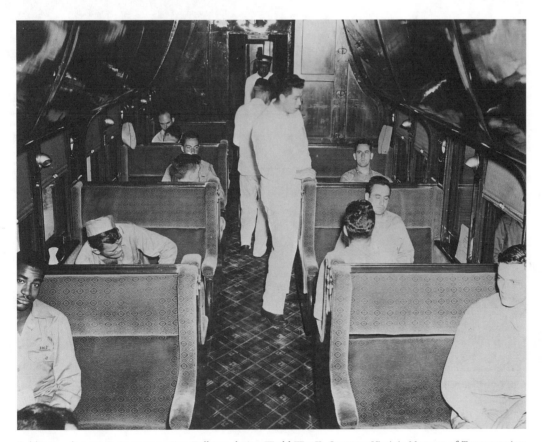

Soldiers underway in an open-section Pullman during World War II. Courtesy Virginia Museum of Transportation, U.S. Army.

What life is like on a troop train...

speeding over the Water Level Route

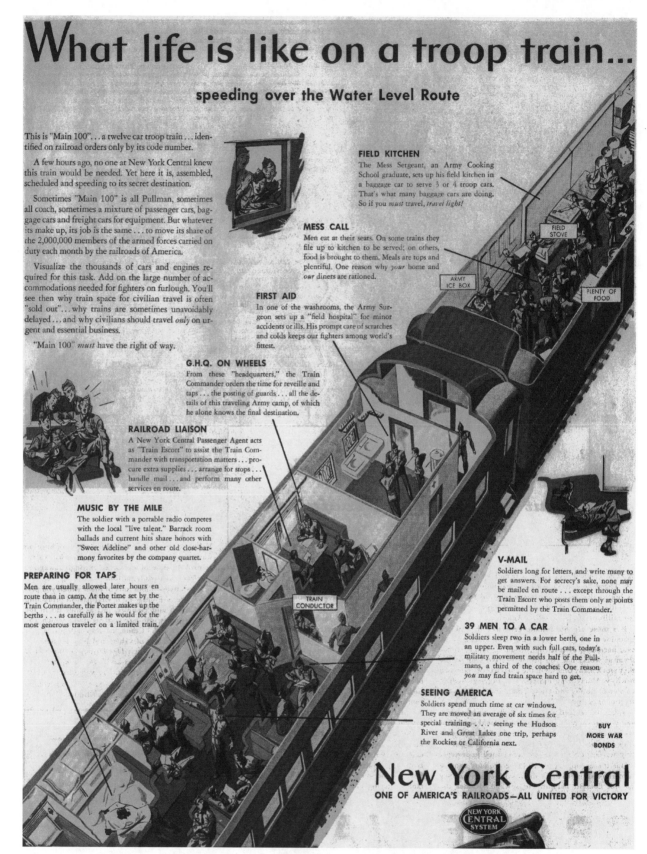

This is "Main 100"... a twelve car troop train... identified on railroad orders only by its code number.

A few hours ago, no one at New York Central knew this train would be needed. Yet here it is, assembled, scheduled and speeding to its secret destination.

Sometimes "Main 100" is all Pullman, sometimes all coach, sometimes a mixture of passenger cars, baggage cars and freight cars for equipment. But whatever its make up, its job is the same... to move its share of the 2,000,000 members of the armed forces carried on duty each month by the railroads of America.

Visualize the thousands of cars and engines required for this task. Add on the large number of accommodations needed for fighters on furlough. You'll see then why train space for civilian travel is often "sold out"... why trains are sometimes unavoidably delayed... and why civilians should travel *only* on urgent and essential business.

"Main 100" *must* have the right of way.

RAILROAD LIAISON

A New York Central Passenger Agent acts as "Train Escort" to assist the Train Commander with transportation matters... procure extra supplies... arrange for stops... handle mail... and perform many other services en route.

MUSIC BY THE MILE

The soldier with a portable radio competes with the local "live talent." Barrack room ballads and current hits share honors with "Sweet Adeline" and other old close-harmony favorites by the company quartet.

PREPARING FOR TAPS

Men are usually allowed later hours en route than in camp. At the time set by the Train Commander, the Porter makes up the berths... as carefully as he would for the most generous traveler on a limited train.

FIELD KITCHEN

The Mess Sergeant, an Army Cooking School graduate, sets up his field kitchen in a baggage car to serve 3 or 4 troop cars. That's what many baggage cars are doing. So if you *must* travel, *travel light!*

MESS CALL

Men eat at their seats. On some trains they file up to kitchen to be served; on others, food is brought to them. Meals are tops and plentiful. One reason why *your* home and *our* diners are rationed.

FIRST AID

In one of the washrooms, the Army Surgeon sets up a "field hospital" for minor accidents or ills. His prompt care of scratches and colds keeps our fighters among world's fittest.

G.H.Q. ON WHEELS

From these "headquarters," the Train Commander orders the time for reveille and taps... the posting of guards... all the details of this traveling Army camp, of which he alone knows the final destination.

V-MAIL

Soldiers long for letters, and write many to get answers. For secrecy's sake, none may be mailed en route... except through the Train Escort who posts them only at points permitted by the Train Commander.

39 MEN TO A CAR

Soldiers sleep two in a lower berth, one in an upper. Even with such full cars, today's military movement needs half of the Pullmans, a third of the coaches. One reason *you* may find train space hard to get.

SEEING AMERICA

Soldiers spend much time at car windows. They are moved an average of six times for special training... seeing the Hudson River and Great Lakes one trip, perhaps the Rockies or California next.

BUY MORE WAR BONDS

New York Central

ONE OF AMERICA'S RAILROADS—ALL UNITED FOR VICTORY

1943 New York Central magazine advertisement.

1943 Minutemen

UNTIL this war is won, saving minutes here may mean saving lives on distant battlefields—and the railroads are making minutes count.

For every minute of the day and night, they move a million and one-third tons of freight a distance of one mile—most of it military weapons and supplies and the raw materials, the food and fuel necessary to keep production going at top speed.

Every minute of the day and night, the railroads keep track of the movement of 2,000,000 freight cars—marshaling them where they're needed—keeping them moving.

Every minute, day and night, fifteen new freight trains are made up and started on their runs somewhere in America.

BACK THE ATTACK WITH WAR BONDS

Every minute of the day and night, railroad men — modern minutemen — are at work on the biggest job in transportation history — to meet the nation's need.

Railroad work is essential work — war work.

• • • •

DECEMBER 10 "CLOSING DATE" FOR CHRISTMAS PACKAGES. This year — when war traffic has first call on all shipping services — it is more important than ever to send your Christmas packages early.

Pack them adequately, wrap and tie them securely, address them right and get them started (to points in the United States and Canada) by *December 10.*

AMERICAN RAILROADS
ASSOCIATION OF
ALL UNITED FOR VICTORY

Magazine advertisement. Courtesy Association of American Railroads.

Interior of 1940s Pullman Sleeping Car showing daytime use.

taxes. That amount completely paid for the quartering and provisioning of 2½ million soldiers for one year! In other words, the railroads paid the federal and state government $7 in taxes for every $1 they paid shareholders. In 1945, railroads gave the federal government $6 million a day in taxes. Rather than the burden they were to the Treasury during the government takeover during World War I, under private ownership during World War II, the U.S. railroads became revenue generators for defense.

— Attempted Work Stoppage —

The only time the government intervened was during a threatened "work stoppage" toward the end of 1943. When the unions demanded a wage increase and made gestures of closing down operations, Secretary of War Henry L. Stimson issued an executive order on December 27, 1943, taking possession of the nation's railroads. For two weeks, until January 8, 1944, the government forced railroad employees to work. Operations, however, were entrusted to the previous owners and management. The government did require the railroad companies to grant a 9¢ hourly raise, overtime conversion, and more vacation time. The 1,450,000 railroad workers welcomed these benefits. There were no longer any threats of strikes or work stoppages.

As with other industries, railroads and their workers were strained to the uttermost due to the severe labor shortage dur-

ing the war. While railroad employment increased by 4 percent in 1943, it was still short of demand. The railroads hired about 115,000 women and 36,000 Mexicans to help fill the gap. At the same time, high schools dismissed approximately 24,000 boys from class early to work daily in switchyards. The need was critical, because the railroads sent 300,000 workers into the military and at least another 100,000 were furloughed to work in other specific defense industries. The railroads recruited men beyond military age who were still able-bodied. Of the 1,400,000 railroad employees working in 1945, about half had no railroad experience prior to December 1941.

— The Military Railway Service —

After World War I, the Army created its own railroad battalion. Fort Eustis, Virginia, became a training center for Army conductors, engineers, and track workers. The fort had a complete railroad facility consisting of cars, locomotives, and a switchyard. Since all activities had to occur on base, the training center became known as the "MG&B" or "Main Gate and Back Railroad." The "MG&B," however, was not enough to prepare railroaders for the war years ahead.

More than just individual volunteers and draftees, the railroads contributed personnel to Uncle Sam in the Military Railway Service. Headquartered at Fort Snelling, Minnesota, the U.S. Army organized 43,000 experienced railroaders into ten Grand Divisions, 50 Battalions, and ten Shop Battalions.

During World War II women assumed railroad jobs formerly done by men. Courtesy Canadian National. #44111.

Turntable operator, Dunsmuir, California, WWII. Courtesy Southern Pacific Shirley Burman College.

Rank depended upon age and years of experience. The army called up the men for the Railway Service by railroad. Southern Railway workers were activated first in March 1942.

The Military Railway Service was designed to repair and build tracks and equipment in war zones, and to supply soldiers as they advanced on the front. They rebuilt the Alaska Railroad to supply soldiers during the Aleutian campaign. Members saw service in North Africa, India, the Philippines, Australia, Italy, France, Belgium, Germany, and Japan. They followed U.S. soldiers up the boot of Italy and began repairing tracks one week after the landing in France on D-Day — June 6, 1944. They rolled trains into Paris only four days after the first troops entered the city.

Before the Normandy invasion, the U.S. Military Railway Service furnished 700 fifty-ton flat cars and over 400 locomotives for the English railways. They helped run trains and adapted the equipment to English specifications. On D-Day itself, they ran 34 hospital trains to speed wounded soldiers from shore to hospitals in England.

Much has been made of the "Red Ball Express," the long line of trucks that supplied General Patton's tanks as they raced toward Germany in fall, 1944. The other part of the story is that the Military Railway Service ran 31,000 tons of gasoline and supplies a distance of over 200 miles in less than a week. The Service moved four entire divisions of the Third Army with their supplies into the flank at the Battle of the Bulge in December 1944, to assure the United States of a victory. The railroaders actually carried artillery ammunition right to the front under the heaviest of enemy fire.

— The Depot: Home Away from Home —

Back in the United States, railroad stations became centers for the traveling soldiers and sailors. Some stations set aside special waiting rooms for the traveling military. In many large stations the USO (United Service Organization) provided entertainment and a congenial atmosphere. Some railroad depots set up "canteens" to furnish refreshments for the personnel or troop trains. Perhaps the most famous of all was the North Platte Canteen in Nebraska. North Platte was a major stop on the Union Pacific near where the line branched off to Denver, California, and the Pacific Northwest. Shortly after Pearl Harbor, Miss Rae Wilson organized donations from nearby citizens to provide free coffee and refreshments to the traveling service personnel. When she became ill, Mrs. Adam Christ, the wife of a Union Pacific engineer, continued the project.

People from 122 communities in Nebraska and Colorado donated items to the canteen. They fed troops no matter what time their train pulled in. There was no segregation at the North Platte Canteen. Anyone wearing a uniform and helping to win the war was welcomed. It was the one time that the Pullman Company "blinked" or maybe even "winked" — as the porters were often invited into the depot with the soldiers for some rest and refreshments. After all, the Pullman porter wore a uniform too. . . .

The North Platte Canteen, among others of course, provided the kind of stops soldiers enjoyed for other reasons. Sometimes soldiers would designate one or two to find a local bar to bring liquor back for everyone. Military Police later told harrowing stories of chasing the men around moving freight trains. Sometimes, too, a sympathetic conductor would hold up a train a minute longer just to make sure everyone was on board.

Between Christmas Day 1941, through April 1, 1946, the women of North Platte, Nebraska, and surrounding communities served over six million service personnel traveling under military orders.

Molly Pitcher, 1944

Molly Pitcher, Revolutionary heroine, symbolizes the spirit of America's women who take over the work of men at war.

Women are doing a big job on the Pennsylvania Railroad

More than 48,000 experienced Pennsylvania Railroad men have entered our armed forces. Yet, wartime's unusual needs for railroad service are being met . . . thanks in great part to more than 23,000 women who have rallied to the emergency. From colleges, high schools and homes, these women—after intensive training—are winning the wholehearted applause of the traveling public.

You see them working as trainmen, in ticket and station masters' offices and information bureaus, as platform ushers and train passenger representatives, in dining car service. Yes, even in baggage rooms, train dispatchers' offices, in shops and yards and as section hands. The Pennsylvania Railroad proudly salutes these "Molly Pitchers" who so gallantly fill the breach left by their fighting brothers-in-arms.

★ 48,128 in the Armed Forces
★ 248 have given their lives for their Country

Pennsylvania Railroad
Serving the Nation

BUY UNITED STATES
WAR BONDS AND STAMPS

Pennsylvania Railroad World War II advertisement. The small print reads that the Pennsy has 48,128 employees in the military and 248 have given their lives to date.

U.S. Army locomotives stored in Wales, United Kingdom, in 1944. Courtesy California State Railroad Museum. #26060.

World War II U.S. Army Hospital Car. Courtesy California State Railroad Museum. #13200.

Ward cars only half the length of standard railroad cars. They were manufactured for use on European rails during World War II. Courtesy Virginia Museum of Transportation, U.S. War Department.

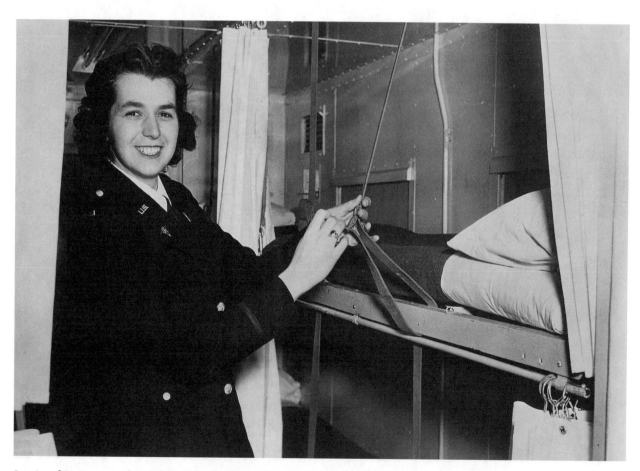

Interior of European-use hospital car. Courtesy Virginia Museum of Transportation, U.S. War Department.

Interior of standard U.S. Army Hospital Car during World War II. Courtesy Virginia Museum of Transportation, U.S. Army.

North Platte Canteen. Courtesy Union Pacific Museum Collection.

North Platte Canteen. During World War II the people of North Platte, Nebr., donated food to serve over six million service personnel. Jim Crow laws or segregation was never tolerated at the canteen. Courtesy Union Pacific Museum Collection.

— Bring the Boys Back Home —

Following the victory in Europe in May 1945, the government had to concentrate its attention on winning the war against Japan. It had to bring a number of military personnel home and then send them to the Pacific Coast. The military needed more Pullmans for travel. In July 1945, President Harry S Truman ordered the removal of all Pullman sleeping cars from civilian trains traveling less than 450 miles. With the war ending sooner than expected due to the dropping of the two atom bombs on Japan that August, the larger number of available Pullmans carried service personnel home. The military wanted to return as many soldiers and sailors as possible by Christmas 1945. By spring 1946, the major troop train movements of World War II became history.

— Technological Developments —

During the war most railroads had to rely upon expanding the technological developments of the late 1930s. They increased the number of track miles under Centralized Traffic Control (CTC) to over 3,000 by the end of 1942. CTC eliminated many bottlenecks. They also installed more power switches and fitted more steam locomotives with the power-increasing "poppet valves." A few railroads managed to purchase some diesels, but production numbers were limited by the government right from the beginning of the war. Even under these strict limitations the number of diesels grew from 1,200 in 1941 to 3,800 by 1945. The major locomotive manufacturers could build as many steamers as they wanted given wartime steel restrictions. In keeping with national fervor, the *Mikado* steam locomotive's name was quickly changed to *MacArthur* in honor of the general of the army in the Pacific!

During the war the military used model railroad layouts to train quartermasters to load and unload supplies at depots. At the same time the largest model manufacturer, Lionel, discontinued making equipment for the general public after 1942. They used their precision tools to manufacture compasses and other navigation equipment for the Navy.

The military also designed the jeep, or more properly the "scout car," according to railroad specifications. The wheelbase was 4 feet 8½ inches. In an emergency, the tires could be deflated and removed. The jeep could then be run on its rims on railroad tracks.

— Accidents —

In spite of the heavy traffic, there were only a few large-scale accidents. In December 1942, a Canadian Pacific troop train rear-ended a passenger train at Almonte, Ontario. Thirty-six people were killed and 200 hurt. In the United States, about 7 P.M. on September 6, 1943, the Pennsylvania Railroad's *Congressional Limited* had an overheated axle bearing. It cracked, snapping the 16-car train in half. One coach hit a signal tower and split in two. Seventy-nine died, and 117 were injured. Barely ten and a half hours later, the New York Central's *Twentieth Century Limited*'s locomotive boiler exploded near Canastota, New York. The engineer and two firemen were killed instantly, and seven employees were injured. No passengers were hurt in the ten-car derailment, because the

ground adjacent to the tracks was swampy and soft. There was no suspicion of sabotage in either accident.

— Plans for after the War —

Toward the end of the war, the railroads carried out surveys and made plans to purchase new equipment. It became abundantly clear that passengers preferred the new streamlined, diesel locomotives. Soldiers and sailors returning from the war, however, had other ideas. Rather than looking forward to traveling in sleek new trains, they dreamed of owning their own automobiles. They wanted the freedom to leave and return whenever they wanted, and directly from their own homes, rather than waiting at the station for the railroad's schedule. Perhaps, too, the younger service personnel never experienced the luxurious streamliners. Trains to most of them after four years in the military meant being herded into a crowded, uncomfortable box with blacked-out windows and going someplace unknown.

— Victory Rode on Trains —

North American railroads, particularly in the United States, won World War II even before the bombing of Pearl Harbor. The railroads united the nation's economy and enabled it to produce and deliver war materiel. The United States had the only natural resources and industrial capacity of the Allies in 1942. Germany controlled the European continent and parts of Africa. Japan conquered East Asia from Siberia to Malaysia. Although England was industrialized, it needed resources from abroad. During the early years of the war, the German submarine menace was quite successful in preventing material from reaching the British Isles.

Australia and the Soviet Union had resources, but they were in remote areas. Neither had a rail network sufficient to bring the war materiel into large-scale production and deliver it where needed. Only the United States, and to some degree Canada, could do so efficiently and in quantities enough to win the war. The growth of the U.S.'s railroad network in the nineteenth century, and its capacity to deliver in the first half of the twentieth, enabled it to become the "Arsenal of Democracy" in every sense of the term. The railroads were essentially an "army" unto themselves.

More than impressive statistics, the railroads were a central part of life during the war years. Families sent their "children" off to war from the railroad station and greeted them there again when they returned. At times Western Union had the grim task of notifying families that their soldier or sailor was wounded or killed in battle or the good news that he or she was coming home. Many times telegraphers had to remain through their shift after receiving a message that one of their own family members was wounded or killed in battle. At last, it was the trains which brought thousands — no, millions — of America's young men and women home to their own families, victory celebrations, and the promise of a new life after the war.

The railroads of Canada and the United States had their finest hour in the fight for freedom against the world of European and Asian dictators. They brought the Allies victory as much as any army. They were, indeed, the "The Lifeline of the Nation."

Modern Times

Historical Survey

When the soldiers and sailors returned home after the Second World War, they wanted to have their own houses and cars. The GI Bill passed by the U.S. Congress granted veterans funds for college and vocational education. The economy changed from war production to manufacturing consumer goods. Many of the labor–management conflicts that had been postponed during the war erupted in a series of strikes. Congress passed the Taft-Hartley Law which prohibited "closed shops" (union membership required) and required an 80-day "cooling-off" period during disputes.

In foreign policy, the United States faced the growth of communism in the late 1940s and early 1950s. The Soviet Union took over countries in Eastern Europe and communist rebels conquered China. In 1950, the communist North Koreans invaded South Korea. The United States became the chief force in defending South Korea from communism. After a truce in 1953, a "cold war" atmosphere lasted between communist and free countries into the 1980s.

In 1957, the Soviet Union launched the first man-made object, called *Sputnik,* into space. Afterward a "space race" ensued between the United States and the Soviet Union. At the same time, both used the latest technology for defense purposes. President Dwight Eisenhower began the construction of a national defense interstate highway system. His idea was to make the military more mobile and not as dependent on the railroads. This interstate system greatly encouraged people to travel more by car.

In domestic matters, the U.S. Supreme Court issued a decision to desegregate public schools in 1954, and allot greater civil rights for those arrested for a crime. At the same time, African-Americans began a movement for desegregation of other aspects of society. Congress passed a number of civil rights acts during the next few years to hasten the pace of change.

After the assassination of President John F. Kennedy in 1963, President Lyndon B. Johnson began a program called "The Great Society." He declared a war on poverty with direct assistance by the federal government to the poor. He also started Medicare, a government health insurance program for the retired. There were numerous education programs and various forms of government assistance for many levels of society.

Congress gave President Johnson the authority to assist South Vietnam in fighting an invasion by communist guerilla forces from North Vietnam. By 1967, there were over a half-million service people in Vietnam fighting a brushfire war.

By 1970, over 40,000 U.S. service people lost their lives in southeast Asia. There were many protests against the war, mostly led by college students. There were also riots in the larger cities led by African-American youth venting anger over their own living conditions.

President Richard M. Nixon, the man who ended the Vietnam War, was forced to resign the presidency in 1974. After a burglary in the Democratic Party headquarters during the 1972 election by Republican Party members, President Nixon was implicated in a plot to cover up the crime and was accused of obstruction of justice. Nixon's resignation from office was the first ever of a U.S. president.

The Democratic candidate, Jimmy Carter, won the 1976 election. President Carter's administration was during an inflationary period as well as a recession in the economy. Many businesses were leaving the country seeking cheaper labor in Asia. Moreover, Japan's auto industry became a definite threat to domestic manufacturers. U.S. manufacturing declined in general. The late 1970s also led to a decline in the United States's prestige abroad and a number of its citizens were held hostage by Iran for months.

The hostages returned to the United States at the moment Ronald Reagan took the oath of the presidency in 1980. The Reagan administration halted inflation and renewed large expenditures for the military. President Reagan used "supply-side economics" to stimulate the economy. He cut taxes so people could invest more in business.

President Reagan's main goal in foreign policy was to put an end to Soviet communism. He began a plan for the use of laser technology to prevent Soviet missiles from reaching U.S. soil. This "Strategic Defense Initiative" or "Star Wars" compelled huge changes in the Soviet system to keep pace with this new technological development. The inflexible Soviet system soon fell apart as new leaders tried to initiate the necessary changes. President Reagan's vice president, George Bush, succeeded him in 1988.

When Iraq invaded Kuwait in the Middle East, President Bush organized an effective international coalition. The United Nations forces removed Iraqi troops in a military action known as "Desert Storm."

After a brief recession, citizens elected Democrat William J. Clinton president in 1992. President Clinton's main emphasis was on government economics and social programs. He attempted to institute a general government health plan for all citizens. While his administration continues to enjoy a favorable economy, it has been plagued with scandals and accusations of impropriety and wrongdoing. In 1998, he became the second president in U.S. history to be impeached.

U.S. society has changed greatly since the 1950s. The availability of birth control in pill form permitted women to have greater control over conception. The Supreme Court's decision to permit abortion at will gave women greater control over the reproductive process. Additional rights were sought and a women's liberation movement began in earnest by 1970. Women entered formerly male professions, seeking careers to become everything from ministers to fighter pilots.

Young people saw a "generation gap" between themselves and their parents. The "Me Generation" no longer regarded traditional social conventions as guiding principles. They regarded the Vietnam War as an example of the hypocrisy and corruption of their elders, and they believed themselves to be the sole arbiters of true ethics. Conventional religions lost meaning for many.

Youth sought a more carefree life. In rejecting traditional values, they wore jeans as a matter of identification. Many turned to or experimented with hallucinogenic drugs to escape boredom and to seek greater thrills in life. The new "rock music" emphasized rhythmic beat rather than melody. It was much simpler in form and lent itself well as a part of the drug culture. In fact, some music was called "acid rock," and there were drug references in many lyrics.

During the early 1950s, television quickly took the place of radio as a home entertainment center. People purchased quick-preparation "TV dinners" so they would not miss their favorite programs. Television news programs became a primary source of information, and newspapers began a significant decline in circulation by the 1980s.

The invention of the transistor in the 1950s made electronics less expensive and broadened applications. Transistors became very important in the development of the computer. First used in business and industry, computers became household devices by the late 1980s. More than a calculating instrument, the computer quickly became an important means of communication with "electronic mail" and a world-wide connective matrix called "Internet."

There is no doubt that U.S. society and values have changed greatly since the Second World War. The pace of life has quickened, and people no longer adhere to traditional values and family expectations. The economy changed from manufacturing to an emphasis on service. From an oil-exporting country in 1950, the United States became dependent on foreign petroleum by the 1970s. With many manufactured products being made abroad by the 1980s, many domestic factories became empty and abandoned. With more women in the workplace and growth in the child daycare industry, fewer people remained at home during daytime hours. Partially due to the high incidence of divorce and the increase in single-parent families, people sought both entertainment and social events outside the household.

Canada gained complete independence from Great Britain after the Second World War. In 1949, the Supreme Court of Canada was recognized as the highest court in the land. Canadians could no longer appeal cases to the English Privy Council. Although mostly symbolic, this recognition ended the last English compulsory legal formality. In 1965, Canada adopted the Maple Leaf flag. Canada today is a voluntary member of the British Commonwealth of Nations.

During the 1950s, Canada adopted a policy of using nuclear energy to generate electricity. It also completed the St. Lawrence Seaway project in 1959, which links the St. Lawrence River with the Great Lakes for ocean-going ships. During the 1960s Canada embarked on a series of socialist projects. In 1961, it adopted socialized medicine.

Canada experienced a recession in the 1960s only to regain a favorable economy by exporting raw materials and wheat products to Asia in the 1970s. It also completed a trans-Canada highway.

During the 1960s Canada became politically divided between its English and French-speaking peoples. The French-speaking population demanded greater recognition of their language and culture. In 1969, Canada passed a bilingual law which established both English and French as official languages. During the 1970s some French Canadians began a separatist movement. Some committed acts of terrorism as well as legal protests for the French-speaking areas to become an independent country. Since then French-speaking Canadians have been unsuccessful in independence referendums at the ballot box. The issue, however, will remain part of the Canadian political scene for some time to come.

The Twilight of the Railroad Era

Everyone throughout the world, including many of the vanquished, greeted the end of World War II with great expectations for the future. In 1945, Canadian and U.S. railroads were financially in better shape than they had been since the 1920s. Even though much of their rolling stock needed to be replaced, they expected to be part of postwar industrial growth. For the next generation, however, the railroads experienced a decline. The economy and society changed and, with government restrictions, the railroads were prevented from competing fairly. In other words, they had to fight with both hands tied behind their backs.

— Statistical Decline —

The statistics told a grim story. In 1945, almost all intercity traffic in the United States traveled by rail; only one-third rode the train by 1957. By 1960, the Pullman Company carried only one-fourth of what it had during the war. After 1960, the decline became more pronounced so that by 1970 the railroads carried but a trickle of intercity traffic. Through a number of vigorous programs and the occurrence of "Expo 1967," the Canadian National was able to increase passenger travel for a few years. It then fell off in the 1970s. Freight fared little better. From 1945 to 1960, rail freight declined almost 30 percent, and it continued to drop. By the 1970s, the railroads carried less than 40 percent of the nation's freight.

The railroads lost a huge number of personnel and dropped from being the United States's and Canada's largest nonagricultural employer. Right after World War II, the U.S. railroads employed about 1,400,000 workers. By the late 1950s, that number decreased to 780,000, and less than 700,000 by the early 1960s. Track maintenance workers, or "gandy dancers," dropped from 167,000 in 1950 to around 45,000 by 1967. The increase in the use of diesels accounts for the large decline in numbers for the most part. Roundhouses were closed, and it took far fewer workers to maintain and operate a diesel than a steam locomotive. Moreover, the diesel did not "pound the rail" as did the steamer, so less track maintenance was necessary. It is also true, however, that many railroads deferred track maintenance as an economy measure.

— Competition —

During the war years, competition from airplanes, trucks, busses, and automobiles was curtailed through gasoline rationing and military priorities. Indeed, the train was the most efficient way to move people and goods. The railroads experienced a revival, and they wanted to believe that it would continue into the future. It was a false hope. With gasoline rationing over and new technologies available, citizens looked to other means of transportation.

The car permitted people to leave and to return and carry with them as much as they wanted — a trunkful — with ease and without the assistance of a Redcap. The car also gave a greater sense of freedom. The driver and passengers could take alternate routes without changing tickets or schedules. Moreover, no one cared if coffee spilled or someone left a snack on the seat. People could wear more comfortable clothing; there was no need to dress up for dinner. And just as important, gasoline was cheap and plentiful.

The factories that had made jeeps and tanks quickly turned to producing cars in record numbers each year. The banks, which owned stock in the railroads, realized a far greater and quicker return on their money by granting automobile loans. Of course, after a few years, the driver wanted a new, more modern car, and, again, another loan.

— Highway Construction —

Both federal and state governments began programs of massive highway construction. Even secondary roads in rural areas were paved. In the 1950s, the federal government began to construct the Eisenhower Interstate Highway System. The Interstate System was proposed as an alternate means to move military personnel, materiel, and weapons during a national emergency. In other words, the military was to become independent of the railroads which served the nation so well during World War II. The four-lane highway had gradual inclines and curves to safely permit driving at speeds up to 80 miles an hour or more. Its entrances and exits were limited for safety, and its overpasses were at a height to permit the carrying of large and high items by trucks. Of course, the Interstate System was used by the general public, and it was another enticement to use the family car on long drives. Canada also constructed a national highway system linking major cities across the country.

New highways encouraged bus companies to compete with the railroads. Busses became larger and more comfortable. With technological advances, many installed air conditioning and, by the 1960s, some even had restrooms. The bus became a cheaper form of transportation even for long-distance trips.

— The Airlines —

The airlines did the most to rob the railroads of intercity passenger traffic. After World War II, the airliner grew larger, faster, and more comfortable than the standard D.C. 3. The Lockheed Constellation and D.C. 7 carried more passengers and some luxuries. Airlines advertised pretty hostesses to serve meals and alcoholic beverages right at the passengers' seats. Air travel, which was once used only in an emergency or when time was a major factor, became more commonplace. The use of radar on board commercial aircraft lessened cancellations and gave the flying public more confidence. During the late 1950s, commercial passenger jet travel became available. The jet cut travel time in half, could fly right over bad weather systems, and was much quieter and did not "rattle" like propeller planes. People wanted to travel in the new planes whenever possible. One version, the 747, actually featured lounge areas in a "bubble" above the regular seating. Airlines advertised all the conveniences of the train and arrival at the destination in only a fraction of the time.

In 1950, airlines already carried almost 25 percent of all intercity distance passengers. By 1960, just after the introduction of the commercial jet, airline passenger traffic jumped to over 60 percent. By the end of the decade, it was well over 80 percent. In other words, from 1950 to 1970, air travel grew over ten times, while the rails cut almost all services by one-half. Many trains by the late 1960s had more crew than passengers.

What made matters worse, the competitors to the railroads were government-funded. Cars, trucks, and busses used highways which were both constructed and maintained at government expense. By 1966, the federal government subsidized air travel by a huge $1.4 billion. By 1968, government subsidies for highway and waterway as well as air totaled a whopping $19 billion per year in the United States. In the meantime, the railroads had to maintain their own roadbeds out-of-pocket and pay an enormous percentage in taxes. In 1946, however, the federal government did rescind its almost century-old perogative to pay only half-price to the railroads for carrying its personnel and goods. The government soon, however, shifted its traffic to truck and airplane.

— U.S. Air Force One —

Perhaps only symbolic, by 1960 the president of the United States no longer traveled by train. The "Whistle Stop" speeches and appearances of presidential candidates were replaced by hurried jet travel among many major cities in one day. The famous private car of the presidents, the *Ferdinand Magellan*, spent almost its entire time in storage. President Franklin Delano Roosevelt liked trains and greatly enjoyed the *Magellan*. President John F. Kennedy, a youthful president representing the generation who fought in World War II, traveled exclusively by jet — U. S. Air Force One. The U.S. railroads lost their most prestigious passenger! President William Jefferson Clinton did travel from Washington, D.C., to the Democratic Convention in Chicago in the *Magellan* in 1996. The trip was for publicity rather than policy purposes. It is interesting to note that when Queen Elizabeth II of England visited the Dominion of Canada in 1951, she and her staff traveled by train.

— Dieselization —

Along with all the lopsided competition, the railroads experienced problems in its own and serving industries. In the years following World War II, the price of coal jumped dramatically. The railroads could not, due to government regulations, adjust their prices accordingly. A major coal strike in the United States in 1949 slowed down some major railroad operations, and it almost crippled the Canadian

National — the price increases and strikes did much to encourage dieselization.

As diesels became more prominent, the railroads reduced and changed their work forces accordingly. The largest numbers were among those in steam maintenance facilities. The transition from steam to diesel greatly affected the economies of small towns like Oelwein, Iowa, to cities like Altoona, Pennsylvania, where a large share of the population worked on the "iron horses." The Norfolk & Western managed to hold on to their steam locomotives the longest. Being a major coal carrier, its fuel was cheaper and readily available. They also built a huge "flow through" steamer service facility at Roanoke, Virginia, which could almost rival the modern diesel service centers. This "lubratorium" boasted that it could lubricate and flush a boiler within an hour! It prepared and dispatched a record 141 steamers in one day! The N&W was the last major railroad to convert to diesel in the late 1950s. In fact, the N&W continued to build its own steam locomotives until 1953. The last steam locomotive ordered from an independent major manufacturer was in 1949. In spite of its brilliant last stand at Roanoke, the steam locomotive gave way to the diesel, and the last group of professional shop artisans closed their doors. There was little or no compatibility between the work and tools of the steam locomotive hostler and the new diesel-electric technician.

Sounds of a century of railroading changed. The piercing, sometimes haunting, steam whistle gave way to the plaintive diesel air horn. The puffing and chugging noise of an approaching steamer was replaced with the monotonous hum of the diesel engine.

— Labor Unrest —

Locomotive firemen, however, took a historic stand. The need for a fireman on a diesel locomotive was questioned with the newly styled units as early as 1937. The railroads recognized the union's argument about safety factors at that time. During the economic squeeze of the postwar years, both Canadian and U.S. railroads raised the question again. They saw the elimination of the fireman's position as a means of saving money. In fact, as late as the 1950s, the U.S. railroads had to observe rules made during World War I. Passenger engine crews completed a day's work after traveling 100 miles, and freight engine crews 150 miles. As speeds increased and with the advent of the diesel, trains could travel those distances within a few hours. In other words, the nonessential fireman received a full day's pay for four or even fewer than three hours of work.

When the railroads announced their intention to eliminate the fireman's position, the unions threatened to strike. Given the obsolete work rules, the railroads accused the employees of "featherbedding." In contrast, a jet plane crew absorbed only 16 percent of its passenger revenue, while a train crew would cost over 40 percent by the 1960s.

In 1956, Canadian Pacific employees staged a strike. The Canadian government formed a Royal Commission to investigate the issue. The Commission permitted the letting go of firemen on freights, but retained the position on passenger trains for a few more years. The Canadian National announced a plan to eliminate the position through attrition. Both U.S. railroads and unions underwent a series of studies on the fireman issue into the early 1960s. Finally, in August 1963, President Kennedy announced "Arbitration Award 282" which called for the end of the fireman's position beginning in spring 1964. It recommended reductions be made through retirement, resignation, or death. Some railroads offered generous retirement and severance packages to hasten the process.

The fireman issue was political as well as economic. From a railroading perspective, another great tradition had ended. The fireman was a future engineer. His experience in the cab opposite the engineer was an ideal apprentice system, symbolically a son following in his father's footsteps. Along with the roundhouse where the iron horse was groomed, the well-earned fireman's seat faded into history.

Engineer's seat of a SD40 diesel-electric locomotive.

— The Pheasants' Revenge —

For years railroaders who worked in the baggage car of a local passenger train in the Midwest enjoyed a steady diet of pheasant for dinner. When passing through farm fields, the engineer would stop the train and signal the baggage car attendants that pheasants were nearby. As the birds took off in flight, the attendants grabbed their shotguns, downed the birds, and retrieved them.

The crew had a chef prepare the pheasant at the hotel for dinner. They did the same on the way back home. This worked splendidly for the well-fed crew. One day, however, the railroad's superintendent was riding that particular train. The crew was not aware of their important passenger, and they did their usual pheasant routine. From that day on they had to content themselves with chicken after their run.

New Jersey Central GP7 photographed in April 1997. Red and white livery was used in last years of CNJ before merger into Conrail.

— The Diesel Revolution —

There is no doubt that the diesel or diesel-electric locomotive brought about the second revolution in railroad motive power — second only to Peter Cooper's *Tom Thumb* and the other early steam locomotives. The diesel itself, however, would undergo its own evolution in the years after World War II. Although General Motors's Electro-Motive Division clearly had a lead in diesel manufacturing, others came on the scene. In 1944, Fairbanks-Morse, which had earlier built gasoline railcars, planned to manufacture locomotives. It produced a series of 1,000 horsepower switch engines and some road diesels with General Electric and Westinghouse traction motors. Never a major contender, it ceased production in 1958.

By 1950, Baldwin (BLH) had absorbed the Lima Locomotive Company and used Westinghouse equipment to build diesel-electrics. The American Locomotive Company (ALCO) produced a 2,000 horsepower unit that could be used in both freight and passenger service. An alliance with General Electric gave ALCO an early boost in the market. GE later, how-

New Jersy Transit U34CH "U Boat" at Hoboken, N.J. Courtesy Railroad Avenue Enterprises. Photo by Bob Pennisi.

Union Pacific *City of Los Angeles* streamliner pulled by "Elegant E" Units. Courtesy Union Pacific.

ever, preferred to build its own locomotives. ALCO went out of business shortly thereafter, although it continued to build diesels through a subsidiary, the Montreal Locomotive Works in Canada, until 1969. Although Baldwin had won some lucrative contracts and built over 3,000 diesel locomotives, it, too, closed its doors in 1956. Baldwin tried to market "customized diesels" as they had steamers. By the 1950s, this practice was clearly obsolete.

— General Electric and General Motors: The Second Generation —

General Electric emerged as the only substantial competitor to EMD. During the mid-1950s, it produced high horsepower units for the Erie and later Union Pacific Railroads. In 1959, its 2,500 horsepower U25B or "U Boat" was a success.

In 1949, EMD introduced its 1,500 horsepower GP7 or "Geep" (pronounced *jeep*). The GP7, and its later version, GP9, functioned equally well as a switcher and as a road diesel. Although manufactured for sale initially to short lines, it became a workhorse for all railroads. Unlike cab units that had to be turned around, its cab permitted good visibility in both directions. It did not need a streamlined appearance, since most freight trains were still running at relatively slow speeds during the 1950s. United States railroads purchased over 6,000 "Geeps" and some were still in use during the 1990s. EMD continued its GP series with higher numbers in the 1970s and 1980s. Some later model numbers used alternating current (AC) as new silicon rectifiers came into common use. A rectifier changed the alternating current to direct current for use in the traction motors. EMD introduced its Special Duty (SD) series in 1951. The SD7 featured Flexicoil three-axle, quad truck mounts. It had a larger radiator and

an additional fan and vent. Its six instead of four traction motors provided greater power and speed.

In 1948, steam locomotives still made up 75 percent of the motive power in the United States. By 1955, fifty major railroads had already discarded all their steamers. In two years, 1957, diesels accounted for 90 percent of all railroad power. The most notable exception was Union Pacific's use of the "Big Boys" on Sherman Hill. By 1967, there were only 21 steam locomotives left on the nation's registry of motive power. Some were kept for excursion and railfan trips.

The Canadian Pacific began its dieselization in 1949, and the Canadian National quickly followed. CPR began its program in British Columbia, and CN worked its way westward. By 1955, CN purchased 1100 road diesels. Both railroads were completely dieselized in 1960 well ahead of some of their friends to the south.

— The Railroad Hour —

Dieselization was only one part of the railroads' attempt to operate more efficiently and to attract passengers and shippers. During the early 1950s the U.S. railroads sponsored the network radio program "The Railroad Hour" hosted by the famous vocalist Gordon MacRae. The program featured famous entertainers and kept the public up to date about rail activities. It was one way to keep trains in the nation's consciousness.

— The Dome Car —

Following World War II much of the rolling stock needed repair or replacement. Many roads purchased cars with new designs. The Chicago, Burlington, & Quincy pioneered the "Vista Dome" car. This car had a glass bubble in its ceiling where passengers could sit and look out above the car. The

Rail Diesel Car "Budd Train," Reading Railroad's *Wall Street* at Bound Brook, N.J., 1970. Courtesy Railroad Avenue Enterprises. #3517.

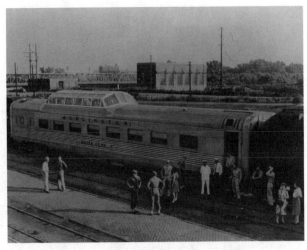

1945, Burlington Route's *Silver Dome* — the first dome car. Forty more were ordered within six months. Other railroads soon followed with their own version. Courtesy BNSF.

CB&Q saw it as a great advantage on its *California Zephyr* which went through the Rocky and Sierra Nevada Mountains. Other western railroads followed with their own dome cars.

— New Sleepers —

Railroads recognized the public's desire for more private sleeping quarters than the traditional open-section Pullmans. Many name trains offered roomettes, bedrooms, drawing rooms, and master bedrooms. All had toilets and wash basins. The master bedroom also had a private shower. To offer some convenience at a lower fare, the Chicago, Burlington, & Quincy and the Baltimore & Ohio began what was to be called the "slumbercoach." This sleeping accommodation was essentially a scaled-down roomette with 24 single and eight double compartments. The beds were quite small (24 x 73 inches), but each unit had its own lavatory facilities. In order to sleep 40 people, the units were on two levels. For example, the "head and feet" portion of the top unit were above bottom units. The top unit was reached by permanently fixed steps. The "slumbercoach" was an economical way to travel, and other railroads adopted it on overnight runs. The Budd Company experimented with the first "slumbercoach" in 1953, and Pullman entered the market in 1956.

Although passenger ridership declined in the 1950s, some U.S. name trains did relatively well. The *California Zephyr,* on its Chicago, Burlington, & Quincy, Denver & Rio Grande Western, and Western Pacific Railroads rolled through the scenic Feather River Canyon. They advertised that their *Silver Lady* went "through the Rockies" rather than around them. The Santa Fe *Super Chief* was still known for its fine dining, and movie stars took the Union Pacific's *City of Los Angeles.* The New York Central's *Twentieth Century Limited* still lived up to its grand reputation. Many former "all Pullman" trains added coaches in the 1950s and 1960s. It was still more comfortable to take a train somewhere rather than be cramped on a propeller-driven airplane with a weather-dependent schedule. When commercial passenger jets became common in the early 1960s, railroad passenger traffic declined quickly

in the United States. At the same time, railroad management faced high labor costs.

— Modern Image for Canadian National —

The Canadian National and Canadian Pacific were a bit more successful in their passenger market. During the mid-1950s, the CPR purchased 173 new long-distance stainless steel cars for long-distance service. Many were "vistadomes" to provide riders with an optimum view of the Canadian Rockies. The Canadian National purchased 260 regular cars, mostly coaches. In 1955, the Canadian National modernized its image by creating a new logo. The letters CN were linked together, which looked to some like a worm. It introduced the cross-country *Super Continental* the following year. During the 1958 recession, the CN reduced its schedule to only two continental trains and sold its shipping lines.

In 1962, CN introduced its "Red, White, and Blue" fare rate system. Each color stood for a different, reduced passenger fare. Meals were included for all first-class passengers, and the CN began to experience an increase in traffic. CN restored over 700 passenger cars and streamlined its Montreal to Quebec, *Le Champlain.* It also advertised its Montreal to Toronto *Rapido* as the "fastest train on the continent," and in 1968 experimented with a turbo train on some runs. In 1964, CN experienced a 20 percent increase in passenger traffic. During "Expo 1967" in Montreal, both CN and CPR experienced an increase in ridership. In fact, CN had to lease passenger equipment from U.S. railroads for a brief period. CN gained a 25 percent increase in passenger traffic that year. The next year, 1968, however, passenger revenue fell off. CPR continued with only one transcontinental, *The Canadian,* and CN reduced its to two: *The Panorama* and *The Super Continental.*

Ridership continued to decline in the 1970s. In both Canada and the United States, passenger service became a revenue-losing situation with no upswing in sight. Railroads in both countries were glad to turn their passenger operations over to government corporations during the decade. In 1970,

1954 magazine advertisement for the Union Pacific Railroad.

1947 magazine advertisement for the New York Central.

The Jersey Central Railroad had several ferries to cross the Hudson River between lower Manhattan and Jersey City, New Jersey. They carried passengers to meet Jersey Central, Baltimore & Ohio, and Reading Lines trains. Courtesy Edward O'Donnell.

the United States created the National Rail Passenger Corporation or Amtrak. As a cost-saving venture, CN and CPR published a joint passenger timetable in 1976. In 1978, CN and CPR sold their passenger equipment to the Crown Corporation, VIA Rail Canada.

— Bear'n It on the CPR —

In fall 1969, a forty-car freight train stopped on siding at Castle Mountain. The conductor and brakeman began to cook some eggs for breakfast since they knew that they were going to be waiting for some time. As they began eating, they felt a slight tilt of the car. They thought it was the section foreman climbing the steps to get a cup of coffee.

When they turned around, they saw a huge black bear with two cubs. In shock, the men climbed into the cupola and out of the window. Now standing outside the caboose, they could see the bears eating their breakfast and thrashing about the cabin. One of the bears even sat at the conductor's desk for a while.

When the train took off, the bears rode it to Massive, Alberta, where the brakeman was able to dislodge them by wielding a bamboo stick. The interior of the caboose was totally destroyed.

— Amtrak —

The Rail Passenger Service Act of 1970 permitted U.S. railroads to carry only freight and divest themselves of pas-

senger service. It created a corporation, Railpax, which managed 219 daily passenger trains over 23,000 miles of track. Its official name, National Rail Passenger Corporation, quickly became better known as Amtrak. ("Railpax" was discarded; it lent itself too easily to jokes and an unseemly connotation.) Amtrak received $40 million in direct federal grants and another $190 million from participating railroads. The railroads' contribution could be in terms of locomotives and rolling stock rather than cash. Amtrak began operations in May 1971, with 1,190 used passenger cars and 326 aging locomotives. In its first year it maintained 219 train schedules — fewer than half of those operating prior to its existence. The initial railroad members were: the Burlington Northern, Baltimore & Ohio, Chesapeake & Ohio, Gulf, Mobile & Ohio, Illinois Central, Louisville & Nashville, Milwaukee Road, Missouri Pacific, Penn-Central, Richmond, Fredericksburg & Potomac, Santa Fe, Seaboard Coast Line, Southern Pacific, and Union Pacific. Auto-Train and Denver & Rio Grande Western held out until 1983. Amtrak began to consolidate its passenger transfers at Penn Station in New York City and Union Station in Chicago.

Amtrak ordered new Amfleet cars for some of its routes. It ordered double-decker cars for its Chicago-West routes. For the most part, passengers rode on the upper level, and the bottom deck was for entry, luggage, and lavatory facilities. These cars were similar to the ones used on the Santa Fe in the 1960s. It also began to convert existing cars' electrical systems to Head-End Power (HEP). Cars would be dependent upon the locomotive's generating electricity for heat, air conditioning, and light. HEP conversion was completed in 1983. Amtrak had to use the single-level "Heritage Cars" on its eastern routes because of tunnel clearances. In 1973, it placed its first order for SDP 45 passenger locomotives with GM. It later purchased 200 F40PH rated at 3,000 horsepower. It used the former Pennsylvania Railroad *GG1* for service in the New York City and Washington, D.C., corridor. The "G" began to be replaced by a Swedish design AEM-7, known as the "Mighty Mouse," "Meatball," or "Toaster" by railroaders. It became the workhorse of the corridor. From 1972 to 1980, Amtrak increased its passenger numbers from 16.6 million to 21.2 million, and its passenger miles from 3.0 billion to 4.6 billion per year. States and cities contributed by remodeling passenger stations.

Amtrak continued the tradition of name trains of the former passenger-carrying railroads. For example, Amtrak runs the *Crescent* between New York and New Orleans, and *California Zephyr* between Chicago and Los Angeles. In some cases the original timetable train numbers were retained.

— VIA —

VIA Rail Canada began a similar operation in July 1978. By October, Canadian Pacific transferred 500 employees to the new Crown Corporation to take over passenger service of the western continentals. By 1979, VIA ran all intercity trains using former Canadian National and Canadian Pacific equipment. It reduced its fleet and began converting its railcars to Head-End Power. The cars were also remodeled for more comfortable cross-country travel. VIA uses both CN and CPR tracks and makes connections with Amtrak in some border cities. During the 1970s and 1980s, both Amtrak and VIA contracted agreements to operate commuter lines. In the United States, state governments formed corporations to provide commuter service.

— Freight Operations —

Freight operations also suffered. By 1962, freight ton-miles declined to levels like those of the Great Depression in the mid-1930s. Trucks and air-freight grew at an astounding rate at the expense of the railroads. In fact, much of the fuel tax and property tax railroads paid went to construct highways. The railroads actually helped build their own demise: they transported much of the material used to build the Interstate Highway System in the 1950s and 1960s. During those years the railroads barely held on to 37 percent of intercity freight. They gave up on less-than-a carload (LTC) service. Many large railroad companies tried to save money by delayed maintenance — particularly roadbeds — and investment in nontransportation industries. In the United States, the merger seemed to be a solution. Since there was duplicate rail service to many cities, merging competing lines and creating larger, more efficient companies seemed to be a solution. According to the Transportation Act of 1940, railroads could propose their own mergers to the Interstate Commerce Commission should benefits exceed those of competition to a given area. From World War I through the 1940s, there were few mergers. From 1957 through 1968, the number of separate railroad companies dropped from 635 to 375, and more followed during the succeeding years.

— Merger Mania: Round One —

"Merger Mania" began when the Louisville & Nashville Railroad (L&N) sought a merger with the Nashville, Chattanooga, and St. Louis in 1955. In 1959, the Norfolk & Western Virginian merged with the Norfolk & Western. Their side-by-side tracks created a more efficient double-track system. In 1960, the Erie Lackawanna was formed from the Erie and Delaware, Lackawanna, & Western. In 1963, Baltimore & Ohio and Chesapeake & Ohio became one, and added the Western Maryland in 1968. In 1967 the Atlantic Coast Line and the Seaboard Airline became the Seaboard Coast Line. Seaboard Coast Line later joined with the L&N, B&O, and C&O to form the Chessie System.

— The Penn Central —

The biggest merger of this early phase was the combining of the Pennsylvania and the New York Central to form the Penn Central in 1968. The two eastern giants had discussed the possibility of a merger for over a decade. The influx of manufactured products from Japan in the 1960s, along with hard economic times in the northeast, closed industries alongside their tracks. The two railroads finally received clearance from both the ICC and a legal decision from the Supreme Court to merge. The new Penn Central had 21,000 miles of track — the largest in the country at that time — and hoped to achieve a cost savings of over $80 million a year. Also, the Pennsylvania brought with it investments in other industries.

The two rivals did not make a happy marriage. Old competitive feelings still ran strong among the employees. Most Pennsylvania workers belonged to a "Red Team," and most New York Central railroads belonged to the "Green Team." Infighting was common at the higher corporate levels. Moreover, trackside and in-cab signals were different, so it was a major leap to integrate locomotives and crews. In some instances, freight would be delivered to the "wrong yard" in some cities. Furthermore, when the bankrupt New York, New Haven, & Hartford asked the Interstate Commerce Commission to release it from passenger service, the ICC ordered it merged into the PC. Service continued to deteriorate. By 1970, PC averaged 22 derailments a day! PC initiated bankruptcy motions in 1970.

The Penn Central bankruptcy caught the nation's attention to the railroads' plight. A major portion of the northeast railservice was now in question. Some legislators began to speak in terms of "nationalization" of the railroads as a means of keeping them alive. A number of bills were submitted to various congressional committees to solve the problem. It was Union Pacific's vice president William McDonald who proposed a workable solution. McDonald suggested that Congress form a new corporation to take over the Penn Central. The federal government would own the majority of stock, although it could go public sometime in the future. He also suggested that Congress create a new "planning agency" to recommend trackage cuts and other efficiencies so that the new company would not be burdened with PC's structural problems.

EMD SW1200 switch engine or "Yard Goat." Over 1,000 of these 1,200 horsepower locomotives were built between 1954 and 1956.

— Conrail —

In January of 1974, Congress signed into law the making of the Penn Central into a new railroad, Consolidated Rail Corporation or Conrail. The Act also created the United States Railway Association (USRA) to bring about efficiency before Conrail became incorporated formally in 1976. The USRA reduced duplicate trackage and placed other bankrupt roads — the Lehigh Valley, the Central of New Jersey, and the Reading, among others — within the Conrail System. It also granted trackage rights into New York City for the Delaware & Hudson Railroad. Congress granted Conrail $2.1 billion for "start-up costs." Most of the money was used for track and equipment repairs. Conrail's chairman, Edward G. Jordan, had to return to Congress for another almost $5 billion to keep the railroad operating.

— Other Mergers —

While the creation of Conrail attracted most of the nation's attention, other mergers were underway. In 1968, the Chicago & North Western absorbed the Chicago and Great Western, and in 1970 Burlington Northern (BN) was created from the Chicago, Burlington, & Quincy, the Spokane, Portland, & Seattle, the Great Northern, and Northern Pacific. James Hill's dream had now become a reality. The Illinois Central and the Gulf, Mobile & Ohio became the Illinois Central Gulf in 1972, and in 1980, the BN absorbed the St. Louis & San Francisco (Frisco). Large railroads took over smaller lines in the hope of operating them more efficiently and with a profit. These mergers were, in a sense, the reaction of an industry fighting for its life. Some mergers benefited all roads con-

cerned, while others would simply be absorbed by yet larger companies in the years ahead.

— Technology —

Even before the merging tendency, some of the larger railroads turned to modernization and technology to make themselves more cost efficient. The Pennsylvania Railroad was the first to use television to monitor freight yard activities as early as 1954. By the 1960s the telegraph gave way to telephone, and Canadian National and the Illinois Central began their own microwave communication systems. Many railroads turned to computers to eliminate the mountains of paperwork.

Railroads modernized freight yards or constructed new, huge classification sites such as Union Pacific's Bailey Yard at North Platte, Nebraska. These yards used automatic retarding devices to control movement of cars, hot box detectors, and undercarriage inspection units. By the mid-1960s new freight cars used Timken roller bearings which greatly decreased axle problems and derailments due to overheating. More efficient brake valves were installed. Disc brakes were used on passenger cars by the mid-1950s, but the technology would have to wait for more cost-effective installation on freights.

— Automatic Car Identification System —

By the 1970s both Canadian and U.S. railroads were using the Automatic Car Identification System (ACI). All locomotives and freight cars had a 13-stripe label along their sides. As the car entered or left a freight yard, a device would

Loading Intermodal Containers. Courtesy Canadian National. #EF2433-34.

Unit Train with modern aluminum cars. Courtesy Canadian National. #EF2856-6.

"read" the label and send the information to a central office. A computer then stored the car's whereabouts for reference. Any car or locomotive could be located, sometimes within minutes. The tracking system also became known as TeleRail Automated Information Network or TRAIN.

— Piggyback —

"Intermodal" or "Piggyback" was one way the railroads could compete with the trucking industry. The idea originated from the U.S. Army's carrying trucks and tanks on flat cars during the Second World War. The Canadian National began a systematized "Piggyback" operation in 1953. In the United States, the first large-scale transporting of trailers on flatcars (TOFC) began on the Pennsylvania Railroad in 1954. The New York Central quickly followed and modified tunnels, bridges, and loading facilities on a large scale. From 1960 through 1968, Piggyback volume increased by 300 percent. By the 1970s the container on flatcar (COFC) came into existence. Rather than a trailer, a sealed container could be loaded from a ship onto a train for transportation almost anywhere. Soon "land bridge" operations were in effect in both Canada and the United States. Shipments from Europe to Asia or vice versa would cross the Atlantic, then be loaded on trains across North America and loaded again on freighters for Japan and other countries in East Asia.

During the 1960s, the railroads began a serious competition with trucks in transporting cars from Detroit to dealers throughout the country. During the 1920s and 1930s, railroads simply loaded new automobiles into boxcars. The process was both cumbersome and time-consuming. By the 1940s and 1950s, trucks took most of the business away from the railroads. In 1960, the railroads introduced special freight cars with racks to load and unload automobiles efficiently. By 1970, the railroads had recaptured 50 percent of the transportation of newly manufactured autos.

There had been some experimentation with transporting trailers or containers directly on the rails, i.e., without flatcars. In the 1940s the Evans Company of Detroit advertised its "Auto Railer" as the rail freight transportation of the future. The Chesapeake & Ohio engineering department developed the first practical "Road Railer" in 1955. The Federal Railroad Administration (FRA), however, would not approve the Road Railer for long-term or regular use for safety reasons. The FRA required that the vans have ladders and roof running boards as a regular boxcar. The idea would have to wait until the government relaxed the rules in 1980.

— Unit Train —

The "unit train" was another innovation. The unit train consists of all the same cars, mostly hopper cars, that pick up a bulk commodity at its source and deliver it to another site for processing. Unit trains often make a circular trip. Some unit train commodities are: coal, grain, rock, potash, and garbage. The Southern Pacific operated an oil unit train with hoses connecting the series of tank cars. Unit trains are most efficient when there are rapid loading and unloading facilities. In 1988, the Georgetown Railroad of Texas invented the "Dump Train." This unit train could unload 1,000 tons of a bulk commodity in less than an hour. The hopper cars unload from a conveyor in sequence.

The unit train was the railroad's response to the development of coal-slurry pipelines in the late 1950s. The Baltimore & Ohio and the Denver & Rio Grand Western pioneered the unit train in the early 1960s. The Canadian Pacific operated the First Canadian unit train in 1967, although Canadian National advertised them after World War I.

"Mini Trains" are 10 to 15 car unit trains. They usually pick up grain from elevators and haul it to a central site for joining with a larger train. They compete effectively with trucks.

— National Transportation Act —

In 1967, the Canadian government passed the National Transportation Act. This act deregulated a good portion of freight rates. Canadian railroads could negotiate "agreed charges" with certain customers. With the growth of Japanese industry, both the Canadian Pacific and Canadian National were in a position to increase traffic and revenue. The rail-

Intermodal yard at Omaha, Nebr. Amtrak station in background. Tracks are Union Pacific in foreground and BNSF at Amtrak station.

Coal Unit Train emptying cars at the Mid American Energy facility, Port Neal, Iowa. It takes 2.7 minutes to empty a car.

roads transported natural resources to the Pacific Coast for embarkation overseas. In the United States, the Interstate Commerce Commission permitted significant increases in freight charges.

— The U.S. Department of Transportation —

In 1966, the U.S. Congress created the Department of Transportation (DOT) with its head having a secretarial post in the presidential cabinet. The DOT develops national transportation policies, coordinates service, stimulates technological advances, and helps to solve transportation problems. The DOT has regulatory authority over land, water, and air transportation in the United States. The DOT also has supervision over air and noise pollution, environmental concerns, and accessibility for the disabled. The Federal Railroad Administration is a division of the Department of Transportation.

— The Federal Railroad Administration —

The Federal Railroad Administration (FRA), gives exclusive attention to the U.S. rail industry. The FRA oversees the role of the railroads in the overall national transportation network, defense, and emergency needs, and the mass transit system. Safety is the primary concern. The FRA employs 360 inspectors to check trains, rail yards, and equipment. They work in cooperation with thousands of railroad company inspectors. The FRA has authority to levy fines and, in extreme cases, close down rail operations. The FRA is involved in new equipment testing and in investigating rail accidents. It also promotes state and local railroad safety programs. Since 1971, the FRA oversees the finances and operations of Amtrak.

— National Transportation Safety Board —

The National Transportation Safety Board (NTSB) investigates mostly airline and maritime accidents. It does, however, reserve the right to investigate railroad accidents when-

ever one of the following is involved: passenger trains, any fatality, hazardous materials, and an accident of repetitive nature. Created in 1967, the NTSB relied on the DOT for funding and administrative support. In 1975, it became an independent agency by act of Congress.

— Operation Lifesaver —

In 1972, the Union Pacific Railroad announced a campaign to educate the public about railroad safety — particularly for automobiles at grade crossings. The program became known throughout the nation as "Operation Lifesaver." Its theme is "Look, Listen, and Live," as Operation Lifesaver reminds people to look and listen for trains when they approach a railroad track.

Operation Lifesaver also asks the public to report any damage to railroad crossing signs and equipment. It asks railroads to close crossings that have fallen into little use. Some estimates credit the program with having saved over 12,000 lives since its beginning. While such a specific claim may be difficult to prove, there is no doubt that Operation Lifesaver has increased the public's awareness of railroad safety issues.

— Social Considerations —

Both Canadian and U.S. railroads had to respond to social change. During the 1960s and 1970s, the railroads were urged, if not required, to hire women and minorities. Women now sought blue collar or operational positions in both countries. With the growth of nationalism by the French in Quebec Province, the Canadian Railroads had to become more bilingual and seek to hire more people of French heritage.

Railroads were also forced to become more conscious of the environment through both legislation and public pressure. Although it produces less smoke than a steam locomotive, the diesel's exhaust is a greater pollutant from a chemical point of view. Moreover, without retaining devices, the diesel leaks quantities of oil along the tracks. The railroads responded to both issues in a timely manner. Retaining tanks were installed on locomotives which virtually eliminated spillage along the rails. Computerized controls helped make the diesel perform more efficiently and, therefore, release fewer pollutants into the air. Railroads placed greater emphasis on maintenance and monitored their equipment to adhere to environmental standards.

— Pullman Company —

The airplane and truck made a severe impact on associated railroad services in both the United States and Canada. The decline in passenger traffic was not the only problem faced by the Pullman Company. Due to a court decision, Pullman had to separate its car operations and its car building into two different companies. In 1947, Pullman sold its operations to the 57 railroads which used its service. By the late 1950s both the Pennsylvania and New York Central railroads began to operate their own sleeping cars. Other railroads followed suit, and the Pullman Company stopped attending the cars completely by 1968. The railroads themselves attended the sleepers, while Pullman maintained and serviced the cars for another year.

— Railway Express Agency —

The Railway Express Agency also went into decline. Even though it operated at a profit into the 1950s, it lost traffic to other companies. When it negotiated a new contract with member railroads in 1959, it was permitted to use trucks and airplanes to keep up with competition. After operating at a deficit in the 1960s, the agency was sold to its five head executives, who changed its name to REA Express. Its traffic declined to about 1 percent of the entire industry, and its directors attempted a series of lawsuits against the railroads and United Parcel Service. It lost an exclusive agreement with the airlines for its air-express operations. By 1975, REA Express went out of business with charges of embezzlement among its officials. The Canadian railroads also ceased their express operations by the mid-1970s.

— Ol' Tramp's Free Train Ride —

Upon acquiring an exceptional purebred female poodle, a pet shop owner in Kansas City decided to buy a mate for it. They had heard that a breeder in Minneapolis had the best line of the most talented and groomed poodles in the country. They placed their order and were willing to pay the price for the "best of the best."

The breeder sent his very best by Railway Express with the following instructions: "One dog — feed 3X per day." Hours later the crate arrived at Oelwein, Iowa, for transfer to another line. Two Express agents saw the instructions and fed and watered the dog. Since they had some extra time, they decided to let the dog run around the freight room to get some exercise. Besides, ol' Tramp, a mangy mixed breed dog that hung around the office, would probably enjoy some company.

A few minutes later another agent entered the building, and the poodle scampered through the open door and es-

caped. The agents searched for over two hours, but could not find the dog. At that point they realized they had to put the dog crate on the next train to Kansas City within minutes! They then had an idea . . . Why not put Tramp on the train!?!? The addresses on the crate were two businesses, so the dog was not anyone's pet. No one would miss Tramp. Besides all the freight card read was: "One dog — feed 3X per day."

Tramp arrived at the pet shop in Kansas City the next day. For the entire week telegrams flew fast and furious between Kansas City and Minneapolis. There were all kinds of accusations, denials, and downright nasty comments. How could a fancy poodle turn overnight into a dog of many breeds and no talent?

Finally the pet shop owner sent Tramp back to Minneapolis in the same crate labeled: "One dog — feed 3X per day." In the meantime the poodle found its way back to the freight station and slept in Tramp's favorite corner. When the agents saw the familiar crate again, they let Tramp out and replaced him with the poodle.

The breeder and the pet shop owner never figured out what happened. And ol' Tramp got a free train ride. . . .

— U.S. Railway Mail Service —

The U.S. government transformed the Railway Mail Service into the Postal Transportation Service in 1949. That same year the Post Office began to move a significant amount of first-class mail by air. As the railroads dropped passenger trains, the post office did not renew mail-carrying contracts. With the introduction of zip codes and central sorting facilities, there was no need to categorize mail on the moving train. The last Railroad Post Office Car operated between New York City and Washington, D.C., in June 1977. Canada had ended its postal agreements with its railroads several years earlier.

By 1980, the Canadian and U.S. railroads ceased to be passenger and public mail and package carrying services. They became exclusively freight haulers — with a few exceptions as commuter railroads. In fact, during the late 1970s, many commuter operations were being assumed by local, state, or provincial agencies. Without mail, express, and passenger services, railroads disappeared from being in the public view and consciousness. They became an industry separated from daily life. Rather than a daily — if not hourly — occurrence, trains were less frequent and a nuisance to the general public.

— End of an Era —

Both Canada and the United States had changed. In 1949, R. C. Weir published the children's book *The Wonderful Train Ride.* According to the story, Aunt Mary trusted her nephew and niece, Billy and Kay, to the Pullman porter at New York's Grand Central Station for a cross-country train ride — alone — to their parents in Los Angeles. The children experienced all the facilities and joy of a first-class cross-country train trip. In the same year both the Guy Lombardo and Tommy Dorsey

175

Orchestras recorded the hit song "Down By the Station." The lyrics spoke of the enjoyment of a train ride: "You'll get a treat when you order a seat on the ole choo-choo." Of course, Glenn Miller's "Chattanooga Choo Choo" was still played on the radio and phonograph claiming that "there's nothing finer than dinner in the diner." Country and western singers celebrated the train. The Lionel Company grossed huge sales at Christmastime with all kinds of new cars that performed every railroad activity imaginable. Two other manufacturers, American Flyer and Marx, became prominent in the model train market.

In slightly more than a generation, Lionel model train sales began to slump. Children's books focused on the airplane, and no one would entrust their child to a stranger for a four-day cross-country trip. Country and western music sang about truck driving, and motorists bought Citizen Band (CB) radios to communicate with others in an attempt to escape "speed traps."

The downtowns that grew around the train station began to sprawl out to shopping centers with large parking lots. People no longer took the train to a larger town or city on Saturday to buy that "something special." People now waved good-bye at their doorstep or at the airport, not at the depot where their relatives and friends boarded a Pullman. The television also ended the necessity of commuting to the city for entertainment. Movie stars now appeared "live" on the screen in one's own home.

While people noticed the end of the passenger train, and that freights moved slower and became less frequent, some still believed the railroads were "greedy companies" run by the "Robber Barons" of old. By the 1970s, the years of regulation and subsidies to competing industries took their toll. If the formation of Conrail made many people realize that there was a problem, there is no doubt in anyone's mind that the railroad era was at an end with the demise of the Rock Island Railroad in March 1980.

After years of attempting a merger with the Union Pacific, bankruptcy proceedings, and attempts at a new image, the Chicago Rock Island and Pacific folded. Its 7,000 miles of track no longer linked the large cities of the Midwest (Chicago, Dallas, Minneapolis, and Denver). A major company simply went out of existence. The Rock Island's demise forced the U.S. government to take a serious look at the plight of the industry which helped build the nation.

Chapter 16.

Trains Today

During the 1980s, railroads entered a new era. No longer engines of U.S. and Canadian culture or creators of a social pattern, railroads today are purely business enterprises. There are three major characteristics of this period: greater application of technology, the tendency toward large mergers, and fewer personnel to carry out more work.

— Staggers Act —

The death of the Rock Island Railroad signaled that the U.S. railroads were in a crisis situation. Only a few larger roads could be considered healthy financially. That same year, 1980, Representative Jim Florio of New Jersey introduced legislation to partially deregulate railroad freight shipping charges. Named after Harley Staggers of West Virginia, the "Staggers Act" permitted railroads to offer discounts to large-volume customers without needing prior approval from the Interstate Commerce Commission (ICC). The railroads could also raise any rate that fell below a significant percentage of expenses. Although the ICC had oversight control of the new rates, it lost much of its regulatory power. In short, the Staggers Act was the first important legislation which led to the revival of the railroad industry in the United States.

The Canadian railroads had enjoyed such freedom since the National Transportation Act of 1967. Twenty years later, the Canadians passed the Transportation Act of 1987, which gave their railroads almost complete control over freight rates. Canadian trains could now effectively compete with trucks, planes, and boats.

— Amtrak —

Amtrak also benefited from new government legislation. In 1976, Amtrak received ownership and control of the New York City–Washington, D.C., "corridor." Amtrak now had greater assurance of meeting its schedules. It also received government contracts to haul mail throughout the country, and already had a small express business.

The Reagan administration distanced itself from Amtrak during most of the 1980s. President Reagan believed that U.S. passenger rail service should stand or fall on its own merit and not be tied to continuous government assistance. Congress declared that Amtrak had to pay half of its operating expenses from public fares. Through a vigorous program, Amtrak was able to pay for 79 percent of its operating expenses from fares by 1992 — which was a higher percentage than other railroad passenger services in the entire world. Ridership grew to about 42 million people per year. Amtrak enjoyed great popularity during its Graham Claytor presidency.

By the mid-1990s Amtrak experienced financial and political difficulties again. The federal government is unwilling again to continue its funding. Former Amtrak president Thomas Downs began a policy of "weeding out" unprofitable trains and turning to the states to fund improvement projects. Such historic trains as the *Broadway Limited* no longer appeared on timetables. Other runs went from daily to only a few times a week.

Environmental legislation also had its effect on Amtrak. Legislation outlawed the dumping of toilet waste directly onto the tracks — a time-honored practice in the industry. Heritage car toilets often froze in winter. Moreover, the Heritage cars used east of the Mississippi were beginning to show their age.

At a time of great financial stress, Amtrak designed and ordered new "Viewliner" sleeping cars for its eastern runs. The Viewliners have the latest in wheel truck and disc brake technology, and they also have batteries to keep lighting and air conditioning on when the engine is changed. The Viewliner has a "cathedral effect." The ceiling is much higher than the Heritage car, and there is a second, smaller window above the lower, larger one. The second window permits the occupant in the upper berth to look out at night when not sleeping. There are basin and toilet facilities in each room as well as a small TV. (Of course, the best picture is the one moving outside the window.) As with some earlier equipment, modern passenger cars have more of the appearance of the jet airplane. Perhaps designers believe that the appearance is "more modern" or that people are more familiar with a rounded shape. This design is quite a switch from the 1930s and 1940s when airlines tried to imitate the comfort and convenience of riding on a train. Viewliner toilets and basins are self-contained and do not empty onto the tracks.

The Amtrak crew finds working conditions much easier than their Pullman predecessors. Although car attendants have similar responsibilities, their hours are more regular. Instead of working 400 hours a month as in the 1920s, the modern attendant works the equivalent of a 40-hour week. He or she undergoes about 100 hours of training before being permitted to work a train. While trying to curtail expenses, Amtrak does an adequate job in its lounge and dining cars. Some trains have a better dinner reputation than others.

In the mid-1990s, in the face of threatened further cutbacks and even a "shut-down" in some government circles, Amtrak is looking toward the future. In mid 1996, it initiated advance credit card payment directly by phone or computer. This is the biggest innovation since 1985, when Amtrak consolidated its ticket sales with the airline travel-agent reporting system.

Amtrak *Acela* train. Courtesy Amtrak.

BOMBARDIER
TRANSPORTATION

Wide lower berth of an Amtrak Viewliner bedroom.

Upper level of bi-level lounge car on Amtrak *California Zephyr*.

Amtrak was also the beneficiary of Pennsylvania's $18.7 million of Federal Transit Administration funds. Amtrak and Pennsylvania planned to upgrade the Philadelphia to Harrisburg trackage and to purchase self-propelled diesel multiple unit cars or DMU — a reminder of the RDG or Budd Train concept. The new DMU is designed to travel the Keystone Corridor at speeds up to 110 miles per hour.

— Amtrak's *Acela* —

In spring 1999, Amtrak unveiled its 150-mile-per-hour *Acela* Northeast Corridor train. A product of Bombardier, it reached 165 miles per hour at the AAR testing facility at Pueblo, Colorado. The new train has a schedule of three hours from Boston to New York and two hours and 45 minutes from New York to Washington, D.C.

The high-speed train is designed to attract customers who usually travel by air. The consist has two locomotives at front and back ends—with one first-class and four business-class cars which hold a total of 304 passengers. The train features wide seats, computer facilities, phone, and fax. The café car has a "pub-like" atmosphere.

With the inauguration of its "fleet of modernism," Amtrak has eliminated the traditional names of its northeast trains. The *Clocker, Keystone,* and *Congressional* are now known as *Acela,* a new name to emphasize passenger service into the twenty-first century. The five current northeast services are divided into *Acela Regional* and *Acela Commuter* divisions.

Amtrak also plans a Midwest Regional Rail System (MWRRS). With Chicago as a hub, MWRRS will serve nine states with over 3,000 miles of track. New trains with modern interiors and many conveniences will run in certain areas at 110 miles per hour. Amtrak projects an eight million person ridership annually. In the meantime, in late spring 1999, it has resumed daily service to Oklahoma with a new train, *The Heartland Flyer.*

In 1999, Amtrak received $140 million from state, federal, and other sources to re-electrify the line from Philadelphia to Harrisburg, Pennsylvania. Amtrak plans to run trains at 110 MPH over those tracks. A new station is being built at the Harrisburg airport.

Amtrak's future looks bright. Ridership grew by 5.1 percent for the second quarter of 1999. Core revenues increased by 9.3 percent. In April 1999, Amtrak ordered 129 more RoadRailer units from Wabash National Corporation. Amtrak's new president, George Warrington, initiated a new employee-training program which emphasizes customer service. There was marked improvement in customer service by spring 1999.

Amtrak is the United States's long-distance rail passenger service. While a few private companies have tried luxury trains from time to time, only Amtrak has lasted beyond the "railroad era." Its traffic between New York City and Washington, D.C., is more than the equivalent of 7,500 fully booked 757s or 10,000 fully booked DC 9s. It holds more than 70 percent of Philadelphia, Wilmington, and Baltimore's share of the air-rail market. Amtrak ridership in 1999 was 22 million people. When including commuter contract services, its total ridership increases to 75 million

With Mt. Shasta in the background, two Genesis locomotives pull modern bi-level passenger cars. Courtesy Amtrak.

Amtrak E60 electric locomotive.

Amtrak AEM 7 at Union Station, Washington, D.C. It is more affectionately called by other names: "Mighty Mouse," the "Meatball," and the "Toaster."

Dome Car. Courtesy VIA.

Courtesy VIA, Rail Canada, Inc.

people. These numbers should grow larger with the *Acela* program.

Amtrak has its critics in government, and sometimes passengers complain of scheduling and delays. Nevertheless, Amtrak is the only viable long-distance rail passenger service option in the United States at the beginning of the twenty-first century.

— VIA —

Canada's VIA Rail has suffered financially over the past years. Many of the services of the original *Canadian* and *Atlantic* were lost in the transition. VIA Rail rebuilt the 157 Budd cars it received from United States Railroads. It also changed to Head-End Power in the early 1990s.

VIA's "Chateau Sleepers" and "Manor Sleepers" still retain the open Pullman-style sections as well as roomettes and drawing rooms. Trains *Canadian*, *Ocean*, *Chaleur*, and *Skina* are equipped with Skyline Dome Cars. They also have end-of-train observation cars in service for first-class passengers. VIA also purchased and refurbished coaches from several U.S. railroads, including the Richmond, Fredricksburg, and Potomac, the Pennsylvania, Atlantic Coast Line, and the New York Central. VIA also operates a seasonal, tri-weekly RDC or Budd train between Sudbury and White River, Ontario.

VIA's cross-continent trips through the Canadian Rockies are a major tourist attraction. In fact, several private companies operate trains through the Rockies with overnight stays at hotels. In that way, tourists have the advantage of an all-daylight run. Canada's VIA Rail has connections, though not through-service, with Amtrak at Montreal, Toronto, and Vancouver. In 1999, VIA Customers traveled over 950 million passenger miles.

— Conrail —

In one sense, the creations of Amtrak and VIA Rail were the "merging" of passenger service into one large corporation for the respective nations. This merging trend continued among U.S. railroads right into the 1990s. When L. Stanley

Crane became president of Conrail in 1981, he restored faith in the merger as the means of saving the railroad industry.

Crane renegotiated work contracts with the labor unions. Rather than confrontations, he exhibited a spirit of cooperation. He convinced the unions to agree to four- and even three-person crews on trains. He then concentrated Conrail's marketing on coal, grain, and intermodal service. Conrail's finances were in the black by the end of 1983. The Reagan Administration sold the government's stock publicly. In 1985, Norfolk Southern (NS) made a $1.8 billion bid for Conrail, but was thwarted by Crane, the unions, and CSX. Conrail stock was sold in 1987 at a public offering.

Conrail's finances fell into a slump by the 1990s. Norfolk Southern and CSX entered into a bidding war for the northeast railroad. Both wanted direct access to the New York City and Boston markets. Conrail resisted the NS offer again through the "fine print" of Pennsylvania law, the state in which it is incorporated. At the same time, Burlington Northern president Robert D. Krebs made sounds of purchasing NS and creating a true transcontinental south of the Canadian border.

In spring 1997, Conrail, CSX, and Norfolk Southern arrived at an agreement. CSX would take over tracks from Boston to Cleveland through Albany and Buffalo, or the route of the former New York Central. Norfolk Southern would have the tracks of the former Pennsylvania through Harrisburg and West.

When the Surface Transportation Board (STB) approved the breakup of Conrail, CSX became the third largest railroad in the United States, with 23,000 miles of track. Norfolk Southern is fourth with 21,400 miles. The STB granted Canadian Pacific rights to New York City through the Delaware & Hudson Railroad. Other regional carriers received trackage rights.

Because of operations problems of the UP/SP merger, the STB required weekly detailed reports from CSX and Norfolk Southern. The STB demanded that both railroads move slowly to avoid problems. The STB and both railroads set June 1, 1999, as "Day One" for the end of Conrail and the takeover by the two eastern giants.

Lounge Car. Courtesy VIA, Rail Canada, Inc.

Bedroom. Courtesy VIA, Rail Canada, Inc.

This Kansas City Southern SD50 locomotive carries the heralds of the "NAFTA Railway."

— Conrail Lives —

Although most of Conrail was divided between CSX and Norfolk Southern, certain trackage remains part of a "shared assets" agreement. Conrail track in certain areas of Michigan, Pennsylvania, and New Jersey gives both railroad giants access to customers along those lines. It also includes important rail yards in Camden, Newark, and south of Trenton. The Detroit district includes Detroit, Dearborn, Sterling Heights, and Carleton. Headquarters remain in Philadelphia, and the Conrail name lives on.

— Merger Mania: Round Two —

The Conrail merger drama is only the most recent phase of the amalgamation trend. In 1982, Union Pacific absorbed the Western Pacific and merged with the Missouri Pacific. Management gave the order that they did not want to see one item with the WP herald left on it! Union Pacific then took over the Missouri-Kansas-Texas (KATY) system in 1988 and the Chicago & North Western in 1995. When the Union Pacific took over the Southern Pacific in 1996, it became the largest railroad in track mileage (36,500) in the United States. (The Southern Pacific had brought with it the rights-of-way of the former Denver & Rio Grande Western and Cotton Belt.)

By summer 1997, Union Pacific experienced difficulties in getting trains through the former Southern Pacific trackage in Texas. Traffic in places came to a standstill, and the whole situation was labeled "gridlock" or "meltdown." Customers along the line demanded more shipments of products, and the exchange with the Mexican rail connection Transportacion Ferroviaria Mexicana S.A. de C.V. (Grupo TFM) at Laredo became a trickle. The freight yard at Houston was antiquated, and could not handle the load. Some former SP employees resigned and hired on with rival BNSF (see below). There was also a locomotive shortage.

Union Pacific encouraged employees to transfer to Texas and planned to hire more to solve the problem. The railroad spent over $500 million to upgrade tracks and facilities. In the meantime, the Federal Railroad Administration cited safety problems, customers threatened lawsuits, and even some Union Pacific stockholders threatened a class-action suit.

Texas was not the only problem area. There was another bottleneck in western Iowa. The former Chicago & Northwestern lines from Minneapolis and those from Chicago met at California Junction. With increased traffic, trains were delayed. The UP temporarily routed the Chicago trains over the Iowa Interstate Railroad. Union Pacific then began to double-track the Chicago line which relieved the congestion.

In 1995, the Burlington Northern merged with the Santa Fe to create the Burlington Northern Santa Fe (BNSF) with 30,852 track miles. Another important merger was the

Seaboard Coast Line, the Louisville & Nashville, and other short lines forming the Seaboard System in 1982, and the Seaboard System joining the Chessie System to create the CSX with 26,328 track miles. In the Midwest, the Soo Line took over 3,100 miles of the bankrupt Milwaukee Road trackage. The remainder of the Milwaukee Road's rails were either torn up or purchased by BN and other companies. In short, the 70 or so large U.S. railroad companies in 1968 have been reduced to a handful of east and west giants. Burlington Northern–Santa Fe, Union Pacific, and the Illinois Central, along with the Kansas City Southern, dominate the midwest and west. CSX and Norfolk Southern with their "merger prize" Conrail serve the east. The tendency toward monopoly, the dream of Harriman, Hill, and Commodore Vanderbilt, seems to be coming true. . . .

— NAFTA —

The North American Free Trade Agreement (NAFTA) took effect at the beginning of 1994. NAFTA created the largest "free trade zone" in the world by gradually removing tariffs on goods traded among Canada, Mexico, and the United States. Most trade restrictions are to be lifted gradually through 2004. Commissions in each country monitor environmental and labor concerns.

NAFTA has greatly increased north–south trade. Kansas City Southern's NAFTA Railway runs from Springfield, Illinois, to New Orleans, Dallas, and Houston. Kansas City Southern Industries invested in Mexico's Northeast Railroad Transportation, Ferroviaria Mexicana (TFM), and Gateway Western. It has capitalized on a 16.1 percent growth rate in trade between the United States and Mexico. With a similar growth rate in Canadian trade, Kansas City Southern is in an ideal position. In 1998, Kansas City Southern and Canadian National have agreed to coordinate marketing and train operations at interchanges in Springfield, Illinois, and Jackson, Mississippi. In summer 1999, Kansas City Southern and TFM started the *NAFTA Express*. This intermodal train makes the trip from Laredo to Mexico City in 32 hours. The *Express* will expand deliveries to other cities in the near future.

Consolidation seems to be a trend even in the short-line or local railroad industry. There have always been a number of smaller railroad companies which connect a factory or town with a larger carrier. These "feeders" could operate at a modest profit as a "Mom and Pop" company which does not have to abide by union rules. During the late 1980s, while the larger roads were selling off nonprofitable trackage, another purchased the rails and formed a new entity in the railroad industry.

— RailTex —

RailTex of San Antonio, Texas, began as a railroad-car leasing company in 1977. In 1984, its president, Bruce Flohr, purchased the bankrupt San Diego & Imperial Valley Railroad, a 45-mile line with two locomotives. He then put his theories into practice. Flohr believed in marketing, giving managers full authority, and customer service. He hired three salespersons for the SD&IV line and turned it into a profitable venture. He then began purchasing more feeder railroads. In

Anatomy of a merger. Burlington Northern EMD SD40–2 teams up with a General Electric Santa Fe locomotive to pull a heavy freight in the Midwest.

1995, RailTex bought the Central Vermont from Canadian National, and renamed it New England Central.

RailTex revenue soared from $16.5 million in 1989 to $38 million in 1992. In 1996, Flohr's operation owned a total of 3,500 miles of track and 29 holdings in Canada, Mexico, and the United States. RailTex also has almost 13 percent ownership of the 4,400-mile Centro-Atlantic Railroad in Brazil. Revenue from operations approached $100 million in 1996.

Each RailTex railroad keeps its own local identity. As with short lines, RailTex does not have to abide by union rules and salary scale. RailTex can operate the short lines at a healthy profit. Flohr believed in cross-training workers and strict adherence to safety regulations. Moreover, his workers were encouraged to act as sales representatives and to generate business. They received end-of-year bonuses for encouragement. Flohr's personal dynamism and cordiality made RailTex a bright, new concept in a more than century-old industry.

— RailTex and RailAmerica —

After Flohr announced his retirement in 1997, RailTex chose Ron Rittenmeyer to become its president. Having associated with larger companies, Rittenmeyer changed Flohr's family style of management to a more Wall Street mentality. The company subsequently lost a number of devoted employees to other roads. Nevertheless, RailTex stood as the largest U.S. short-line company.

In late 1999, RailAmerica, another short-line company, offered to purchase RailTex. Formed in 1986, RailAmerica owns railroads in the United States, Canada, and Chile. It also has a freight concession in Australia. The offer has been

approved by stockholders and the Surface Transportation Board. RailAmerica tends to centralize its operations and give its short lines less independent identity than did RailTex. RailAmerica is now the largest short-line company in America, controlling over fifty-one railroads.

— Canadian National and Canadian Pacific —

Although there was no merger of the two largest Canadian railroads, Canadian National (CN) and Canadian Pacific Railway (CPR), they experienced revenue growth and undertook major projects in recent years. Business grew with Japan and other Asian countries. Internal traffic increased as well as freight to and from the United States. Canadian National at one point announced a $212 million profit. The National Transportation Act of 1987 permitted the Canadian railroads to respond more quickly to rate changes in the United States.

With a softer economy in the late 1980s and early 1990s, CN began a program of downsizing and modernization. By 1994, the Canadian government began to prepare CN for privatization. Privatization was officially announced in February 1995, and by the following November, the government released its 83.3 million shares of stock for sale on exchanges in Montreal, New York, and Toronto. The sale netted the government $2.2 billion.

CN is in the process of purchasing 394 new locomotives over the next fifteen years. In April 1995, it completed a new St. Clair Tunnel between Sarnia, Ontario, and Port Huron, Michigan. The new tunnel has a 26-foot 6-inch diameter which can accommodate double-stack containers. It saves 24

RailAmerica

183

Canadian Pacific Rogers Pass Project. Courtesy Canadian Pacific Railway.

Rogers Pass Project. Mount Shaughnessy Tunnel. Courtesy Canadian Pacific Railway.

A track inspector uses a "High-Railer" truck which can travel on both highway and track. Note the small, flanged guide wheels which hold it onto the rails.

hours on runs from Halifax, Nova Scotia, to Chicago. In the 1980s, the Canadian Pacific began a major reconstruction in Rogers Pass. It completed the 9-mile MacDonald Tunnel in 1989, the longest in North America.

In the mid-1990s, Canadian Pacific Railway concluded an agreement with CSX to share the "Iron Highway." Trailers could be loaded or unloaded on special flatcars without lifts or other special equipment. In 1999, Canadian Pacific inaugurated its own "Expressway Service" to promote cooperation rather than competition with the trucking industry on inter-city short-haul service. "Expressway Service" combines the "best features" of both forms of transportation.

In the late 1990s, Canada had 16 regional railroads and some trackage of the Burlington Northern Santa Fe, CSX, Conrail, Norfolk Southern, and Wisconsin Central. BCR is the largest regional with 1,440 miles extending from North Vancouver to Fort Nelson, British Columbia. Connections are made with CN at Prince George and with both CN and CPR at Vancouver.

With "rationalizing" or abandoning unprofitable trackage, Canadian National remains the fifth largest rail system in North America with 17,143 miles. Canadian Pacific Railway has 11,505 miles, including ownership of the Soo Line in the Midwest. CN and BC Rail have also developed modern telecommunication divisions. With acquisition of new and more efficient motive power, the Canadian railroads are preparing themselves for the new century.

— NAFTA Sparks CN-IC Merger —

NAFTA encouraged Canadian National to look southward. In July 1999, Illinois Central and Canadian National merged into an international north–south system. Besides gaining a huge share of southbound trade, Canadian National was able to obtain an ice-free port for Canadian exports. The merger created a 20,400-mile system which extends from Halifax to Vancouver and southward to New Orleans. It also includes the former Chicago Central and Pacific line from Chicago westward to Sioux City and Council Bluffs, Iowa. Just as important, the merger provides a connection with Mexican rails.

Canadian National announced the purchase agreement of Illinois Central in February 1998, for $2.8 billion. In August of the same year CN purchased 75 percent of IC stock. The U.S. Surface Transportation Board approved the merger in March 1999 to take effect on July 1 the same year. CN and IC operated as distinct systems for marketing purposes for one year. CN promised to keep the Illinois Central corporate name alive. Illinois Central identified itself for decades as the "Main Line of Mid America." With this merger CN could alter the slogan to the "Mainline for a Larger America."

— North American Railways, Inc. —

In December 1999, Canadian National Railway (CN) and Burlington Northern Santa Fe (BNSF) announced a proposed

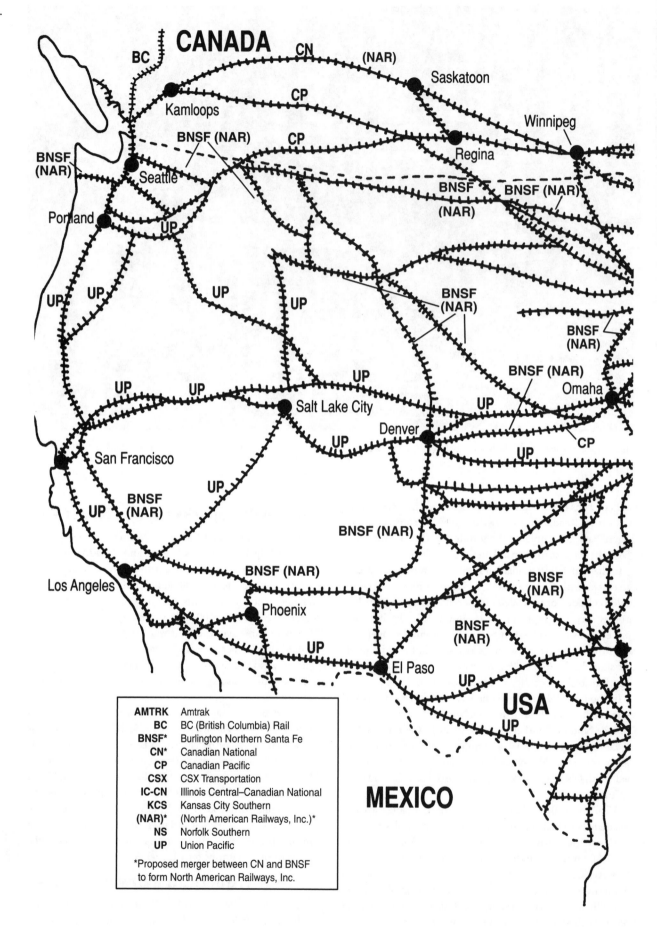

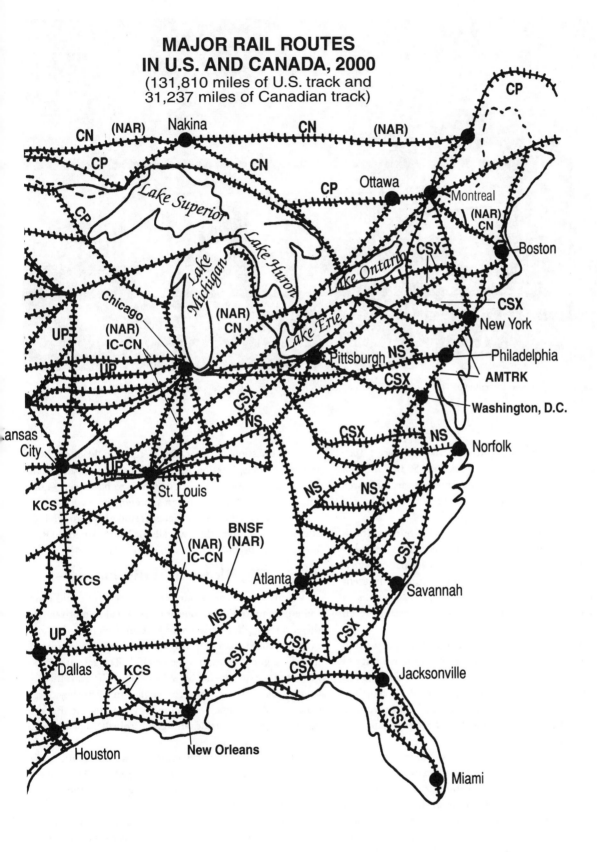

MAJOR RAIL ROUTES
IN U.S. AND CANADA, 2000
(131,810 miles of U.S. track and
31,237 miles of Canadian track)

Union Pacific Super Turbine locomotive. The two units generated 8,500 horsepower and were known as "The Big Blows." Courtesy Union Pacific.

merger. The new company, North American Railways, Inc., would be the largest on the continent, with 50,000 miles of rail and 67,000 employees. Combined revenues are estimated at $12.5 billion. The merger is defined as a CN purchase of BNSF.

The Canadian court system and the U.S. Surface Transportation Board must approve the merger before it can become a reality. This approval may not be automatic because of the operational difficulties experienced during some recent mergers of large systems. BNSF, however, did accomplish a relatively smooth integration of the former Burlington Northern and Santa Fe lines in 1995.

North American Railways, Inc. is to be headquartered in Montreal, Canada, with Canadians forming the majority of its Board. BNSF president Robert Krebs would remain as non-executive chairman of the new company for a short period of time. CN chairman Paul Tellier is still chief executive officer of CN and would become chief operating officer of North American Railways.

The proposed merger argues that it would increase Canadian exports and facilitate trade, especially with Mexico. The combination gives U.S. shippers better access to European trade; products can be carried by rail from the west coast directly to Halifax, which is North America's deep-water port closest to Europe. The Canadian corridor is most important for a growing U.S. double stack market. BNSF argues that the merger is the best way to compete with the trucking industry.

Along with service, operations, and legal questions, there are also some political concerns. The largest U.S. shippers' group, the National Industrial Transportation League, asks about the need for yet another merger. Some congressmen and senators question whether the merger would affect other modes of transportation as well as other railroads. Some politicians question whether it is wise to have over 34,000 miles of U.S. rails controlled in a foreign city.

If the proposed merger progresses smoothly through legal and political hurdles, the plan calls for North American Railways, Inc. to become a reality in mid-2001.

— Big Blows and Big Jacks —

During the steam era almost every railroad could claim something unique about one or more of its locomotives. The diesel era brought about standardization. Union Pacific, however, still could boast of having two unique and powerful engines: the gas turbines and the DD40A. The gas turbine began as an experiment by ALCO and General Electric Companies using aircraft technologies. In 1949 they developed a 4,500 horsepower engine for Union Pacific. Because of the design of its outside railing, subsequent models became known as "Verandas."

Later, General Electric developed a two-unit 8,500 horsepower Super Turbine. It weighed almost 850,000 pounds and was used almost exclusively to pull freight trains through the Wasatch Mountains. The turbines, however, had a few drawbacks. They consumed 600 gallons of fuel an hour. Old locomotive tenders had to be used as tanks to contain enough fuel for them to make the trip. Moreover, the heavy Bunker C fuel was thick and corrosive. To save fuel, the Super Turbine used a self-contained 600 horsepower standard diesel engine to move around a freight yard for servicing. It was impossible to use more than one turbine unit in a tunnel; the second unit would snuff out due to lack of air. The Super Tur-

The 6,600 horsepower Union Pacific *Centennial* diesel locomotive. The 6900 was the first *Centennial* used in regular service. Courtesy Union Pacific Museum Collection. #56805.

F40PH in push-pull service with New Jersey Transit. This particular locomotive has a Caterpillar diesel. Newark, N.J., May 1997.

bine's exhaust temperature would reach 850 degrees Fahrenheit, and they made an enormous noise. Railroaders called them "Big Blows."

Since the cost was almost the same to maintain a diesel locomotive whatever its size, Union Pacific experimented with a General Electric twin-diesel component using the same chassis. In other words, two U25B diesel engines powered the single locomotive to achieve 5,000 horsepower. In the late 1960s, Union Pacific ordered a series of 6,600 horsepower units from EMD using the same twin-engine idea. Since the unit's first service was to pull a train to UP's Golden Spike Centennial Celebration at Promontory, Utah, they quickly became known as *Centennials*.

The *Centennials* were more properly known as DDA40s, and they were the most powerful single-unit land vehicle at that time. They weighed 545,000 pounds and could achieve 90 miles per hour. Because of their size and weight, railroaders called them "Big Jacks."

— *Little Joes* and FL9s —

There was a small, second generation of electric motors following World War II. In 1946, Josef Stalin, leader of the Soviet Union, ordered electric locomotives EP4 and EF4 from General Electric. With the blockade of Berlin and Cold War policies, the United States banned their export.

General Electric changed the locomotives from a 5-foot to 4-foot 8½-inch gauge and marketed them to the Milwaukee Road's 654-mile Rocky Mountain Division. At 3,300 volts, they delivered a continuous 5,110 horsepower and could muster 5,550 horsepower for one hour. The Milwaukee Road rigged a connection so that they could be used in tandem with diesel electrics. The *Little Joe* remained in service until the end of electrification in 1973. *Little Joe*'s cousins, class W-1 and EL-2B, were purchased and used by the Great Northern Railway and Virginia Railroad respectively.

From 1956 through 1960, EMD produced 60 FL9 locomotives exclusively for the New Haven Railroad. The FL9 produces 1,800 horsepower. They were unique, because they could run on diesel, overhead catenery, or hotshoe from a third rail. The FL9 was ideal for New Haven's operations into New York City. The Connecticut Department of Transportation operated several FL9s until 1999, in the last New Haven paint scheme of reddish-orange, black, and white.

— Third and Fourth Generation Diesels —

Diesel locomotives greatly affect the profit margin and safety with their efficiency. GM's Electro-Motive Division GP series reached into the '50s and '60s models. General Electric competed with its U and Dash lines. Horsepower increased along with anti-pollution measures. Both companies raced at first for higher horsepower units. Morrison Knudsen's MK Rail, which initiated the competition, bowed out to concentrate on manufacturing switch engines.

The true second generation in diesels actually caused a pause in the horsepower wars. In 1972, EMD initiated its "Dash 2" 3,000 horsepower series. The advantages, however, were not just in power. The Dash 2 reduced exhaust emissions and increased traction control. A new truck design reduced wheel slippage. It was the first to use solid state technology to control different functions. This modular control made it easy to repair, and an "event recorder" monitored engine function and other activities — even the use of sanders.

The SD 40–2 quickly became the industry standard for the 1970s. Forty railroads in the United States and Canada purchased these efficient workhorses. EMD sold over 4,400 SD 40–2 units in a little over 20 years.

In 1994 EMD teamed up with the German firm of Siemens AG to introduce AC traction. The 4,000 horsepower SD 70 MAC opened up another generation of diesel technology. The AC motors provide even greater control and tractive power at any speed. Radial trucks and diagnostic systems increase efficiency, and the "Whisper Cab" added comfort for the crew.

The SD 70 has a 4,000 horsepower DC version. This SD 70 M is well-suited for high-speed intermodal trains. In late 1999, Union Pacific placed an order for 1,000 SD 70Ms.

*Little Joe*s at Harlowton, Montana, 1966. Courtesy Railroad Avenue Enterprises.

New Haven triple function FL-9s at New Haven, Connecticut, in 1965. Courtesy Railroad Avenue Enterprises.

Located under the cab are the speed recorder (open box with tape at left) and the event recorder in closed box on top of platform at right.

The more recent SD 90 MAC has a 16-cylinder 6,000 horsepower (rated) H engine. The cooling system uses antifreeze, so it can be shut down in cold weather without having to drain coolant. Two computer display screens have replaced traditional instrument gauges. It uses the Global Positioning System for constant location information, and it automatically transmits "fault and performance" data to repair facilities and railroad headquarters.

By the mid-1990s, General Electric took the lead in locomotive manufacturing and sales. Its C40–8W and C41–8W have microprocessor controls and are rated at 4,000 horsepower. The C44–9W increased the horsepower to 4,400. The more modern AC4400CW also has a leap on sales. GE has developed a "single investor per axle" which, it argues, provides superior tractive force. In 1994, in cooperation with the German firm of Deutz MWM, GE developed the AC6000CW, rated at 6,250 gross horsepower.

Stronger and larger are not always ends unto themselves or always mean better in locomotives. Four or five smaller engines pulling freight have the insurance that, if one unit breaks down, the others can still carry the load with a minimum of difficulty. If one or two high horsepower units fail, half of the pulling power is lost, which will result in a more serious problem. This argument notwithstanding, the horsepower war is on again. Strength aside, the microprocessor and other electronic gear are now a necessary component of modern railroading.

Digital speed indicator in a modern locomotive. Speed is automatically sent to speed recorder below the cab.

The SD40–2 locomotive that brought about the third generation of diesel-electric locomotives. Built by EMD, it generates 3,000 horsepower. Courtesy Union Pacific.

SD70 MAC 4,000 horsepower diesel-electric locomotive built by EMD. Burlington Northern was its first customer for long coal trains. It is also known as the "Big Mac."

EMD SD60M began production in 1989. They are rated 3,800 horsepower and over 500 have been built to date.

Console of an EMD SD70 MAC locomotive. Courtesy Maurice Evans.

— Bombardier Transportation —

Since World War II, Bombardier Transportation has become a major producer of railroad rolling stock. Joseph-Armand Bombardier began the company in Canada in 1942. He first pioneered the manufacturing of snowmobiles. The company quickly expanded into the making of aircraft, light rail, and railroad equipment. Bombardier Transport has manufactured over 10,000 railroad vehicles to date.

— Locomotive #4744 —

While AC traction motors have been used in Europe since the 1970s, they were not employed extensively in North America until the 1990s. Canadian Pacific Locomotive #4744 has the distinction of being the first AC traction diesel-electric on this continent.

Locomotive #4744 was manufactured by the Montreal Locomotive Works (MLW) with a DC traction motor in 1971. It was the only 4,000-horsepower model M-640 of its kind.

In 1984, a four-way partnership of Canadian Pacific Railway, the federal government's Development Corporation, MLW/Bombardier, and Brown-Boveri were formed to develop AC traction. On the 99th anniversary of Canadian Pacific Railway's "Last Spike Day," November 7, 1984, Locomotive #4744 left the Angus shops under power of its new AC traction motors. The first AC traction locomotive served well until 1992, when it developed a cracked block and needed a new crankshaft as well as other expensive repairs. Having proved the worth of AC traction, Locomotive #4744 was then "put out to pasture."

Amtrak has purchased superliners and viewliner cars from Bombardier. The company is currently producing Amtrak's high-speed trainsets (trains built in sets to run as a unit). Bom-

EMD SD9 still at work. The series began in 1954 and is rated at 1,750 horsepower. It is a sister to the SD7 that began the Special Duty series. This model has been modified with a lowered nose.

General Electric AC4400CW-9 locomotive. It produces 4,400 horsepower.

Manufacturing the high speed *Acela* trainset. Courtesy Bombardier Transportation.

bardier has developed a revolutionary tilting technology for Amtrak's *Acela* trains. Bombardier Transportation today is an international corporation with offices in eleven countries.

— Radio —

Radio communication increased both efficiency and safety in the railroad industry. Early attempts to introduce a system even predates Marconi's first success with the radio in 1885. The Lehigh Valley Railroad actually experimented with an "induction system" in the late 1880s. In 1905, the Chicago and Alton used the first truly wireless telegraph on a train.

The Union Pacific began broadcasting from their office building in Omaha, Nebraska, to its local rail yard in 1910, and expanded the system to other locations before World War I. The Lackawanna pioneered radio traffic from New York to moving trains in 1914. They quickly advanced from telegraphy to voice broadcast.

During the 1920s, major electronic corporations assisted several railroads in experimenting with various devices. By 1928, the Pennsylvania Railroad demonstrated locomotive-to-caboose communications. These experiments ended when the Federal Radio Commission canceled the wave bands that the railroads used for broadcasting.

In 1936, the Pennsylvania Railroad began experiments with the "trainphone." The trainphone did not require a federal license, and permitted dependable voice communication all along the train as well as with other trains and towers. It was an "inductive" system that used both rails and telegraph

wires to carry the signal. The system in many ways was superior to radio per se, since tunnels and mountainous areas did not hamper the signal. Its major drawback was that the signal did not carry beyond 100 feet of rails or telegraph wires. That limitation, however, assured privacy of conversation and non-interference from other radio traffic. By 1943, the trainphone was perfected for general use.

After the initial attempts through World War II, true train radio development abated in the United States. The newspaper commentator Drew Pearson revived the concept in 1943. Pearson argued that the wreck of two Atlantic Coast Line trains that December could have been prevented with the use of radio. By early 1944, the Association of American Railroads championed the cause of systemwide radio installation.

The Pennsylvania Railroad's trainphone brought the entire industry up to speed. In 1946, the Kansas City Southern announced plans to introduce trainphones in every locomotive, caboose, and tower. Other railroads followed suit for at least a portion of their trackage.

The trainphone was very beneficial for train operations and safety for almost two decades, but by the 1960s, railroads started to abandon trainphones for more modern microwave transmission. The invention and use of the transistor permitted a reduction in the size of the transmitter/receiver. Today railroad workers carry hand-held radios to communicate with each other and a central office. There is no doubt that radio communications have greatly benefited the railroad industry.

BOMBARDIER TRANSPORTATION

Interior of a modern parlor car (1998).

Modern Long Island Railroad bi-level commuter car. Manufactured by Mitsui & Co. Courtesy Long Island Railroad.

Montage demonstrating use of the "Belt Pack" in a freight yard. Courtesy Canadian National. #E5228–1.

— Automatic Equipment Identification —

While the Automatic Car Identification System greatly helped the tracking of freight cars, it had its drawbacks. The scanning device could not read markings when dirty, and after some time rain and sunshine faded the colors beyond readability. Its computer system was not integrated with others, which caused delays in reporting the location of cars. By the 1990s, the traditional ACI system had become antiquated.

Many of the early ACI problems have been solved recently by an updated version called Automatic Equipment Identification (AEI). Rather than using bar codes, AEI reads a small tag on the side of the car. This tag stores reporting marks, size, and model electronically. AEI uses two types of scanning devices. The "Consist Scanner" is alongside a main track and sends its information after the entire train has passed — in other words, an account of the entire consist. "Tracker Scanners" are used in freight yards. They send information immediately when each car is scanned to help in the formation of trains. While the Consist Scanner has been in use for some time, rail yards are just beginning to install Tracker Scanners. An Electronic Data Interchange System (EDI) is used to transmit the information electronically to receivers anywhere. While the new scanning system is not foolproof, it is far more accurate, very efficient, and saves on the number of personnel needed to operate it.

— Locomotive Remote Control —

By the 1990s, a new form of technology came into use chiefly on yard locomotives and on industrial tracks. Several companies are marketing a device which permits remote control of an "engineerless" locomotive from some nearby point. In other words, a single railroad worker in a yard can do all necessary switching operations. There is no need for the yard worker to signal an in-cab engineer for locomotive movement.

Vectran and Theimeg companies began manufacturing these devices in the 1970s. Cattron and Canac, a spin-off of CN, entered the market later. Most of their customers are steel mills and coal-grain operations. CN is the only major railroad to adopt remote control to a significant degree. In 1996, 62 percent of CN's switching operations were being handled by a remote-control "Belt Pack." It planned to move to 100 percent in the near future. Given recent mergers, CN needs many more years to reach its goal. CP Rail is also using the Belt-pack, but on a more modest scale.

The United Transportation Union (UTU) in the United States has petitioned the Federal Railroad Administration to ban the use of remote-controled devices. It cites safety factors. So far the devices have had limited use in the United States. The Muskingham Electric RR in Ohio operates a partially remote-control train on 20 miles of track between its coal mine and power station. In 1992, the Wisconsin Central (WC) began using remote control to move a train between a rock quarry and its crusher. More recently it introduced remote control on its 77-mile White Pine Line to permit the engineer to set out and pick up cars by himself. Since the UTU petition, WC has stopped plans to increase remote control operations.

Remote control manufacturers argue that their device actually increases safety and reduces accidents. One person is in complete control while stepping between cars. It eliminates the possibility of a misunderstood signal, and decreases the time lag between issuing an order and engineer-locomotive response. If an accident does happen, however, there may not be anyone else around to summon help. There is no doubt that remote-control devices reduce labor costs.

— Flashing Rear End Device —

Another remote radio device changed the appearance of the caboose. The widespread use of axle bearings on freight cars virtually eliminated the "hot box" problem. There was, therefore, no longer the need for a brakeman or assistant conductor to look for problem signs from the rear of the train. Instead the last freight car has a box-shaped rear end device attached to the top side of the coupler. Some had a strobe light and were known as a "Flashing Rear End Device" or FRED for short. FRED transmits air brake pressure and motion information to the engineer. Engineers claim that FRED has greatly helped "slack action" or the different speeds of car sections on longer trains. It also permits the conductor and assistant conductor to sit in the front cab with the engineer. Of course, modern locomotive cabs can accommodate three or even four people in a comfortable and almost soundproof environment. The smaller train crew was accomplished in both Canada and the United States through negotiations with labor unions in the 1980s. The fewer crew members also helped the railroads compete more favorably with the trucking industry in hauling bulk commodities.

— Electronic Air Brake System —

FRED may have only his flashing duty in the future. Technical Service Marketing (TSM) of Kansas City is currently testing an Electronic Air Brake System (EABS) on some trains. EABS is a computerized braking system which connects each car's brakes electronically with the locomotive cab. An electronic impulse is carried by DC current on radio to a computer console or Head End Unit (HEU), commonly called MARY, which controls and monitors all braking functions. The

The Trainlink or MARY is the receiver-transmitter for FRED located in the locomotive cab. This unit was added on an older locomotive. They are built in the consoles of modern locomotives. The "ID code" must match the counterpart on FRED. The unit is commonly called MARY by railroaders today.

Flashing Rear End Device reports air brake pressure to MARY and can apply brakes in an emergency. FRED has replaced the caboose.

RoadRailer

stopping command reaches every car simultaneously, which eliminates the 15- to even 90-second lag time on long trains. It decreases the length of stopping distances anywhere from 30 to 70 percent.

EABS permits greater control of the braking process most particularly for slowing down without stopping on steep grades. It also eliminates defective brake valves or "kickers" which throw a train into a false emergency mode. The Car Control Unit (CCU) is a small box which not only controls and reports the car's braking condition, but also transmits the car's road number and reporting marks.

Burlington Northern Santa Fe is using EABS on some trains. Preliminary reports are highly favorable. The CCU on the last car of an EABS train transmits its brake and reservoir air pressures, which virtually eliminates the need for FRED's technology. EABS promises to be a great safety improvement for the railroad industry. The Association of American Railroads is developing specifications for both cable and radio versions. The new brake technology should soon become the industry standard. FRED, to be sure, will keep his important flashing duties into the future.

— RoadRailer —

The moving of tractor trailers "on their own wheels" by train has a great potential for increasing railroad traffic and revenue. Earlier experiments of using self-contained, flanged wheels on trailers did not produce the desired results. In recent years the concept was modified by placing a separate railroad truck or "bogie" under a trailer. Two trailers would share the same bogie as did the streamlined *Zephyr*, the lightweight passenger train of the 1930s.

One company manufactures the bogies and equips trailers for railroad use: Wabash National makes a Mark V RoadRailer. The company claims ease of transferring a trailer from road to rail. The RoadRailer also has a "coupler mate" so a trailer can be attached to the end of any freight or passenger train.

In one sense, RoadRailer is essentially a trailer on rails without the use of a flatcar. It also eliminates the time-consuming loading and unloading process as well as the necessity of bringing the vehicle to a particular site which has heavy capacity loaders. Although there may be technological adjustments to be made, the "trailer on rails" (TOR) has great potential for the railroad industry. A train with 70 or more trailers can cross the continent far more efficiently, in a quicker time frame, and with far less pollution than each being pulled by its own tractor. The TOR can also alleviate highway congestion and defer road repair for states and municipalities. Amtrak currently hauls mail with RoadRailers.

— Environmental Consciousness —

The railroad industry has placed safety as a primary concern for over a century. It also paid some attention to environmental issues since its inception. For example, railroad companies used the available technologies to prevent fires caused by sparks from smokestacks and heat from hot boxes. In recent years the railroads, and industry in general, have become more conscious of the environment and pollution.

The U.S. government has passed many laws which directly affect the railroads as well as other businesses. The key acts are: The Resource Conservation and Recovery Act, the Comprehensive Environmental Response Compensation and Liability Act, the Clean Air Act, and the Clean Water Act. These laws set standards for transporting hazardous waste, require cleaning contaminated sites, regulate the use of toxic waste, and control the amount of pollutants emitted into air and water.

Since the 1980s, railroads have spent millions of dollars to comply with environmental legislation. They have initiated environmental awareness programs and integrated sound, environmentally friendly practices in day-to-day activities. Both new and veteran employees receive environmental training. Recycling, revising, and reclaiming is being applied. The railroads' leadership has developed environmental policies and

State-of-the-art, solar-powered hydraulic switch.

RoadRailer Mark V is capable of speeds up to 100 MPH in both directions. The "bogies" are removed for road use. Courtesy Wabash National.

The *Powhatan Arrow* of the former Norfolk & Western. It has now been placed in a museum. Photo courtesy of Norfolk Southern Corporation.

guidelines to be used by all employees in virtually all activities. The Union Pacific, for example, has a facility at Council Bluffs, Iowa, that separates petroleum products from rainwater runoff from an engine refueling station. Hopper cars are cleaned with "coal slag" rather than "steel grit" before washing, and the cars are painted with water-based rather than petroleum-based paints. New engine cleaning facilities have reduced water consumption volume up to 90 percent.

Railroads have also spent millions of dollars in fitting new nozzles to fuel locomotives with less danger of spillage. They have retrofitted older locomotives with "retention tanks" to collect fuel and oil which would drip on the right-of-way during normal operating conditions. Some have experimented with using natural gas for fuel. It burns cleaner and totally eliminates the fuel-drip problem. The Union Pacific has begun to locate and identify the many water wells drilled along its line during steam locomotive days. These wells must be closed for both safety and environmental reasons. The railroads have hired teams of employees whose only task is environ-

mental safety. They also carry on audits to monitor compliance. The observance of sound environmental practices not only fulfills the law, it is also cost effective. Recycling saves money and material, and hazard-free property is a safety factor.

GE Transportation Systems has begun a "greening" of its locomotive program. It has greatly improved fuel efficiency and reduced emissions through its electronic fuel injection (EFI) system. It has also engineered a split-manifold cooling system and compartmentalized fuel tanks to prevent pollution in the event of a locomotive accident. Retention tanks keep fuel and other solvents from reaching the roadbed. GE also produces a natural gas–burning locomotive. There is no doubt that the railroads and related industries have responded to environmental concerns in a most positive way.

— Diversity —

The railroad industry has made great strides in increasing the employment and promotion opportunities for women, mi-

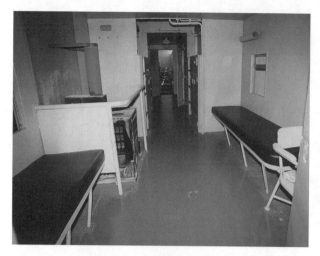

Bunk area of a caboose. Farmers often rode in the caboose when taking cattle to the stockyards.

A caboose. It will soon disappear from commercial railroads.

Veteran engineer Maurice Evans on the deck of an SD40-2 locomotive. The railroad industry today offers many opportunities for women and minorities.

norities, and the physically disabled. More than complying with federal law, some companies recruit from predominantly African-American and Hispanic colleges and universities. They also support scholarship funds as well as such community organizations as the Urban League.

Within the railroad companies, departments support career development and organizations are formed for women and minority groups. Some companies provide assistance for child and elder care. Some railroads affiliate with the American Institute for Managing Diversity in Atlanta, Georgia.

Railroads today see diversity as a strength. A person's distinctive qualities are an enhancement to the workforce. Diversity is also interpreted as marital status, family status, political affiliations, both formal and informal educational background, lifestyle, sexual orientation, disability, etcetera. The railroad industry today is a major supporter of diversity in the workplace.

— End of the ICC —

As the U.S. government created new agencies to ensure compliance with environmental legislation, it eliminated the oldest of its regulatory commissions. The ICC Termination Act of 1995 ended the existence of the 109-year-old Interstate Commerce Commission. Representative John Kasich of Ohio led the cause which was supported by the railroads, the trucking industry, and the Teamsters. The government created the ICC to regulate railroad rates when the train was the only reasonable means of distance transportation. Moreover, the railroads were viewed at that time by the public as the worst of the robber barons and there was a need to curtail their prices. It was a way to control the monopoly the railroad industry held over the U.S. public. Following World War I, the numerous government regulations severely hampered the railroad industry. By the 1930s, the airplane, busses, trucks, and the automobile ended the railroads' monopoly on transportation. In the years following the second World War, the ICC's enforcement of government regulations, as well as taxation, put the railroads at a clear disadvantage over other forms of transportation. Some argue that deregulation should have occurred by 1950.

The Staggers Act of 1980 "took the teeth out" of the ICC's enforcement abilities. According to most, the agency had

Union Pacific's Harriman Dispatch Center in Omaha, Nebraska. The "Bunker" which electronically maps the entire system is below this level.

clearly outlived its usefulness by the end of the decade. The ICC Termination Act of 1995 was initiated as a government cost-saving measure. Its remaining regulatory functions were transferred to the Surface Transportation Board. The termination of the ICC symbolically brings the final end to the "Railroad era" — about a generation too late to be truly useful.

Even with more favorable legislation and union contracts, railroads are still not "out of the woods" financially. Some analysts predict that the decade of cost-cutting is at an end. Train crews have been reduced to the margins of safety and practicality. New diesel technology and other devices are cost-effective and efficient, but they require a substantial capital expenditure. Moreover the railroads are dependent on the cost of oil. Some reports indicate the railroads will not be able to continue to take a sizable market share away from trucks by the early twenty-first century.

The railroad industry's one big problem is that trains can run only where the tracks go. Railroad service is from depot to depot or from spur line to spur line. Trucks run from door to door and highways are everywhere. It is the same thing for passenger service. Trains take people from station to station. The car takes someone from front porch to front porch.

Perhaps wider use of the RoadRailer concept could solve the freight problem.

— ISTEA —

In 1991, Congress passed the Intermodal Surface Transportation Efficiency Act, commonly called ISTEA. Millions of dollars were appropriated for improvements on many areas of surface transportation. For the first time in history the railroad industry received funds for upgrading existing tracks as well as money for planning. In some places tracks were relocated to eliminate grade crossings, and intermodal facilities were increased.

ISTEA assisted the planning of high-speed rail in certain parts of the country. Along with the high-speed project on the east coast, others are being projected in the Chicago area, a Texas Triangle, as well as a "California Corridor" between Los Angeles and San Francisco.

— TEA-21 —

In 1998, Congress voted for the Transportation Equity Act for the 21st Century (TEA-21) which granted $8.2 billion over a six-year period for rail transit. Another $6.1 billion is guaranteed, and the remainder must have separate appropri-

Two F40M2 Commuter Passenger Locomotives, elephant style, at LaSalle Street Station in Chicago. Now a commuter-only station, it once served such lines as the New York Central and Rock Island.

Operations Management Center, Montreal. Modern centralized traffic control. Courtesy Canadian National.

ations acts each succeeding year. TEA-21 authorizes 191 "New Start" projects with an evaluation procedure to determine which would most likely receive further funding for completion.

The money will go to new rail lines as well as improvement of existing ones. Technological improvements are eligible along with the construction of stations and other passenger facilities. TEA-21 encourages joint development: Stations are to be constructed alongside shopping facilities or pedestrian malls. In fact, shopping facilities can be rented within the station itself and revenues kept to offset transit costs.

Programs are being considered in thirty-five cities that no longer have commuter rail services. They range from Charlotte, North Carolina, to Memphis, Tennessee, to Minneapolis/St. Paul, Minnesota. TEA-21 also funds almost $30 million for transit on the state-owned Alaska Railroad with another $40 million for capital improvements. TEA-21 sets aside about $1 billion for research and planning for Magnetic Levitation Technology in both high- and low-speed phases. These funds, however, need to be appropriated each year by Congress from Highway Accounts. Planning and experimentation must be a public–private partnership and involve materials manufactured mostly in the United States.

— Association of American Railroads —

The Association of American Railroads (AAR) represents freight railroads in the United States, Canada, and Mexico. It is the rail industry's principal advocate before Congress, federal agencies, and executive offices. Today the AAR represents 93 percent of all inter-city rail traffic, and Amtrak is the only inter-city passenger carrier with full membership. (Some commuter and other freight railroads have associate membership status.)

The AAR has two subsidiaries: Transportation Technology, Inc. in Pueblo, Colorado, and RAILINC in Cary, North Carolina. Transportation Technology, Inc. is the world's leading railroad research and testing facility. It has both domestic and foreign clients. RAILINC develops and provides information technology programs for the railroad industry.

— High-Speed Rail —

As for attracting more passenger traffic, there have been some attempts at high-speed rail. Several states have carried out feasibility studies. In 1989 Texas established its own High Speed Rail Authority. It awarded the Texas TGV Corporation a franchise to construct a high-speed line connecting Dallas, Fort Worth, Austin, and San Antonio. Lacking private funds, the Texas project died in 1994. President Clinton's administration has encouraged such projects, but none have borne fruit.

Germany and Japan have developed Magnetic Levitation (Maglev) trains in their respective countries. Maglev trains "float in a rut," suspended above the surface, and not on tracks. The Maglev cars reach speeds of 300 miles per hour. They work on the same principles that cause an electric motor to turn — except it runs in a line instead of rotating on an axle. Maglev is very expensive and may not be suitable in some climates. TEA-21 provides funding for the feasibility of high-speed rail, including Maglev, in the United States.

— Railroad Education —

In 1992, officials of American Class I railroads met with administrators from select community colleges. During the next five years they developed a program of college-level courses in railroad operations technology. The railroads wanted to "raise the bar" on the quality of applicants admitted to entry-level positions in the railroad industry. Students would receive an Associate of Applied Science degree in railroading.

The program and certification would not compete with management or proprietary training carried out by the railroads themselves. The program has grown to twenty community colleges in the United States and Canada, offering degrees and certification. These community colleges and railroads have combined into the Railroad Education and Training Association or RETA. Students who complete the Railroad Operation Technologies program have a definite

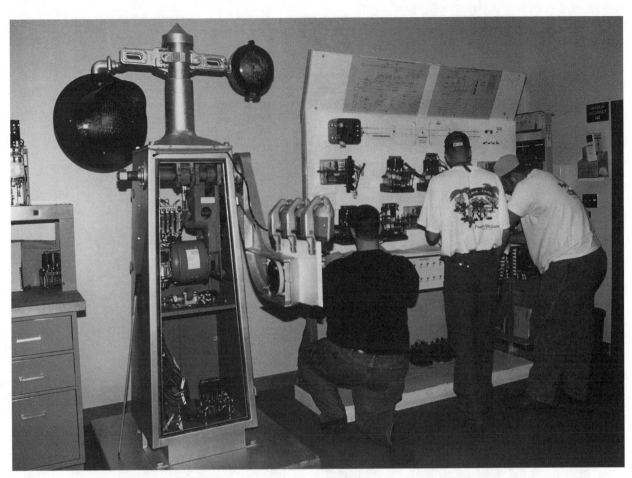

Students learning grade-crossing gate electronics at BNSF training facility (National Academy of Railroad Sciences) in Overland Park, Kansas.

advantage for employment in the industry and for eventual promotion.

For decades, the Association of American Railroads made available kits on railroad education for schools in the United States and Canada. Today the Federal Railroad Administration is providing similar educational programs through its Internet web site. (See www.fra.dot.gov.) The FRA curriculum has lessons that range from preschool through senior high school. It has games, quizzes, photos, artwork, and diagrams, along with text. There are also guides for teachers, so instructors who have no firsthand knowledge of railroading could conduct the program with the class. The curriculum emphasizes safety, possible railroad careers, history, economics, railroad stories, and culture. Instructors find it easy to use, and students enjoy learning more about trains.

— The Railroad Industry Today —

Railroads were part of the growth and development of the industrial revolution. They are products of the coal, iron, and steel eras. While both Canada and the United States still have some heavy industry, the focus is changing. Today's modern economy is dominated by the computer, plastic, and petro-

leum. During the past decade the railroads have adopted the newest technologies very well to survive and even prosper. They will have to keep at the technological forefront into the next century to compete with other modes of transportation.

Today, Canada has 31,237 route miles of track and the railroad employs about 50,000 people. The United States has 170,433 route miles of track and about 131,810 railroad workers. There are 11 class I roads ($256 million-plus in revenue). There are 30 regional railroads which generate $21 to $256 million. According to the latest statistics, the U.S. railroads transport 65 percent of motor vehicles and parts, 60 percent of coal, 50 percent of pulp and paper products, 49 percent of farm produce, and 40 percent of processed food and chemicals. They also account for 30 percent of travelers using public transportation (including commuters).

The flanged wheel on a rail is the most energy efficient way to move just about anything. If the railroad era and mentality could have continued beyond the 1960s, there would be fewer traffic jams, far less pollution of the environment, and a far greater savings of oil and other natural resources. If passenger trains were more frequented, perhaps, too, people would be a bit more congenial.

Chapter 17.

Conclusion

The Past Is the Prologue to the Future

When Charles Carroll of Carrollton lifted the first shovel of earth to construct the Baltimore & Ohio Railroad, he helped create an industry and institution which helped shape the United States of America. The railroad provided an all-season and all-weather transportation system which permitted the young country to grow across the continent.

Before the U.S. Civil War, railroads linked settlements along the Mississippi–Great Lakes water routes with eastern cities. At the same time they provided a means for the creation of other communities located far from navigable rivers.

After the Civil War, the United States constructed transcontinental railroads to the Pacific Coast. These lines literally created towns as they were being built. They were agents encouraging people to move into sparsely populated territory, and thereby created the richest food-producing area in the world. The Great Plains became known as the "bread-basket," the southwest grew cattle to supply a nation of "beef eaters," and California was able to send its cornucopia of agricultural products throughout the entire nation. Railroad tracks also made feasible the shipping of the various metal ores and forest products from the Rocky and Sierra Nevada Mountain areas to factories in the east for processing into manufactured goods for all. In short, the U.S. railroads made a desert bloom into a truly productive area.

By the 1880s, the railroads were the means for the Canadians to link British Columbia with the east and permit the expansion of people into the prairie region. Without the railroads, such economic activities in the center of the North American land mass would have been impossible.

The opening up of the interior of both countries gave the United States and Canada a distinct advantage in the first half of the twentieth century. In the nineteenth century, railroads in other parts of the world were limited by political boundaries or economic backwardness. For example, Europe was divided into several small countries; in fact, before 1870, the area of Germany consisted of almost 50 independent states! England, where railroading began, was a relatively small area. Both Asia and Africa were not economically developed, and when European powers formed colonies, railroad construction was both limited and for a particular purpose.

The United States did not have these disadvantages. Instead, it had a huge and varying land mass to conquer. The same was true for Canada. The freedom born in the United States permitted and even spurred on economic growth by recognizing that people could profit by the fruits of their own

labor. Therefore, investing and working on the railroad became symbolic of the opportunities offered by the new land. It made agricultural and mining activities profitable to all who were willing to work in the New World!

Freedom and the railroads attracted people to the United States and Canada. Fleeing famine and political oppression, the Irish helped construct the Baltimore & Ohio and Erie Railroads among others. The Illinois Central attracted others from Europe. With the transcontinentals, both the United States and Canada amassed campaigns to attract people to populate the new, interior territories.

With tracks leading to most places in the nation, the frontier disappeared in the United States by 1890. The land mass was settled for the most part, and through standard time zones and a standard track gauge, the U.S. railroads permitted the nation to function as one huge economic unit. The United States had all the materials available in one contiguous political setting to become an industrial giant — all made possible by the railroads.

Canada opened its prairie country by the 1890s, and in order to encourage further growth, constructed more rail lines to the Pacific Coast. Canada attracted people from Central and Eastern Europe to start farms on its vast land.

At the beginning of the twentieth century, the Canadian government assumed ownership of a large portion of its rail system. In the United States, Congress passed laws limiting profits and regulating the industry. In both countries, the railroads also had to face new competition from automobiles, busses, trucks, and eventually airplanes. North American railroads made a tremendous effort to attract and keep passengers through technological advances and customer service.

World War II was North American railroads' finest hour. In terms of rationing and efficient movement of both civilian and military supplies, the railroads made heroic efforts to meet freedom's demands. By the creation of such a self-sufficient, tremendous economic unit in the United States, railroads helped win the war as much as any army.

After the war, people in both Canada and the United States turned to automobiles, trucks, and airplanes for transportation services. These new means offered greater independence in scheduling and a significant savings in time. In order to survive both greater competition and continued government regulation, U.S. railroads soon became freight-only haulers. A government-owned entity, Amtrak, assumed long distance

Baltimore & Ohio Motive Power. Courtesy B&O Railroad Museum.

BNSF Employee Appreciation Day. June 1997.

railroad passenger service in the United States. Canada did so a few years later with VIA Rail.

As freight haulers, the Canadian and U.S. railroad industry today has become a leader in technological innovation. Railroads are a most efficient way to transport bulk goods between fixed points. Although railroads no longer have a virtual monopoly on transportation as they did a century ago, they are still absolutely necessary to the economy of both nations. Since the 1980s, they have reclaimed some of the business previously lost to other carriers. Given further technological development, they may continue this trend into the future. In short, they are keeping a great tradition in the economic growth of two great democratic nations.

When Charles Carroll of Carrollton signed the Declaration of Independence, he helped begin modern democracy and the spread of freedom throughout the world. When Charles Carroll of Carrollton lifted the first shovel of earth for the first American railroad, he helped create the institution which provided for the nation's growth and the preservation of self-government in its most perilous days during World War II. Both the nation and the railroads continue his vision at the turn of a new century.

Epilogue

"You couldn't get him off this island of paradise even if you got him a lower berth in a Pullman!"

During 1943, Warner Brothers released a motion picture entitled *Air Force.* The story background is historically accurate for the most part. A flight of B17 "Flying Fortress" bombers took off from California on their way to Hawaii on December 6, 1941. They arrived early on Sunday, December 7, right in the middle of the Japanese attack on Pearl Harbor. At the same time, Japan was also bombing Wake Island, Guam, Midway, and the Philippines.

After the attack, the B17, called *Marianne,* was ordered to fly to the Philippines. They had to refuel on Wake — a clipper airplane refueling station occupied by U.S. Marines. Upon arrival, the crew saw the same devastation they witnessed at Pearl Harbor. They were quickly escorted to report to Major Bagley, the island commander. Bagley was confined to a bed in his office for injuries sustained in the earlier attack.

The captain of the B17 crew, Quincannon, offered to fly Major Bagley and the other wounded off the island. Bagley adamantly refused to leave. He said he "wasn't worth his weight in gasoline." As they were leaving the makeshift hospital room, Quincannon asked the second-in-command, Major Daniels, if there was any way to convince Bagley to leave the island. Daniels turned and jokingly said: "You couldn't get him off this island of paradise even if you got him a lower berth in a Pullman!" The *Marianne* took off without Major Bagley or any of the marines on Wake. They all died in action when the island fell several weeks later.

When the movie played in U.S. theaters, everyone with an education above the first grade understood the situation on Wake, and that Major Bagley turned down the most tempting travel offer possible. Wake is an island: the only way off is by sea or air. From a purely realistic point of view, the B17 flight was a good offer. A "Flying Fortress," (also known as a "Flying Boxcar" because of its bomb-carrying capacity), was a state-of-the-art aircraft in 1941. Daniels could have suggested the "Clipper Airplane" which stopped on the island for refueling. Major Bagley would have had a smooth ride. . . . He also did not suggest a captain-size stateroom on the Queen Mary or some other luxury liner. The greatest travel temptation to the Major — or just about anyone in 1941 — was a lower berth in a Pullman.

Pullman meant "travel in safety and comfort." The lower berth had the smoothest ride and largest area; it also had the window at night. The person sleeping in the lower berth faced the forward direction during the daytime. The porter would attend to the major's needs: shine his shoes, press his clothes, and remind or wake him just before his destination. Just about everyone knew that in 1943, even those who did not have a first grade education.

A generation later, in 1973, the Pullman Company no longer existed. Amtrak's first-class service tried to retain a few sleeping car traditions. First graders heard the word Pullman possibly from their parents or other relatives, or friends' parents. It had little meaning to them, if an explanation did not follow. Maybe they saw the interior of a sleeping car on a late-night, black-and-white movie on television.

Toward the end of the century, almost two generations later, the word "Pullman" has no meaning at all. It could easily be mistaken for a new computer game to succeed Pacman, Poké-mon, or some other cartoon/electronic creature. (Pullman must be pure fiction: it doesn't have a web site. . . .) In fact, most people under the age of 40, or maybe even 50, would not understand the meaning of Major Bagley's comment, if he or she watched the movie *Air Force* on cable or satellite TV. The railroad era has passed. . . .

If the word "Pullman" has lost its full cultural meaning, trains and railroad history still hold a fascination for the North American public of all ages. Tourist lines and museums help people get a taste of the past. There are hundreds of them in Canada and the United States. Most reflect something of a local "fallen flag" or of a previous regional road. Each has something special for its guests or visitors.

While it is impossible to list all of them, a few deserve some mention. Pennsylvania's Steamtown National Historic Site features tours behind steam locomotives. Nearby Strasburg Railroad also offers tours, and the Pennsylvania Railroad Museum in the same town has a great collection of memorabilia as well as two GG1 locomotives. The Baltimore & Ohio Museum in Baltimore has a great collection of locomotives and rolling stock as well as exhibits and archives.

The Grand Canyon Railway runs a daily train from Williams, Arizona, to the rim of the Grand Canyon. The railway uses a rebuilt Mikado steam locomotive. It is the best way to visit one of the "natural wonders of the world." Tour the canyon on a Fred Harvey bus and stay at the Bright Angel Lodge — the last vestiges of the great Santa Fe customer service empire. Yes, the Grand Canyon Railway has a baggage car — and an open-end observation car for photographers.

The American Orient Express is a provate luxury train that visits national landmarks. Nothing but the best is on board.

For narrow gauge enthusiasts, the Durango & Silverton runs through gorges and great scenery. The Cumbers & Toltec Scenic Railroad also offers steam narrow-gauge excursions in New Mexico.

The California State Railroad Museum is located in the restored Central Pacific Railroad Station in Sacramento. It has many Southern Pacific items as well as train rides. The Napa Valley Wine Train has daily dinner excursions through California wine country. It offers numerous vintage wines along with dinner and the scenery of sumptuous grapes.

The Fremont Dinner Train in Fremont, Nebraska is a most

Kansas City Southern's *Southern Belle* private train. It is powered by F7 diesel locomotives.

authentic representation of the dining car of the early 1940s. Dinner and decorations are a gourmet's delight. From time to time, the crew puts on a World War II USO show as well as other '40s style entertainments. It's a great way to "live" railroad history.

Amtrak links most major cities and many small towns. Even though it does not offer "Pullman service," sleeping accommodations are modern and comfortable. Dinner is delicious and at a reasonable price. Even distant locations are an "overnight away," so what's the big hurry? The same for VIA Rail in Canada. A combined Amtrak-VIA vacation would be ideal. And the train's names are even the same as during the "good ol' days."

Once a major industry, the model-train makers no longer enjoy the market of previous years. Children today prefer computer games and space age toys to trains that circle the Christmas tree. Many fathers, however, are avid collectors of the older models. Model train memorabilia collecting is still alive and very well.

While presidents no longer make "whistle stop" campaigns by train throughout the country, President George Bush took to the private rail car for some extra publicity during the 1992 campaign. President Bill Clinton traveled to Chicago by rail to accept his party's nomination in 1995. A spiffy railroad car gets far more attention than a TV picture at a boarding ramp of a one-size-fits-all airplane — even if it is Air Force One. And, oh yes, you CAN still sleep in a Pullman!! The Holiday Inn Crowne Plaza at Indianapolis, Indiana, has renovated thir-

Grand Canyon Railway.

Brotherhood of Sleeping Car Porters Twenty-Fifth Anniversary Parade in Harlem, New York City, in 1950. Front Row: W. C. Hills, Asa P. Randolph, Thomas Paterson, D. LaRoche, and Ashley Totten. Back Row: W. H. Sanderse and H. H. Rock. Courtesy African American Museum and Library of Oakland.

teen 1920s Pullman sleeping cars for guest occupancy. Each car is decorated to the taste of the celebrity's name it carries — from Greta Garbo to Rudolph Valentino. And the hotel is in Union Station where the Pullmans are parked on the tracks they probably occupied for a few minutes each night during the golden age of railroading.

Most people today may not know the meaning of "Lower Berth in a Pullman," but the entire modern world sets its clocks and watches according to the time zones created by American railroads.

Amtrak is right: "There's Something Magic About a Train. . . ."

Fremont Dinner Train.

GLOSSARY

Railroad Slang Terms

Term	Definition
Air Monkey	An air brake repairman.
Anchor Them	Set brakes on cars that have already stopped.
Angel's Nest	Seat in a caboose cupola.
Ape Wagon, Bouncer Buggy, Cage, Chariot, Clown Wagon	Caboose.
Armstrong	Steam engine equipped with an automatic stoker.
Baby Lifter	Passenger brakeman.
Baby Loads	Partly loaded cars.
Baggage-buster	Baggage man.
Bate Can	Lunch bucket.
Balling the Jack	Running fast.
Barn	Roundhouse.
Batter	Overworking a steam engine.
Battleship	A large locomotive.
Beam	Signal light.
Beehive	A yard office.
Bender	A track liner.
Bending Rail, Bending Rust, Bending Iron	Relining a switch.
Big Crummy	Business car.
Big "E"	Engineer or member of the Brotherhood of Locomotive of Engineers.
Big Hole	Applying the emergency brake.
Big Hook	A wrecking derrick.
Big "O" or Big Ox	A conductor or member of the Order of Railway Conductors.

Binders	Hand brakes.
Black Diamonds	Company coal.
Blackie, Hoghead, Hogger, Pig Mauler, Pig Jockey	Locomotive engineer.
Blazer	A journal box packing on fire.
Bleed a Car	Drain the air reservoir.
Blockhead, Ground Hog, Shack, End Man, Squirrel	Brakeman.
Board	A fixed signal usually referred to as slow or order clear.
Bookkeeper	Flagman.
Boomer	Someone who worked for many railroads.
Boxcar	An all-room Pullman.
Brain-plate	A trainman's hat badge.
Breeze	Compressed air.
Bridge Monkey	People who work on bridges.
Brownie Box	Superintendent's car.
Buckle the Bolognies	Connect air hoses.
Bug	A telegraph instrument; also a lantern.
Bug Torch	A trainman's lantern.
Bull Cod	A knuckle lock.
Bullhead, Skipper, Captain, Brains, Corn Doctor	Conductor.
Bullsnake	Yard master.
Bump	To exercise seniority or bumping another employee.
Butterfly	A switching move.
Caboose Bounce or Caboose Hop	Engine and caboose only.
Calliope, Galloper, Hog, Kettle, Skillet, Pig	Locomotive.
Car Jockey, Cinder Cruncher, Dolly Flapper, Cherry Picker, Long Fielder, Yard Goat	Switchman.

Car Peck	Car inspector.
Carry a White Feather	Steam from the safety valve.
Cat's Claw	Spike puller.
Chain Gang	Construction or workers in a gang.
Chase the Red	Go back from stopped train to protect it.
Chew Cinders	Engines do this when reversed in working steam while running.
Chairman or Chink	Car washer.
Choppy	Rough track.
Cinder Dick	A special officer or railroad detective.
Cinder Snapper	Passenger on an observation platform of the rear car.
Civil Engineer	A locomotive engineer out of a job.
Clam Diggers	Railroad employees in the San Francisco Bay area.
Clean the Clock or Wipe the Clock	Emergency air application.
Clean the Slate	Release the air.
Close or Open the Gate	Close or open a switch.
Club a Car	Set the hand brakes.
Club Job	Track where it's necessary to set hand brakes to prevent cars from rolling.
Cock-Loft	Caboose cupola.
Consist	Make-up of the train.
Cooning the Train	Going over the top of cars.
Cornfield Meat	Head-on collision.
Couple the Rubbers	Connect air hoses.
Cowboy Pullman	Drovers' car.
Cow Cage or Crate	A stockcar.
Cow Punchers	Car inspectors.
Cracker Box or Glow Worm	Diesel streamliner.
Crowning It	Coupling a caboose on the end of a freight train.
Crummies	Cabooses.
Cupola or Crow's Nest	Observation area of the caboose.

Cut	A few cars and an engine or just several cars placed together.
Dancing the Carpet	Explaining to the boss.
Deadhead	A fireman's term for brakeman and also a passenger pass.
Deadheading	Not doing one's work, working without a union card; it could also mean getting a return ride and not working.
Deadhead's Home	Smoking car.
Deck	Floor of a locomotive cab. Sometimes it means boxcar roofs.
Decorate	Riding on top of a freight train.
Devil-Claw	A young roadmaster.
Diamond Cracker, Tallow Pot, Grease Ball, Smoke Agent, Water Warmer	Fireman.
Dicks	Special service officers, railroad police; "Cinder Dick."
Die Game	Stalling on a hill.
Die on the law	Crew is at the 12-hour work limit before reaching its destination.
Dinger	Assistant yard master.
Dispatcher's Delight	An attentive telegraph operator.
Dog Catching	Picking up a crew away from a depot when they've reached the 12-hour work limit.
Dog Train	Slow, low-priority freight.
Dogging	Lying down on the job.
Dope	Waste or oil from packing boxes. It could also mean orders or instructions.
Double Heading	Two engines to pull one train. Also means belonging to two unions.
Double the Hill	Cut the train in half and take up each part separately.
Down on the Sand and Beating Her on the Back	Put sand on the rail and reverse lever full forward, throttle wide open.
Drag	Slow freight train.
Drone Cage	Private car.
Drop	Cutting off cars and allowing them to coast to their places when switching.
Dropper	Yardman who rides the cars in hump yards.
Drummer	Yard conductor.
Dummies or Green Backs	Derailing frogs.

Dust the Flues	Sanding flues of oil-burning locomotives.
Dutch Drop	Reversing the engine and passing cars in opposite direction when leaving them someplace.
Dynamite	Emergency application of brakes.
Dynamiter	Applying brakes quickly.
Elephant Tracker	Special officer.
Errand Boy	Roadmaster.
Eye	Signal.
Fireworks	Fuses.
Flag	Assumed name.
Flat Wheel	An employee who limps.
Flimsies	Waybills or it could also mean train orders.
Flying Switch	A switch movement made without stopping.
Foamer	An extreme rail fan (they "foam" at the mouth when they see a train).
Fog-Gauge	A steam pressure indicator.
Freeze the Hub	Cool a heated journal.
Frog	X-shaped track where one line crosses another.
Galloping Rods or Monkey Motion	Valve gear of a steam locomotive.
Gandy Dancers or Gangs	Track workers or track repair gangs.
G-Bum	An habitual drinker.
Go High	Go on top of the cars to relay signals.
Glass	Insulators or more specifically telegraph insulators.
Glory	String of empty freight cars or death by accident.
Gons	A gondola car — a car with an open top.
Graveyard	Trackage for damaged or condemned equipment.
Greenboard	Signal for clear track ahead.
Griever	Local chairman of a labor union.
Guns	Track torpedoes.
Hard Joint	Rough coupling.

Harness	A passenger trainman's uniform.
Hay	Overtime or sleep.
Heel	Braked cars on the end of a track.
Hi-daddy	Line switching in which cars are cut off behind the engine and then the switch is thrown again after the engine is passed.
High Ball	A signal that means to proceed or go ahead which means that the track is clear.
High Ball Artist or Eagle Eye	Engineer who is known for fast running.
High Ballers	A mechanical wig-wag signal on a caboose.
High Iron or Stem	A main line.
High Wheeler	A passenger locomotive.
Hog	Locomotive.
Hole	A side track.
Home Guard	An employee who stays with one railroad.
Hop Toad	Derail.
Hot Box or Stinker	An overheated journal.
Hummer	Someone of outstanding ability.
Hump	A freight yard where cars are pushed and allowed to roll onto various tracks.
In the Corner	A locomotive throttle wide open.
In the Hole	Train on a siding.
Irish Valentine	A train gram, particularly one in a green envelope.
Jack and a Half	Overtime.
Jackpot	Traffic congestion.
Jam-Buster	An assistant yardmaster.
Jeep	A diesel-electric freight engine by Electro-Motive.
Jerk Soup or Jerk Drink	A steam locomotive taking up water while running.
Jerk Water	Anything small or insignificant.
Jim Crow	A rail bender.
Johnny Ball	A telegraph insulator.
Johnson Bar	A hand-operated reverse lever on a steam engine.

Juggler	A freight crew member who loads and unloads less than a car load at station stops.
Juice	Air brakes.
Jungle	A loafing place but also a hobo or tramp's hangout.
Keeley	A water can to cool heated journals.
Keapot	Full pressure of steam.
Kit	The art of cutting off cars and allowing them to roll onto a siding.
King	A freight conductor or sometimes a yardmaster.
Kitty	A railroad station cash fund.
Knock the Stack Off	Working an engine hard.
Knowledge Box	Yardmaster's office.
Knuckle Buster	A monkey wrench.
Lever Jerker	An interlocker leverman.
Lightning, Slinger, Brass Pounder, Wire Tickler	A telegraph operator.
Lincoln Pin	A narrow gauge road.
Liner	A passenger train.
Little Jeff	An independent brake valve.
Lizard Scorcher	The cook.
L. U. G.	An engine that is stored in good condition.
Lung	The draft gear of a car.
Make a Joint	To couple cars.
Make a Pass	To switch cars.
Markers	Rear-end signals or lights.
Master Mechanic's Blood	Valve oil.
Monkey Hop	One who runs on jobs with lots of overtime.
Monkey	A brakeman.
Monkey Suit	A passenger train conductor's or brakeman's uniform.
Mountain Lion	Road master.
Mud	Fuel oil.

Mud Chicken	Surveyor.
Mud Hen or Old Soak	A saturated engine.
Mud Hop	Yard clerk.
Mule	Boiler maker.
Muskrats	Water servicemen.
Non-air	A non-union railroad worker.
Notch	Throttle setting.
Nurse	Hostler.
Nut Cracker	Automatic air brake valve on the engine.
Oil Can	A tank car.
Old Alibi	Road master.
Old Head, Old Rail	A veteran employee.
Old Waterbury or Turnip	A railroad watch.
Old Whiskers	A senior official.
On the Peg	Full boiler pressure.
Paddle	A semaphore signal or shovel.
Palace of Justice	Business card.
Parlor Maid or Parlor Shack	The hind flagman on a freight.
Peck	Twenty minutes allowed for lunch.
Pecker Neck	An apprentice.
Pie Book	A meal ticket.
Pig Pen	Round house.
Pinch Her Down	Reduce speed, usually before a stop.
Pin for Home	Go home.
Plug	Water crane or a short passenger train.
Pocket Deity	Pocket watch (Canadian term).
Possum Belly	A tool box usually under the caboose.
Potato Bug or Pollywag	A motor train.
Pot Belly	A caboose stove.

Pounding Her	Working a locomotive to its capacity.
Prime Mover	The diesel engine of a diesel-electric locomotive.
Pumpkin	BNSF locomotive with orange, dark green, and yellow paint scheme introduced after 1997.
Puncher	To request a reply for correspondence.
Pussy Foot	Special officer.
Put in a Jewel	To put a new bearing on a car.
Rabbit	Derail.
Race Horse	General foreman.
Rail Bird	Any railroad worker.
Rat Holes	Tunnels.
Rattler	A freight train.
Real Estate	Poor coal.
Red Ball or Dancy Grag	Fast merchandise freight.
Red Board	A stop signal.
Reefer	Refrigerator car.
Ribbon Rail	Welded rail or seamless rail.
Ribbons of Rust	Main track.
Ride the Point	Ride the farthest car being pushed by an engine.
Ritz	A Harvey House.
Robissary	A commissary car.
Rocking Chair	Retire on a pension.
Rocking Chair Job	Working on a diesel switcher.
Roof Garden	A mallet locomotive or helping locomotive on a mountain.
Rule G	Nonconsumption of alcohol.
Sacred Ox	A mallet locomotive or helping locomotive on a mountain.
Sag	Bottom of grade, between two uphill sections of track.
Sand House or Sand House Dope	Rumors by workers concerning the future of the railroad.
Saw	A meeting of trains longer than the available siding.

Seashore	Sand.
Shave	To burn weeds on the right-of-way, that is, along the track.
Shiner	A brakeman's lantern.
Shoo-fly	A temporary track around an obstruction.
Shortrail	Derail.
Shorts	Cars left between stations.
Shovel Runner	A steam shovel engineer.
Show Cars	A supply train.
Shuffle the Deck	Switch cars on the house tracks at every station.
Shunting Boiler or Goat	A switching engine.
Side Door Pullman	A boxcar used by a bum for stealing a ride.
Sifting Through the Dew	Traveling at very high speed.
Skunk	A motor car with a striped front.
Slug	Heavy fire in a locomotive firebox or a diesel locomotive without an engineer's cab attached to other units.
Smoke Agent	Locomotive fireman.
Smoker	A locomotive.
Smoking Them or Smoke Orders	A method of getting from one station to another without train orders or moving very slowly and looking for another locomotive along the track.
Snake	Switchman.
Snipe	A track worker.
Snoozer	A Pullman car.
Soft Bellies	Old wooden-framed cars.
Soup Jockey	Cook.
Soup Ticket	A short report thrown from the train reporting its contents.
Soup Wagon	Creosote wagon.
Spar	A pole to shove cars into the clear when switching.
Speedy	Call boy.
Spike Gun	Machine for driving spikes.
Spot	To put a car or locomotive in a particular place. It also means to sleep on a lunch break or rest on company time.

Spotter	An official who snoops around checking up on employees.
Spur	Track with switches at one end only.
Squealer	A journal box or hot box.
Stake 'em By	Shove cars with a heavy pole.
Star Gazer	Brakeman who fails to see signals.
Stem	Mainline.
Stinker	An overheated journal box or hot box.
Strawberry Patch	The rear end of a caboose at night.
String	Several cars coupled together.
Strings	Telegraph wires.
Sunkink	A track out of line due to extreme heat expansion.
Switch Shanty	A gossip.
Tallow Pot	Fireman.
Tank	Locomotive tender.
Tank Town	A small town where a steam locomotive stops for water or it could mean any small town on the line.
Thousand Miler	A starched blue shirt which is worn particularly by workers on different railroads.
Throttle Fever	Desire to be an engineer.
Throttle on Gate	The throttle is wide open.
Throw a Wing-Ding	Drink on duty.
Toad	A type of derail placed on top of the rail.
Token	Train order.
Toonerville	A local freight train.
Top Dresser Drawer	The upper bunk in a caboose.
To Set a Binder	To apply the hand brakes.
Tramp Run	A train which has no particular destination; it picks up and sets out.
Try the Wind	Test the automatic air brakes.
Turnip or Pocket Deity	Canadian terms for a railroad pocket watch.
U-Boat	U25B General Electric locomotive (Universal, 2,500 horsepower, B-type trucks).

Ugly Duckling	First used to refer to GP7 and GP9 locomotives. Now used for any diesel-electric locomotive.
Varnish Wagons, Varnish Car, String of Varnish	Passenger coaches.
Velvet	Welded or seamless rail.
Walk up Against the Gun	To go up a stiff grade with the water injector on in a steam engine.
War Club	An electric lantern.
Wash Out	A violent stop signal made by the arms or by swinging a lantern at night in a low semi-circle across the tracks.
Whale Belly	A steel car or a coal car.
Whiskers on Rails	Frost.
Whistle Stop	A small town.
White Rat	A train auditor.
Whizz	Automatic air brakes.
Windcutter	A streamliner.
Wing 'er	Set brakes on a moving train.
Wipe the Clock	Putting the brakes on emergency.
Yard Bull	A railroad detective.
Yard Goat	A switch engine.
Yellowboard	A caution signal.
Zulu or Zebra	An emigrant outfit.

APPENDIX A

North American Railroad Chronological Table

1825   John Stevens's first steam locomotive in North America.

1826   Bryant's Granite Railway receives charter.

1828   Baltimore & Ohio begins construction.

1829   Stourbridge Lion runs at Honesdale, Pennsylvania.

1830   Quebec Fortress construction railway built in Canada.
        Peter Cooper's *Tom Thumb* runs first time.

1831   First Baldwin locomotive.
        Charleston and Hamburg Railroad operates first scheduled train in North America.

1833   Andrew Jackson rides on the Baltimore & Ohio. First president to ride a train.

1834   First express company started.

1836   First "sleeping car" runs in Pennsylvania.
        Champlain and St. Lawrence begins Canada's first passenger service.

1838   All railroads declared "Post Routes" by the U.S. government.

1839   William Harnden starts express company.

1843   First true sleeping cars on the Erie.

1850   First railroad land grant signed by President Millard Fillmore.

1851   Erie Railroad completed from New York to Dunkirk on Lake Erie.
        First "train order" or regulation of train operations by telegraph.

1852   Philadelphia connected with Pittsburgh.
        Baltimore & Ohio reaches Wheeling.
        Illinois Central began construction.

1853   New York Central formed.
        First passengers travel between New York City and Chicago by rail.

1854   Explorations begun to plan a railroad to the Pacific Coast.

1856   First railroad bridge across the Mississippi River

1859   First Pullman sleeping car in operation.
        First run of railroads to transport soldiers into action. Col. Robert E. Lee takes soldiers by train to end John Brown's raid at Harper's Ferry.

1861   First Union troops arrive by train for U.S. Civil War.

1862   President Abraham Lincoln signs the Pacific Railway Act to construct the first transcontinental railroad.

1863	Brotherhood of the Footboard (Locomotive Engineers) formed.
1864	First run of a Railway Post Office car.
1865	George Baker invents hot water heat for passenger cars.
1866	First refrigerated shipment of fruit under ice. First block signals in operation.
1868	First refrigerator car patented. Janney coupler patented. First Pullman dining car in use.
1869	Completion of first transcontinental railroad at Promontory, Utah. George Westinghouse patents the air brake.
1872	Crédit Mobilier scandal made public. Electric block signal developed.
1876	Fred Harvey begins first restaurant for the Santa Fe. Intercolonial Railway opens in Canada.
1877	First large-scale railroad workers' strike.
1881	First electric light in a railroad car.
1882	William Baker and George Westinghouse use steam from locomotive to heat passenger cars.
1883	Alonzo Mather wins prize for first humane cattle car. Railroads institute time zones and standard time.
1885	Canadian Pacific completed to Vancouver.
1886	Movement to standard gauge: 4' 8½".
1887	Interstate Commerce Commission established.
1890	Steel rails predominate on U.S. railroads.
1891	St. Clair Tunnel opens in Canada.
1893	American Railway Union formed.
1893	New York Central's engine 999 breaks 100 MPH speed limit at 112.5 MPH near Batavia, N.Y.
1894	Pullman strike.
1895	Baltimore & Ohio uses first electric locomotives.
1896	National Transcontinental begins construction in Canada.
1898	Grand Trunk Pacific completed from Winnipeg to West Coast.
1900	Casey Jones killed at Vaughn, Mississippi.
1902	Inauguration of the 20th Century Limited and the Broadway Limited trains.
1910	Mann-Elkins Act extends Interstate Commerce Commission's authority.

1913   End of wooden passenger cars.
        National Transcontinental completed in Canada.

1916   Canadian Royal Commission to study conditions of railroad financial difficulties.
        Adamson Act establishes 8-hour workday for railroad employees.

1917   Esch Car Service Act gives the ICC authority to regulate rail traffic.
        U.S. government takes over railroads during World War I.

1919   Canadian National Railway created out of Grand Trunk Pacific and Canadian
        Government Railways.

1920   Esch-Cummins Act returns U.S. railroads to private owners.

1923   Grand Trunk becomes part of Canadian National.

1925   First successful diesel-electric switching locomotive. Central Railroad of New Jersey #1000.
        First meeting of the brotherhood of sleeping-car porters.

1926   U.S. Railway Labor Act gives employees the right to form their own union.

1927   First all private-room Pullman sleeper.
        Central Vermont absorbed by Canadian National.

1928   Canadian National puts first road diesel-electric locomotive in service.

1929   W. Carrier builds first mechanical air conditioner for a railroad car.

1934   Centralized Traffic Control (CTC) installed.

1934   First lightweight streamliners: Chicago, Burlington, & Quincy's *Zephyr* and the Union Pacific's *M-10000*.
        Pennsylvania Railroad begins runs of its 100 MPH GG 1 electric locomotive.

1935   Electro-Motive Division of General Motors builds first twin diesel units #511 and #512.

1936   Association of American Railroads formed.

1937   Brotherhood of Pullman Porters signs first labor contract.

1939   Canadian railroads move first troop trains.
        Electro-Motive Division displays first diesel-electric freight locomotives.

1942   U.S. has 3,000 miles of track under CTC.

1944   A Pullman sleeper is loaded every three minutes during World War II.

1949   Electro-Motive Division introduces the GP7 locomotive.

1955   First large merger since World War I: Louisville & Nashville merges with the Nashville, Chattanooga,
        and St. Louis.

1960   CN and CPR complete dieselization.

1965   CN extends CTC from coast to coast.

1967   Canada's National Transportation Act permits "agreed charges" for certain customers.

1968   Penn Central created.
        Pullman Company ceases attending cars.

1970	Penn Central files for bankruptcy.
1971	Amtrak begun.
1974	Conrail created out of Penn Central and other bankrupt eastern railroads.
1975	REA Express folds.
1977	Last operation of a Railway Post Office car.
1978	VIA Rail absorbs long-distance Canadian passenger service.
1980	Staggers Act permits U.S. railroads to deregulate shipping rates.
1982	Union Pacific absorbs Missouri Pacific and Western Pacific. CSX formed from Seaboard System and the Chessie System.
1984	Canadian Pacific pioneered AC traction in North America.
1994	Canadian National privatized.
1995	Union Pacific absorbs Chicago & Northwestern. BNSF formed by Burlington Northern and Santa Fe merger. CN completes new St. Clair Tunnel. ICC terminated; some regulatory functions assumed by the Surface Transportation Board.
1996	Union Pacific absorbs Southern Pacific.
1999	Canadian National proposes merger with Burlington Northern Santa Fe to create North American Railways, Inc.
2000	U.S. Surface Transportation Board postpones all Class I mergers until 2001.

APPENDIX B

Chart of Recent Mergers

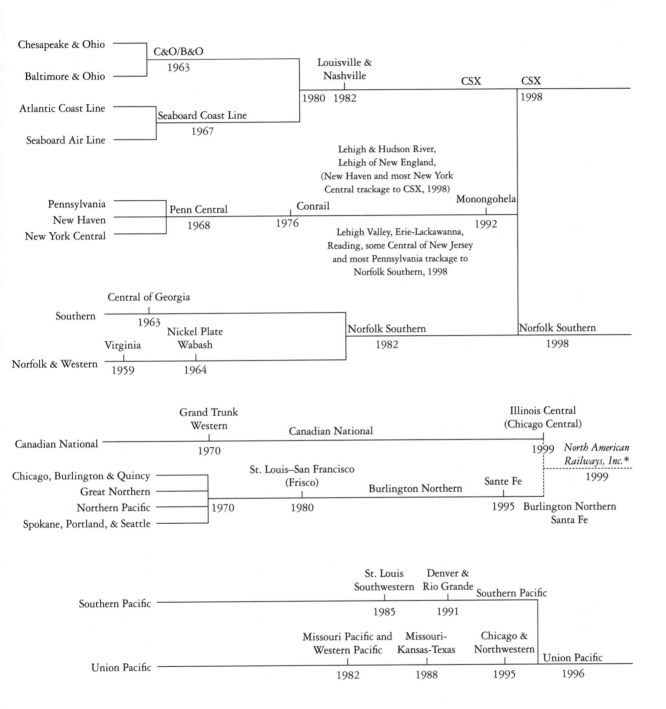

*Proposed merger, subject to approval by authorities in U.S. and Canada.

APPENDIX C

Railway Mileage in the United States

The mileage in this table is of the route and does not include more than one track between points.

Year	Miles of Road Operated	Year	Miles of Road Operated
1830	23	1880	93,296
1831	95	1881	103,108
1832	229	1882	114,677
1833	380	1883	121,422
1834	633	1884	125,345
1835	1,089	1885	128,320
1836	1,273	1886	136,338
1837	1,497	1887	149,214
1838	1,913	1888	156,114
1839	2,302	1889	161,276
1840	2,818	1890	163,597
1841	3,535	1891	168,403
1842	4,026	1892	171,564
1843	4,185	1893	176,461
1844	4,377	1894	178,709
1845	4,633	1895	180,657
1846	4,930	1896	182,777
1847	5,598	1897	184,428
1848	5,996	1898	186,396
1849	7,365	1899	189,295
1850	9,021	1900	193,346
1851	10,982	1901	197,237
1852	12,908	1902	202,472
1853	15,360	1903	207,977
1854	16,720	1904	213,904
1855	18,374	1905	218,101
1856	22,076	1906	224,363
1857	24,503	1907	229,951
1858	26,968	1908	233,468
1859	28,789	1909	236,834
1860	30,626	1910	240,439
1861	31,286	1911	243,979
1862	32,120	1912	246,777
1863	33,170	1913	249,777
1864	33,908	1914	252,105
1865	35,085	1915	253,789
1866	36,801	1916	254,036 (peak year)
1867	39,050	1917	253,626
1868	42,229	1920	252,845
1869	46,844	1925	249,398
1870	52,922	1930	249,052
1871	60,301	1935	241,822
1872	66,171	1940	233,670
1873	70,268	1950	223,779
1874	72,385	1960	217,552
1875	74,096	1970	205,782
1876	76,808	1980	178,056
1877	79,802	1990	146,002
1878	81,747	2000	131,810
1879	86,556		

APPENDIX D

Reporting Marks and Railroad Companies
Recognized by the Association of American Railroads, 1999

AA	Ann Arbor (Mich. Interstate)	BJRY	Burlington Junction
ABC	Akron & Barberton Cluster	BKRR	Batten Kill
ABL	Alameda Belt Line	BLE	Bessemer & Lake Erie
ACJR	Ashtabula, Carson & Jefferson	BLKM	Black Mesa & Lake Powell
ACRI	Algoma Central	BLMR	Blue Mountain
ACWR	Aberdeen, Carolina & Western	BLOL	Bloomer Line
ADBF	Adrian & Blissfield	BMH	Beaufort & Morehead City
AF	Alabama & Florida	BML	Belfast & Moosehead Lake
AGCR	Alamo Gulf Coast	BNSF	Burlington Northern and Santa Fe
AGLF	Atlantic & Gulf	BOP	Border Pacific
AGR	Alabama & Gulf Coast Railway	BPRR	Buffalo & Pittsburgh
AKDN	Acadiana	BR	Bradford Industrial Rail
AKMD	Arkansas Midland	BRAN	Brandon Corporation
AL	Almanor	BRC	Belt Railway of Chicago
ALAB	Alabama	BRFD	Branford Steam
ALM	Arkansas, Louisiana & Mississippi	BRG	Brownsville & Rio Grande International
ALQS	Aliquippa & Southern	BRR	Bootheel Regional Rail
ALS	Alton & Southern	BRW	Black River & Western
ALY	Allegheny & Eastern	BS	Birmingham Southern
AM	Arkansas & Missouri	BSDA	BSDA RR
AMHR	Landisville	BSOR	Buffalo Southern
AMTK	Amtrak	BST	Bay Shore Terminal
AN	Apalachicola Northern	BSV	Boone & Scenic Valley
ANR	Angelina & Neches River	BVRY	Brandywine Valley
AOK	Arkansas-Oklahoma	BXN	Bauxite & Northern
APA	Apache Rwy.	CA	Chesapeake & Albemarle
APD	Albany Port District	CACR	Clarkdale Arizona Central
APNC	Appanoose County Community	CAGY	Columbus & Greenville
AR	Aberdeen & Rockfish	CALA	Carolina Southern
ARA	Arcade & Attica	CALM	Caddo, Antoine and Little Missouri
ARC	Alexander	CALT	Caltrain
ARN	Amaud Railway	CART	Cartier Railway Company
ARR	Alaska Railroad	CASO	Canada Southern
ARZC	Arizona & California	CBC	Chemis de fer Baie des Chaleurs
ASML	Atlanta, Stone Mountain & Lithonia	CBEC	CBEC Ry.
ASRY	Ashland	CBF	Council Bluffs
ATLTA	AT & L RR	CBL	Conemaugh & Black Lick
ATW	Atlantic and Western	CBNS	Cape Breton & Central Nova Scotia Railway
AVR	Allegheny Valley		
AWW	Algers, Winslow & Western	CBRC	Columbian Basin
AZER	Arizona Eastern	CBRM	Chillicothe-Brunswick Rail Maint.
BAR	Bangor & Aroostock	CBRY	Copper Basin
BAYL	Bay Lines	CC	Chicago, Central & Pacific
BB	Buckingham Branch	CCCL	Connecticut Central
BCLR	Bay Colony	CCKY	Chattooga & Chickamauga
BCR	British Columbia Railway	CCRA	Camp Chase Industrial
BDRV	Belvedere & Delaware	CCRR	Claremont Concord
BEEM	Beech Mountain	CCT	Central California Traction
BHP	BHP Nevada	CCUO	Chicago-Chemung

CDAC	Canadian American RR	DCFB	Dodge City, Ford & Bucklin
CEDR	Cedar River	DCRC	Dubois County Railroad Corp.
CEIW	Central Indiana & Western	DER	Dunn Erwin Rwy.
CERA	Central of Indianapolis	DGNO	Dallas, Garland & Northeastern
CFNR	California Northern	DL	Delaware-Lackawanna
CFR	Cape Fear	DLWR	Depew, Lancaster & Western
CFWR	Caney Fork & Western	DME	Dakota, Minnesota & Eastern
CHR	Chestnut Ridge	DMIR	Duluth Missabe & Iron Range
CHRR	Chesapeake	DMM	Dansville & Mount Morris
CIC	Cedar Rapids & Iowa City	DMVW	Dakota, Missouri Valley & Western
CIND	Central of Indiana	DNE	Duluth & Northeastern
CIRR	Chattahoochee Industrial	DQE	De Queen and Eastern
CISD	Colonel's Island	DR	Dardanelle & Russelville
CKRY	Central Kansas	DRHY	Durham Transport
CLC	Columbia & Cowlitz	DRIR	Denver Rock Island
CLNA	Carolina Coastal	DS	Durango & Silverton
CLP	Clarendon & Pittsford	DSRC	Dakota Southern
CM	Central Montana Rail	DSRR	Delta Southern
CMGN	Central Michigan	DT	Decatur Junction
CMPA	Madison	DV	Delaware Valley
CMR	Coopersville & Marne	DVS	Delta Valley & Southern
CN	Canadian National	DW	Deseret Western
CNOW	Columbia & Northern	EACH	East Camden & Highland
CNZR	Central New England	EARY	Eastern Alabama
COER	Crab Orchard & Egyptian	ECBR	East Cooper & Berkeley
COP	City of Prineville	EDW	El Dorado & Wesson
CORP	Central Oregon & Pacific	EE	Ellis & Eastern
CP	Canadian Pacific	EEC	East Erie Commercial
CPDR	Carolina Piedmont	EERX	Eccles & Eastern
CR	Conrail	EFRR	Effingham
CRL	Chicago Rail Link	EIRC	Eastern Illinois
CRLE	Coe Rail	EIRR	Eastern Idaho
CSCD	Cascade and Columbia River	EJE	Elgin, Joliet & Eastern
CSKR	C & S	EJR	East Jersey Railroad and Terminal
CSL	Chicago Short Line	ELKR	Elk River
CSO	Connecticut Southern	ELS	Escanaba & Lake Superior
CSP	Camas Prairie	EM	Edgemoor & Manetta
CSS	Chicago, South Shore & South Bend	EN	Esquimalt and Nanaimo
CSXT	CSX Transportation	EPTC	East Portland Traction
CT	Columbia Terminal	ESHR	Eastern Shore
CTN	Canton	ETC	East Texas Central
CTR	Clinton Terminal	ETL	Essex Terminal
CTRN	Central of Tenn. Ry & Navigation	ETRY	East Tennessee
CTRW	Carlton Trail Railway Co.	EV	Everett
CTS	Cumbres & Toltec Scenic	EVRC	Elkhorn Valley Rail Car
CTT	Comunicación y Transport de Tijuana	EVT	Evansville Terminal
CUOH	Columbus & Ohio River	FC	Fulton County
CUVA	Cuyahoga Valley	FCEN	Florida Central
CVRR	Cimarron Valley	FEC	Florida East Coast
CW	Colorado & Wyoming	FEVR	Fremont & Elkhorn Valley
CWCY	Caldwell County	FGLK	Finger Lakes
CWR	California Western	FMID	Florida Midland
CWRL	Central Western Railway Corp.	FMRC	Farmrail
CWRY	Commonwealth	FNOR	Florida Northern
DAIR	D & I	FRR	Falls Road
DAKR	Dakota Rail	FSR	Fort Smith
DART	Dallas Area Rapid Transit	FVW	Fox Valley & Western
DC	Delray Connecting Railroad	FWCR	Florida West Coast

FWDB	Fort Worth & Dallas Belt	IN	Indiana Northeastern
FWRY	Fillmore Western	INPR	Idaho Northern & Pacific
FWWR	Fort Worth Western	INRD	Indiana
GBRY	Gettysburg	IOCR	Indiana & Ohio Central
GC	Georgia Central	IORY	Indiana & Ohio Railway
GCRY	Grand Canyon	IR	Illinois Railnet
GCSR	Gulf, Colorado & San Saba	ISRR	Indiana Southern
GCW	Garden City Western	ISSR	ISS Rail
GEXR	Goderich-Exeter	JEFW	Jefferson Warrior
GFM	Grupo Ferroviaria Mexicana	JGDR	Jackson, Gordonville and Delta
GFR	Grand Forks Railway	JJRR	Joliet Junction
GFRR	Georgia & Florida	JTFS	Juniata Terminal
GLSR	Gloster Southern	JVRR	Juniata Valley
GMRC	Green Mountain	KBSR	Kankakee, Beaverville & Southern
GMRY	Great Miami & Scioto	KCS	Kansas City Southern
GNBC	Grainbelt	KE	Kansas Eastern
GNRR	Georgia Northeastern	KJRY	Keokuk Junction
GNWR	Genesee & Wyoming	KKRR	Knox & Kane
GR	Grand Rapids Eastern	KLA	Kawartha Lakes
GRR	Georgetown Railroad	KNOR	Klamath Northern
GRWR	Great Walton	KRCX	Kokomo
GSM	Great Smokey Mountain Rwy.	KRR	Kiamichi
GSWR	Georgia Southwestern	KSW	Kansas Southwestern
GTR	Great River	KT	Kentucky & Tennessee
GTRA	Golden Triangle	KWT	KWT Rwy.
GU	Grafton & Upton	KYLE	Kyle
GVSR	Galveston Railroad	LAJ	Los Angeles Junction
GWL	Great Western Lines	LAL	Livonia, Avon & Lakeville
GWR	Great Western	LBC	Lewisburg & Buffalo Creek
GWRC	Georgia Woodlands	LBR	Lowville & Beaver River
GWWD	Greater Winnipeg Water Dist.	LC	Lancaster & Chester
GWWE	Gateway Eastern	LCS	Leadville, Colorado & Southern
GWWR	Gateway Western	LDRR	Louisiana & Delta
HB	Hampton & Branchville	LER	Logansport & Eel River Short-Line
HBRY	Hudson Bay Railroad	LHRR	Longhorn
HCRR	Honey Creek	LINC	Lewis and Clark
HE	Hollis & Eastern	LIRC	Louisville & Indiana
HESR	Huron & Eastern	LIRR	Long Island Railroad Co.
HMCR	Huntsville & Madison County	LKRR	Little Kanawha River Rail
HN	Hutchinson & Northern	LKWR	Lackland Western
HOS	Hoosier Southern	LNAL	Louisville, New Albany & Corydon
HPTD	High Point, Thomasville & Denton	LNW	Louisiana & North West
HRRC	Housatonic	LPN	Longview, Portland & Northern
HRS	Hollidaysburg & Roaring Springs	LRPA	Little Rock Port
HRT	Hartwell	LRS	Laurinburg & Southern
HS	H & S Railroad Co.	LRWN	Little Rock & Western
HSRR	Hardin Southern	LS	Luzerne & Susquehanna
HVSR	Hocking Valley Scenic	LSI	Lake Superior & Ishpeming
IAIS	Iowa Interstate	LSRC	Lake State
IANR	Iowa Northern	LT	Lake Terminal
IATR	Iowa Traction	LTVX	LTV Mining
IBT	International Bridge Co.	LVRR	Lycoming Valley
ICRK	Indian Creek	LW	Louisville & Wadley
IHB	Indiana Harbor Belt	LXOH	Lexington & Ohio
IHRC	Indiana Hi-Rail	LXVR	Luxapalila Valley
ILW	Illinois Western	MAW	Maumee & Western
IMRL	I & M Rail Link	MBRX	Milford-Bennington
IMRR	Illinois & Midland	MBTA	Massachusetts Bay Transportation Auth.

MC	Maine Coast	NEKM	Northeast Kansas & Missouri
MCER	Massachusetts Central	NENE	Nebraska Northeastern
MCLR	McLaughlin Line	NERR	Nashville & Eastern
MCR	McCloud	NHCR	New Hampshire Central
MCRR	Monongahela Connecting	NHN	New Hampshire Northcoast
MCSA	Moscow, Camden & San Augustine	NHRR	New Hope & Ivyland
MCTA	Minnesota Central	NHVT	New Hampshire & Vermont
MDDE	Maryland & Delaware	NICT	Northern Indiana Commuter Transportation District
MDDT	Maryland Mass Transit		
MDLR	Midland Terminal	NIRC	Northern Illinois Rail Commuter District
MDW	Minnesota, Dakota & Western	NJT	New Jersey Transit
ME	Morristown & Erie	NKCR	Nebraska, Kansas & Colorado RailNet
MET	Modesto & Empire Traction	NOKL	Northwestern Oklahoma
METW	Municipality of East Troy	NOLR	New Orleans Lower Coast
MGRI	MG Rail	NOPB	New Orleans Public Belt
MH	Mount Hood	NOW	Northern Ohio & Western
MIDH	Middletown & Hummelstown	NPB	Norfolk & Portsmouth Belt Line
MISS	Mississipian	NPR	Northern Plains
MJ	Manufacturers' Junction	NRI	Nebkota
MKC	McKeesport Connecting	NRR	Nobles & Rock
MMID	Maryland Midland	NS	Norfolk Southern
MMRR	Mid-Michigan	NSHR	North Shore
MNA	Missouri & Northern Arkansas	NSM	Northshore Mining
MNBR	M & B Railroad	NSR	Newburg & South Shore
MNCR	Metro North Commuter Railroad Co.	NSSR	North Shore Scenic
MNJ	Middletown & New Jersey	NTRY	Nimishillen & Tuscarawas
MNNR	Minnesota Commercial	NVRR	Napa Valley
MNRR	Minnesota Northern	NWP	Northwestern Pacific
MPA	Maryland & Pennsylvania	NYA	New York & Atlantic
MR	Midland	NYCH	New York Cross Harbor
MRL	Montana Rail Link	NYGL	New York & Greenwood Lake Railway
MRS	Manufacturers Rwy. Co.	NYLE	New York & Lake Erie
MSCI	Mississippi Central	NYSW	New York, Susquehanna & Western
MSDR	Mississippi Delta	OCTL	Oil Creek & Titusville
MSE	Mississippi Export	OGEE	Ogeechee
MSO	Michigan Southern	OHCR	Ohio Central
MSR	Michigan Shore Railroad	OHIC	Ohi-Rail
MSTR	Massena Terminal	OHRY	Owego & Harford
MSV	Mississippi & Skuna Valley	OLB	Omaha, Lincoln & Beatrice
MTRA	Chicago Commuter Rail Service	OLO	Ontario L'Original
MVRY	Mahoning Valley	OLYR	Olympic
MVT	Mount Vernon Terminal	OMID	Ontario Midland
MWHA	Mohawk, Adirondack & Northern	ONCT	Ontario Central
MWRL	Molalla Western	ONR	Ontario Northland Railway
MWRR	Montana Western	ORR	Osage
NAUG	Naugatuck	OSRR	Ohio Southern
NBER	Nittany & Bald Eagle	OTC	Owensville Terminal
NBSR	New Brunswick Southern	OTR	Oakland Terminal
NCPR	North Carolina Ports	OTT	Ottumwa Terminal Transfer
NCR	Northern Central	OTVR	Otter Tail Valley
NCRC	Nebraska Central	OUCH	Ouachita
NCT	North Charleston Terminal	OVR	Ottawa Valley RaiLink
NCVA	North Carolina & Virginia	PAL	Paducah & Louisville
NCYR	Nash County RR	PAM	Pittsburgh, Allegheny & McKees Rocks
NDCR	NDC Railroad Co.	PBL	Philadelphia Belt Line
NDM	Ferrocarriles Nacionales de Mexico	PBNE	Philadelphia, Bethlehem & New England
NECR	New England Central	PBR	Patapsco & Back Rivers
NEGS	New England Southern	PBRR	Pine Belt Southern

PBVR	Port Bienville		SBK	South Brooklyn
PCHR	Port Colborne Harbour Railroad		SBLN	Sterling Belt Line
PCN	Point Comfort & Northern		SBRR	Stourbridge
PDRR	Pee Dee River		SBVR	South Branch Valley
PHL	Pacific Harbor Line, Inc.		SCAX	Metrolink
PI	Paducah & Illinois		SCBG	Santa Cruz, Big Trees & Pacific
PICK	Pickens		SCE	Scenic
PIR	Pittsburgh Industrial		SCRA	Southern California Regional Rail
PJR	Port Jersey		SCRF	South Carolina Central
PJRL	Penn Jersey Rail Lines		SCTR	South Central Tennessee
PJS	Paperton Junction		SCXF	South Central Florida Express
PLRR	Palouse River		SCXY	St. Croix Valley RR
PNR	Panhandle Northern		SDIY	San Diego & Imperial Valley
PNW	Prescott & Northwestern		SDNR	San Diego Northern Railway
PNWR	Portland & Western		SEKR	Southeast Kansas
POTB	Port of Tillamook Bay		SEMO	Southeast Missouri Port
POV	Pittsburgh & Ohio Valley		SERA	Sierra
POVA	Pend Oreille Valley		SERS	Southeast Rail System
PPHW	Peoria, Peoria Heights & Western		SFR	Southern Freight Railroad
PPU	Peoria & Pekin Union		SFS	Santa Fe Southern
PRCC	Palouse River & Coulee City		SGLR	Seminole Gulf
PRT	Parr Terminal		SGVY	Saginaw Valley
PRV	Pearl River Valley		SH	Steelton & Highspire
PRYL	Port Royal		SIND	Southern Indiana
PSAP	Puget Sound & Pacific		SIRS	Shelbyville Industrial Rail
PSR	Pittsburg & Shawmut Railroad		SJVR	San Joaquin Valley
PT	Peninsula Terminal		SKOL	South Kansas & Oklahoma
PTC	Plainview Terminal		SL	Salt Lake City Southern
PTRA	Port Terminal RR Association		SLC	San Luis Central
PTSC	Port Terminal Railroad of South Carolina		SLGG	Sidney & Lowe
PUCC	Port Utilities Commission of Charleston		SLGW	Salt Lake, Garfield & Western
PVRR	Pioneer Valley		SLR	St. Lawrence & Atlantic
PVS	Pecos Valley Southern		SLRR	St. Lawrence & Raquette River
pvt	Private		SLRS	Switching Management Services
PW	Providence & Worcester		SM	St. Mary's
QBT	Quincy Bay Terminal		SMA	San Manuel Arizona
QNSL	Quebec North Shore & Labrador RR Co.		SMRR	Sisseton Milbank
QRC	Quebec Railway Corp.		SMV	Santa Maria Valley
QRR	Quincy		SO	South Orient
RARW	Rarus		SOM	Somerset
RBMN	Reading, Blue Mountain & Northern		SPTA	Southeast PA Transportation Authority
RCC	Red-Mont		SRC	Strasburg
RJCM	R. J. Corman, Memphis		SRN	Sabine River & Northern
RJCN	R. J. Corman, Allentown		SRNJ	Southern Railroad of New Jersey
RJCP	R. J. Corman		SRS	Southeast Rail System
RJCR	R. J. Corman, Pennsylvania		SRY	Southern Ry. of British Columbia
RJCW	R. J. Corman, Western Ohio		SS	Sand Springs
RRCO	Rochelle		SSAM	Sault Ste. Marie Bridge Co.
RRVW	Red River Valley & Western		SSC	Southern Switching
RS	Roberval and Seguenay		SSDK	Savannah State Docks
RSM	Railroad Switching Serv. of Missouri		SSLV	Southern San Luis Valley
RSNR	Red Springs & Northern		ST	St Rail System
RSR	Rochester & Southern		STAT	Stewartstown
RSS	Rockdale, Sandow & Southern		STC	Simpson Timber Co.
RT	River Terminal		STE	Stockton Terminal & Eastern
RVSG	Rio Valley Switching		STLH	St. Lawrence & Hudson
SAN	Sandersville		STMA	Saint Maries River
SB	South Buffalo		STR	Shawnee Terminal

SUAB	Southern Alabama
SUN	Sunset
SVRR	Shamokin Valley
SW	Southwestern
SWKR	SWKR Operating Co.
SWP	Southwest Pennsylvania
SWR	Southwind
TASD	Terminal Railway, Ala. State Docks
TBRY	Thermal Belt
TCKR	Turtle Creek Industrial
TCRO	Tri-County Commuter Rail Authority
TCT	Texas City Terminal
TCWR	Twin Cities & Western
TE	Tacoma Eastern
TFM	Transportacion Ferroviaria Mexicana
TKEN	Tennken
TM	Texas Mexican Rwy.
TMBL	Tacoma Municipal Belt Line
TMSS	Towanda-Monroeton Shippers Lifeline
TN	Texas & Northern
TNER	Texas Northeastern
TNMR	Texas – New Mexico
TPW	Toledo, Peoria & Western
TR	Tomahawk Railway
TRC	Trona
TRIN	Trinidad
TRRA	Terminal RR Assoc. of St. Louis
TSBY	Tuscola & Saginaw Bay
TSE	Texas South-Eastern
TSRD	Twin State
TSRR	Tennessee Southern
TSU	Tulsa-Sapulpa Union
TSWR	Toppenish, Simcoe & Western
TTIS	Transkentucky Transportation
TTR	Talleyrand Terminal
TXGN	Texas Gonzales & Northern
TXNW	Texas North Western
TXOR	Texas & Oklahoma
TXTC	Texas Transportation
TYBR	Tyburn
UCIR	Union County Industrial
UCRY	Utah Central
UMP	Upper Merion & U Plymouth
UP	Union Pacific
URR	Union Railroad
USG	U.S. Government
UTAH	Utah Rwy.
UTIL	Utility
VALE	Valley
VCY	Ventury County
VIA	Via Rail Canada
VR	Valdosta
VRR	Vaughan
VRRC	Vandalia
VSRR	Virginia Southern
VTR	Vermont
WACR	Washington County
WBCR	Wabash Central

WBSH	Wabush Lake Railway
WC	Wisconsin Central
WCLR	Waccamaw Coastline
WCOR	Wellsboro & Corning
WCTR	WCTU Company
WE	Wheeling & Lake Erie
WGCR	Wiregrass Central
WHOE	Walking Horse & Eastern
WHRY	Windsor & Hantsport
WKR	Western Kentucky
WMI	West Michigan
WNFR	Winifrede
WPRR	Williamette & Pacific
WPY	White Pass and Yukon Corporation Limited
WRRC	Western
WS	Walkersville Southern
WSOR	Wisconsin & Southern
WSR	Warren & Saline River
WSRY	Winamac Southern
WSS	Winston-Salem Southbound
WTJR	Wichita, Tillman & Jackson
WTLR	West Texas and Lubbock
WTNN	West Tennessee
WTRM	Warren & Trumbull
WTRY	Wilmington Terminal
WUT	Wichita Union Terminal
WVN	West Virginia Northern
WVRR	Willamette Valley
WW	Winchester & Western
WWRC	Wilmington & Western
WWV	Whitewater Valley
WYCO	Wyoming & Colorado
YARR	Youngstown & Austintown
YB	Youngstown Belt
YDC	Yankeetown Dock
YKR	Yorktrail
YSLR	Yolo Shortline
YVRR	Yadkin Valley
YW	Yreka Western

Commuter Operators

AMTK	Amtrak
CALT	Caltrain
DART	Dallas Area Rapid Transit
LIRR	Long Island Railroad Co.
MBTA	Mass. Bay Transportation Authority
MDDT	Maryland Mass Transit
MNCR	Metro North Commuter Railroad Co.
MTRA	Chicago Commuter Rail Service
NICT	Northern Indiana Commuter Transportation District
NJT	New Jersey Transit
SCRA	Southern California Regional Rail
SDNR	San Diego Northern Railway
SPTA	Southeast PA Transportation Authority
TCRO	Tri-County Commuter Rail Authority
VIA	Via Rail Canada

APPENDIX E

Railroad Movies Available on VHS for "The Armchair Conductor"

Many movies made in the 1920s through the 1960s contain scenes that take place on trains. During that time, riding on trains was a usual occurrence, and, therefore, a natural part of a movie plot or novel. Some movies actually featured a famous train, railroad, or equipment. In the 1980s and 1990s, train scenes were still ideal for a particular impact. The following list contains movies that are available at local video stores or for purchase by mail order. Here is a feast for the "armchair conductor."

North American Train Movies

Broadway Limited (Victor McLaglen, Marjorie Woodworth, ZaSu Pitts, Dennis O'Keefe, Patsy Kelly) Hal Roach Studios in cooperation with the Pennsylvania Railroad made the movie in 1941. It has a lot of steam action and many interior scenes showing off Pennsy equipment. It has a fabulous "crossing the diamonds" sequence leaving Chicago's Union Station, and it keeps getting better. There is an appearance of a GG1 toward the end of the movie. It is a light comedy and great railroad entertainment. A must-see.

Danger Lights (Jean Arthur, Louis Wolheim) *Danger Lights* is about the Depression-era camaraderie on the Milwaukee Road. It has lots of steam action and a thrilling scene of a locomotive running at full speed toward the end.

Denver and Rio Grande (Edmond O'Brien, Sterling Hayden, Laura Elliott, J. Carrol Naish, ZaSu Pitts) Featuring a number of big western stars of the 1940s, the movie depicts the rivalry of the Denver and Rio Grande and Santa Fe Railroads.

Emperor of the North (Ernest Borgnine, Lee Marvin, Keith Carradine) Hobo life had its heroes, and the Emperor of the North knows all the tricks. It has lots of steam action and is both authentic about hobo life and entertaining.

The General (Buster Keaton) *The General* is a somewhat humorous "silent screen" account of the Andrews Raid. It is quite inaccurate from a historical perspective but it is nonetheless entertaining.

Grand Central Murder (Van Heflin) A murder takes place in the famous New York Central's Manhattan terminal. It shows private cars, track alignments, and the dispatch center. It is a classic 1940s railroad and murder script—a real "whodunnit."

The Great Locomotive Chase (Fess Parker, Jeffrey Hunter) A truly accurate account of the Andrews Raid. It is very entertaining and shows vintage equipment. It is a must for nineteenth-century rail enthusiasts.

The Harvey Girls (Judy Garland, John Hodiak, Preston Foster, Ray Bolger) *The Harvey Girls* features some of the biggest movie actors and actresses of the 1940s. It has authentic scenes of the Fred Harvey restaurants and puts forth the theme that the "Harvey Girls" civilized the West. It also shows vintage Santa Fe equipment.

The Horse Soldiers (John Wayne, William Holden, Constance Towers) John Wayne stars as a Union officer penetrating Confederate lines. The movie shows authentic Confederate railroad equipment and its destruction by Union soldiers.

The Hurricane Express (John Wayne) The "Wrecker" destroys the trains of a Depression-era railroad company. In serial form, this movie is one of John Wayne's earliest starring roles. It is loaded with steam action and train wrecks. Wayne, of course, brings the "Wrecker" to justice. Try to put the clues together to discover the "Wrecker's" identity before Wayne does.

Kansas Pacific (Sterling Hayden, Eve Miller) Another 1940s meeting of a western star with the rails. The story is about the construction of the Kansas Pacific just before the Civil War. It brings out the emotion of "Bleeding Kansas" even though the movie used "modern" railroad cars.

Narrow Margin (Gene Hackman, Anne Archer) Try to hide from the Mafia on a trans-Canadian train! The movie shows off the interior of VIA cars and is pure excitement. The movie is a must-see for VIA fans and all rail fans.

Paradise Express (Grant Withers, Dorothy Appleby) This 1930s classic describes the competition between a short-line railroad and a trucking company. There is sabotage, theft, and, of course, boy meets girl. It has a lot of steam action and shows the problems of running a railroad under receivership.

Prison Train (Fred Keating, Linda Winters, Val Stanton) Take a transcontinental ride to Alcatraz during the 1930s. The movie has very poor acting, but lots of steam action. Overlook the plot and just enjoy the train. . . .

Runaway Train (Jon Voight, Rebecca De Mornay, Eric Roberts) No one in the cab, and a freight train is running at full throttle. The modern movie shows the problem of clearing track and trying to slow down a speeding train.

Silver Streak (Sally Blane, Charles Starett) This movie stars the Burlington Route's *Zephyr*. It shows the mechanics as well as the train running at speed. It is a lot of fun, with a "boy meets girl" plot, 1930s style.

Silver Streak (Gene Wilder, Jill Clayburgh, Richard Pryor) There's comedy, murder, and even "train chasing" in this Los Angeles to Chicago trip made in the 1980s. It features modern equipment and a spectacular locomotive crash in Union Station. It is a fun movie.

Three for Bedroom "C" (Gloria Swanson, James Warren) Two people claim to have reservations for Bedroom C. The third is Swanson's pre-teen daughter. Anyone can guess the results. This lighthearted comedy shows off the interior of the early 1950s Santa Fe Super Chief—even scenes in the Turquoise Room. What the plot lacks, the train makes up for. . . .

Twentieth Century (John Barrymore, Carole Lombard) Named after the New York Central's famous *Twentieth Century Limited*, the movie is actually an adaptation of a stage play. The train scenes occur about one-third through the movie, and most take place in the lounge car and Pullman bedroom. The equipment is of the early 1930s.

Under Siege II (Steven Seagal, Eric Bogosian) A maniac and his commando team hijack a modern train. They manipulate a satellite "doomsday machine" from the train, and Seagal saves the day. It has many good interior scenes. It also has a lot of unnecessary profanity.

Union Pacific (Barbara Stanwyck, Joel McCrea, Anthony Quinn) Cecil B. De Mille created an epic movie about the building of the first transcontinental railroad. There is a good portrayal of "Hell on Wheels," although the movie takes a few historical liberties. It is a Hollywood archetype. A must-see.

Without Reservations (John Wayne, Claudette Colbert) Wayne meets Colbert on a train (possibly *Commodore Vanderbilt*) going from New York to Chicago. The movie has great interior scenes of Pullmans and diner and lounge cars. After a transfer in Chicago, they continue their journey on the Santa Fe *Sunrise Limited*. Wayne is a Marine flyer who just returned from World War II. The movie is a gem and a must-see for anyone who likes trains and/or John Wayne.

Foreign Train Movies

Berlin Express (Merle Oberon, Robert Ryan, Paul Lukas) In the days following the end of World War II in Europe, the U.S. military controlled German train movements. The movie has lots of spy action, intrigue, and a good depiction of German rolling stock.

The Cassandra Crossing (Burt Lancaster, Sophia Loren, Ava Gardner, Richard Harris) A trans-European Express is traveling with a deadly virus on board. It has a spectacular ending.

The Lady Vanishes (Margaret Lockwood, Michael Redgrave, Paul Lukas) Just before World War II, several English subjects travel from Switzerland through Germany—with a spy on board. It has excellent scenes of coaches, bedrooms, and the dining car. Yes, the lady does vanish and the intrigue is to find her. The master of suspense, Alfred Hitchcock, directed it.

Night Train to Munich (Rex Harrison, Margaret Lockwood, Paul Henreid) A captured scientist, a spy in Nazi uniform, and a beautiful girl take a train under guard to Munich. It has a lot of suspense and some gentle humor. No one can resist a 1939 night train ride to Munich.

The Pearl of Death (Nigel Bruce and Basil Rathbone) This Sherlock Holmes movie is the archetype of train mysteries. Besides murder, the movie has great interior scenes of a London to Edinburgh express. The movie depicts English rail travel in the immediate post–World War II period. A must-see.

Romance on the Orient Express (Cheryl Ladd, Stuart Wilson, John Gielgud) Two American women travel the modern *Orient Express* seeking adventure and romance. One meets a new lover and another reunites with a former flame. The movie shows off one of the most luxurious trains in the world.

Shanghai Express (Marlene Dietrich, Clive Brooke) Marlene Dietrich is the best of all possible mysterious women and she is riding a train! The train travels through Civil War China during the late 1930s. The movie describes train travel in war-torn China.

The Train (Burt Lancaster) A freight train loaded with French art is being taken to Germany during the last days of World War II. The Resistance does a magnificent job in preventing it from leaving France. The film also has one of the most spectacular train crashes ever filmed.

Current Canadian Pacific freight. Courtesy Canadian Pacific Railway.

BIBLIOGRAPHY

The sources included below are those that are available to the general public at a bookstore or library. Some company publications are mentioned that are available to the general public. Copies of U.S. railroad legislation can be obtained through a representative or senator. Railroad magazines provide articles on both current and historical topics. These include: *Trains, Railroad and Railfan, Vintage Rails, Pacific Rail, News, Rail News, Railway Age,* and the former *Passenger Train Journal. Life Magazine* had many articles and reports on railroad events—with photos—during the 1930s and 1940s.

Abdill, George B. *Civil War Railroads: A Pictorial Story of the War Between the States, 1861–1865.* Bloomington and Indianapolis: Indiana University Press, 1999.

Ames, Charles Edgar. *Pioneering the Union Pacific: A Reappraisal of the Builders of the Railroad.* New York: Appleton-Century-Crofts, 1969.

Amtrak. *Amtrak—Transportation's Critical Link.* December 1996.

———. *1995 Annual Report.*

Armstrong, John H. *The Railroad, What It Is, What It Does: The Introduction to Railroading.* Fourth edition. Omaha, Nebr.: Simmons-Boardman Books, Inc., 1998.

Association of American Railroads. *Highlights of American Railroad History.* Washington, D.C.: The Association, 1954.

———. *Railroad Land Grants: A Sharp Deal for Uncle Sam.* Washington, D.C.: Information and Public Affairs, 1983.

Bain, William E., ed. *B & O in the Civil War.* Denver: Sage Books, 1966.

Bernet, Gerard E. *The Hard Coal Carriers.* Flanders, N.J.: RAE Publishing, 1994.

Berton, Pierre. *The Great Railway.* Toronto: McClelland & Stewart, 1974.

Black, Robert C. *The Railroads of the Confederacy.* Chapel Hill: University of North Carolina Press, 1998.

Botkin, Benjamin Albert, and Alvin F. Harlow, eds. *A Treasury of Railroad Folklore.* New York: Bonanza Books, 1989 (1953).

Burlington Northern Railroad. *Historical Background Information: Major Burlington Northern Predecessor Companies.* St. Paul, Minn.: Burlington Northern Railroad, 1980.

Canadian National, *CN Today.* Montreal: CN Public Affairs and Advertising, nd.

———. *Growing Up with Canada.* Montreal: Canadian National, Public Affairs and Advertising, 1987.

———. *1995 Annual Report.* Montreal: Canadian National, 1996.

Casey, Robert J., and W. A. S. Douglas. *Pioneer Railroad: The Story of the Chicago and North Western System.* New York: McGraw-Hill, 1948.

Castner, Charles B., Ron Flanary, and Patrick C. Dorin. *Louisville & Nashville Railroad: The Old Reliable.* Lynchburg, Va.: TLC Publishing, 1996.

Chorlian, Meg. *Orphan Trains.* Petersborough, N.H.: Cobblestone Publishing, Inc., 1998.

Cohen, Ronald D., and Stephen G. McShane, eds. *Moonlight in Duneland: The Illustrated Story of the Chicago South Shore and South Bend Railroad.* Bloomington and Indianapolis: Indiana University Press, 1998.

Combs, Barry. *Westward to Promontory: Building the Union Pacific Across the Plains and Mountains.* New York: Crown Publishers, 1986.

Corliss, Carlton J. *Main Line of Mid-America: The Story of the Illinois Central.* New York: Creative Age Press, 1950.

CP Rail. *CP Rail System Chronology,* 1989.

Cupper, Dan. *Horseshoe Heritage: The Story of a Great Railroad Landmark.* Halifax, Pa.: Withers Publishing, 1993.

Cushing, Raymond, and Jeffrey Moreau. *America's First Transcontinental Railway: A Pictorial History of the Pacific Railroad.* Pasadena, Calif.: Pentrex, 1994.

Daniels, Winthrop More. *American Railroads: Four Phases of Their History.* Princeton: Princeton University Press, 1932.

Davis, Burke. *The Southern Railway: Road of the Innovators.* Chapel Hill: University of North Carolina Press, 1985.

Davis, George B., Leslie J. Perry, and Joseph W. Kirkley. *The Official Military Atlas of the Civil War.* New York: Gramercy Books, 1983.

DeNevi, Don. *America's Fighting Railroads: A World War II Pictorial History.* Missoula, Mont.: Pictorial Histories Publishing Company, 1996.

Derleth, August William. *The Milwaukee Road: Its First Hundred Years.* New York: Creative Age Press, 1948.

Drury, George H. *The Historical Guide to North American Railroads.* Waukesha, Wis.: Kalmbach Books, 1994.

Durham, Robert K. *The Jersey Central Railroad.* Auburn, Pa.: R.K. Durham, 1996.

Fitzsimons, Bernard. *150 Years of North American Railroads.* Secaucus, N.J.: Chartwell Books, 1982.

Bibliography

Foster, Gerald L. *A Field Guide to Trains of North America*. Boston: Houghton Mifflin, 1996.

Fries, William. *Train Wrecks & Disasters: A Pictorial & Chronological History as Reported by the Press*. New Port Richey, Fla.: W. Fries, 1994.

Fundamentals of the Steam Locomotive. Omaha, Nebr.: Simmons-Boardman Books, 1992.

Glazebrook, G. P. de T. *A History of Transportation in Canada*. New York: Greenwood Press, 1969 (1938).

Goddard, Stephen B. *Getting There: The Epic Struggle Between Road and Rail in the American Century*. Chicago: University of Chicago Press, 1996.

Gordon, Sarah. *Passage to Union: How the Railroads Transformed American Life, 1829–1929*. Chicago: Elephant Paperbacks, 1998.

Gray, Carl R. *Railroading in Eighteen Countries: The Story of American Railroad Men Serving in the Military Railway Service, 1862 to 1953*. New York: Scribner, 1955.

Halberstadt, Hans. *Modern Diesel Locomotives*. Osceola, Wis.: Motorbooks International Publishers & Wholesalers, 1996.

Halberstadt, Hans, and April Halberstadt. *The American Train Depot & Roundhouse*. Osceola, Wis.: Motorbooks International, 1995.

Haney, Lewis H. *A Congressional History of Railways in the United States*. New York: A. M. Kelley, 1968 (1908).

Harlow, Alvin F. *Steelways of New England*. New York: Creative Age Press, 1946.

Harper's School Geography. New York: Harper & Brothers, 1885.

Harwood, Herbert H., Jr., and Robert S. Korach. *The Lake Shore Electric Railway Story*. Bloomington and Indianapolis: Indiana University Press, 2000.

Hatcher, Colin K. *The Northern Alberta Railways*. Calgary: B.R.M.N.A., 1981.

————. *The Northern Alberta Railways, volume two*. Calgary: B.R.M.N.A., 1987.

Hawthorne, Nathaniel. "The Celestial Railroad" in *The Portable Hawthorne*, ed. Malcolm Cowley. New York: Penguin, 1976.

Heath, Erle. *Seventy-Five Years of Progress: Historical Sketch of the Southern Pacific*. San Francisco: Southern Pacific Bureau of News, 1945.

Hedin, Robert, ed. *The Great Machines: Poems and Songs of the American Railroad*. Iowa City: University of Iowa Press, 1996.

Henderson, Louis T. *Trains: A Children's Picture Book of Trains and Stories About Them*. Chicago: M.A. Donohue & Company, 1935.

Hofsommer, Donovan L. *Katy Northwest: The Story of a Branch Line Railroad*. Bloomington and Indianapolis: Indiana University Press, 1999 (1976).

Holbrook, Stewart Hall. *The Story of American Railroads*. New York: American Legacy Press, 1981 (1947).

Holley, Noel T. *The Milwaukee Electrics: An Inside Look at Locomotives and Railroading*. Second edition. Edmonds, Wash.: Hundman Publishing Company, Inc., 1999.

Holt, Marilyn Irvin. *The Orphan Trains: Placing Out in America*. Lincoln: University of Nebraska Press, 1994.

Hungry Wolf, Adolf. *Canadian Railway Stories: 100 Years of History and Lore*. Skookumchuck, B.C.: Good Medicine Books, 1985.

Husband, Joseph. *The Story of the Pullman Car*. Grand Rapids, Mich.: Black Letter Press, 1974 (1917).

Jacobs, Timothy. *The History of the Pennsylvania Railroad*. New York: Smithmark Publishers, Inc., 1994.

————, ed. *The History of the Baltimore & Ohio: America's First Railroad*. New York: Smithmark Publishers, Inc., 1994.

Jensen, Oliver Ormerod. *The American Heritage History of Railroads in America*. New York: American Heritage/Wings Books, 1993 (1975).

Johnson, F. H. *Brief Record of the Development of the Milwaukee Road from the Chartering of Its First Predecessor Company in February 1847 to Date, July 1944*. Chicago, Ill.: Public Relations Dept., Milwaukee Road, 1944.

Johnston, Carole Turner. *Trains West*. Sioux City, Iowa: Quixote Press, 1996.

Klein, Aaron E. *Encyclopedia of North American Railroads*. Secaucus, N.J.: Chartwell Books, 1994 (1985).

————. *New York Central*. New York: Smithmark, 1994 (1985).

Koucky, Rudolph W., MD. "The Buffalo Disaster of 1882," in *North Dakota History*, 50, no. 1, 1983.

Kyner, James Henry. *End of Track*. Lincoln: University of Nebraska Press, 1960.

Lewis, Robert G. *The Handbook of American Railroads*. Second edition. New York: Simmons-Boardman Publishing Corporation, 1956.

MacKay, Donald. *The People's Railway: A History of Canadian National*. Vancouver: Douglas & McIntyre, 1992.

MacKay, Donald, and Lorne Perry. *Train Country: An Illustrated History of Canadian National Railways*. Forest Park, Ill.: Heimburger House Publishing Company, 1995 (1994).

Maiken, Peter T. *Night Trains: The Pullman System in the Golden Years of American Rail Travel*. Baltimore: Johns Hopkins University Press, 1992 (1989).

Marre, Louis A., Jerry A. Pinkepank, and George H. Drury. *The Contemporary Diesel Spotter's Guide*. Milwaukee, Wis.: Kalmbach Books, 1995.

Marshall, James. *Santa Fe, the Railroad that Built an Empire*. New York: Random House, 1945.

Martin, Albro. *James J. Hill and the Opening of the Northwest*. St. Paul: Minnesota Historical Society Press, 1991 (1976).

240

McKissack, Pat, and Fredrick McKissack. *A Long Hard Journey: The Story of the Pullman Porter.* New York: Walker and Company, 1995 (1989).

Meader, Stephen W. *The Long Trains Roll.* New York: Harcourt, Brace & World, 1966 (1944).

Middleton, William D. *Landmarks on the Iron Road: Two Centuries of North American Railroad Engineering.* Bloomington and Indianapolis: Indiana University Press, 1999.

————. *South Shore: The Last Interurban,* revised second edition. Bloomington and Indianapolis: Indiana University Press, 1999.

————. *"Yet there isn't a train I wouldn't take": Railway Journeys.* Bloomington and Indianapolis: Indiana University Press, 2000.

Moon, Gypsy. *Done and Been: Steel Rail Chronicles of American Hobos.* Bloomington and Indianapolis: Indiana University Press, 1996.

Morgan, David Page. *Fast Mail, the First 75 Years: A History of the Burlington Railroad's Mail Service between Chicago and Council Bluffs–Omaha, 1884–1959.* Mobile Post Office Society, 1959.

Morris, Juddi. *The Harvey Girls: The Women Who Civilized the West.* New York: Walker and Company, 1997.

Nock, O. S. *Railways at the Zenith of Steam.* New York: Macmillan, 1970.

North, Paul. *American Steam Locomotives.* New York: Bookman Publishing, 1988.

Osterwald, Doris B. *Cinders & Smoke: A Mile by Mile Guide for the Durango & Silverton Narrow Gauge Railroad.* Lakewood, Colo.: Western Guideways, 1995.

Overton, Richard Cleghorn. *Burlington Route: A History of the Burlington Lines.* Lincoln: University of Nebraska Press, 1976 (1965).

Pickenpaugh, Roger. *Rescue by Rail: Troop Transfer and the Civil War in the West, 1863.* Lincoln: University of Nebraska Press, 1998.

Porterfield, James D. *Dining By Rail: The History and the Recipes of America's Golden Age of Railroad Cuisine.* New York: St. Martin's Griffin, 1998 (1993).

Potter, Janet Greenstein. *Great American Railroad Stations.* New York: Preservation Press, 1996.

Prince, Richard E. *Atlantic Coast Line Railroad: Steam Locomotives, Ships, and History.* Bloomington and Indianapolis: Indiana University Press, 2000 (1966).

————. *Seaboard Air Line Railway: Steam Boats, Locomotives, and History.* Bloomington and Indianapolis: Indiana University Press, 2000 (1969).

Railway Association of Canada. *Atlas: Canadian Railways.* Montréal: The Association, 1996.

————. *Canada's Railways: Now and the Future.* Montréal: Railway Association of Canada, 1996.

————. *Perspectives on Productivity and the Canadian Railway Industry.* Montréal: Railway Association of Canada, 1999.

Rand McNally. *Atlas of the United States.* New York: Rand McNally & Co., 1935.

Rand McNally and Company. *Handy Railroad Atlas of the United States.* Chicago: Rand McNally, 1988.

Randall, J. G. *The Civil War and Reconstruction.* Lexington, Mass.: Heath, 1969.

Reed, Robert Carroll. *Train Wrecks: A Pictorial History of Accidents on the Main Line.* Atglen, Pa.: Schiffer Pub., 1996.

Rehor, John A. *The Nickel Plate Story.* Milwaukee, Wis.: Kalmbach Publishing Co., 1994 (1965).

Riley, C. J. *The Encyclopedia of Trains & Locomotives.* New York: MetroBooks, 1995.

Rose, P. S. *Steam Engine Guide.* Lancaster, Pa.: Stemgas Publishing Company, 1989 (1910).

Rowland, Kate Mason. *The Life of Charles Carroll of Carrollton, 1737–1832 with His Correspondence and Public Papers.* 2 vols. New York: G.P. Putnam, 1898.

Schafer, Mike. *Caboose.* Osceola, Wis.: Motorbooks International, 1997.

————. *Streamliner Memories.* Osceola, Wis.: MBI Publishing, 1999.

————. *Vintage Diesel Locomotives.* Osceola, Wis.: Motorbooks International, 1998.

Schafer, Mike, and Joe Welsh. *Classic American Streamliners.* Osceola, Wis.: Motorbooks International, 1997.

Schulte, Christopher. *The Dictionary of Railway Track Terms.* Omaha, Nebr.: Simmons-Boardman Books, 1993.

Simons, Richard S., and Francis Parker. *Railroads of Indiana.* Bloomington and Indianapolis: Indiana University Press, 1997.

Solomon, Brian. *Railroad Stations.* New York: MetroBooks, 1998.

Starr, John William. *Lincoln & the Railroads.* New York: Arno Press, 1981 (1927).

————. *One Hundred Years of American Railroading.* New York: Dodd, Mead & Company, 1928.

Stevens, Jolene. *A Second Century Begins: A History of the Sioux City Stock Yards.* Sioux City, Iowa: Sioux City Stock Yards, 1987.

Stewart, Robert, Ann Fortheringham, and David Jones. *Canadian Pacific Remembers.* Montréal: Communications & Public Affairs, CP Rail System, 1995.

Stover, John F. *The Life and Decline of the American Railroad.* New York: Oxford University Press, 1970.

————. *The Routledge Historical Atlas of American Railroads.* New York: Routledge, 1999.

Strapac, Joseph A. *Cotton Belt Locomotives.* Bloomington and Indianapolis: Indiana University Press, 1999 (1977).

Sulzer, Elmer G. *Ghost Railroads of Indiana.* Bloomington and Indianapolis: Indiana University Press, 1998 (1970).

————. *Ghost Railroads of Kentucky.* Bloomington and Indianapolis: Indiana University Press, 1998 (1967).

————. *Ghost Railroads of Tennessee.* Bloomington and Indianapolis: Indiana University Press, 1998 (1975).

Tayler, Arthur. *Illustrated History of North American Railroads: From 1830 to the Present Day.* Edison, N.J.: Chartwell Books, 1996.

Bibliography

Taylor, Jerry. *A Sampling of Penn Central.* Bloomington and Indianapolis: Indiana University Press, 2000 (1973).

Thompson, Slason. *A Short History of American Railways: Covering Ten Decades.* Chicago: Bureau of Railway News & Statistics, 1925.

Tigges, John. *Milwaukee Road Steam Power.* Polo, Ill.: Transportation Trails, 1994.

Tigges, John, and Jon Jacobson. *Milwaukee Road Narrow Gauge: The Chicago, Bellevue, Cascade, & Western: Iowa's Slim Princess.* Boulder, Colo.: Pruett Publishing Company, 1985.

Train Shed Cyclopedia. Novato, Calif.: N. K. Gregg, 1972.

Turner, Charles Wilson. *Chessie's Road.* Alderson, Wis.: The Chesapeake & Ohio Historical Society, 1993 (1956).

Turner, George Edgar. *Victory Rode the Rails: The Strategic Place of the Railroads in the Civil War.* Lincoln: University of Nebraska Press, 1992 (1953).

Union Pacific Railroad. *The Harriman Dispatching Center,* nd.

———. *Rails Across America.* Omaha, Nebr.: Union Pacific Railroad, 1986.

———. *Union Pacific Corporation and the Environment.* Bethlehem, Pa., nd.

Union Pacific Railroad Company. *Union Pacific Railroad, a Brief History.* Omaha, Nebr.: Colonial Press, 1969.

Van Metre, Thurman William. *Transportation in the United States.* Brooklyn: The Foundation Press, 1950.

Vance, James E. *The North American Railroad: Its Origin, Evolution, and Geography.* Baltimore: Johns Hopkins University Press, 1995.

Wabash National. *Road Railer, Mark V Training Manual.* Lafayette, Ind.: Wabash National Corporation, 1995.

Watt, William J. *The Pennsylvania Railroad in Indiana.* Bloomington and Indianapolis: Indiana University Press, 2000.

Weber, Thomas. *The Northern Railroads in the Civil War, 1861–1865.* Bloomington and Indianapolis: Indiana University Press, 1999 (1952).

Weir, Ruth Cromer. *The Wonderful Train Ride.* Chicago: Rand McNally, 1947.

Welsh, Joe, with Jim Boyd and William F. Howes Jr. *The American Railroad.* Osceola, Wis.: MBI Publishing Company, 1999.

White, John H. *The American Railroad Freight Car.* Baltimore: Johns Hopkins University Press, 1995 (1993).

———. *The American Railroad Passenger Car.* Baltimore: Johns Hopkins University Press, 1978.

Wilner, Frank N. *The Amtrak Story.* Omaha, Nebr.: Simmons-Boardman, 1994.

———. *Railroad Land Grants: Paid For in Full.* Washington, D.C.: Association of American Railroads, 1984.

———. *The Railway Labor Act & the Dilemma of Labor Relations.* Omaha, Nebr.: Simmons-Boardman Books, 1991.

———. *Railroad Mergers: History, Analysis, Insight.* Omaha, Nebr.: Simmons-Boardman, 1997.

Winkler, Fred Andrew. *Railroad Conductor.* Spokane: Pacific Book Company, 1948.

Withuhn, William L., ed. *Rails Across America.* New York: Smithmark Publishers, 1993.

Wormser, Richard. *Hoboes: Wandering in America, 1870–1940.* New York: Walker and Company, 1994.

———. *The Iron Horse: How Railroads Changed America.* New York: Walker and Company, 1993.

Yenne, Bill. *Southern Pacific.* New York: Smithmark Publishers, Inc., 1994.

INDEX

Page references in italics refer to illustrations.

ABOUT THE AUTHOR

Rudolph Daniels received his Ph.D. in History from Pennsylvania State University in 1971. He has taught in Europe and the United States. He has written numerous articles, and *Trains across the Continent* is his third book. At the request of the U.S. Department of Transportation, Daniels completed a pre-school through 12th grade railroad curriculum for the nation's schools.

Daniels is a much sought-after speaker on railroad history and other topics. He is Assistant Dean for Special Projects and teaches Railroad History at Western Iowa Tech Community College, Sioux City, Iowa, 51106; phone (712) 274-6400 or (712) 276-3185.

Author Rudolph Daniels.